William Wycherley
and the Comedy of Fear

William Wycherley and the Comedy of Fear

John A. Vance

Newark: University of Delaware Press
London: Associated University Presses

© 2000 by Associated University Presses, Inc.

All rights reserved. Authorization to photocopy items for internal or personal use, or the internal or personal use of specific clients, is granted by the copyright owner, provided that a base fee of $10.00, plus eight cents per page, per copy is paid directly to the Copyright Clearance Center, 222 Rosewood Drive, Danvers, Massachusetts 01923. [0-87413-708-X/00 $10.00 + 8¢ pp, pc.] Other than as indicated in the foregoing, this book may not be reproduced, in whole or in part, in any form (except as permitted by Sections 107 and 108 of the U.S. Copyright Law, and except for brief quotes appearing in reviews in the public press).

Associated University Presses
440 Forsgate Drive
Cranbury, NJ 08512

Associated University Presses
16 Barter Street
London WC1A 2AH, England

Associated University Presses
P.O. Box 338, Port Credit
Mississuaga, Ontario
Canada L5G 4L8

The paper used in this publication meets the requirements of the American National Standard for Permanence of Paper for Printed Library Materials Z39.48-1984.

Library of Congrss Cataloging-in-Publication Data

Vance, John A., 1947–
  William Wycherley and the comedy of fear / John A. Vance.
    p. cm.
  Includes bibliographical referenes (p.   ) and index.
  ISBN 0-87413-708-X (alk. p[aper)
  1. Wycherley, William, 1640–1716—Criticism and interpretation. 2. Fear in literature. 3. Comedy. I. Title.
PR3777 .V36 2000
822'.4—dc21
                                              99-089589

PRINTED IN THE UNITED STATES OF AMERICA

For Jimmy
"a Corinthian, a lad of mettle, a good boy"
—*Shakespeare*

[T]here is no such thing as perpetual tranquility of mind while we live here, because life itself is but motion and can never be without desire, nor without fear, no more than without sense.
—Thomas Hobbes, *Leviathan*

Contents

	Introduction: "'Tis less to undergo the ill, then fear"	9
1.	Into the Labyrinth: *Love in a Wood*	17
2.	On the Edge of Discovery: *The Gentleman Dancing-Master*	48
3.	"Plagues and Torments": *The Country Wife*	81
4.	"Surrounded with so many fears and griefs": *The Plain-Dealer*	130
5.	Conclusions: "More Fears, Plagues and Torments Yet in Store!"	175
	Notes	185
	Bibliography	246
	Index	255

Introduction:
"'Tis less to undergo the ill, then fear"

LONG CONSIDERED ONE OF THE BRIGHTEST LIGHTS IN THE GALAXY OF Restoration comic dramatists, William Wycherley still poses more difficulties for those trying to identify his appeal than do his starmates Dryden, Etherege, Vanbrugh, and Congreve. What is it that attracts readers to his work? What is it that earns Wycherley—the author of but four plays—the distinction of being one of England's very best comic playwrights, regardless of literary period? His vigorous satire? His irreverence? His bawdiness? His vivacious characterizations? Even, perhaps, his morality? From a time when he was condemned for his general indecency and "profligate and heartless" plays—most memorably by Collier and Macaulay—Wycherley has since received the critical scrutiny reserved for only the most significant authors.[1] For over thirty years now, Wycherley criticism has been quick to emphasize his "penetrating social criticism," "moral concern," and "personal ambivalence toward his age." Many have argued that he "set out quite openly to teach his audience," unmasking his characters "to show how far what we are deviates from what we should be"; that he was "clearly more censorious of Restoration society than [were] most of his contemporaries"; and that his satire "almost reaches the level of fanaticism"—this "bitter and enigmatic" playwright "savagely" attacking his society and age in plays that "are cool statements of his colossal, though smiling, misanthropy."[2] Whether considering Collier's and Macaulay's immoral Satan or the modern critics' satirical savior, one may easily conjure an image of a snarling Wycherley, holding his nose as he depicted the vice and folly of his time and conclude that, for all his comic brilliance, Wycherley's artistic spirit was predominantly dark, pessimistic, and—when appropriate—vicious.

This book takes serious issue with such an impression. It argues that Wycherley was not so much an *attacking* playwright but a *thinking* one, a comic dramatist little concerned with larger social, political, or moral questions,[3] but one fascinated instead by the workings and motivations of fallible and insecure men and women—by that which is constant, pervasive, and obsessive. He did not so much intend his art to expose, warn, or teach, but rather primarily to *depict* what he found both exhilarating and disturbing. Wycherley's presentation of the inevitable in human thought and behavior marks his genius and ultimate dramatic success—his "attitude" toward life being not one of pessimism but rather one of exuberant penetration. This study moreover contends that far from being his "gloomiest" or "grimmest" statement, *The Plain-Dealer* is in many respects his most optimistic expression—given the limits of optimism imposed by the unappeasable world Wycherley unveils in his comedies.

When writing on a Renaissance or Restoration playwright, one must confront head on the daunting argument that these plays reflect standard dramatic form of the time, well-established character types, and popular farcical constructions—as suggested by Robert Hume's forceful assertion that "character is not Wycherley's primary interest, and hence his plays make poor subjects for quasi-clinical psychological analysis"—and in Rose Zimbardo's unequivocal position that Wycherley's characters "are not meant to simulate 'real' people; they are rather meant to designate certain rhetorical positions determined by the poetic form."[4] In reply, one might first note that even those who have examined Wycherley from traditional or otherwise conservative perspectives have not denied the playwright's interest in the psychological and ambiguous. Katharine Rogers believes that he is different from many of his contemporaries "in his grappling with reality—real human nature, as distinct from social surface." James Thompson, while arguing for limits to Wycherlean ambiguity, does admit that one appeal of the playwright is his "intriguing indeterminacy." Jocelyn Powell furthermore notes of *The Country Wife* that it is "a commentary on the workings of the human animal." And A. M. Friedson sees *The Plain-Dealer* as "an example of Wycherley's skill as an analyst of human behavior."[5] In addition, there are a strong and hearty number who more directly and emphatically address both the complexity of Wycherley's art and the plays' reflection of deeper psychological considerations.[6] As Anthony Kaufman argues, "Although the comic playwrights of the Restoration have been accused of a narrowness of vision, the truth is that they were not afraid to portray the abnormal personality." Finally, Meredith Anne Skura succinctly heads off another conservative cliché by reminding us that "the poets discovered *psychoanalysis* before Freud did."[7]

Even though many agree that Wycherley is simply excellent in revealing what lies beneath the surface, their concentration remains nonetheless on the playwright's satiric exposure of, as James Sutherland concludes, "the vulgarity and triviality and sheer animalism" that festers below the outward social demeanor.[8] But whereas Wycherley happily pulls back the folds of laughter, wit, and social portrait, he is *not* for the most part judgmental as to what he finds. He is more the scientist than the moralist—he examines and displays but makes few overt, moral, or didactic statements about his discoveries. Wycherley's art is primarily a psychological one that extends to the reader (and even an audience) an invitation to consider motives, thought processes, and dysfunctions that are stimulated by, affect, and create external action. It seems a truth everywhere evident, though often suppressed, that regardless of how much the critic wishes to concentrate discussion of the drama elsewhere, the reader's interest in individual characters cannot be restrained—nor should it be, for Wycherley's plays inform us that such was his overriding interest as well. He does not simply push forward his women and men as satiric mouthpieces or objects of derision, but instead twits or torments them into revealing themselves, by extension exposing that which is more compelling.

That Wycherley was a man of the Restoration, that he wrote in a familiar dramatic form, that he borrowed from continental drama and his own English tradition,[9] that his characters were indicative of Restoration types, that he may have wanted for a number of personal and financial reasons to compose successful stage comedies, that his plays were written more to be staged than read—are all givens; but the *result* of his dramas as *literature* is the concern of this book. Consequently, my references throughout will more often be to "the reader" and not always to "the audience."[10] It should be blatantly obvious that any serious reading of these plays can be rendered utterly useless by a dramatic performance of them, in which the rules and objectives may be appreciably different.[11] I must disagree, then, with Scott McMillin's assumption that "Readers of a play are in a difficult position, because they are reading something that was not primarily intended to be read. Plays are performances, and they need actors, a stage, an audience before they fully exist. Hence, reading plays ought to make one feel a bit silly . . . until one develops an imagination to witness a printed drama as a performed event."[12] I feel a bit silly only by having to repeat what seems so plainly evident: that the very nature of their being printed as texts transforms these plays from stage vehicles to dramatic literature demanding to be read and analyzed as such. In addition, Wycherley was well aware that earlier English dramatists were in fact being read in the 1670s and being analyzed through either the more casual or the more intense process of literary criticism. Regardless then of any immediate use of his comedies as simple stage fare, Wycherley very likely assumed his works would be read, if not carefully scrutinized, by more sophisticated minds.

Wycherley's plays are not simply reflections of his age or society; instead they hold up a glass to the serious and at times profound human desires and frailties—not so much greed, vanity, pettiness, and hypocrisy, but rather frustration, helplessness, impotence, and fear. The title of this study is accordingly meant to convey not only the playwright's understanding of fear as a primary stimulus for behavior and human interaction but also the contradictory, oxymoronic nature of life—the unsettling, incongruous, indeterminate actions, rituals, and perceptions of which men and women are so clearly capable. Wycherley therefore shares a sensitivity to the word *fear* we find most evident in Hobbes and especially Rochester:

> For hunger or for love they fight and tear,
> Whilst wretched man is still in arms for fear.
> For fear he arms, and is of arms afraid,
> By fear to fear successively betrayed;
> Base fear, the source whence his best passions came:
> His boasted honor, and his dear-bought fame;
> That lust of power, to which he's such a slave[.]
> . . . .
> The good he acts, the ill he does endure,
> 'Tis all from fear, to make himself secure.[13]

Fear and its variants *fearful* and *afraid* appear too frequently in Wycherley's four plays to be dismissed as just stylistic preference.[14] The fear (apprehension and dread) stems mainly from a pervasive insecurity that cannot be denied, although it may be transformed, temporarily at least, into a number of aggressive manifestations. For Wycherley's characters, the truths about human debility are too frightening and unbearable to be openly recognized or articulated. As a result, truth is avoided and spurned, forcefully and at times frantically by the women and men who hide behind a number of comforting and protective facades—social conventions, literal masks, misdirection, and indirection in overt action, gesture, language, and thought. Most of Wycherley's characters (major and minor) have active and often destructive imaginations and a considerable shrewdness of design. Male relationships are with little exception fraught with insecurity, division, regressive and self-destructive behavior—whereas among the females one invariably discovers a delightful and healthy sense of sorority. But one also finds among the women a more acute understanding of fear and an acceptance that propriety is necessary to human interaction, and the imaginative characters accordingly construct forms of propriety where none actually exist.

It is no revelation to state that Wycherley was intrigued by sex—not merely the entertaining or shocking aspects of the act as much as the knowledge that the instinctual sexual drive serves as catalyst and influence—often with destructive as well as "life-giving" effects. Peering beyond the frequent comic chaos, we can find Wycherley's sensitivity to the psychological subtleties of sexual relationships and one's ability or inability to cope with his or her sexual essence as well as that of others—

friend as well as foe. In Wycherley's plays, the sexual forces demand satisfaction regardless of the consequences—for the males a satisfaction usually violent and oppressive; for the females one normally erotic and liberating. The comedies moreover reveal a central motif of coitus interruptus, both literal and figurative—one that adds to the tension and frustration the reader, viewer, and character all may share. Yet we often respond enthusiastically to the sexual energy and exuberance sweeping us along, no matter how much debris we may pick up along the way. Often the playwright ushers us into a labyrinth in which the normal dramatic markings are spun the wrong way. To walk within Wycherley's labyrinth demands vigilance, caution, and skepticism; traditional expectations often will simply not do.

In this book I do not deny, nor do I wish to depreciate, Wycherley's considerable comic gifts: the humorous and pleasurable moments are of course ubiquitous—no one could deny them—some relying heavily on stock devices and long-tested confrontations to encourage a laugh. But at the heart of that comedy lies something less comic, though no less pleasing—something more compelling, something often calling on laughter to break the tension and discomfort Wycherley's plays force on the reader.[15] Unlike the later comedies of Goldsmith and Sheridan, where we can revel in unbounded joy, riding merrily along with Tony Lumpkin or straining to catch another pillaging of the language by Mrs. Malaprop, in Wycherley our laughter is frequently short-lived—the mood forced to undergo rapid change—because we are encouraged to consider more intently a number of rugged and nasty truths about human nature. Wycherley always makes demands upon us—he forces us to sit up and engage with him—whereas with Goldsmith and Sheridan we can sit back and relax, assured that we will be joyously entertained. Their comedies leave us refreshed and contented; Wycherley's leave us plainly exhausted—though, without question, far more intellectually stimulated.[16]

William Wycherley
and the Comedy of Fear

1
Into the Labyrinth: *Love in a Wood*

WYCHERLEY'S FIRST COMEDY OFFERS THE SAME CHALLENGE POSED BY such plays as *Love's Labour's Lost*—to find something worthwhile in an early minor work by a major playwright. Were not Shakespeare the author of *The Two Gentlemen of Verona*, the argument might go, who then would have had much to say about it? But as industrious critics have successfully mined Shakespeare's earliest comedies, so too have Wycherley's commentators at least attempted to discover the gold in *Love in a Wood, or, St. James's Park*. Some have opted to place this work within the context of early Restoration stage history, to distinguish it from its possible sources,[1] while others have searched for the genesis of later Wycherlean characters as a way to avoid dismissing the play as deservedly forgettable.[2] However, beyond these historical and structural contexts, *Love in a Wood* introduces the major concerns and motifs that permeate all four of Wycherley's comedies: the destructive interaction between males, the dread of humiliation, the fear and avoidance of truth, and the accompanying need for indirection. We moreover discover the exuberance of Wycherley's female characters and the playwright's proficiency in luring his audience and readers into an unkempt labyrinth filled with unexpected turns and blocked exits.

One longstanding assumption is that Wycherley built his first comedy upon a tripartite structure of low, middle, and high-plot characters—presenting harsh criticism and satire in the low, a reflection of realism in the middle, and the right-way alternative in the high-plot group.[3] Still, such divisions unnecessarily restrict one's perspective of the play and distort its design. Wycherley's intermingling of the characters from the "three plot" groups and easy transition from one to another reveal that there is in essence only one world, one set of impulses common to men and women regardless of station. High-plot characters may be less rumpled and soiled, but the basic instincts are the same for the resplendent as well as for the untidy. And a good place to begin challenging these and other views is with a reevaluation of the irrepressible Lady Flippant, often filed away in the "low-plot" group as just one more of a voluminous number of hypocritical characters inhabiting seventeenth-century comedies—Wycherley's version, as it were, of Shadwell's Lady Vaine in *The Sullen Lovers* (1668). But despite the temptation to judge her on satiric or otherwise moralistic grounds, Lady Flippant is simply one of Wycherley's most delightful creations, a woman who evinces a vigorous sexual energy that is constantly at war with her basic insecurities.[4] She knows the price self-advertisement exacts on a woman's dignity and is sensitive to the horrors of being alone—or being *perceived* as alone. If Mrs. Joyner is correct—"Then your frequent, and publick detestation of Marriage, is thought real; and if you have had no Offer, there's the thing Madam" (I.i.32–33)[5]—then we may conclude that these "flippant" remarks against marriage are but part of a mask, a form of propriety that offers balm to a bruised ego likely frustrated at being unable to satisfy a normal sexual urge (she reminds us that her "person" is still in "good repair") and therefore feels keenly a rapid lessening of self-esteem. It is just too easy to dismiss her as the traditional oversexed hypocrite, the kind of character we are not supposed to like and assume the playwright does not either.[6]

Lady Flippant's jocular depiction of her modus operandi introduces as well another central motif of the play—the often painful and frustrating ritual of courtship and indirect release of sexual energy and tension, a Dionysian movement apparently ordered and invigorating yet also frenzied and destructive. Clearly, Flippant's purpose and energy are impossible to suppress: "Tis well known no Woman breathing could use more Industry to get her a Husband than I have . . . [so] that no quarter of the Town might be ignorant of the Widow *Flippant*" (I.i.15–19). Because she holds that a widow's money is her "chiefest Bait" (l.43) and thus (as is often the case with the males) the metaphor for her sexual appeal, Flippant accordingly dangles her assets and then pulls the purse strings shut, hoping to enclose men in her trap as well as keep them effectively away from the source of her power: "Husbands are got like Bishopricks, by saying no" (45–46). But we observe how quickly her strength gives way to her insecurity, embodied in the terrifying prospects of lost independence and, to her horror, the loss of her coach—that which symbolizes more than prosperity and self-reliance, for its rolling wheels connote the kind of motion that invigorates and the kind of freedom that appeals to Wycherley's women, a freedom they greatly fear relinquishing: "a Lodging is as unnecessary a thing to a Widow that has a Coach, as a Hat to a Man that has a good Peruque" (65–67). We see early in his first play, then, that Wycherley offers little that is sedentary and satiated; rather in his comedies almost all will be agitated and unfulfilled. In addition, the coach reflects the playwright's strong association of the female with enclosures. Although most often linked with incarceration, here the image is one of independence and security: a widow "is most properly at home in her Coach, she eats, and drinks, and sleeps in her Coach" (68–69).[7]

Lady Flippant's brother, Alderman Gripe (with his anachronistic appearance and sordid preoccupations) is certainly on one hand Wycherley's contribution to the body of Commonwealth and Puritan characters who served admirably as comic butts—begun in earnest with Robert Howard's *The Committee* (1662).[8] Yet, with the duplicitous and zealous Gripe there is much more to consider. His impeding the "Freedom" of his sister (1.76) and his besotted interested in young Lucy, daughter of the "old cheating jilt" Mrs. Crossbite, stimulates an aggressive desire for power and dominance—the first of Wycherley's males to do so. Even in his insincere and competitive "praising" of Mrs. Joyner as well and as often as she "praises" him, Gripe demonstrates that like other Wycherlean males, he calls upon whatever means available (creatively metaphoric or regressively primitive) to assert and then protect his masculinity. To him Mrs. Joyner is, among other things, the "flowr of Matrons," the "Muffler of Secresy," the "Cup-board of Charity," and the "Rivet of sanctify'd Love or Wedlock." (Not to be outdone, she repays each "compliment" in kind: he is the "Head-band of Justice," the "Bellows of Zeal," the "Fob of Liberality," and the "Picklock and Dark-Lanthorn of Policy" [I.i.110–35]). Other than the reference to things that lock and otherwise restrict ("Muffler of Secresy," "Cup-board," "Head-band," and "Picklock"), if the actors deliver their lines in a perversely erotic way, the moment takes on a far more intriguing dynamic than that of simple hypocritical bantering, for it would then be vigorous, bawdy, and nasty.[9] And as a further illustration of the female enclosure motif, Gripe's fearing his daughter Martha's exposure to the coxcomb Dapperwit leads to his locking her up as a safeguard, a gesture that typifies the male anxiety over losing his female possessions and accordingly the representative of his manhood. Still, Gripe's fear stems less from what he perceives as an aroused male's interest in his daughter as it does from Martha's own sexuality, which he must realize is perilously close to revealing itself publicly as well as privately; he believes she is waiting only for the opportunity to act as her instincts encourage her to.

Wycherley's female characters are all the more intriguing because their overpowering sexual vigor—which they exude in thought, metaphor, and gesture, as well as in behavior—is almost always in contrast to the often infantile, repressive, and debilitating sexuality of the males. Unlike the men, who generally cannot help enhancing their own and others' sexual dysfunctions, the women move undaunted and unalterably toward a state where passionate needs may be satisfied. They naturally resist any attempts to inhibit those desires and eventually discover means by which to subvert the patriarchal authority custom and law have bestowed on their keepers. To Gripe, shoving his daughter (or, in Pinchwife's case, his young wife) behind a closed door means pushing her into a womb-like enclosure, where she can be of little threat because her sexual essence has yet to be "born": "I was forc'd to lock up my Daughter for fear of him, nay, I think the poor *Child* her self was afraid of him; come hither *Child,* were you not afraid of Dapperwit?" (emphasis added; I.i.149–52). The "fear" is of course his own, even though he tries vainly to shift the emotion to one who doesn't feel it. Gripe is similarly apprehensive that Dapperwit will "contaminate" the female on whom he wishes to release his own peculiar brand of sordidness—Lucy Crossbite. Like Horner, Pinchwife, and Manly, Gripe instinctively understands that other males seek his destruction and transformation into some manner of cuckold. His motivation is not to "redeem" the helpless Lucy from "the Jaws of that Lyon," as he boldly announces, but rather to feast on her "little" body all by himself (167–71).[10]

In Sir Simon Addleplot, another charter member of the "low-plot" group, Wycherley suggests that masculine discord is more than a simple demonstration of the Hobbesian naked aggression many have identified in Restoration drama.[11] There are a few exceptions (most significantly, Freeman's commitment to Manly in *The Plain-Dealer*), but throughout Wycherley's four plays the males harbor an active hostility toward their brothers, which manifests itself in frequent attempts to abuse or render them impotent (whether actually or metaphorically), such destruction being a pervasive motif and virulent preoccupation. Males rarely band together for any positive goal; they move toward their objective not in harmonious step but in a circular motion, probing for weaknesses, looking for something to exploit. Hobbes's observation—"the way of one Competitor, to the attaining of his desire, is to kill, subdue, supplant, or repell the other"[12]—is continually given life in Wycherley's social world.

Addleplot's exhilaration comes more from winning the game of manipulation than in obtaining the monetary goals he claims to seek—and typical of his sex he insists on labeling and categorizing others and segregating himself from any conception of brotherhood. As a result, he takes exception to Mrs. Joyner's observation, "Why will you keep Company with him [Dappwerwit] then, I say? for to be plain with you, you have followed him so long, that you are thought but his Culley" (I.i.206–8). That is, Addleplot's horror at being thought indistinct from Dapperwit prompts an immediate reassertion of his separateness: "I his Culley? . . . Lord that I should be thought a Culley to any Wit breathing" (210–11).[13] And other than the amusing irony that he still cites Dapperwit as an authority ("as *Dapperwit* says"), therefore beginning here as well Wycherley's habitual and often subtle undercutting of his male characters, Addleplot reflects the fear of being labeled himself—

for to be labeled is to be powerless—in the control of others. Labeling is judged a most useful weapon by those (especially Manly in *The Plain-Dealer*) debilitated by their own insecurities.[14]

The more rambunctious males—Vincent, Ranger, and Dapperwit (from the "middle-plot" group)—easily demonstrate their relationship to their "low plot" brothers by continuing the preoccupation with male aggression:

> Dap. But why shou'd you force Wine upon us? we are not all of your gusto.
> Vin. But why shou'd you force your chaw'd jests, your damn'd ends of your mouldy Lampoones, and last years Sonnets upon us, we are not all of your gusto?
> Dap. The Wine makes me sick, let me perish.
> Vin. Thy Rymes make me spew.
>
> (I.ii.6–12)

Other than "mouldy," "sick," and "spew" reflecting the unhealthy aspects of male relationships, the exchange makes clear that the characters must measure up to certain qualities their sex has deemed "masculine"—wit,[15] posturing ("one-upness"), courage, virility, success, and—if all else fails—the ability to imbibe impressive amounts of ale and wine. Yet, even those who show proficiency in some or all of these skills often fail to gain commendation, as is evident in Dapperwit's remark to Ranger about Vincent: "He may drink because he is obliged to the Bottle, for all the wit and courage he has, 'tis not free and natural like yours" (20–21). The "flattery" of Ranger at the end of Dapperwit's observation (one recalls the Gripe-Joyner exchange), as well as his gesture of fraternity, does not obscure the inherent need to fragment whatever approaches masculine solidity. And that Vincent may be "obliged" to drink satisfies Dapperwit by "testifying" to Vincent's apparent dependence and resulting inferiority. Ranger's rejection of this assessment, I would argue, owes more to his refusal to be at one with the pompous wit than to any praiseworthy affection for Vincent. In addition, we have Dapperwit's admission that he is using Sir Simon in his courtship of Gripe's daughter Martha: "*Addleplot* is but my Agent whilst he thinks me his; he brings me Letters constantly from her, and carries mine back" (I.ii.110–12)—taking clear delight in the thought of Addleplot performing the role of sexual lacky. That this plan of course later backfires on Dapperwit is representative of Wycherley's interest in the self-destructive impulse that forces a man subconsciously or unwittingly to push himself, usually as he tries to push another, toward a rendezvous with his own humiliation.

Dapperwit's railing at the "ignorant dull age," which allows for few "patient" or "faithful" friends, is mere transference; as Wycherley demonstrates particularly well in *The Plain-Dealer*, compressing one's feelings of insecurity and hostility into a convenient barb at the present age or contemporary "society" provides a handy release of personal frustration. It has nothing to do, really, with the playwright's assessment of his "Age." And Dapperwit's remark, "'Tis disobliging to tell a Man of his faults to his face" (I.ii.49), underscores the characters' fervent commitment to avoiding truth, a point reinforced by Ranger's desire to keep Lydia unaware of his plans to hunt "some fresh Game" in St. James's Park that night. He claims that women "are poor credulous Creatures, easily deceived" (79), but such a patronizing assessment only underscores the power the female has to upset the male's equilibrium. Lydia "follows" Ranger to his "haunts," thereby usurping much of his power by permitting him no privacy within an "exclusive" male sanctuary. In addition to Vincent's presenting to Ranger the frightening vision of the avenging woman—"She'll be even with you when you are married I warrant you" (words that still have resonance in the play's final two scenes)—the allusions here depict the male as the hunted sex, another motif prevalent in all four of Wycherley's plays.

As did Dapperwit earlier, Ranger fires his piece at the helpless and absent Addleplot (the pattern of "two [or more]-versus-one" another favorite Wycherlean device), informing the company that Sir Simon's career is in decline: "He was once the sport, but now the publick grievance of all the fortunes in Town; for he watches them like a younger Brother that is afraid to be mump'd of his snip" (I.ii.101–2). In other words, Ranger describes Addleplot as a "Disabled Debauchee"—not king but counselor, not sinner but sage, not participant but voyeur. And furthermore conspicuous is Ranger's own joy in imagining another male's sexual frustration. Those willing to disrupt and fuel discord seem everywhere; as Ranger adds, "But this is an ill place to conceal a Mistress in, every Waiter is an Intelligencer to your Rivals" (138–39). And yet these characters always evince the kind of rugged exuberance that makes Wycherley's plays so attractive to the modern reader. Wycherley's men and women do not sit and dazzle us with their conversation; they move, react, and expend energy—with a vitality that is almost always primal and/or sexual. For example, Dapperwit says of Martha, "the poor young Wench is taken with my person, and wou'd scratch through fowr walls to come to me" (I.ii.114–16). The comic vanity of such a boast is undoubtedly appealing, and Michael Mohun may well have added an exaggerated gesture or raised the level of affectation in his speech to increase the laughter from his audience.[16] But the erotic implications of the assessment are just as conspicuous. As one of many Wycherlean males with active imaginations, Dapperwit has in effect described the ultimate male fantasy: that an aroused woman would be so taken with his "person" that she would resort to violence to satisfy her animalistic cravings (the allusion to scratching certainly being emotive). Despite Dapperwit's amusing misinterpretation of her interests, Martha *is* a sexual creature, not in any misogynistic Juvenalian context, but rather in a more captivating sense of a powerful woman (pounding through four walls), one who will not be denied what she feels is naturally her right, and one who will eventually escape her incarceration.[17] As his Hippolita, Margery Pinchwife, and Lady Fidget indicate, Wycherley was far more intrigued by, rather than critical of, the image of the dauntless and sexually driven female. But such a conclusion is indeed difficult to accept when we view the playwright as the traditional satirist with censure and correction foremost on his mind.

Wycherley's plays allow the males very little respite from irrepressible women—evident here by the return of Lady Flippant, who desires an admission of jealousy from Dapperwit. Her insistence in this matter testifies to her inexhaustible energy and ability to make things happen—to effect reaction and affect the course of events by simple will and hammering repetition. And clearly, she wins this power skirmish: defenseless and weakened, Dapperwit is unable to stem her eagerness with either his disclaimers or his insults. Surely, Flippant does more than draw her weapon on the unarmed, for she and the better equipped Ranger engage in a discussion ripe with suggestive language—intitiated, of course, by Lady Flippant:

> *Flip.* ... I do not know a man of you all, that will not thrust a Woman up into a corner,[18] and then talk an hour to her impertinently of marriage.
> *Ran.* You wou'd find me another man in a corner, I assure you, Madam, for you shou'd not have a word of marriage from me, whatsoever you might find in my actions of it; I hate talking as much as you.
> *Flip.* I hate it extreamly.
> *Ran.* I am your man then, Madam, for I find just the same fault with your Sex as your do with ours. ... Since you are a Lady that hate marriage, I'll do you the service to withdraw the company, for those that hate marriage, hate loss of time.
> (I.ii.261–79)

Likely flushed by the metaphoric sexual tustle, Flippant is unwilling to let Ranger depart: "Will you needs go then? the gentlemen are a going, Sir *Simon,* will you let 'em" (300–301). And to keep Ranger and the others from leaving, she entertains them with a song about the male's desire for sexual *carte blanche:*

> A Spouse I do hate,
> For either she's false or she's jealous;
> But give us a Mate,
> Who nothing will ask us, or tell us.
> (305–8)

This ditty prevents for the moment the mass egress and elicits praise from Ranger, which need not be taken sarcastically, especially if one visualizes a physically attractive Lady Flippant:[19] "The Song is edifying, the Voice admirable, and once more, I am your servant, Madam" (324–25). And yet a replacement of the feminine for the masculine pronoun in the song depicts the marital state Wycherley's strongest women (Hippolita, Lady Fidget, and Alithea particularly) desire and work to realize.

The second act opens in St. James's Park—at night, the darkness being that most alluring mask under which men and women may hide identities, longings, fears, and the truths about themselves. But even in darkness the activity level is intense; the pace stimulating. Rochester's *Ramble in St. James's Park* (likely composed about the same time as Wycherley's play) is the most memorable depiction of such coursing—one certainly helpful in understanding the sexual connotations many perceived in references to the Park.[20] Wycherley's scene is obviously almost angelic in contrast to Rochester's graphically carnal portrait,[21] but both poem and play concede that sexual intensity defies restraint and demands expression. And Wycherley reminds us as well that "moral" defenses are weakened and the instinctive urges more pronounced when one escapes into the darkness, into the security of the enclosure—whether it be coach, bedroom, or the more fertile environment of St. James's Park—all securely hidden from the penetrating eye of propriety.[22] And the influence of the darkness and the understood license of St. James's Park pushes the characters toward a kind of Dionysian baptism[23]—with Lady Flippant's calling Addleplot a "modern Satyr" only encouraging the mythic analogue. And she makes clear which sex dominates in the ritual: "For now anights the jostling Nymph is bolder, / Then modern Satyr with his Cloak o're shoulder" (II.i.100–101)—the ceremonial expression stimulating the female desire for freedom in the forgiving and liberating confines of nature.[24] Lydia's remark to Flippant that "There does not pass a night here, but many a match is made" (II.i.73–74) assumes that lovers as well as potential husbands are the hunted quarry.

The movements begin to accelerate—the ladies walk in front of the gentlemen; the men "follow them"; the women leave the men behind as they "re-enter" the place from which they left; the men then "re-enter" and "walk slowly towards" the women; Flippant "runs away"; Lydia follows; the men follow as well; Flippant "re-enters," and so on. Entering, exiting, following, evading, turning, and returning characterize the motion in the park, and even when the men and women lite long enough for an exchange, the evasive tactics continue, the sense of movement progresses—all suggesting the restless and frustrated nature of this social terrain. Instinctive and defensive gestures of concealment are furthermore evident: Addleplot enters "muffled in a Cloak"; Lady Flippant then "puts on her Mask." When they perceive "torches and music," Addleplot and Flippant maintain their disguise, and the dancers accompanying the light and song stay hidden behind their "vizards." The constant "asides" in this scene only heighten the reliance on indirection and the fear of revelation. Faces are turned away or to the side; eyes peer from the darkness or behind a mask or garment. As Ranger observes, "And now no woman's modest, or proud, for her blushes are hid" (II.i.11–12).

Lady Flippant's comments, especially, provide additional evidence of the elusive and obfuscatory way of Wycherley's world. To Addleplot she asks, "[W]ho are you? don't you know me?" When he answers that he does not, she replies, "I am glad on't, for no man e're lik'd a Woman the better for having known her before" (II.i.103–8)—both a literal and "biblical" connotation of "to know" being relevant. Indeed, she is very quick to express fear of revelation: "I must not discover my self" (157–58). Although Wycherley clearly distinguishes between general male and female conduct and impulse, both sexes share this anxiety over being found out, scrutinized, and thereby rendered less powerful. For the women, however, the various masks (vizards, darkness, indirection) also emancipate them; here Flippant is more free to speak erotically to those in her company, sheltering while at the same time expressing her sexual essence within the protective aspects of language, particularly within double entendre:

Flip. Do they come? are they men certainly?
Lyd. Prepare for an assault, they'l put you to't.
Flip. Will they put us to't certainly? I was never put to't yet;[25] if they shou'd put us to't, I should drop down, down certainly.
Lyd. I believe, truly, you wou'd not have power to run away.
Flip. Therefore I will not stay the push; they come, they come, oh the fellows come!
(II.i.82–89)

Figuratively at least, Lady Flippant reveals a considerable erotic aggressiveness and anxiety—both crashing together in a moment of spirited chaos. And the suggested references to body positioning and sexual intercourse testify to the free sharing of such talk among women—a stark and significant contrast to the destructive or furtive sexual references made typically by the males.[26] In Wycherley, the reluctance to articulate *openly* such desires is not a by-product of theologically or socially bred guilt; rather it is the necessary tribute to some form of legality or propriety, which serves as a self-check—a way to avoid giving in to the volatile Dionysian urges that would blur the distinction between the social and natural human being—something Wycherley's females particularly fear.[27]

Lady Flippant need not, then, be portrayed as an elderly dowdy, an ancient coquette, a forerunner of Lady Wishfort, a woman who spends time in front of her mirror looking for cracks that must be walled up or relishing the attention of some pathetic and sexually superannuated gentlemen. This bold "jostling Nymph" (100) plays better as more physically attractive than Addleplot's depiction suggests (possibly being only in her early thirties).[28] Although she requires the security and indirection her mask provides, Flippant's passionate effervescence (which leaves us disappointed in many ways with the virtuous Christina) is impossible to miss:

> *Flip.* I love of my life men should deal freely with me; there are so few men will deal freely with one—
> *Sir Sim.* Are you not a Fireship? [prostitute] a Punk, Madam?
> *Flip.* Well, Sir, I love Raillery.... This is the time and place for freedom, Sir.... those that deal freely indeed, take a woman by—
> *Sir Sim.* What, what, what, what?
> *Flip.* By the hand and lead her aside.
>
> (117–31)[29]

Terminating her thought and enticing Addleplot to complete it through *aposiopesis* is a thinly disguised sexual teasing, serving to stimulate his imagination and then frustrate his expectations ("By the hand . . . ").[30] Wycherley is simply not interested in offering another sparkling battle of wits, the kind he would have found between Etherege's Sir Frederick Frollick and the Widow Rich or between James Howard's Welbred and Lady Wealthy.

The remainder of the Park scene only reinforces this state of Dionysian agitation: torches approach, Lady Flippant leaves, the dancers arrive, and Addleplot goes about "peeping, and examining the Womens cloaths." The dancers, musicians, and Addleplot leave only to be replaced immediately by Flippant and Lydia, with Vincent and Dapperwit in close pursuit. The eye cannot rest comfortably in this labyrinth, for quickly Flippant begins to move away only to be jerked back (literally as well as figuratively) by Lydia, who is then pulled the other way by Flippant: "Monstrous impudence, will you not come?" (181). Another pair of hands seeks to prevent movement, as Vincent grabs Flippant and adds a threat of further physical harm into an already chaotic yet invigorating situation: "I never suffer any violence to be us'd to a woman, but what I do my self; she [Lydia] must stay, and you must not go" (182–83). This clash between the sexes moves far beyond the witty thrusts and parries most brilliantly realized in Dorimant and Harriet or Mirabell and Millament. In fact and despite his allusion to violence, Vincent's attempt at satirical wit undercuts his "masculine" assertion of power: "coyness in a woman is as little sign of true modesty, as huffing in a man, is of true courage" (185–87). It is certainly not lost on the women that Vincent is at that moment both physically and verbally "huffing." And while Dapperwit encourages Lydia to remove her mask, he punctuates his request with awkward yet threatening attempts to grab at her disguise: "now I shou'd see your face, let me desire you to pull off your Mask" (214–15). But Lydia finds no reason why her face should light "the World," the metaphorical evasion of brightness making clear Wycherley's preference for the shadows, for the darker underside of life. And always there is fear:

Ran. What, play with your quarrey till it fly from you.
Dap. You frightned it away.
. . . .
Ran. 'Tis she, 'tis she, I was afraid I saw her before, let us follow 'em, prithee make haste, 'Tis *Lydia*.
Lyd. They follow us yet I fear.

(295, 302–5)

The frantic pace in St. James's Park does not altogether diminish, as we might expect, when the scene shifts to Christina's apartment. In her brief appearance there, Lady Flippant once more invigorates the environment, even if she does not stimulate Christina, that "young Lady scarce eighteen, of extraordinary beauty" (II.iv.74–75). Flippant moreover pays court to the dominant and rigorous aspects of her personality: "if 'twere not for a Woman that could make an excuse with assurance, how shou'd we whedle, jilt, trace, discover, countermine, undermine, and blow up the stinking fellows, which is all the pleasure I receive, or design by them; for I never admitted a man to my conversation, but for his punishment certainly" (II.ii.70–75). One may find appropriate, as does Christina, a quick dismissal of this observation as wishful thinking (if not blatant hypocrisy), but the volatility of Flippant's imagery breathes considerable life into her assertion, especially, again, if one views her to any degree sexually appealing—more perhaps like Etherege's Mrs. Loveit. And even if her howl frightens more than her bite, the sound at least makes us take notice: "I have been defending our cause. . . . I do so mumble these prating, censorious fellows, they call Wits, when I meet with them." She is the Diana in Wycherley's mythology—lover of the hunt, protectress of women, and more: "I am the revenger of our Sex, certainly" (iii.64–71). Flippant's points are too good, her spirit too formidable, to be so easily dispensed as a "low" plot hypocritical character, the mere target of satire. Rather than exposing her to ridicule, Wycherley is pushing her forward, allowing her to invigorate the play with impunity.

Later, Wycherley treats us to another delightful illustration of Flippant's faithful obedience to her sexual promptings. Attempting to write "as a Clerk," the besieged Addleplot can barely put pen to paper before Flippant begins "jogging" him (a playfully "violent" prelude to the sex act—she hopes). But the "Dull Rascal" (IV.i.77) cannot be stimulated toward the proper response, which leaves an increasingly impatient Flippant to lament his passivity: "There are some Clerks wou'd have understood me before this." Sir Simon can only protest the muscular force that pushes against him in a delightful reversal of gender roles (and a reminder of Flippant's earlier allusion): "if you squeeze me so to the wall, I cannot write" (81–84). And then, after another "jogging," comes the awaited assertion of his masculinity—"you'l never leave, till you have made me sawcy":

Flip. I wou'd I cou'd see that.
Sir Sim. I vow and swear then, get you gone; or i'le add a black patch, or two, to those on your face. . . .
Flip. Will you, Sir, will you?—

as she "Jogs him again" (IV.i.91–96). As if testing her mettle, Sir Simon threatens to kiss her if she passes the "Creviss" on the floor—which of course she does. His assessment, "she kisses as tamely as Mrs. *Ticklish,* and with her mouth open too" (101–2), belies the fact that she is being provocative; her mouth parts but refrains from "mouseling" the eager Addleplot. Her feigned horror at Sir Simon's threat, "If you come again, I shall do more to you then that," only trumpets forth her teasing nature: "You do more to me then that; if you'l do more to me, then that—," as she "throws down his Ink, and runs out" (IV.i.107–10).

Addleplot returns "holding up his hands," telling Mrs. Joyner that he followed the fleeing Daphne into the next room, ostensibly to avenge his spilled ink: he "threw her down upon the bed; but in short, all that [he] could do to her, wou'd not make her squeek"—to which the matchmaker responds, "She was out of breath man, she was out of breath" (115–26).[31] We are left to wonder if he is exaggerating, as men are wont to do, the point to which the moment progressed. Was he potent enough even to titillate Lady Flippant's insatiable sexual appetite? Is his reference to spilled ink a comment on the emptiness of his "inkhorn"—or a premature ejaculation? Is Flippant's subsequent attack of the "rude unmannerly Rascal" sincere? Is she merely trying to guard her reputation with feigned moral outrage? Or might she be angry because in his attempt "Jonas" failed to go far enough or to satisfy her, if he even attempted to go that far?[32] Regardless, after Simon reveals himself, saying that he took the disguise of Jonas only "to be near her," Flippant replies, "What a beast was I, I cou'd not discover it" (138). Her moral "indignation" now suddenly evaporates, and after Joyner tells Addleplot "alas, poor Lady, she cannot resist you," Flippant admits, likely with a flirtatious sparkle in her eye, "'Tis my weakness"—signifying not so much her desire for Addleplot but rather for sexual interaction with men, whatever its nature—actual, metaphorical, or subliminal (146–48). Finally, one sees in Flippant's aside, "When I come home again, I'le laugh at you soundly" (IV.i.157–58), an enticing ambiguity. If she makes the comment with a giggle, her words may refer to Addleplot's poor attempt at disguise. If she says them more provocatively, with a trace of erotic malice, her remark could then refer to his inability to make her "squeek" sexually.[33] Sir Simon is understandably perplexed and fearful: "Has *Joyner* betray'd me then? 'tis time to look to my hits" (159–60). And if Flippant means her threat in a more malicious way, Addleplot runs the risk of having his impotence hung out for the world to see—in Wycherley, the most pervasive male fear.

Addleplot's hopes for shoring up his fragile masculinity rest in his relationship with Martha, daughter of the old Puritan Gripe. Imprisoned by her father ("be sure you stay within now; if you go out, you shall never come into my dores again"), Martha naturally wishes to escape and experience the world she has been denied by patriarchal oppression. She questions "Jonas" about his alter-ego, Addleplot, making a number of references (subtle and direct) to Sir Simon's gullibility, ignorance, foppishness, financial insolvency, and contraction of the "modish distemper." It takes Martha only a few short moments to emasculate him metaphorically, the second time in this scene that he has failed as a man. "Jonas" does not deny that Addleplot has the French pox: "He can cure it with the best *French* Chyrurgion in Town" (IV.i.207–9), thereby providing us with another reason (if chancres, lesions, or a rash were visible to her) why Lady Flippant may have been angry with him, why she did not squeek, and why she would laugh at him "soundly" when she returned home—such a possibility being again reflective of Wycherley's love of misdirection as well as indirection.

The introduction of the "high-plot" Christina—Christ-like, it appears, in her being falsely accused—suggests again that in Wycherley surface impressions are almost always misleading. Initially, one should pay attention to the words of Christina's impertinent servant Isabel: "it is in my power, it seems, to make you in part happy, if I cou'd but hold this villanous tongue of mine, but then let the people of the Town hold their tongues if they will, for I cannot but tell you what they say" (II.ii.13–16). Even though part of Isabel's motives are self-serving—being low in society's hierarchy she relishes the power to inform and be depended on—her words (looking forward to Lucy in *The Country Wife*) also imply a more sisterly altruism. She wants Christina to show the vitality that characterizes a powerful and healthy woman. Christina's virtue, which actually is passive and inhibiting, makes her the target of those who either distrust the protestation of such fidelity or see her behavior as too individualistic, as rejecting of the sorority. Christina cannot be normal; she must have "grown mad," as the town talk suggests (32). Even Lady Flippant's greeting, "Hail faithful Shepherdess" is likely tinged with mock-heroic sarcasm (51). Whereas it may seem almost perverse to fault someone with Christina's overt sensibilities ("thou sure wou'dst prize my only faithful heart"), in Wycherley's world those women who strive for some distinction apart from their sex deny their feminine nature—and they appropriately pay a price for such self-imposed isolation.[34]

As Lydia barely escapes the pursuing Ranger and instinctively seeks shelter at another woman's door, we find movements such as "Coming back," "pursu'd," "retire," "coming up," "returns," "follow," "run away," "seek out," and "go" illuminating the truth that life cannot be as controlled and repressed as Christina's demeanor might suggest. Ranger's interview with Christina (whom he thought he had chased from the park) exploits the device Shakespeare used so effectively in *Twelfth Night*—that is, having a character (Toby Belch in Shakespeare, Lydia here) writhing in discomfort as he or she is humiliated within earshot, unable to make his or her presence known.[35] Ranger strums the Petrarchan accompaniment by praising the "glorious" and matchless beauty Christina, only to have his chivalric instrument unstrung by the very fact that Christina had not strayed from her chamber for him to have seen: "A pox, I have hang'd my self in my own line" (166)—certainly not the only male character in Wycherley to do so. And the eagerness of Ranger's blatant flattery does not obscure the nearly constant references to the face, eyes, and to the fear of self-revelation. Wycherley's characters are fascinated by what they fear; they avoid looking directly at each other yet make continuous reference to sight and to the face. Here Christina's resolution is to "see the face of no man" until her love, Valentine, returns; and Lydia begs of her, "keep me from the sight" of Ranger (II.ii.87–90).[36]

1: INTO THE LABYRINTH 31

Wycherley's dramatic landscape teems with spies or those who suspect themselves of being spied upon, regardless of the irony that in the many references to sight the characters are often hidden by the darkness or by a door or corner. And once more a scene ends with a reminder of that most conspicuous emotion:

> Chri. I fear, Madam, you are as liable to mistakes, as your Kinsman [Ranger].
> Lyd. I fear, I am more subject to 'em. . . .
>
> (191–93)

The return of Valentine adds but one more dark stroke to the canvas rather than brightening it with the presence of another "high plot" member. We expect one who is dashing and brave, yet this young lover is bubbling with anxiety: "I fear'd my Mistress, not my Life." In his imploring Vincent to provide evidence of Christina's fidelity so that he may "clear those doubts [he] went away with" (II.iv.17–19)—the spectre of infidelity normally rendering the male at least psychologically clumsy—we note that Valentine's concerns have so debilitated him that even the paragon of virtue, Christina, fails to earn his trust. But she is after all a beautiful woman for whom Valentine feels a physical desire, and that attraction dominates all sense, leaving him vulnerable to the fear of impotence that affects such seemingly different characters as Don Diego, Gerrard, Pinchwife, and Manly. That he fears infidelity from one as virtuous as Christina is simply irrelevant to his emotions. In addition, Valentine has taken Clerimont's insult to Christina as an overture to win her affection and, reflective of basic masculine hostility, wounded him in a duel. Vincent reminds Valentine that he is still in the habit of "turning the daggers point" (39) on himself, after having attempted to convince him that Christina was a "Penelope" (32):[37] "I say she put her self . . . in her chamber, this month for you—shut out her barking Relations for you—has not seen the Sun, or face of man, since she saw you" (40–43)—an identification that, more interestingly, buttresses the incarceration motif and reminds us that Christina is really outside the sorority and thus a difficult character to appreciate. Because of the often unnatural and suffocating associations of feminine incarceration, there can be little sympathy for one who "put[s] her self" in her chamber.

It is next Valentine's turn to hide behind the door, as Ranger begins his account of the lovely woman of mystery he has just visited. The scene balances nicely with the one at Christina's apartment, points to Ranger as a catalyst for much of the comic anarchy, and reinforces Wycherley's emphasis on the characters' inability to perceive matters clearly: "I do not know her"; "do you know who lives there?" (II.iv.63–72). Whereas Vincent offers the correct assessment—that Christina has never left her apartment—Valentine covets the more destructive scenario shaped by the implications of Ranger's romantic interest in her: "Here's your *Penelope,* the woman that had not seen the Sun, nor the face of Man, since my departure; for it seems she goes out in the night, when the Sun is absent" (108–10). Valentine's parting couplet—"Hunger, Revenge, to sleep are petty Foes, / But only Death the jealous Eyes can close" (123–24)—typifies, even as a commonplace, the kind of sourness and bite that marks male relationships in Wycherley's comedies. I find it difficult, then, to see Valentine as comprising with Christina a heroic alternative or manifesting a "noble Caroline past" within the "Restoration" realism of the play.[38] And because he has no effect on Valentine's assumptions, we may conclude that Vincent is relatively impotent in his environment.[39] Given the unalterable truths of human nature, such characters, no matter how admirable, are powerless in a world that responds to more instinctive and confrontational emotions and impulses.

"High," "Middle," and "Low" plot worlds merge as the loquacious Dapperwit seeks to parade his "mistress" Lucy Crossbite before his "friend" Ranger. Dapperwit boasts of having hid his "Jewel" from the eyes of all but his friend: "[N]othing but you cou'd have wrought upon me for a sight of her" (III.ii.1–7). Appropriately distrustful of such a "fraternal" gesture, Ranger quickly replies, "I do not believe you." We soon tire of Dapperwit's tag-line, "let me perish"—and only wish he would. In Dapperwit we see no Fopling Flutter, Novelty Fashion, or Sir Wilfull Witwould, for Wycherley's "fops" lack that palpable good nature that generally marks Etherege's, Cibber's, and Congreve's creations.[40] Accordingly, Ranger's insults directed at Dapperwit's poetry and gullibility do little damage, for they fail to strike at the heart of his sensibilities. And the pandering of his mistress to Ranger, as it were—"the Devil take me, if good men (I say no more) have not been upon their knees to me, to see her, and you at last must obtain it" (III.ii.24–25)—is also an attempt to humiliate his fellow male, for by "accepting" the woman, Ranger would be beholden to Dapperwit for having assisted him in the satisfaction of his sexual desires. Indeed, Dapperwit assures Ranger that he takes "as much pleasure to bring Lovers together, as an old Woman; that as a Bankrupt Gamester loves to look on, though he has no advantage by the play; or as a Bully that fights not himself, yet takes pleasure to set people together by the ears; or as—" (IV.ii.41–45), all clearly reflecting far more than an apparent fondness for simile.[41] Dapperwit's torment of Ranger moreover includes a description of Lucy as a smoargasboard of sexual delights: "Such neck and breasts"; "Such feet, legs, and thighs"; "a mouth no bigger then your Ring"; and "then so neat, so sweet a Creature in bed, that to my knowledge, she do's not change her Sheets in half a year" (III.ii.58–65). And Dapperwit even pulls back those sheets for his "friend":

"or as hard as to put you to bed to *Lucy,* and defend you touching her" (19–20). Ranger cannot help getting tangled in these metaphoric bedclothes, for while Dappwerwit is knocking on Lucy's door he asks, "Will she not open"—intentional or not, an extension of the sexual word play that has been simply impossible to ignore. Dapperwit of course revels in Ranger's apparent interest and immediate frustration (Lucy refuses to come to the door)—thus allowing him to control, at least for the moment, one considered more traditionally masculine and superior in wit.⁴²

Emerging as protector of the "innocent," Mrs. Crossbite yanks Dapperwit back to his proper place: "I wonder at [your bringing] . . . your Friend here to witness your disgrace" (III.ii.132–34)—seeking first to strip the fop of his economic preeminence: "What, you have Mortgaged my Daughter to that Gentleman; and now wou'd offer me a snip to joyn in the security" (136–37). "[H]olding down her head," the "demure" Lucy, following her mother's example by rejecting Dapperwit, leaves the suitor no course but to vent his humiliation on another male—the disguised Addleplot, who arrives only to be struck, kicked, and called a "Sot," an "impudent Rascal," and a "rascally, insolent, pen and ink-man" (III.ii.205–10). When so defeated, Wycherley's males invariably reach for some tangible form of consolation—here, Dapperwit turns his eye immediately toward Martha as a way to "support the loss of this young Jilt [Lucy] here" (235–36).

On another front and more graphically depicting the parasitic, destructive, and ritualistic nature of human interaction, Mrs. Joyner shrewdly exacts money from Gripe toward the purchase of clothing and trinkets, the symbolic sexual preliminaries with which to arouse Lucy. Parodying the virgin sacrifice, Joyner leads Gripe deliberately from the introduction to the preparation and then to the threshold of consummation—the last destined to be frustrated. In this dark and often uncomfortable scene—a far cry from the naughty exuberance one finds in St. James's Park—the sexual word play unveils that which is both sadistic and masochistic. Still, Gripe's sordid actions and allusions speak more to the truth of human relations than do any ideal posturings of the virtuous (even Christina)—Wycherley's presentation of human nature being anything but fastidious. Lucy's reluctance to join Gripe, who beckons and implores with perverse sweetness ("come and sit down by me"; "You must sit down by me"; "To please me, you must sit, Sweetest" [III.ii.335–40]), not only stimulates him further but also gives Joyner the opportunity to bring into the open his most intense erotic fantasy: "A poor bashful Girl, Sir; I'm sorry she is not better taught" (343). This blatant appeal to sadism titillates Gripe's regressive sexuality, for Lucy is a "poor" (financially insecure) and "bashful" (complacent and intimidated) *girl,* who might be in need of better teaching from her new master: "I am glad she is not taught; I'le teach her my self" (344). Teaching, after all, demands discipline, as Lucy herself is quick to suggest: "but if I shou'd be dull, and not move as you wou'd have me, you wou'd not beat me, Sir, I hope?" (345–47). Certainly masters then beat their servants, and teachers their pupils, but given the context of the discussion, the Puritan surely envisages such a "beating" as part of his unsavory sexual reverie, in which his victim would be expected to "move" as he would have her. "Beat thee, hony Suckle," he responds, "I'le use thee thus, and thus, and thus" (348–49).[43] Rather than reflecting any surprise or revulsion at Lucy's allusion to being beaten, Gripe's reaction instead portrays him as one totally captivated by the darker connotations of the exchange.[44]

Evaluating Gripe's kissing of Lucy as a "commitment," the resourceful Joyner demands and the Puritan begrudgingly provides more and more cash with which to dress Lucy properly. The moment is vintage Wycherley in that so much of the humor exploits the characters' frustrations—Gripe's sexual obsession resulting in his forgetting how much money he has so far given Joyner—and the metaphoric dressing running contrary to Gripe's vision of an undressed and therefore helpless Lucy. After he locks the door and hears Lucy "beg" of him "what, will you lock me in, Sir? don't lock me in, Sir" (380–81), Gripe's thoughts again slip to the sadistic. He has been aroused by her reference to beating; he has now incarcerated her to establish his supremecy; and he continues figuratively the progression toward the realization of his sexual cruelty: "'Tis a private lesson, I must teach you fair." He even converts her reference to his "Fidle" and "Kitt" into allusions to his sexual organ: "I'le shew it thee presently Sweetest" (382–84).[45] And in the midst of this carnally rugged moment, Wycherley includes one of his most ubiquitous motifs, coitus interruptus. Gripe takes Lucy into his arms only to have her cry out ("don't hurt me, Sir, . . . Oh, Oh, you will kill me!") and Mrs. Crossbite and two male attendants (denying their fellow male his pleasure) break through to her rescue (387–89). Although her motives are tainted considerably, there is evidence here that even the often unappealing Mrs. Crossbite is at least a fringe member of the protective sisterhood.[46] Without question, these scenes portray the deformed, sordid, and bestial environment of the "low" world—with its lying, blackmail, and lust; but can it really be argued that such goings on are indigenous to such a world—one in need of a good bit of exposure and lashing? One doubts any serious reader or theatre patron could have sequestered Gripe into a closet marked "Puritan" or "Cit" without seeing that he represents a primitive quality common to all of society's ranks.

Later, Joyner torments Gripe with the threat of revelation; she will tell the world of his "filthy lusts" and "fleshly carnal seekings" (IV.i.25,

30)—and we certainly enjoy his bemoaning the loss of the five hundred pounds he has paid to Mrs. Crossbite as hush money.[47] Knowing that money has often served as substitute for sexual virility, Gripe offers more coins to reassert his masculinity, but the shrinking of his purse only enlarges the perception of his impotence. And here as well is another manifestation of the male's self-destructive tendency as the tight-fisted Gripe pays for the services of one who blackmails him: "[T]hou hast made me pay thee for betraying me" (7–8). Desperate to retrieve the five hundred pounds given to Mrs. Crossbite, Gripe puts his trust in Joyner, who will attempt to link herself to his future and couple him with insolvency and further humiliation. And her promise to make up for her losses with *her own,* not Lucy's, body (69–70)—another gesture of female assertiveness at the expense of the male—only adds revulsion to his considerable humiliation: "No, no, I'le rather take your word, Mrs. *Joyner*" (71).

The movement to Lydia's lodging does little to cool the glowing embers of frustration and avoidance, the word *conceal* spoken three times in the first four lines of the scene. Whether it be through the frequent use of "Asides" or "Aparts," a fractured exercise in wit, the use of paradoxical language, the cover of darkness, the sanctuary of a coach or St. James's Park, or a letter signed with another's name (such as the one Leonore delivers to Ranger), the characters filter almost all they say and often contemplate through an artificial construct, fearful of any direct expression that would leave them vulnerable in a world that seeks out and then devours the weak.[48] Even knowledge is gained indirectly and at some cost: to her observation that men wish to keep women ignorant, Lydia adds, "but 'tis that encreases our inquisitiveness, and makes us know them ignorant, as false" (III.iii.48–49). And it is Lydia who so accurately reflects the playwright's fascination with the influence and effects of fear: "Misfortunes are least dreadful, when most near. / 'Tis less to undergo the ill, then fear" (131–32).

In this scene, Wycherley once more uncorks the effervescent Lady Flippant. Initially she serves as confidant for Lydia, who shares her trepidation over Ranger's violating her privacy: "[T]he discovery of my anger to him now, wou'd be as mean as the discovery of my love to him before" (III.iii.6–7). Flippant moreover entertains Lydia, as well as the audience, with her usurpation of the familiar masculine complaint: "Though I did so mean a thing, as to love a fellow, I wou'd not do so mean a thing as to confess it. . . . [D]o you think me so ill bred, as to love a Husband" (8–16). Lydia's reply is not, I would argue, censorious but rather similarly playful: "You had a Widows heart, before you were a Widow I see."[49] Flippant's response would fit comfortably within the confines of *The Country Wife:* "I shou'd rather make an adventure of my honour, with a Gallant, for a Gown, a new Coach, a Neck-lase, then clap my Husbands cheeks for them, or sit in his lap; I shou'd be as asham'd to be caught in such a posture, with a Husband, as a brisk well bred of the Town, wou'd be, to be caught on his knees at prayers, unless to his Mistress" (18–23). The image of the kneeling male before his mistress speaks to a dynamic of power appealing to Lady Flippant and all the women in these plays. What makes matters difficult is not Flippant's *lack* of pulchritude (once more, she may well be physically attractive), but rather her frequent lack of modesty and subordination to propriety. With Dapperwit's "here's my eternal persecution" (32–33), we find the gender roles once more reversed—Daphne is in hot pursuit of her Apollo "from one side of the Stage, to the other"—energizing the scene with spirited chaos and the right measure of fear. Dapperwit is completely overmatched: "unmerciful, Lady *Flippant,*" and then "softly" to Ranger, "I promis'd to bring you off, but I find it enough to shift for myself" (61–62). And whereas the chasing and grabbing has caused her to be "out of breath," Flippant emerges as a Medusa or Artemis before the Acteon-like Dapperwit, who is certainly no Perseus. "I have been defending our cause," she says; "I have beat him out of the Pit"; "I am the revenger of our Sex, certainly" (64–65, 71)—her estimation punctuated by Dapperwit's "And the most insatiable one, I ever knew" (72). Indeed, her desire for erotic expression is inexhaustible; she serves as one of Wycherley's most formidable women—one who encroaches on the male landscape, visibly altering its terrain.

The frenzied activity at Lydia's moves its way to Vincent's lodgings—where "high" and "middle" plots again meet. Regarding Isabel's assurance that her lady had not been to the Park the previous evening and that "she had not stirr'd out since [his] departure," Valentine's reply suggests the difficulty in Wycherley's world of arriving at a state of certitude: "Will not Chamber-maids lye, *Vincent?,*" to which Vincent responds, "Will not *Ranger* lie, *Valentine?*":

> *Val.* Do you think a Woman, having the advantage of her Sex, and Education, under such a Mistress, will want impudence to dis-avow a truth, that might be prejudicial to that Mistress?
> *Vin.* But if both testimonies are fallible; why will you needs believe his? we are apter to believe the things we wou'd have, then those we wou'd not.
> (IV.iii.1–16)

Valentine's overtures to misanthropy look forward to Manly, and his distrust similarly debilitates him—he is afraid to act because he senses the incomprehensible nature of things, especially in matters touching upon his personal life: "If she be innocent, I shou'd be afraid to surprize her, for her sake; if false, I shou'd be afraid to surprize her, for my own" (26–27). Again like Manly, Valentine is a character who creates—one who shrouds his insecurity and feelings of impotence in fictive constructs. And when he capitulates and "retires to the dore behind" to learn indirectly of Ranger's designs on Christina—that is, after he has been encouraged by Vincent to "go watch her house, see who goes out, who in" (33)—we witness once more the sequestered object of ridicule bubbling with frustration as he listens to a tale that reflects poorly on his manhood. Furthering the confusion, Ranger laughs at Vincent's skepticism and jealousy regarding Christina's coming: "Incredulous envy; thou art as envious, as an impotent Letcher at a Wedding" (64–65). In addition to linking the "middle-ploters" to those like Gripe ("impotent Letcher"), the simile is most apt in its suggestion of a deep-seated masculine joy in envisioning other males as sexually inept, forced to live vicariously as voyeurs—helpless, powerless, and forever sexually frustrated. In defense of his manhood, Vincent laughs at the letter Ranger has shown him from "Christina" (actually Lydia). Ranger says he "trusts" him with such a secret because he *distrusts* him otherwise to serve his best interests: "Thou art as envious as a Rival," Ranger continues, "but if thou art mine, there's that will make you desist [gives him the letter]; and if you are not my Rival; intrusting you with such a secret, will, I know, oblige you to keep it, and assist me against all other interests [i.e., other male rivals]" (68–72). The men continue their posturing, wending around each other, each wishing to appear superior—Vincent with his "knowledge," Ranger with his "virility"—both bluffing and calling each other's bluff.[50]

In the midst of this squall comes the "gentle paragon" Christina, who immediately "pulls off her Mask." But this unveiling does little to clear anyone's vision, for misinterpretation and vanity immediately shape another mask to replace the literal one she wears. Still behind the door, Valentine remarks, "'Tis she; curs'd be these eyes, more curs'd, then when they first betray'd me, to that false bewitching face" (126–27). The confusion intensifies as Christina seeks Valentine, her face "blushing" to think of so chasing him, with both Valentine and Vincent believing, however, that she refers to the departed Ranger—suggesting again that all the references to eyes, sight, and the face ironically stress the character's *inability* to confront or discover the truth. With Wycherley moreover stirring into the recipe several pinches of sexual entendre, Christina tells Vincent, while Valentine is secluded behind the door, "pray call him out, that he may excuse it, and take it on himself, together with my shame." ("How impatient she is!," muses Vincent.) "Or do you delay the happiness I ask," she continues, "to make it more welcom? I have stay'd too long for it already, and cannot more desire it" (135–44). We find here a rare moment for Christina, in which something approaching a natural passionate energy is allowed some escape from her often stifling and pristine demeanor.[51]

The discomforting ballet continues as the characters project their limitations and insecurities: "You could not know"; "How cou'd she know?"; "You wou'd not be known"; "do you know me?"; "You knew me not"; "how cou'd he know me." Although men and women in this play often project an assured and worldly wisdom, Wycherley is always quick to undercut such apparent certainties. Ranger then returns, Valentine retreats to his hiding place, and Christina again dons her mask—but in her need to reestablish a sense of propriety she pulls it off again in the hope of correcting Ranger's assumptions and deterring his misapplied sexual energy. Yet, Ranger demonstrates that such gestures as the removal of a literal mask are generally ineffective: "Take but t'other vizard off too; I mean your anger" (250)—all followed by Valentine's coming forward to confront his rival, only to be thrust back by Vincent "before he was discov'rd by Ranger" (274). Finally, three more dancers (Lydia, Leonore, and Dapperwit) trapse upon the scene, remaining on stage only long enough to misconstrue what they have observed. Ranger's remark is well to the point: "I shall never be master of my Senses more" (311–12). However, as the women and men begin to disperse, there appears a tantalizing hint that out of this chaos some order may emerge: Ranger vows to leave off "Intrigues, honourable or dishonourable, and all sorts of rambling" (329–30). Is this a calm of mind, all passion spent?—or merely a temporary reaction to having been pulled, tossed, and embarrassed in the dance? And even the simple couplets that end the fourth act reinforce the playwright's concerns with veiled sight and the destructive aspects of human relationships:

> Just as at Blind-mans Buff, we run at all,
> Whilst those that lead us, laugh to see us fall;
> And when we think, we hold the Lady fast,
> We find it but her Scarf, or Veil, at last.

The commencement of the final act returns the "low-plot" group, who parody a kind of higher medieval pageant, with Addleplot as a "knight" (in the archaic sense, that is) and Martha as his lady in waiting. "Sir Jonas" is keeper of the key to Martha's chastity belt—that preserver of virtue and the knight's guarded masculinity. This mask (or "masque") of a by-gone era enters another level of absurdity as Addleplot remarks to Martha, "I wou'd have kept the Maiden-head of your lips, for your sweet Knight, Mrs. *Martha,* that's all; I dare swear, you never kiss'd any man before, but your Father" (V.i.11–13). Though "incarcerated," Martha feels free enough to torment her keeper: "My sweet Knight, if he will be a Knight of mine, must be contented with what he finds, as well as other Knights" (14–15)—the emphasis of the last phrase suggesting once more the sexual anguish of the restrained male, with his manhood insulted and "other Knights" or "friends" assisting in the emasculating process. Martha's showering "Sir Dapperwit" with hugs and kisses, forces Addleplot to beg her discretion: "Then reserve your kindness, only, for your Worthy Noble, Brave, Heroick Knight; who loves you only, and only deserves your kindness" (25–27). Addleplot's absurd overtures toward chivalry testify that his language and allusions have a self-destructive effect, even as he tries to protect and assert himself with them. He stands foolishly reflecting the play's preoccupation with disguise and fear of revelation: "A Pox, I must make haste to discover my self, or I shall discover, what I wou'd not discover": "So marry'd Wight, sees what he dares not blame;/And cannot budge for fear, nor stay for shame" (46–47, 57–58).

Lest we forget that we are still stumbling along in the labyrinth, Wycherley has Martha initially *defend* Gripe: "Do not speak ill of my Father," she tells Dapperwit; "he has been your friend, i'm sure"—and then quickly condemns him with "His hard usage of me, conspir'd with your good Meen, and Wit, and to avoid slavery under him, I stoop to your yoke" (72–76). Although we are tempted to applaud Martha because of her desire to escape her imprisonment, we find it difficult to commend her for seeming to choose at least a partial bondage to Dapperwit. But Martha is like Wycherley's most resourceful female characters, those who can wield power and maintain considerable freedom even *within* the inhibiting confines of the traditional male-female relationship. She accordingly shows wisdom in judging a marriage to a Dapperwit far preferable than a life dominated by an oppressive father—for the less fearful Dapperwit at least has a spark of exuberance in him, though he is a fool; whereas the sordidly aggressive Gripe suggests more a negation of life.

In Wycherley's comic panorama, the night truly has a thousand eyes. Addleplot enters the park and observes that "after all my seeking, I can find those I wou'd not find" (V.i.177), while Dapperwit is behind the door with Martha, spying on Addleplot. Sir Simon wishes now to shed his disguise as Jonas and present his true identity, but as expected he takes off his mask only to have another one placed on him by someone else. The darkness, his voice, and Martha's insistence that he *is* Jonas have trapped him in a disguise he cannot remove. Prompted by the antifraternal instinct, Dapperwit refuses to clear up the confusion, and "Jonas" simmers in the juices of his own plot, facing the prospect that Dapperwit has stolen Martha from him: "Wilt thou let her do so ill a thing,

Dapperwit, as to marry thee? open her eyes, prethee, and tell her I am a true Knight" (252–53). But Addleplot's "trial" of Martha's worth and his wish that her eyes be opened do not refute Wycherley's contention that delusion is protective: as Addleplot is forced to admit, "[I am] ruin'd by my own Plot," yet "I will plot on still, a plot of prevention" (256–57).

Following the arrival of Mrs. Crossbite, Mrs. Joyner, and Gripe (the Puritan stimulated by the darkness and the trees),[52] the ever optimistic Vincent asserts to the downtrodden Valentine, "I am prepar'd to lead you out of the dark" (291–92)—a remark that immediately strikes with apparent significance. Is this the playwright speaking or simply one of his fallible characters? Will Wycherley now begin to extricate us from the labyrinth? Vincent attempts to explain to Valentine how the confusion came about, and after the reader stumbles over the word *fear* thrice in only six lines (319–25), Vincent feels compelled to jog his hesitant friend by insisting, "Open but your eyes, and the Fantastick Goblin's vanish'd, and all your idle fears, will turn to shame" (324–25). No other assertion seems to have as much importance to the issues and motifs Wycherley has featured throughout his first play. Because the characters have avoided opening their eyes all along, one can only wonder if this remark heralds redemption and reconciliation—or will it be ignored and relegated to the refuse heap of sound advice well given but not absorbed or embraced wholeheartedly. Will Wycherley be accommodating and go the way of the fictive world in which conversions are often easily made (one thinks of another comedy with redemptive overtones set in the woods: *Midsummer Night's Dream*) or will he be truer to the spirit of the real and complex world in which such atonements are temporary or partial at best?

The answer is not long in coming. Vincent—he who gave such sage counsel on *direct* confrontation with the truth—will examine Ranger and later Dapperwit *indirectly* so that Valentine may be convinced of Christina's virtue.[53] Already we determine that he who gives such good advice cannot actually follow it, the unalterable incongruity of human nature being unsupportive of Vincent's facile though altruistic view of things. Whereas his advice to Valentine was made with vigorous certainty, his observation is way off the mark—that is, that all may be righted with direction or plain speaking and that the fears he describes are mere fantastical goblins. These fears are much deeper rooted, not to be chased away by simple, even if welcome, admissions of honesty. In short, Vincent fails to appreciate the basic human reliance on indirection to cover debilitating insecurities.

The agitation of the characters only intensifies as Ranger arrives, followed by Christina and Isabel, who are followed by Lydia and Leonore. Aparts and asides are sprinkled liberally throughout the rest of the scene—further evidence that the indirection and anxiety continue unfazed by Vincent's seemingly climactic observation. With further references to sight, the characters look at each other, from the front, back, and sides, hoping to discern a sign of each one's true feelings, searching for something that will allow them to maintain an edge or gain power. But the moonlight masks rather than illuminates because, as Vincent observes, it "scarce affords light enough to distinguish a man from a tree" (357—58). "How can you know *Ranger*, then?" asks Valentine (359). Indeed, how can anyone truly know anyone else? Vincent's earlier remark to Valentine seems more and more, then, something to be marveled at for its absurdity than praised for its sagacity. What chance does the reformer or satirist have, we might wonder, if such advice from relatively attractive individuals is shown so ineffectual? What Vincent says of Christina—she who was at home "surrounded with so many fears and griefs" (354)—again serves an emblematic function—extending to all four of Wycherley's comedies.

There is no cessation of movement as Valentine follows Ranger and Christina, along with Lydia and the maids. "They all go off together in a huddle, hastily," but then three break off from the others, moving quickly past each other, exchanging brief glances, nods, and asides—all in a cotillion of indeterminacy, going nowhere but moving almost frenetically. And the relationship between the masking and the dread of discovery remains paramount: "I wish that Cloud may yet with-hold the Moon," Valentine says to himself, "that this false Woman [Christina], may not discover me, before I do her" (382–84). In a space of some sixty lines, Vincent's neat advice to "Open but your eyes" has been knocked down and trampled amid the confusion, hesitation, and posturing. Only to avoid the fear of masculine disgrace—the result, he believes, of his love's infidelity—does Valentine wish to reveal himself to Christina (who believes, of course, that she is talking to Ranger): "'Tis rather a tryal of my self then her; I cannot undergo it . . . I cannot hold; I must discover my self, rather then her infamy" (387–93). But because he is masked by the darkness and unwittingly by Christina's believing him to be another, he does not come forward but instead holds back, allowing her to unravel the mystery in an oblique, rather than direct, manner. Certainly the more he hears, the more convinced Valentine becomes of Christina's sincerity, but the fact that he allows her to go on for as long as she does speaks to his unwillingness to emerge from the protective darkness: "My joy, and pity, makes me as mute, as my shame; yet I must discover myself" (431–32).

But just as we sit back and expect the predictably saccharine reconciliation between the lovers, Christina stuns us with her reaction to Valentine's revelation of his identity: "How! is it you? then I am not satisfy'd":

Val. Will you be worse than your word?
Chris. I gave it not to you.
(441–43)

As Valentine holds her by the hand, she "seems to struggle to get from him" (448). If anything in the play qualifies as entrapping the reader, this reaction certainly does.[54] Just what is going on here? Other than thwarting reader and audience expectations, Wycherley demonstrates again just how inimical is the notion of direct discourse. Initially, Christina is humiliated at having "discover'd" herself to Valentine in such a manner. It is one thing to praise him and voice her love and devotion indirectly through a conversation with "Ranger," but to know that she has so opened herself to Valentine makes her painfully aware that, at least for the moment, she has sacrificed her equality, if not power, in their relationship—because such openness is always tantamount to vulnerability. Her curt response and her pulling away from his hand are instinctive gestures toward a reassertion of her potency, and they help at least momentarily to give her the kind of interest and vitality her more exemplary status does not afford. Since the protective mask was stripped from her, exposing her directly, she begins to shape another one with this apparently inexplicable aloofness. More than simply sustaining the farcical confusion, Wycherley well demonstrates that aspect of human nature that, out of a survival instinct, drives women and men to act irrationally and inconsistently. Valentine's comment to Vincent, "who is blind now? who deceiv'd now?," refers on the surface to his friend's confusing Lydia with Christina, but the irony is that we could truthfully answer: "Well, everyone is."

Ranger, who earlier vowed to end this form of "rambling," encourages "Christina" (Lydia) to admit her true feelings: "but now, when no body sees us, nor hears us, why this unseasonable shyness?" (462–64). No one character rises above the indeterminate landscape; no one character can manipulate from a position of strength; almost everything happens by accident. As Ranger begins to speak kindly of Lydia, who in a moment of considerable power lets him talk and talk and talk ("I do resolve, if I can find her again, to keep her for ever" [484–90]), we can only wonder if, like Christina, his lyric will change when Lydia reveals herself to him. And indeed the pattern is repeated—once more indicating that the three worlds of the play are more similar than traditional assumptions suggest—Lydia repeats Valentine's words, "now cannot I hold out any longer, I must discover my self" (491–92). And we might also anticipate that Ranger's inconstant nature, to which he has so brazenly admitted, makes hollow his promise to "keep" Lydia "for ever." But we should have learned by now to avoid following such "well-marked" paths in Wycherley's labyrinth, for the playwright snares us once more with Ranger's parting words to "Christina": "But, Madam, because I intend to see you no more, i'le take my leave of you for good and all; since you will not speak, i'le try if you will squeek" (493–95). He hopes to make her squeal with sexual delight or gasp in some kind of erotic horror at his manhood, but she only has time to "squeek" (shriek) with apparent anger and fear as he attempts to "throw her down."[55]

This is without question midsummer night's madness; yet Ranger's recourse to violent sexual gratification is more an integral part of Wycherley's world than the apparent sincerity and loyalty we earlier found in Christina. This is an environment in which sexual impulses are expressed in various and often disturbing ways. Lady Flippant's bawdy insouciance, Christina's purity and narcissistic sublimation and repression, Martha's anxiety, Lucy's near-sadistic and maschochistic word play, Dapperwit's transferral of the sexual drive to wit and vanity, Gripe's perverted longings, and now Ranger's seemingly spontaneous though more likely calculated passionate aggression all form the sexual dynamics of the play. Here again, however, the result is frustration—a coitus interruptus that hardly leaves the reader smiling comfortably, but rather grinning with both pleasure and discomfort at what has transpired. Such jagged edges as this may prevent our seeing the play as a smooth though conventional—or pastoral—comedy, but what we have instead is far more captivating and engaging than we might have initially assumed.

Upon discovering Lydia as the victim of his intended rape ("Is it she! *Lydia* all this while?"), Ranger feels as defeated and stripped of power as did Christina earler in the scene. But whereas Christina recovered lost ground with her haughty air, Ranger does so by quickly shifting the focus of guilt to Lydia: "you thought I did not know you now, because I offer'd you such an unusual civility.... Certainly, therefore, I wou'd have taken my revenge, you see, for your tricks" (502–8).[56] Typical of Wycherley's males, Ranger calls on verbal aggression as well as physical intimidation to regain lost potency—which he seeks to punctuate by taking her by the hand:

Lyd. Come not near me.
Ran. Nay, you need not be afraid, I wou'd ravish you, now I know you.
(518–20)

Are we or Lydia to take comfort in such assurances? And what do we make of her willingness to take the blame?: "And yet, *Leonore*, I think 'tis but justice, to pardon the fault, I made him commit?" Rather than being the traditional naiveté and self-effacement of "romance" heroines, the explanation in Wycherley's world is more likely that she has been so stimulated by his transgression that she flushes with a new feeling of arousal and power, which may be detected in her remark, "though I made the blot,[57] your over-sight has lost the game" (525–26)—the game being the sexual union. She must realize that, although he has transferred guilt and claimed knowledge all along, his sexual assertions here have been circumvented and his weaknesses revealed, giving her enough to maintain equality, if not ascendency, in their relationship.

All that seems left, then, is Dapperwit's arrival and announcement of his recent marriage to Martha, "an Heiress worth thirty thousand pound, let me perish" (539–40). He invites everyone, as it were, to a post-game reception that will include the now secondary ritual, as Ranger implies, of the other couples' marriages. Wycherley therefore resolves the crises, as staged drama demands, but he does not bundle his package tightly. The reader experiences relief at the end of this scene but only in the sense that the perplexing and feverish activity has finally terminated; there are no smiles at the prospects of tried and true young lovers at last united. We have witnessed two "reconciliation" scenes involving the pairs of lovers: The first, which features the "ideal" couple, Christina and Valentine (what two more benign and hopeful names could Wycherley have chosen?), ends in Christina's anger, discomfort, denial, retraction, and struggle to break free. The second scene offers a union of the more "realistic" lovers, Lydia and Ranger, which is marked by duplicity, misstatement, violence, and apparent stupidity and self-effacement. And now we have been informed that Martha, having long sought freedom from her tyrannical and perverted father, has recently become the wife of a vain coxcomb.[58]

The final scene begins, oddly enough, with what one might actually expect: the reaction of Gripe to his daughter's marriage: "Oh graceless Babe, marry'd to a Wit! an idle, loytering, slandering, foul-mouth'd beggarly Wit" (V.ii.2–3). But whereas there is pleasure in seeing Gripe's plans so foiled,[59] we must at least accept the wisdom of his assessment; for just an instant we are forced against our wills to appreciate that his view is correct. (And, as a testament to the indomitable ego, Addleplot hopes to latch on to Lady Flippant as a measure of consolation for having lost Martha to Dapperwit.) The defensive posture the reader has likely assumed—owing to Wycherley's surprises, twists, and turns—at least prepares one for the next shock: Martha's admission that she married Dapperwit only because she was "six months gone with Child" and saw no promise for another husband (23–25), a revelation that only corroborates the suspicion that she was always aware of her options and sought a marriage that, under the circumstances, offered her the best chance at some power and freedom. Dapperwit has certainly heard nothing about the pregnancy: "How's that!" (28). This is obviously the ultimate comic irony in the "Minister's Daughter" vein,[60] and it appears to work as even further comeuppance for Dapperwit: "Who wou'd have thought, *Dapperwit,* you wou'd have marryed a Wench?," muses Ranger (29–30). But Dapperwit's reaction once more defies prediction: he is content with her thirty thousand pounds and blithely insists that the celebration go on. After all, as he tells Gripe, "I cannot be without a Woman" (48–49), as he avoids the frightening implications of her condition—that is, he has been victim of another male's potency, thus emphasizing visually, even if unfairly, his own shortcomings. Dappwerwit is able to make the transfer of sexuality to money, that frequent sanctuary for displaced masculine virility. He can be "manly" because he has what the other man lacks: Martha's person and her father's money. And the victory over Gripe helps compensate for any loss of ego and of course the "loss" of his "wench" Lucy (47). And Gripe's lament, "My Daughter, my Reputation, and my Money gone" (50), teasingly implies that at least now he has his priorities in the correct order—although his very next words totally smother that newborn thought: "but the last [money] is dearest to me."[61] And to our amazement, Gripe joins in the merriment by deciding to marry Lucy, get his "five hundred pound again," and beget heirs "to exclude my Daughter, and frustrate *Dapperwit."* Gripe too finds a way to reconstruct his razed masculinity, comprehending that the rebuilding process, paradoxically, can only be accomplished by destruction. He now feels comfort and security in the old chestnut, "cheaper keeping a Wife then a Wench" (50–55).

Dapperwit suggests a dance, indicating that as the play ends the rituals continue; no real order has been restored or, better yet, introduced. There is certainly a feeling of cohesion; this is after all one of the few plays that mates so many pairs of males and females (five)—only Mrs. Joyner and Mrs. Crossbite are left without their "Jacks" (though they had them years earlier). But such coupling does little to plaster over the frustration and fear characteristic of the play as a whole. The antagonism between the males, for example, remains conspicuous in Gripe's sadistic revelation to his new son-in-law that he will marry Lucy, the wit's mistress, and thereby deny him in the end all of that thirty thousand pounds. Dapperwit has as a result ordered a dance celebrating his own ruination. Lucy Crossbite remains silent, hidden somewhere in the shadows of this scene. What her reaction will be when the time comes to entertain Gripe's demands is unclear, although she has already demonstrated an ability to manipulate the old Puritan; we may trust that women like her mother and Mrs. Joyner (out of both altruistic and selfish reasons) will assist her in maintaining whatever dominion she can establish, for the alternative is too frightful to consider: incarcerated literally and spirittually by Gripe. (Surely we need not fear for Lady Flippant in a marriage to Addleplot; she would be far too much woman for Sir Simon to handle, more a Restoration Wife of Bath than a Patient Griselda.)

Our parting glimpses of Valentine, Christina, Ranger and Lydia are also less than reassuring. Valentine wonders why Christina is still angry but feels confident that tomorrow, after the marriage, she will "put me out of all my fears." Her response—"I am afraid then you wou'd give me my revenge, and make me jealous of you; and I had rather suspect your faith, then you shou'd mine" (99–102)—suggests a more complaisant woman than when we saw her last, but (owing to her haughtiness and capacity for anger) one cannot conclude with certainty that her remarks are said with genuine warmth and affection. And we can rest assured that she will be quick to show Valentine her more acerbic side should troubles arise between them. And both Valentine and Christina mention the word "fear," thus keeping that truth of life clearly in focus. Playfully it seems, Ranger tells Lydia that after the wedding he will have his turn "of watching, doging, standing under the window, at the dore, behind the hanging or—" which implies more of the same behavior we have witnessed throughout the play and the subtle realization that she is in fact a formidable woman, expressing her physical charms more openly to others than he might wish. Nor does her reply make us confident that their union would be ideal: "But, if I cou'd be desperate now, and give you up my liberty; cou'd you find in your heart to quit all other engagements, and voluntarily turn your self over to one woman, and she a Wife too? cou'd you away with the insupportable bondage of Matrimony?" (107–10), indicating that she is already establishing a set of rules that will provide her with the best chance for freedom within marriage—the beginning of a proviso in which she expects much, one spoken mildly perhaps but with a tone reflective of a woman weathering herself for a storm rather than anticipating sunny conjugal bliss. Appropriately, Ranger ends the play with an intriguing couplet: "The end of Marriage, now is liberty, / And two are bound—to set each other free"—one ripe with paradox suggestive of the often indeterminate nature of life and one that reflects what women both fear losing most and most hope to obtain in the marital relationship.

Love in a Wood provides enough evidence to mark it as a first play;[62] for example, the possibilities for some characters are not always fully realized and the motifs speak at times a little too loudly for the best kind of comic writing. Surely, some of the surprises are unprepared for and some of the characters and relationships may leave us unfulfilled, but these are the results, it seems to me, of Wycherley's interest in demonstrating the often tormenting, incomprehensible, and antagonizing way of the world rather than their being the consequences of a playwright's maiden effort. In his probing beneath the social and superficial aspects of human interaction, Wycherley shows how so much is prompted by the need for and preoccupation with power and sexual gratification and how fears and anxieties are reflected and then worked out, often with unsatisfactory results. These characters are not as fragmented and divorced as many critics have believed, for as Hobbes observed, "Nature hath made men so equall . . . [that] when all is reckoned together, the difference between man, and man, is not so considerable."[63] Although he determines that men and women move and behave in ritualistic patterns, Wycherley shows that life does not always follow expected and predictable paths, clearly marked and easily traveled. And therefore, we leave it to Ranger to provide the appropriate emblem for *Love in a Wood:* "[W]e are . . . way-lay'd, with Surprizes, Trapans, Dangers, and Murdering dis-appointments" (IV.iii.332–33).

2
On the Edge of Discovery: *The Gentleman Dancing-Master*

THE CONGESTED NATURE OF THE CHARACTERS AND INTRIGUES IN *Love in a Wood* may well have encouraged Wycherley to trim his numbers when he came to write his next play, *The Gentleman Dancing-Master*. Even so, he continued unabated his exploration of the motivations and conduct of volatile and fearful men and women. As the title of his first play suggests frenzy and confusion, the title of his second conjures the stimulating and often disturbing associations of dancing. That is, from Pepys's agonies over the relationship between Pembleton and his Elizabeth to Samuel Johnson's apparent disdain for the antics of the dancing master in the next century, we find that dancing masters were often viewed suspiciously and that dancing itself, although at times perceived as an emblem of harmony, served as a more dignified sibling of sexual expression, often as a convenient way to decorate ubiquitous physical desire.[1] For example, in Vanbrugh's *The Relapse* (1696), Worthy entreats of "good Berenthia" to "lose no time, but let us begin the dance as fast as we can"—to which she replies, "Not till the fiddles are in tune, pray sir. Your lady's strings will be very apt to fly, I can tell you that, if they are wound up too hastily. But if you'll have patience to screw 'em to their pitch by degrees, I don't doubt but she may endure to be played upon" (III.ii.233–40). And a number of bawdy verses of the seventeenth century, such as "Why Do You Trifle, Fy Upon It?" (ca. 1610) make even more explicit connections between the sex act and "a merry Jig."[2]

But such associations had been made long before the seventeenth century. Juvenal's Sixth Satire also makes clear that dancing masters and the dance (with accompanying music) were closely linked to promiscuous sexual activity, as represented by Bathyllus, the ballet dancer under Domitian, who elicited from women a number of highly agitated responses: "One can't control her bladder, / Another suddenly moans in drawn-out ecstasy / As though she was coming."[3] The early Christian period often united dancing with the deadly sin of Lust, and in the medieval *exempla* were frequent threats and even administration of cruel

2: ON THE EDGE OF DISCOVERY 49

punishments to those who chose to dance—especially women. In the Renaissance, folk dancing was only deemed acceptable in the ballroom when its more erotic properties were concealed. The seventeenth century witnessed a strong Puritan reaction against the dance, particularly from men like William Prynne, who called for the excommunication of dancing masters and an end to all dancing.[4] And even in his first play, Wycherley equates dancing with Gripe's perversions: as Lucy says, "Are you a Dancing-master then, Sir? but if I shou'd be dull, and not move as you wou'd have me, you wou'd not beat me, Sir, I hope?" (III.ii.345). Clearly, then, many seeing or later reading *The Gentleman Dancing-Master* would by precedent as well as by inclination view dancing in the play in its provocative as well as its literal sense.

The comedy opens with young Hippolita, true to her namesake, voicing frustration over the restrictions placed on her and her sex: "To confine a Woman just in her rambling Age! take away her liberty at the very time she shou'd use it! O barbarous Aunt! O unnatural Father! to shut up a poor Girl at fourteen, and hinder her budding; all things are ripen'd by the Sun; to shut up a poor Girl at fourteen!" (I.i.1–6). Her lament is about all the exposition one needs, but it serves to establish immediately the motif of the incarcerated woman, restrained by authority figures who would suppress and inhibit her natural desires and expressions.[5] (And Wycherley perhaps takes a lead from Shakespeare in a possible pun on "*ripen'd* by the *Sun*": "sun" to *son*—a young male.) She is even kept from attending church "because the men are sometimes there!" (20–21). Arthur Friedman and others have provided the reasons why Hippolita is but fourteen years of age.[6] However, we might add that Wycherley likely wished to depict as young a female as possible who is still believable as a *sexual* creature, interested in expressing herself erotically (budding or ripening, as she says)—an age reflecting a more natural rather than socially influenced female.[7] The play's basic structure of course invites the expectation that she will escape the bondage and watchful eyes of her aunt Mrs. *Caution* and father James *Formal* (a name shelved for the Spanish alias "Don Diego"), and we guess early that neither caution nor formality (propriety) will be able to suppress the liberating instincts of this young Amazon.[8] Even the possibility that her escape may result from some improper act does not inhibit a desire to see her free and able, as she puts it, to "take a Ramble to the Park" (10)—ultimately to St. James's, we guess.

Hippolita's actions and aspirations are clearly self-centered, but in a healthy, not a debilitating sense:

Hipp. Not see a man!—
Pru. Nor come near a man!—

Hipp. Nor hear of a man—
Pru. No, Miss, but to be deny'd a man!
(24–27)

The repetition of *man* certainly emphasizes what Hippolita's intended husband, Monsieur de Paris, is not, and Prue's accompaniment (she is surely speaking for her mistress as well as for herself) "and to have no use at all of a man!" reflects well the aggressiveness and desire for dominion we find in almost every one of Wycherley's female characters. Hippolita resists domestic tyranny (the arranged marriage) and follows her basic inclinations toward freedom. She is resourceful, vivacious, irrepressible, and as yet unspoiled by the demands of social behavior, although not oblivious to them. We are soon aware that Wycherley has no real intention of giving us a story-book stage romance, complete with a modern-day Perseus on hand to rescue the imperiled Andromeda—even if the play's structure suggests just that. Considering the purely sexual motivations and the fears that drive women and men, we may safely conclude that benign affection and mutual respect will cut few furrows in Wycherley's dramatic landscape.

Prue believes her mistress has known "little of the World" because she would apparently refuse a fool for a husband; after all, even though he is dull, Monsieur is "handsom enough to lye with in the dark," and in the daylight Hippolita may "take the priviledge of a Wife" (47–51). Being "of the world," Prue understands that if the husband is vain but complaisant he may be easily maniplauted, thereby permitting the woman the kind of freedom she requires in a marriage. Surely, marrying Monsieur is better than being "shut up as long as you live" (61–62) in the house of another kind of male—the more malevolently egotistical, one such as Don Diego. But at this point Hippolita is less naive than she is delightfully uncivil and rebellious, whereas to her father and aunt she is incorrigible and uncontrollable and must therefore be imprisoned—in her room now, in a marriage to Monsieur de Paris soon enough. She entertains us with her uncompromising feminism, even though the images she presents are at times unnatural for one of Wycherley's female characters: "but rather than marry my Cousin, I will be a Nun in the new Protestant Nunnery they talk of, where (they say) there will be no hopes of coming near a man!" (67–70).

The moment we set eyes on Monsieur de Paris (the former Anglo, Mr. Parris), we have every confidence that he will be the conduit through which Hippolita will meet another and so gain her freedom, for it is he who tells his cousin about Gerrard, the mere "*English*-man," who is handsome, tall, "witty," "brave," "well-bred," intelligent (although he has none of the "French graces," such as skill in dancing or in French song)—in short, virile, which of course stimulates Hippolita's interests. Understanding intuitively the destructive aspects of male relationships, Hippolita must realize that Monsieur will lead Gerrard to her if he believes doing so would serve Gerrard ill.[9] To torment her cousin and to indulge in delightful prospects, she informs Monsieur that her prison cell (her chamber) has a "door into the Gallery, which looks into the the backyard of a Tavern, whence Mr. *Gerrard* once spying me at the Window, has often since attempted to come in at that Window by the help of the Leads of a low Building adjoyning, and indeed 'twas as much as my Maid and I cou'd do to keep him out—" (160–65). She hardly depicts a starry-eyed Romeo below her balcony, but rather a sexually driven predator, aroused at the sight of the young female, emerging from the backyard of a tavern, climbing like a nipped cat over all obstacles, forcing himself against the barriers that stand in his way—a basic, raw sexual energy driving him forward. (We later find that he has "broken" glass to arrive in her room [II.i.85–88].) This is our first impression of Gerrard, but recalling the playwright's inclination for misdirection in *Love in a Wood*, we should distrust such a portrait. In any event, the image of the young Lothario "spying" Hippolita from afar and having that sight stimulate his sexual desire introduces the voyeuristic motif that so permeates the play.[10]

Suggesting that Wycherley abhors a vacuum of antagonists in his plays, the "oppressive" Mrs. Caution, arrives as Monsieur leaves—with Hippolita's "command" to him that Gerrard come and prevent her marriage to Paris! (210–15)—Wycherley being more conscious here about keeping the scene less cluttered with bodies. Appropriate to her name, Caution seems censorious of all the "giggling" she hears (241), to which Hippolita retaliates with an allusion to her own "youth" and her aunt's "crabbed old age" (252). The puckish Hippolita chooses to open her formal assault, however, with ambiguity and paradox: "I never lived so wicked a life, as I have done this twelve-month, since I have not seen a man" (263–64). How could this be, asks her keeper, since you have "not seen a man" all that time?" Hippolita responds, "No, I have done no ill, but I have paid it with thinking" (267). In her attempt to frustrate her aunt (and I would add to draw her out a bit and loosen what Hippolita sees as an all-too-suffocating mask of propriety), the young Amazon refers to the strong association of thought and morality made in works such as *The Whole Duty of Man* (1670), but oddly Mrs. Caution takes the less-rigid position of a Milton (in *Aereopagitica*): "O that's no hurt; to think is no hurt" (268). And well she might believe so, for she reveals that she has had similar erotic thoughts, not only in dreams (the "Widow's Comfort," as she terms it) but awake, when she has been unable to sleep.[11] In effect offering her niece sisterly advice, Caution also permits

Hippolita, for these brief moments at any rate, to be her confessor and comforter—the kind of communication between women Wycherley finds most healthy and natural. She rationalizes that when sexual contemplations are relegated to dreams one is exonerated from any charge of impropriety. But having those images come to mind while awake and in bed is quite another matter—something that imposes the formidable conflict between the natural and the proper.[12] More than the typical dowdy, *senex irata,* or sexual hypocrite, Mrs. Caution is a more intriguing study, a woman who because of the various inhibitions imposed by her surroundings and training, is left to express her erotic sensibilities indirectly and secretly in late-night reveries.[13]

The motives for Mrs. Caution's inordinate concern and interest in her niece's sexual imaginings are complex: first there is an understanding that sexual frustration is unhealthy and enervating; but also present is envy for the young woman's vitality and undaunted attitude and the opportunity to satisfy any physical urges—an opportunity Caution feels has passed her by.[14] Hippolita tells her aunt, "But I did not only dream, Ih—" (sighing) (278). We may be tempted to conclude the *aposiopesis* as follows: ". . . I also had sexual relations with a man in this house." Her aunt realizes of course that such would be impossible owing to the constant surveillance (by herself and Don Diego) under which Hippolita has lived. Her highly agitated response, "How, how! did you more than dream! speak, young Harlotry; confess," likely suggests instead her fear that Hippolita has masturbated—a release for pent-up sexual energy, we may assume, Caution has herself considered, if not actually practiced—for her reference to *waking* sexual thoughts at least encourages our considering that possibility.[15] But Caution is frightened by the open admission of any sexual activity and the articulation of erotic dreams and fantasies: they must succumb to propriety; they must be masked in some way. As a result, she is highly relieved when Hippolita explains, "I did not only dream, but I was pleased with my dream when I wak'd" (282–83). Again, her aunt's reply suggests much, "Oh is that all?" Ironically, her fear for something more sexually graphic has disarmed her "puritannical" pose, and she has now unwittingly endorsed her niece's sensual daydreams and the enjoyment of those dreams.[16] Wistfully dwelling, we might guess, on her own daydreams, Mrs. Caution recovers enough to tell her niece of the evils of the modern "masquerading Age," in which women give up their freedom and remain "Virgins" only in disguise (300–305). Despite her allegiance to "caution," then, she demonstrates a sensitivity to a women's loss of power and freedom in the social world—even while being partly responsible for the incarceration of her niece. Wycherley again informs us that his characters' names may misinform as well as predict.

Wycherley now presents the eager Gerrard listening attentively as Monsieur de Paris repeats what Hippolita had given him to say—that if he is interested in her, the Englishman is to appear at her window at six in the morning to prevent her marriage to an "unnamed" suitor. The "French" arachnid delights in luring the confident English fly into the trap, even though we see Gerrard as properly on guard: "I should be unwilling to be fool'd by this Coxcomb" (I.ii.36–37). Gerrard at least begins as a "truewit," for he properly appreciates that males cannot trust one of their own sex, but he is aroused enough by the prospects of the young Amazon to inquire further into her family background, discarding all skepticism the moment he realizes her father is a "rich *Spanish* Merchant" (40–41). Behind this apparent shift from caution to enthusiasm— "I will be an easie Fool for once" (44)[17]—is the young man's greed and sexual curiosity, although we cannot discount another less direct impulse that drives him forward: the pleasure in taking the father's daughter as well as his money, an exercise in power and manipulation, another of the destructive aspects of male relationship—one evident at the conclusion of *Love in a Wood*. Gerrard is conscious that his business is analagous to hunting: "To be caught in a Fools Trap—I'le venture it" (47)—that is, if the possibilities for bagging attractive game remain good. Even his decision to venture on the expedition shows him more than a "robust and honest Englishman,"[18] for he suggests one who is adventurous, egocentric, and avaricious—qualities matched by his ostensible quarry Hippolita. Our interest in the confrontation is as a result heightened, even though Wycherley will disappoint those who expect that Gerrard will, by nature of his masculine charm and strength, eventually *win* the young woman's heart.

Reflective of masculine aggression whatever the context, Gerrard and Martin "gang up" on Monsieur, who feels compelled to provide a substantial defense of his "Frenchness" and aversion to all that is English (50–140), a section of the play in which Wycherley perhaps tries too hard to exploit ethnocentric humor[19]—even though Monsieur shows considerable fear of revealing his true "Englishness." Regardless, the scene at the French House turns more appealingly frenetic at the moment the waiter announces the arrival of the whirlwinds Flounce and Flirt—Gerrard's anxiety immediately evident in his fear of being the prey rather than the hunter: as he says to the waiter, "[T]ell your Master, if he cannot protect us from the Constable, and these midnight-Coursers, 'tis not a House for us" (I.ii.146–47). The Waiter's panic when told to confront the tempestuous duo testifies to their Amazonian nature: "They'll not be satisfi'd with that, they'll break open the door"; last evening they had roamed "all over the house" for two noblemen, who "were fain to hide themselves in the Bar under my Mistresses Chairs and Peticoats." "[D]o the Women hunt out the men so now?" asks a nervous Monsieur (149–53). These women (along with Hippolita) emphatically challenge all concepts of male ascendency—as Martin admits, "And we are not so much afraid to be taken up by the Watch, as by the t[e]aring midnight Ramblers or Houza-Women" (159–60). Again, it is certainly tempting to depict Flirt and Flounce as ugly harridans, large of bulk,[20] using more powder on their faces than might a volley of cannon. The visual treat would be unforgettable, but to view them as more like Penthesileas than as Medusas would only heighten the effect and significance of their appearance. They upset the financial security of men; they ridicule convention; and they affect the flow of business. An aggressive *and* sexually attractive woman is far more redoubtable to a man than an obese or homely female easily dismissed as something outside the realm of desirability. (And they have both been kept by wealthy Lords [177–78].) Their tumultuous entrance—they strike the waiter as well as "kick" and curse—refusing to be stopped by those who would lock them *out* (as opposed to the normal pattern of locking women *in*) moreover illustrates the determination most of Wycherley's women have to escape incarceration and assert themselves erotically and powerfully.[21]

These women, intensified manifestations of Hippolita, rhetorically (and to some extent literally) capture and bind the males in the room. Flounce says to Gerrard, "You need not be afraid, Sir, we will use no violence to you, you are not fit for our Service; we know you—," to which her sister Amazon adds, "The hot Service you have been in formerly, makes you unfit for ours now; besides, you begin to be something too old for us we are for the brisk Hoaza's of seventeen or eighteen" (188–92).[22] To understand better Don Diego's wish to keep his daughter bound to his influence, we should consider the example of Flirt and Flounce, for it is this kind of unbridled sexuality that he fears his daughter possesses, something he would be unable to control once it is given rein. Moreover, when the two men inform the women that they cannot join them for supper—Martin pointing out, "Besides, we have supp'd"—Flounce immediately squelches such feeble attempts at assertiveness: "No matter, we only desire you shou'd look on, while we eat, and put the glass about, or so" (242–43). Her demeanor assumes (in good "gender-turn-about" fashion) that these men are good only for amusement, service, and decoration.

Suggesting further the fragmentation of male relationships, Gerrard and Martin retire, leaving a helpless Monsieur to serve at the women's pleasure. They toy with him, order for him, feed him, and take delight in his servitude: "I kiss your hand obligeant, Madam," he says to Flirt before he begins ordering in French (293). Monsieur must appreciate the frightening implications of the women's decision: "I think we had

2: ON THE EDGE OF DISCOVERY

beter carry the Gentleman home with us" (318–19), surely dreading what they would likely expect of him and doubting if he could in any way satisfy such a pair as this.[23] As if to make him even more pliable, Flirt announces "I have a passion for you, Sir. . . . An extreme passion, dear Sir, you are so *French,* so mightily *French,* so agreeable *French*" (350–54). This "Gallic" fly has now lighted on the *English* web: "Well then," a momentarily more confident Monsieur concedes, "I'le venture my body wit thee for one night." But the merry black widow has other ideas: "For one night, don't you believe that, and so you wou'd leave me to morrow; but I love you so, I cannot part with you, you must keep me for good and all, if you will have me. I can't leave you for my heart" (358–62). Flirt's mock-helplessness only underscores the power she wields in the sprouting relationship. Rather than a comically grotesque interlude, this scene prepares us well for Hippolita's imperial domination of Gerrard.

Upon first meeting the young Amazon, Gerrard seems the conventional Lothario: "She is beautiful beyond all things I ever saw" (II.i.60). However, she immediately assumes a pose of both aloofness and innocence, which puts her in the best postion to keep him off balance and thereby establish her power: "[I]f you do not like your reception, I cannot help it; for I am not us'd to receive men" (II.i.57–59). Gerrard then makes the mistake of mimicking Hippolita's initial verbal tag of "I'de have you to know" (68–70)—prompting a measured reply: "What do you mock me too? I know I am but a home-bred-simple Girl; but I thought you Gallants of the Town had been better bred, than to mock a poor Girl in her Fathers own house" (71–73). Such feigned modesty lures Gerrard several steps further into the snare, and she will clearly make him pay for his attempt at verbal superiority.[24] Hippolita also makes evident in an aside that such artifice is not so much learned as it is instinctive: "if dissimulation were not very natural to a Woman, I'm sure I cou'd not use it at this time; but the mask of simplicity and innocency is as useful to an intriguing Woman, as the mask of Religion to a States-man, they say" (91–95).

The moment that most encourages our judging her primarily as a traditional ingenue is the following exchange, which continues Wycherley's interest in sight and truth avoidance:

Ger.   Why do you look away, dearest Miss?
Hipp. Because you quarrell'd with me just now for frowning upon you, and I cannot help it, if I look upon you.
Ger.   O let me see that Face at any rate.
Hipp. Wou'd you have me frown upon you? for I shall be sure to do't.
Ger.   Come, I'le stand fair: you have done your worst to my heart already.

> *Hipp.* Now I dare not look upon him, lest I shou'd not be able to keep my word. [aside]
> *Ger.* Come, I am ready, and yet I am afraid of her frowns. [aside] Come, look, Ih—am ready, Ih—am ready.
> *Hipp.* But I am not ready. [aside]
> *Ger.* Turn, dear Miss, Come, Ih—am ready.
> *Hipp.* Are you ready then, I'le look? [Turns upon him] No faith, I can't frown upon him, if I shou'd be hang'd. [aside]
>
> (II.i.96–111)

And soon after, Gerrard says to himself, "So I have look'd upon her so long, till I am grown bashful too; Love and Modesty come together like Money and Covetousness, and the more we have, the less we can shew it. I dare not look her in the face now, nor speak a word" (126–29). Certainly, Hippolita may be likened to Etherege's Harriet and Congreve's Millamant in her assuming a more independent and haughty demeanor in order to disguise a genuine affection for the male, but Hippolita is younger than they and thus closer to instinct than to social experience and her attitude is not quite that of Harriet's "I feel as great a change within, but he shall never know it" or Millamant's "Well, if Mirabell should not make a good husband, I am a lost thing;—for I find I love him violently."[25] Although attracted to Gerrard, Hippolita is not simply in love with him in the familiar sense, and even the "love" she later claims to feel is secondary to the realization that he is a vehicle by which she may escape her imprisonment and exercise her freedom and dominion.[26] In any event, the apparent "struggles" she has with her feelings here clearly evaporate the more she is in Gerrard's company.

Both realize, though especially Hippolita, that a loss of power is the lot of those who reveal too much; accordingly, when she observes Gerrard's bashfulnes (a sign of vulnerability), she feels more confident to say (and not in an aside), "[W]hen once we Women find the men bashful, then we take heart; now I can look upon you as long as you will" (134–35). Hippolita's natural intelligence informs her already that she has an excellent chance of remaining the ascendent partner in the relationship. Gerrard is therefore not living up to expectations; that is, we expected to find him a more vigorous, aggressive, and witty English male, one who would let nothing deter him in his desire for the young woman. But once he moves from voyeur (looking at her from another vantage point) to participant (in the room with her), he loses most of his nerve; he stumbles and hedges, revealing less an irresistible charm than a basic insecurity. And for all her seeming girlish delight in his appearance—"[I] like this man strangely, I was going to say lov'd him"—Hippolita keeps in mind what is most important to her: "Courage then, *Hippolita*," she steadies herself, "make use of the only opportunity thou canst have to enfranchise thy self: Women formerly (they say) never knew how to make use of their time till it was past; but let it not be said so of a young Woman of this Age" (119–23). She is convinced that she must not wait: "[C]ourage, I say, *Hippolita,* thou art full fourteen years old, shift for thyself" (124–25), comprehending that she must act before the conservatism and lassitude of age make her unable to break free from a perpetual bondage. A Lady Flippant might tell her that such anxiety is unfounded, but then again, an only slightly older Margery Pinchwife might have something else to say.

That Hippolita finds the allure of power and malice more irresistible than the diversions of innocent love is apparent the moment Gerrard attempts to kiss her hand: "Nay, there 'tis you men are like our little Shock-dogs, if we don't keep you off from us, but use you a little kindly, you grow so fidling, and so troublesom, there is no enduring you" (II.i.146–48). Her patronizing reply seems at least to arouse Gerrard's passive sexuality: "O dear Miss, if I am like your Shock-dog, let it be in his priviledges" (149–50). His almost immature, even if playful, obsequiousness aside, we might wonder just what are those "priviledges" to which he alludes? Being stroked and petted and used as companion and bedwarmer immediately come to mind, and Hippolita's mischievous retort suggests as much: "Why, I'de have you know he [the shock dog] does not lye with me" (151). But Wycherley's audience and first generations of readers would have known that in poetry and loose talk lapdogs do and suggest far more. For example, a few lines from Robert Gould's *Love Given O're* (1682) highlight the bawdy possibilities of the woman-lapdog relationship:

> How, when into their Closets they retire,
> Where flaming Dil——s does inflame desire,
> And gentle Lapd—s feed the am'rous fire:
> Lapd—s! to whom they are more kind and free,
> Than they themselves to their own Husbands be.[27]

Considering Wycherley's frequent employment of sexual entendre, we may assume that both Gerrard and Hippolita understand the bolder applications of the allusion; and, because there is both pleasure and security in such oblique references, Hippolita adds, likely with devilish emphasis, "I always kick him off from the Bed, and never will let him come near it" (153–54). The infamous "it" moves elusively as it so often does in ambiguity—allowing the "safe" meaning as "the bed" as well as the proximity of her vaginal area. Although Gerrard mistakenly believes Hippolita is too young to appreciate the "other" meaning of such things ("poor Creature, a Wonder of Innocency" [161])—thus clearly testifying to his failure as a perceptive character and intellectual equal of his love interest—Hippolita *is* aware of the sexual implications of what she says and believes that Gerrard will apprehend her bawdier meaning: "Why cou'd you be so good-natur'd as to come after my Shock-dog in my Love? it may be indeed, rather than after one of your Brother men" (158–60). Her handling of this rather indelicate matter displays the facility with which she can arouse and frustrate Gerrard and her genuine delight in doing so. And her reference to his "cuckoldry" creates an image unlikely to vanish after his marriage to her. In essence, she uses her "innocence" and "helplessness" (her weapons of indirection) masterfully to *encourage* him to act:[28] "I cou'd let you kiss my hand, but then I'm afraid you wou'd take hold of me and carry me away" (167–68).

We shake our heads in both wonder and amusement at Hippolita's attempts to stimulate her reluctant or slow-witted suitor.[29] When she *repeats* "I am sure you would carry me away if I shou'd [let you kiss my hand]," he only replies, "Be not afraid of it," leaving Hippolita to offer in an aside, "Nay! I am afraid of the contrary; either he dislikes me, and therefore will not be troubled with me, or what is as bad, he loves me, and is dull, or fearful to displease me" (177–82). Here we find that Hippolita's asides have gone from the traditionally sweet and revealing "I like him extremely" to the more overtly censorious. And her frustrations only increase as Gerrard hesitates, seemingly too sluggish to appreciate her entendres and hints about rescuing her from "prison":

Hipp. Nay, I am sure you wou'd carry me away, what shou'd you come in at the Window for, if you did not mean to steal me?
Ger. If I shou'd endeavour it, you might cry out, and I shou'd be prevented.
Hipp. Dull, dull man of the Town, are all like thee. He is as dull as a Country Squire at Questions and Commands. No, if I shou'd cry out never so loud; this is quite at the further end of the house, and there no body cou'd hear me.

(184–91)

Disappointed, as we are, that Gerrard is too lifeless to grasp either her or her design, Hippolita resorts to a more blatant temptation to encourage action. If he shows little prospect of titillating her erotic interests, he can still assist in gaining the freedom she desires: "Nay, I know you come to steal me away; because I am an Heiress, and have twelve hundred pound a year" (194–95).[30] And indeed Gerrard is now properly stimulated: "Come, come, my Dearest, let us be gone: Fortune as well as Women must be taken in the humour" (225–26)—his exuberance here serving more as further insult to rather than redemption of his character. In the last moments of the initial meeting, then, we find Gerrard sinking in rhetoric as well as in esteem: "My Soul, my Life, 'tis you have Charms powerful as numberless" and Hippolita conversely rising: "Well, well get you gone then" (217–18, 221). Wycherley has titillated us with Hippolita's direct and indirect sexual dialogue and the possibilities of a consummation of her desires—if only in the metaphoric realm—only to have us witness a young woman aroused and a young male apparently impotent. The mention of money, not Hippolita's sexual word play, sparks Gerrard. That she asks "have you any Brothers?" (209) speaks splendidly to his disappointment as a male, and one wonders not only if Hippolita can bring him around but whether he is worth the effort.[31]

Usually, the sudden arrival of a Prue, Don Diego, or Mrs. Caution would prompt some aggravation at the interruption, but now that the emphasis of the scene has left the bed and dressed itself in banker's clothing, we might experience something closer to relief. Even so, the appearance of Diego begins another stage in the ritual—one more energetic on the one hand, as Gerrard begins to lead Hippolita around in an actual dance, but also darker in its implications. For all his evident comic vanity, Diego has sought to restrict the women in his life—his daughter, his widowed sister Caution, and even his deceased wife: "'twas as much as I cou'd do to keep up her Mother" (II.i.5–6), implying that he has always been apprehensive about a woman's freedom.[32] His sober, somber, censorious, and inhibited "Spanish" demeanor, shaped by fifteen years in the country, is his great comfort—to be "Spanish" allows him to escape "English" reality and reshape a life in his own image—the kind of egotistical and perversely creative activity that marks many of Wycherley's male characters, Horner and Manly especially. And he shares with Pinchwife that constantly agitated and breathless quality of one whose eyes constantly dart about,[33] always suspicious, always obsessive. Diego's reactions are influenced by his fear of losing control over the women in his life—unfavorably reflecting on his masculine power to shape and create—and confronting, through his daughter's free expression, the unsettling truths about the female's sexual nature.[34]

Gerrard ostensiblty leads the dancing, the surrogate sexual activity, but it is Hippolita who directs the couple's movements: "stir not from me; but lead me about, as if you lead me a Corant" (II.i.233–34).[35] Even her father's fury and drawn sword fail to shake the resourceful young Amazon, who continues undaunted and in command: "Take no notice of them; but walk about still, and sing a little, sing a Corant" (250–51). Prompted by instinct, Diego lunges at Gerrard, who then draws his own weapon, both men going through another ritualistic exercise, this time with another substitute for sexual virility, the phallic sword, threatening but doing no harm, until the fearless ("Mind him not, but dance and sing on") Hippolita ceases hostilities by transforming Gerrard into her "Dancing-master"—a most ironic touch, for Gerrard is hardly "dancing" in either a literal or figurative sense. Hippolita's re-creation of Gerrard in one respect portrays him as the effeminate or sterile version of the dancing master in order to keep her father and aunt at bay; while in another it serves to propel him, by having him emulate the virile dancing master of myth and literature, into a Dionysian celebration of potency, into a more aggressive and natural sexual response.[36]

Highly attuned to the sexual association of "dancing," Mrs. Caution wishes to trap Gerrard by posing questions, the answers to which would betray his identity. (And she is not at all squeamish about seeing him "dead" once he "confesses" to sexual indiscretion, suggesting again the frenzied associations she has with the act [293–94].) But in Wycherley those who demand direct replies often provide their adversaries the means by which to escape, as do both Caution and Diego here. His vanity bruised and his power threatened (although he draws twice more on the younger male), Diego assumes the role of Spanish inquisitor, asking the same questions his sister had already posed: "What will you be wiser than I?" he says to her (313). The length of this squabble speaks to the static nature of Diego, who pushes and pulls, gaining only the ground he has recently given up, in effect providing his daughter time to come up with an explanation—time to shape another mask by which to obfuscate the truth. And it is significant that Hippolita, not Gerrard, concocts the story that Monsieur de Paris wants her proficient in dance before the wedding. Gerrard, knowing she has saved him for the moment, now admires her "Wit" (296–97). Yet for all her evident power and ingenuity, one is always aware that she dreads the loss of her freedom, which would leave her perpetually incarcerated, spiritually as well as physically, under the watch of her father.

After a little stammering at the commencement of his interrogation—"Why, how, how, how should I come hither" (302, 323)—Gerrard's remaining relatively silent (and relying on the young woman to rescue him) for about one hundred lines is another indication of his insufficiency as a virile male character. Even Diego's voiced anxiety—"he has dishonour'd my Family, debauch'd my Daughter" (354–55)—only emphasizes Gerrard's shortcomings, as does Hippolita's telling her father that Monsieur has "sent" Gerrard so that she could "recover [her] Dancing a little before our Wedding" (361–62). Gerrard must listen without protest as Diego in effect schools him by informing Hippolita that he hopes the young man "does not use the Dancing-masters tricks of squeezing your hands, setting your Legs and Feet, by handling your Thighs, and seeing your Legs" (392–94). That Diego envisages the more sexual manifestation of the dancing master informs us as well as it does Hippolita that he may be more worldy wise than his Spanish demeanor lets on. But even more telling is the cataloging of sexual activity here evincing a vicarious and peculiar delight in the progression of the sexual act, starting with hand squeezing and then moving toward the fondling of the woman's thighs. Don Diego, the widower and as far as we know the celibate (celibacy being appropriate to his "Spanish" sobriety), is a voyeur both in imagination and reality, the most perverse aspect of his actions and thoughts being that the woman involved in such a voyeuristic reverie is his own daughter. It is one thing to state "Do not allow him to lay one hand on any part of your body but your hands, arms, and waist"; and quite another to admonish her using the emotive language he chooses here.[37]

In his insistence that "Hippolita "shou'd learn to dance," Diego appears, despite himself, to be giving tacit approval to her erotic activity, because of the associations he himself has made between the dance and sexual movement. Though he would fear losing control over her, he is enough obsessed by her budding sexuality to wish it displayed: "it shall be so, and I'le see you dance my self. . . . [T]o your bus'ness, teach her, her Lesson over gain, let's see" and "Come, come, let's see your *English Method*, I understand something of Dancing my self—come" (401, 411–15). But Gerrard fails once more to measure up: "I shall betray you yet, dearest Miss, for I know not a step, I cou'd never dance" (417–18). Hippolita's playful admission to her father that she cannot proceed in the dance because she is "asham'd" elicits from her father an answer that unwittingly suggests a most liberal attitude toward sex: "You must not be asham'd, Child, you'll never dance well, if you are asham'd" (420–23). However, he increasingly sounds like an agitated voyeur aroused to the height of impatience: "Come, come, I say, go to't" (425). And to reinforce this motif, Wycherley has Diego move to the next room where he can "peep" in through a crack in the door and watch his daughter's actions. Hippolita wishes to remain at least this once safely confined behind an impenetrable wall: "Nay, Father, you peep, indeed you must not see me, when we have done you shall come in" (440–41).

Gerrard's moving toward Hippolita now that they are alone ("Let me adore you, dearest Miss, and give you—"[446]) offers hope that his dormant virility has been awakened, but still paramount is the passive quality of his words "*Let* me *adore* you" more than his attempt to embrace her. At any rate, she refuses his embrace, perhaps sensing that he wishes to make up for his previous ineptitude with a mere pittance of affection—as one might in a later era seek atonement with a small bouquet of flowers. In addition, we cannot forget that his prime motivation is still Hippolita's purse rather than her person and that his seeming romantic gesture is actually a financial one: "we have yet an opportunity, and the Gallery-window is yet open" (455). Too shrewd, however, to leave on his terms, Hippolita's assumption of helplessness is again comically ironic, sarcastic, and relevant, as she tells him that men promise their young women hours of amusement at the "Court, the Playhouse, and Hide-Park," but once they "have got 'em" in their "Clutches" they "carry 'em to *York-shire, Wales,* or *Cornwall,* which is as bad as to *Barbadoes*" (461–66). Although we have little concern that she could be so tricked and manipulated, her words still present the omnipresent fear of imprisonment, for in those "wild" places men may more easily keep their spouses restricted and apart from the freedoms the city offers strong and resourceful women: "rather than be served so, I wou'd be a Pris'ner in *London* still as I am" (466–67). Her spirited nature needs not only its release but also the environment and inspiration only London can provide.

Wycherley never lets the reader lose sight of Hippolita's invincibilty and dauntlessness and Gerrard's tentativeness and insecurity:

Ger. Pray, sweet Miss, then let us make the better use of our time, if it be short; but how shall we do with that Cousin of yours in the mean time, we must needs charm him?
Hipp. Leave that to me!
Ger. But what's worse! how shall I be able to act a Dancing-master? who ever wanted inclination and patience to learn my self.
(478–83)

Hippolita joyfully plagues him further by making the connection between lovemaking and dancing a little more obvious: "A Dancing-School in half an hour will furnish you with terms of the Art. Besides, Love (as I have heard say) supplies his Scholars with all sorts of Capacities they have need of in spight of Nature, but what has Love to do with you?" (484–87). Her attempts to prompt a more aggressive masculinity include her feeding Gerrard a good dose of humiliation, especially since he was unable to digest her constant offerings of sexual innuendo. In short, Hippolita has established the relationship on her terms, and her caution is warranted for she truly doubts that "Love" is Gerrard's "Master" (492): "Since we poor slavish Women know / Our men we cannot pick and choose"— and truly fears the inescapable bondage to which women *may* be subjected: "Though all we gain be but new slavery; / We leave our Fathers, and to Husbands fly" (524–25, 552–53). We might wish to discount Hippolita's later concern that if he discovers her deception, her father might well, being of a "Spanish" disposition, "kill" her or at least punish her severely (thoughts moreover expressed by Monsieur—III.i.106–7; IV.i.326–

27). Nevertheless, the fear is very real to Hippolita—that somehow Diego will destroy her spirit by continued incarceration or violent physical action: "I must be obedient *as long as I am with him*" (549—emphasis added)—words given validity by Diego's subsequent remark on the union of Monsieur and his daughter: "'tis all one whether she loves him now or not; for as soon as she's marry'd, she'd be sure to hate him: that's the reason we wise *Spaniards* are jealous and only expectè, nay will be sure our Wives shall fear us, look you" (IV.i.86–90). Hippolita's attraction to the bumbling Gerrard, then, is only enhanced because she sees that he is, although handsome and far less offensive than Monsieur, the kind of husband who could not thwart her freedom and power—a husband that she, not her father, has chosen.

Following Hippolita's further ridicule of Gerrard (this time in front of Monsieur)—"[A]fter I had a good while pleas'd myself in jesting and leading the poor Gentleman you sent into a Fools Paradise" (III.i.78–79)—Wycherley once more sets his characters in motion, as Don Diego "walks leisurely round" Monsieur, "surveying him, and shrugging up his shoulders" while the fop "makes Legs and Faces" (III.i.128–29)—the popinjay's wing-flapping suggesting the infantile nature of Monsieur's narcissistic sexuality. The pitched battle here between the French and Spanish forces (III.i.132–285), again shamelessly cashing in on the audience's ethnocentrism, does not preclude its connection to Wycherley's more significant concerns. Each man's name-calling and slight of the other's manner and dress (Pantaloons versus Spanish hose) seeks to strip the enemy of his protective covering—both fragile egos finding security within the adopted identity—for each understands that to pick at threads of cloth is to unravel the other's "manhood."[38] And always there is emphasis on self-destruction: first in Monsieur's insulting the very man he must of course please and then in Mrs. Caution's observation, "What have you a mind to ruine your self, and break off the Match" (193–94). Warming to his advantage, Diego insists that his nephew begin ceremoniously to strip himself of his French "Dress, Stammering, and Tricks"—adding more sadistically (one might picture the villain's requisite smirk) "he that marry's my Daughter shall at least look like a wise man, for he shall wear the *Spanish* Habit" (235–36). Fittingly, the women (Hippolita, Caution, and Prue) leave "laughing" at the hapless Monsieur—female derision being the ultimate humiliation for the beaten male. According to Diego's conditions, Monsieur must dress like a Spaniard yet speak now like an Englishman—an ironic linguistic mockery of Gerrard, as well as a sartorial undoing, for in effect Monsieur will have to ape Diego, but without any of his "Spanish" power.

With the return of Gerrard and the women, Diego orders the couple to recommence their ritualistic movements—prompted both by Mrs.

Caution's suspicions and by his daughter's troubling admission to him: "I have a great respect for my [Dancing] Master" (III.i.349). We listen once more to Gerrard's protestation (to Hippolita) that he is incompetent (impotent) in the dance and to her assurance that she will lead him through the motions.[39] Diego moreover provides a fitting gloss on Gerrard's manhood by reminding him that Dancing Masters often "talk" more than they dance (353–55). As earlier, Diego encourages the ritual with excitement and impatience: "about, about with her, man. . . . Hey, hey, more fooling yet, come, come, about with her. . . . [M]ove her, I say, begin Hussie, move when he'll have you"; "Come, move I say, and mind her not. . . . Come, move on, she's mad. . . . Come, One, two, turn out your Toes" (III.i.374–94). The tension is clearly palpable as Wycherley leads us to the edge of discovery, when masks may be lifted and the characters forced to confront frightening realities. But Diego's voyeurism is even more demanding of our attention as he orchestrates the movements, vicariously taking part in the figurative sexual movement ("turn out your Toes"), engaging in that stimulating yet frustrating activity of the disabled debauchee, the sexual superannuary. Based on their previous meeting, Diego must judge Gerrard as inept and consequently someone to attack, insult, humiliate, and in the metaphoric world of the dance—someone to replace. Diego's response to his sister's contention that Gerrard is "no more a Dancing-master than I am a Maid"—"What! will you still be wiser than I?" and "What, will you see further than I?" (III.i.358–60; IV.i.691)—at least suggests that he is being deliberately obtuse to keep the ritual alive, thereby furthering his sadistic and voyeuristic ends. We may accordingly find more sinister than comic his claim that Gerrard cannot manipulate him: "What, you laugh I warrant to think how the young Baggage and you will mump the poor old Father; but if all her dependence for a Fortune be upon the Father, he may chance to mump you both, and spoil the Jest"; "I cheated by any man!" (III.i.325–28, 587). Also measuring Gerrard's vulnerability, Prue reacts to Diego's command to his daughter, "Hussie, move when he'll have you," with "I cannot but laugh at that, ha, ha, ha" (382–83). Is she laughing merely at the fact that Gerrard is stumbling about in the dance? Or is she, too, like Caution, thinking of lovemaking, envisaging either Hippolita's movements during sexual intercourse or, more likely, the amusing image of an apparently dull-witted Gerrard attempting intercourse with Hippolita?

Eventually the Englishman appears at least somewhat properly stimulated, for with the encouragement of Hippolita and to the horror of Caution he squeezes the young Amazon's hand, then her bare arm, then her thigh—the very progression to which Diego alluded. In this Dionysian activity, lovers move continuously, back and forth, side to side, turning out, turning in—all under the father's direct observation and with his fervent advocacy (unlike so many other "cuckolds" of stage tradition, he is not oblivious to the action going on beneath, above, or behind him): "Fall back, fall back, back, some of you are forward enough to fall back" (397–98). Despite her father's commands, Hippolita's reflects her aggressive and dominant personality in her unwillingness to "fall back when he [Gerrard] bids her" and her more natural acceptance of the charge to "Come forward"—a movement that arouses *her* enough to squeeze *Gerrard's* hand (401–2, 409–10). And Diego concedes that his daughter remains unbridled: "she moves forward pretty well; but you must move as well backward as forward, or you'll never do any thing to purpose" (412–14). Simply, the sexual implications of this dance cannot be divorced from even the character's *conscious* understanding, as now evident in the intensity of Mrs. Caution's reaction: "See, see, she squeezes his hand now, O the debauch'd Harletry!"; "What will you bawd for your Daughter?" (410–11, 441). The aunt's own passionate sensibilities make her more than uncomfortable at the near incestuous implications of her brother's involvement: "are you at your beastliness before your young Daughter?" (415–16)—in short, an entirely mad scene punctuated effectively by the laughter of Prue.

Understandably, Caution has an inhibiting effect on Hippolita: "my Aunt puts me quite out, I cannot dance while she looks on for my heart, she makes me asham'd and afraid together" (III.i.424–26)—a reaction mainly attributable to the older woman's having accurately perceived this ritual as sexual—a perspective shaped by Caution's own erotic encounters: "I will not go out, my conscience will not suffer me; for I know by experience what will follow" (443–44). Finally, after Diego thrusts his sister out, leaving the "lovers" alone, we know that all sexual activity will *end,* not continue, with his departure—despite Gerrard's laughable claim of "we'll make good use of your time when you are gone" (445–46). Indeed, all action occurs *outside* the door, for Caution has now worked herself up to a froth: "I right! no 'tis your dainty Minx, that Jillflirt your Daughter here that is right, do you see how her Hankerchief is ruffled, and what a heat she's in?" (532–34). Certainly it is she, not Hippolita, whose linen is mussed. Remarking that his sister has been "loose" and "unchaste" in her youth (529–30), Diego maintains some emotional distance by relying on the vehicle: "She has been dancing," while his sister is closer to the tenor: "Ay, ay, *Adam* and *Eves* Dance, or the beginning of the World, de' see how she pants?" (535–37). In her response to her brother's observation that Hippolita pants because "She has not been us'd to motion"—"Motion, motion, motion, de' call it? no indeed, I kept her from motion till now, motion with a vengeance" (539–40)—Caution comes very close to making the equation openly between dancing and sexual activity, and she seems to be losing more than maintaining the needed propriety of speech. Mrs. Caution's presence in the play thus stimulates what might otherwise be a more controlled and slower-paced plot to break Hippolita away from her father. She barges in, stirs matters up, strikes fear in the hearts of Gerrard and Monsieur, encourages her brother's anger and vanity—all giving the play a kind of uneasiness and vitality it would lack without her. She is no less dynamic than the irrepressibles Flippant, Flirt, and Flounce. Without question, her resolve is fierce: "I shall not budge, royally I shall not" (IV.i.429); and here (and earlier) she literally "thrusts" Gerrard "away": "I say he shall not take her by the hand, he shall touch her no more; while I am here there shall be no more squeesing and tickling of her palm,[40] good Mr. Dancing-master, stand off" (III.i.558–60). At one point it takes the physical efforts of both Don Diego and Monsieur to "thrust" *her* out.[41]

As for Caution's niece, Hippolita *allows* Gerrard to feel powerful and manly: "Methinks you shou'd be contented in making bold with his Daughter; for you have made very bold with her, sure"; "I do not doubt your confidence, for you are a Dancing-master"; "if I am such a confident Piece, I am sure you made me so" (III.i.455–56, 458–59, 464–65). Yet, she subtly undercuts such praise of his "virility" with reminders of her inexperience: "I am sure I cou'd not look upon a man before." What distinction, after all, could Gerrard feel as a lover if he was the very *first* man she's laid eyes on—Ferdinand to her Miranda (466–67)? She also contradicts him whenever the mood strikes: "Say you so!"; "I say you have no reason to say so yet" (474, 499)—moreover becoming thrilled at the prospect of leaving the house in a coach-and-six, not simply (and more romantically) leaving with Gerrard on horseback (515). And, like Martha before her, Hippolita almost inexplicably defends her father to her suitor: "you are a fine Gentleman to abuse my poor Father so" (449). These contradictory remarks demonstrate Wycherley's continued delight in leading his readers as well as Gerrard through the labyrinth—and suggest even the unthinkable possibility that Don Diego, for all his unsavory characteristics, is more "manly" than is the young English suitor. Despite Hippolita's assertions, such as "Well, Father, think what you will, but I know what I think" (IV.i.99), Diego does after all have control over her (the only one of the three males in the play who does)—and even the powerful (Hippolita) must respect the strength of their major adversary. On the other hand, like the young Lothario experiencing a modicum of romantic success, oblivious to the fact that his young lady has entirely managed it, Gerrard displays unjustifiable cockiness: "I hope I shall make bolder with her yet" (457). Hippolita's tells him that his "bold" action in coming through the window (and we might recall how he was manipulated into doing that) made her more "confident" as a woman, and we detect once again the playful "Kitten" (as Prue called her earlier) toying so deliberately with her mousy prey. Ever the observant one, Gerrard informs her, "I do not think you confident, you are only innocent" (470).[42]

Upon his return, we detect no abatement of Don Diego's lust for dictating the ritual and humiliating further the fumbling dancing master: "I will not be put off so"; "Come, sing to her, come begin"; "I say begin, I will not excuse you, come take her by the hand, and about with her" (III.i.552–57).[43] With every imperative is another reminder of Gerrard's impotence ("you know I cannot sing a Note, Miss," 546–47) and Diego's obsession with the movement and his vicarious role in it.[44] The dance becomes even more frantic with the couple's starting and stopping, the intrusion of the volatile Diego, and the physical interruption (and thus *participation* in the ritual) by Mrs. Caution, who "thrusts" Gerrard "away" from her niece: "he shall not touch her, he has touch'd her too much already" (562–63). Here as elsewhere in the play (and throughout *Love in a Wood*) we find no satisfactory release of the passionate energy in a literal or figurative sense; rather, Wycherley builds upon the sexual tension and anticipation, frustrating his characters (and the reader) with various forms of coitus interruptus.

An emasculated Monsieur, owing to his radically new "Spanish" appearance, returns to the ridicule of the laughing Hippolita and Prue: "[W]hen we poor men are your Gallants you laugh at us your selves, and wen we are your Husband, you make all the World laugh at us" (IV.i.18–20). Diego assails his helpless opponent from another flank, refusing Monsieur's wish at least to "unite France and Spain" in his habiliments. The vanquished begs for terms but is refused; the surrender must be unconditional: "I have said, look you, your Dress must be *Spanish,* and your Language *English,* I am uno Positivo" (IV.i.43–44). In making a sniveling display of himself—"do but spare me my Crevat. . . . have some mercy" (108, 111)—Monsieur certainly lacks the *je ne sais quoi* of a Fopling Flutter or Lord Foppington, but in his ridiculous guise he more accurately reflects the reality of Wycherley's harsher world, in which the males are required to destroy another, however the means. And his pathetic attempt to hang on to his "identity" by donning the French crevat (and thereby rescuing himself from ultimate degradation) is countered by Diego's pulling it off, in effect breaking further his nephew's spirit—wrecking Monsieur's imaginative play-world and refurbishing it with Diego's own nightmarish vision. The nastiness in many ways mitigates the delightful spectacle before us, and Diego adds dancing to this ritual of humiliation, ordering the Black servant to play dancing master and lead Monsieur in the dance: "Black, teach him now to make a *Spanish* Leg. . . . Black, do what you can, make the most of him, walk him about" (144, 150)—the supreme indignity of being led about by one's social and, as perceived, racial inferior. The strong link between dancing and sexual activity only adds to the highly discomforting aspects of the display.

And now, following this clear demonstration of Diego's power (Monsieur and the servant continue their bizarre dance even after he has left the room), Wycherley shifts attention to another of his vibrant female characters—the maid Prue, who laments the chambermaids' plight of "carking and caring, the watching and sitting up, the trouble and danger of our Mistresses Intrigues! whilst they go away with all the pleasure" (IV.i.167–69). She continues her lament as the dancing proceeds, thus forcing one to shift back and forth between the occular treat of Monsieur and the Black servant staggering about and the intriguing implications found in the words of the stationary Prue. And her musings do more than provide a *raison de être* for her interest in Monsieur; they more importantly reinforce the sexual agitation and unfulfillment that are often the characters' lot in these plays. Wycherley reminds us that Prue, regardless of her social position, is like her other sisters—not only a loyal associate, but a woman often stimulated by what she sees, hears, and envisions in her dreams and fantasies, one who constantly looks to release her highly pent-up erotic intensity.[45] The voyeurism and vicarious reveries to which she must resort, however, are far less gratifying to her than they are to Don Diego, who draws power and security from his form of indirect participation. This healthy woman is shamefully "left in the Lurch here with a Couple of ugly little Black-a-more Boys in Bonets and an old wither'd *Spanish* Eunuch, not a Servant else in the house" (180–82), her options being merely perversions rather than healthy sexual experiences. She is incarcerated with ugliness and impotence; she lacks the opportunity to express herself more naturally and in her own way accordingly voices the greatest fear of women in Wycherley's plays.

As does Hippolita, Prue must resort to a "lesser evil" (her "Mistress's leavings," Monsieur de Paris) to avoid the horrors of spiritual and sexual demise among the members of the household. Even so, her "deliverer" has only frustrated her advances: "I have pull'd off his Perruque, unty'd his Ribbons, and have been very bold with him, yet he would never be so with me; nay, I have pinch'd him, punch'd him, and tickl'd him, and yet he would never do the like for me" (203–6). Prue understands the periodic need to mix a little pain with pleasure and even to employ visual eroticism: "I have taken an occasion to garter my Stockins before him, as if unawares of him; for a good Leg and Foot, with good Shoos and Stockins, are very provoking" (213–16). But the lack of inhibition in Prue's admission cannot release her from the necessity of indirection, for not only must she don an elaborate cosmetic mask of "Bees-wax and Hogs-grease"[46] but she must confront Monsieur by filtering her passionate energies through a fictional "dream" she had about him. Yet because he fails to pick up on her hint, Prue is forced to be more direct: "Why then methoughts last night you came up into my Chamber in your Shirt, when I was in Bed, and that you might easily do; for I have ne're a Lock to my door" (244–46). Monsieur's obliviousness to this admission, the flimsiest of indirection, allows Wycherley to take the fictive sex act further, right to the point of consummation: "I'm sure I cry'd out, and wak'd all in tears, with these words in my mouth, You have undone me, you have undone me! your Worship has undone me" (259–61). But Prue pushes even further, smothering Monsieur with billowing hints, hoping that life will somehow imitate art: "Indeed it was so lively, I know not whether 'twas a Dream or no: but if you were not there, I'le undertake you may come when you will, and do any thing to me you will, I sleep so fast" (264–66).

Although sharing her mistress's (and Lady Flippant's) exasperation at the male's inability to comprehend even blatant sexual suggestion, Prue shoves matters about as far as she can to the precipice of discovery—to a direct request to be taken sexually: "my door hath neither Lock nor Latch to it: if you shou'd be so naughty as to come one night, and prove the dream true"; "Then by that I should come into your Worship's Chamber, and come to bed to your Worship"; "But if I shou'd do such a trick in my sleep, your Worship wou'd not censure a poor harmless Maid, I hope; for I am apt to walk in my sleep" (278–88). Even though her inflection likely enhances these titillating visions, Monsieur's passivity serves only to provide another kind of coitus interruptus: "I'le be sure to lock my door every night fast," he says incredulously (IV.i.290). (And Monsieur's reference to the locked door shows in another interesting sense how walls, doors, and locks are so often in Wycherley the working metaphors of a woman's life.) At the moment Prue decides to toss aside all manner of indirection—"I must come roundly and downright to the bus'ness" (291–92)—Gerrard stumbles on the scene, the unwelcome agent of interruption and antifraternalism. Although we are reconciled by our knowledge that Monsieur is hardly worthy of Prue and that she may have remained unsatisfied even had he understood and attempted to act on her hints, one can hardly fail to appreciate the way she inundates the scene with her exuberance, thereby making Monsieur's tepidity even more aggravating.

Monsieur's debasement moves ever forward as he apologizes to Gerrard for the "trick" he has played on him and begs his forgiveness, insisting that he be "obliged" to Gerrard as a fit kind of penance (IV.i.345). And after Hippolita sends her cousin out, Gerrard gleefully observes, "So, so, to make him hold the door, while I steal his Mistress is not unpleasant" (IV.i.461–62)—well aware that the Gallic fool is the only person he rises above in the play. Moreover, Gerrard's fear of discovery and fleeting time, as reflected in his *carpe diem* commonplaces, makes simple and pleasurable Hippolita's disarming and tormenting him with her dallying—"But I am not ready"—and allusions to "rosy" lost opportunities: "'Twas well for me [my Father came in upon us]; for on my Conscience if he had not come in, I had gone clear away with you when I was in the humour" (483–87). An insatiable Hippolita simply cannot resist any exercise of her power: "But, Sir; you cou'd believe I was in earnest in the morning, when I but seemed to be ready to go with you; and why won't you believe me now, when I declare to the contrary? I take it unkindly, that the longer I am acquainted with you, you shou'd have the less confidence in me" (497–98). At this point, Gerrard has no choice but to follow Monsieur's lead and set himself up for further ridicule:

Ger. . . . What, won't you go with me then after all?
Hipp. No indeed, Sir, I desire to be excus'd.
Ger. Then you have abus'd me all this while?
Hipp. It may be so.
Ger. Cou'd all that so natural Innocency be dissembl'd? faith it cou'd not, dearest Miss.
Hipp. Faith it was, dear Master. . . . you saw I cou'd dissemble with my Father, why shou'd you think I cou'd not with you?
. . . .
Ger. And I must never hope for you?
Hipp. Wou'd you have me abuse you again?

(IV.i.519–36)[47]

Even though young Hippolita is quite proficient in her bitchiness, we still have difficulty sympathizing with Gerrard, who is certainly no George Barnwell. And in response to Hippolita's now telling Gerrard that she is no heiress, commentators have traditionally rallied to his side, stating that he displays sincere affection for her when he sighs and admits that he is captivated not by money but by love. How that sigh is expelled, however, is open to debate; in any event, we are undoubtedly encouraged, based on established—and subsequent—dramatic practice (e.g., "Sentimental Comedy"), to expect the emergence of a new romantic relationship from this point on. But we should have known better. Wycherley astounds us once more by having Hippolita turn the screws tighter rather than loosening them: "What, wou'd you take me without the twelve hundred pound a year? wou'd you be such a Fool as to steal a Woman with nothing?" (549–51). A beleagured Gerrard reacts as a man will when reason and decorum fail him: "I'le convince you, for you shall go with me; and since you are twelve hundred pound a year the lighter, you'll be the easier carried away" (552–54).[48] Is this, as Prue suggests, a prelude to rape or abduction, the primitive signifier of fear and fractured masculinty? Is this lifting of Hippolita instead a welcome demonstration of Gerrard's vitality, something she has worked to force out of him? Or might this be a futile and childish reaction resulting from frustration and insecurity? Does Hippolita laugh at his actions, feign horror, or smile with delight? Regardless, we know one thing: it has been Hippolita who has forced the response, Hippolita who has manufactured the more virile outburst. In addition, we cannot rest long contemplating the meaning of this mildly violent and erotic moment, because it is immediately *interrupted* by Don Diego and Mrs. Caution.

Gerrard's brief moment of ascendency—if so it may be judged—is obliterated by a return to his more nervous and confused demeanor: "How now! you seem to be out of humour, Friend," says Diego, to which the younger man responds, "Yes, so I am, I can't help it" (IV.i.561–62). Nor does the "Spaniard" relax his obsession with Hippolita's dancing: "Hussy, wou'd you not do as he'd have you! I'le make you do as he'd have you" (579–80), at the same time his sister cannot help breaking down the metaphoric barriers in order to speak more plain: "'Tis a lye, she'll do all he'll have her do, and more too, to my knowledge" (582–83).[49] Perhaps Caution's explosive language and his own physical response to Hippolita's machinations have a beneficial effect on Gerrard, for presently he shows some mettle, his dullness perhaps finally and finely sharpened by anger, frustration, and humiliation. Are we once more, then, at the edge of discovery? Will Gerrard finally be direct? To Diego he observes, "She pretends she can't do what she shou'd do, and that she is not in humour, the common Excuse of Women for not doing what they shou'd," and then in asides to Hippolita, "Hold your piece, I say, silly Woman. . . . I am in a pretty humor to dance. I cannot fool any longer, since you have fool'd me" (597–605).[50] Even so, he makes his remarks somewhat indirectly, to Diego instead of Hippolita in the first instance, and in asides in the others. Further vitiating Gerrard's "moment" is the entrance of Monsieur, who triggers Diego's demand that Gerrard dance again with his daughter, placing Gerrard in that uncomfortable environment where he shows himself deficient. And Gerrard moreover admits that he cannot play the violin, another kind of impotence in the metaphoric context of music and dance, thus compelling him again to respond violently—especially after hearing Diego chide him for his weakness: "What, are you a Dancing-master, and cannot play!" (671). Gerrard winds up "the strings till they break, and throws the Violin on the ground," spouting damnations against womankind: "Next to the Devil's the Invention of Women, they'll no more want an excuse to cheat a Father with, than an opportunity to abuse a Husband" (682–84).

Gerrard's misogyny provides him the comfort of the broad generalization (he can avoid a confrontation with the more vexing particularization)—as a release of his anger and as a vehicle by which to regain his lost manhood (his sense of it, that is). But his words also suggest his weakness, in that such an admission, such a display of emotion, such a nod toward direct discourse, makes him more open to all who hear him—and thereby more vulnerable rather than powerful. Besides, the forces Gerrard confronts are much stronger than he. Hippolita senses—and I believe is stimulated by—the challenge and instinctively begins a counteroffensive not only to protect herself but to "save" him as well: "for Heaven's sake for this once be more obedient to my desires than your passion" (607–8). So pressed, Gerrard can only retreat: "I am in no good Dancing humour indeed" (611), but is made by Diego to participate further in the ritual of degradation, his indignation rising at his inability to maintain any advantage: "I am become her sport, one, two, three, Death, Hell, and the Devil" (635–36), while the volcanic Mrs. Caution fights off Monsieur's attempt to restrain her: "Do you see how she leers upon him and clings to him, can you suffer it?" (638–39). Wycherley again places his characters in a near-orgiastic state, replete with chaotic action and breathless speech. We had assumed a change of direction as Gerrard took some steps toward manhood, but of course we were disappointed in that expectation, reminding us that we are in the labyrinth still.

Gerrard's inability to follow up on his brief flurries of mental and physical assertiveness is moreover apparent in his willingness (or concession) to subject himself once more to Hippolita's dominion and abuse—with the additional blessing of her father:

> *Ger.* But you'll make a Fool of me agen: if I shou'd come, wou'd you not?
> *Hipp.* If I shou'd tell you so, you'd be sure not to come.
> *Don.* Come, come, she shall not make a Fool of you, upon my word: I'le secure you, she shall do what you'll have her.
> . . . .
> *Ger.* But, Madam, will you have me come?
> *Hipp.* I'd have you to know for my part, I care not whether you come or no; there are other Dancing-masters to be had. . . .
>
> (706–14)

Her whispering "a little good advice" in his ear to ease his "shame" barely mitigates the effects of her remarks, nor the implications of Diego's "assurance" that "she shall do what you'll have her"—namely, that he is not man enough to have it so, and worse still Hippolita's reminder that "there are other Dancing-masters to be had." Diego notices that his daughter whispers something to Gerrard but is content because all happens before him, under his direct supervision: "Well, well, let her whisper before me as much as she will to night, since she is to be marry'd to morrow" (728–29). That Hippolita, for all her desire to flee from Diego, is truly her father's daughter is most evident in the pleasure she takes in her manipulations, so wonderfully obvious in the similar wording of their charge to Gerrard as the fourth act concludes:

Don. And be sure you bring the Fiddlers with you, as I bid you.
Hipp. Yes, be sure you bring the Fiddlers with you, as I bid you.
(740–41)

Even the pathetic Monsieur (still being led about by his "Master," the Black servant) finds opportunity to add to Gerrard's distress: "What, out of humour, man! a Dancing-master shou'd be like his Fiddle, always in Tune. Come, my Cousin has made an Ass of thee, what then, I know it" (V.i.6–8). Able now to reclaim a modicum of power at another's expense, Monsieur informs Gerrard of the elaborate scheme he and Hippolyta had cooked up to make a fool of the young suitor, accentuating his confession with inane laughter. Gerrard now painfully concludes that the one person over whom he assumed a superiority has left him checkmated: "The Fool has reason, I find, and I am the Coxcomb while I thought him so" (19–20). The "good humor" Monsieur exudes in his "fooling" indeed "begins to be tyrannical": "Ha, ha, ha, that thou shoulds't be gull'd so by a little Gipsey, who left off her Bib but yesterday; faith I can't but laugh at thee" (64–69). Monsieur first "comforts" his rival by attacking all women and implying that the young man is not alone in his abuse, but then ridicules the notion of brotherhood by laughing directly at Gerrard for his gullibiilty. Of course the young Englishman has a more predictable response at the ready, as he strikes, kicks, and draws on Monsieur in one more effort to regain, through violence, what is left of his ravaged ego. But again the gesture (which includes his slashing at Monsieur's legs, while Paris "leaps"—another kind of dance) does little good, seeing that Monsieur, in the context of physical contest, is just too easy of a mark. Gerrard cannot satisfy the expectations of his gender until he has outflanked Don Diego and disarmed Hippolita.

The young Amazon's arrival quells the battle, vexing Gerrard further with her "concern" for Monsieur: "What, you have not hurt my Cousin, Sir, I hope" (111). Gerrard can only admit "How she's concern'd for him; nay, then I need not doubt, my fears are true" (112–13). Hippolita playfully yet still cruelly torments the man who had just earlier called her names, attempted to expose her, and lifted her up as if to abduct her: "But I am afraid," she remarks to Monsieur, that "you have hurt my Master, Cousin, he says nothing; can he draw his breath?" (122–23). Monsieur begs of Hippolita, "faith don't abuse him any longer," which, with its probable sarcastic or patronizing emphasis, prompts Gerrard's second show of anger: "He counsels you well, pleasant-cunning-jilting-Miss for his sake; for if I am your divertisement, it shall be at his cost, since he's your Gallant in favour" (132–34). His name-calling may be deemed a positive step in his redemption (as a masculine hero), but still his revenge is most indirect and his thinking completely erroneous: "I say pleasant, cunning, jilting Lady, though you make him a Cuckold, it will not be revenge enough for me upon him for marrying you" (142–44). Unable to face for long the actual cause of his debasement, Gerrard can only attack Hippolita through an agent.

Throughout her suitor's verbal tirade, Hippolita remains imperturbable, giving back in kind: "How, my surly, huffing, jealous, senseless sawcy Master?" (V.i.145). Her calling him "Master" can only remind him that he is anything but, and she chastizes him for believing she would ever wed one such as Monsieur. With the weapon of rationalization yanked from his grip, Gerrard is left simply to claim that she is like all women who marry those who make the best cuckolds (an interesting kind of self-condemnation), again finding sanctuary in these brief moments of sweeping misogyny. And, as always, Hippolita is adroit and acerbic in her reply: "Indeed, Master, whatsoever you think, I wou'd sooner chuse you for that purpose then him" (155–56), a remark that skirts briefly the edge of flattery before plunging deeply into derision. The prospects for Gerrard's future are laid out before him—and one wonders if he could ever truly forget such a remark after his marriage to this young Amazon.

We moreover note that, as Hippolita sends Monsieur off as a buffer between her and her family (and discovery), she announces *her* decision to shift direction: "Go . . . whilst I put my Master into a better humour" (168–69). What she says to Gerrard is to his and our considerable surprise: "Well, Master, since I find you are quarrelsom and melancholy, and wou'd have taken me away without a Portion, three infallible signs of a true Lover, faith here's my hand now in earnest, to lead me a Dance as long as I live" (179–82). This "capitulation" to Gerrard has been happily explained as follows: her severe behavior all along was intended to showcase the "Patient Gerrard," and because he has so successfully proved worthy as a faithful lover, he earns the admission of her true feelings and subsequent devotion. I find it most difficult to accept such reasoning, which forces us to see Wycherley simply following tired convention or extricating himself from difficulty with a sudden reversal as awkward as any *deus ex machina*. At what point did Gerrard surmount the final hurdle? How has he shown himself admirable? And do we really see them as equals, each being truly worthy of the other?

Certainly, the approaching end of the play demands resolution; Wycherley had neither the liberty nor inclination to close the curtain with Hippolita still frustrating Gerrard and exploiting his weaknesses. But her kindly response, I would argue, is based on several more significant factors. Without question, she finds Gerrard comely enough and most pliable—in short, the kind of husband who would allow more freedom than restriction in marriage. She understands that the game must end, but also that her desire for escape must be fulfilled. Her "magnanimous" gesture (showing in her unpredictability how easily she can turn Gerrard one way and then another) only embellishes her mystery and thus her ascendency. (We recall her remark that "passion un-masks every man" [V.i.163–64].) Her behavior throughout makes clear—regardless of her telling Gerrard that he will "lead" her in the dance—that she is secure in her strength and confident that she will never lose it. If she has put him through a test, it has not been to determine his sincerity and love—those are *our* expectations, based on a cheery view of romantic union, not at all Wycherley's interest—but rather to determine if she can guarantee herself relative freedom in a marriage to him.

And as we would expect, Gerrard responds with hesitency and insecurity: "But, Dearest, I would be assur'd of what you say, and yet dare not ask the question. You h——do not abuse me again, you h——will fool me no more sure" (V.i.185–87). We find now that Wycherley has cleverly entrapped the reader (who expects some kind of tender exchange) as successfully as Hippolita has snared Gerrard: for she demonstrates how quickly she wishes to publicize her omnipotence: "Yes but I will [fool you] sure.... For I say you are to be my Husband, and you say Husbands must be Wittals and some strange things to boot" (188, 190–91)—dashing Gerrard's early expectations and making him responsible for the present state of things. The beaten Gerrard will "venture" the match, even though at his "peril," "fore-warn'd" and "fore-arm'd" of what a life with Hippolita holds in store. He will be no Theseus triumphant over the Amazonian queen; Hippolita simply will not allow it. Further deteriorating the image of a benign and obediant wife-to-be, Hippolita establishes the ground rules: "a Husband's jealousie, which cunning men wou'd pass upon their Wives for a Complement, is ... but an affront to their Honour.... So that upon the whole matter I conclude, jealousie in a Gallant is humble true Love, and the height of respect, and only an undervaluing of himself to overvalue her; but in a Husband 'tis arrant sawciness, cowardise, and ill breeding, and not to be suffer'd" (205–8; 210–13)—admonitions that speak much to the motivations and actions of Alithea in *The Country Wife*. The amusing though frightening implication of this speech is that Gerrard as a "gallant" has very little liberty at all, and yet as a husband he is promised even less.

Having been duly lectured, Gerrard can only concede, "But, Madam—... I stand corrected gracious Miss" (209, 214). Still, Hippolita is not through; she chastizes him for not having enough sense to know for what purpose she intended the "fiddlers" (actually Gerrard's acquaintances): "What do you think I intended to do with them? (221). She has conceived the plan to escape from her father's house; she has assumed command of the operation, as her use of military metaphors implies; Gerrard often appears as an underequipped foot soldier. As her father's and aunt's in their particular ways, Hippolita's is an obsessive nature that accelerates matters, exuding considerable energy and exhausting those around her. She brims with self-confidence and self-esteem and shifts her pose from commander to, appropriately, Amazon queen, wanting again for Gerrard to tell her that money is not the basis of his desire for her (she seems to have trouble believing such a good thing could be true): "can you yet, as I said, be so desperate, so out of fashion, as to steal a woman with nothing?" (241–42). In her making doubly sure, she reminds Gerrard in still another way of his debility: he must concede that he is "so desperate" and "so out of fashion." Now apparently convinced, Hippolita feels free to display a more queenly generosity by bestowing on him the bounty of twelve hundred pounds, for she "pities" his having a wife "put upon" him "with nothing." This imperious gesture (the money, she knows, will be at her disposal as well) can hardly be viewed a deserving reward for Gerrard's "patience."[51]

Even the most benign amorous activity—here Gerrard's kissing his mistress's hand as in supplication—is interrupted, this time by Don Diego, who is highly uncomfortable with such direct physical contact, especially since he has not ordered, controlled, or witnessed its initial stimulation. In any event, he decides that now is the time to push matters toward a climactic point: "I see it plain, he is no Dancing-master, now I have found it out, and I think I can see as far into matters as another: I have found it now, look you" (285–87). If one concludes that Diego never suspected Gerrard as being anything but a dancing master, that he believes dancing masters only teach dancing, and that his sister's warnings were mere ravings, then one can believe Diego suddenly comes around when he witnesses Gerrard kissing his daughter's hand. But he has perceived Gerrard as more than a dancing master; he has associated the dance with sexual activity and articulated his knowledge of the sexual propensities of dancing masters; he could not have been such a simpleton to dismiss totally his sister's warnings; and he has witnessed his daughter touching and rubbing Gerrard's hand and Gerrard her hand, arm, and leg earlier in the play. Furthermore, Diego says the words openly to Gerrard, Hippolita, and Monsieur, prefacing his remarks with "Umph, umph, no, no"—*not* in an aside, which would better suggest a sudden revelation. He assumes the *role* of the naive father—thereby wearing his own mask of innocence—as a way to exit the voyeuristic world he has joyously inhabited. He needs some external stimulus to propel matters to their end, and he uses this innocuous kiss on the hand as his pretext, as something "legal" on which to act. This tangible symbol of Gerrard's intentions is most disturbing, for now Diego must consider that the young man has, beyond occasional sour language directed at women, some kind of aggressive sexual tendencies and accordingly might well be a threat to the father's dominion over his daughter—although even this interpretation is mitigated somewhat by Gerrard's timid language (likely heard by Don Diego): "Dear Miss, you but encrease my fears, and not my wealth"; and "My fear was prophetical" (254, 288). And Monsieur's confession that Gerrard is indeed no dancing master only helps to prompt Diego's drawing on the young suitor, the natural and thus inevitable expression of male hostility reaching its climax as Monsieur "betrays" Gerrard for his own gain, leaving his rival no choice but to flee, as Diego showers Monsieur with contempt and threatens him with monetary emasculation and Gerrard with death. Gerrard then seeks to "lead" Hippolita only to have her resist (334). And into this chaotic whirlpool, shifting from the sexual to the violent, arrives the Parson, who one expects will be an agent of peace and order, the catalyst for resolving present tensions. But he remains passive, saying nothing, only to be shoved in another room by Monsieur. Merely a messenger of information, the Parson serves simply as another decoy to the reader—another dead end in Wycherley's labyrinth.

But weapons may be fashioned from a genealogy tree as well as an oak, as we discover in an amusing, yet no less intense, debate between Don Diego and Monsieur about the former's "impressive" family lineage, which of course exposes Diego's humble ancestry, thus lifting his Spanish disguise to reveal his less-than-noble English pedigree. Embarrassed and enraged, Diego draws his sword—the shortest route available toward reasserting his manhood—but he lunges at Gerrard, not at Monsieur. Wycherley once more trips us up, leading our eyes one way only to have the action take place somewhere else. Diego tranfers his anger at Monsieur back to the last male over whom he had ascendency: Gerrard, who is still looking nervously for a way out of the house. To Diego, Gerrard serves as the nearest reminder of the time when he was securely a man of noble Spanish blood, and not the more pedestrian James Formal. And Monsieur's seeming bravery in drawing on Diego is belied by his self-reassurance that "Sure he will not shew his valour upon his Nephew and Son-in-Law, otherwise I shou'd be afraid of shewing mine" (400–401). In addition, Monsieur offers Diego a calming hypothetical: "I say, suppose he had done, done, done the feat to your Daughter. . . . I say, suppose he had, . . . ; well, I am ready to marry her however" (413–14, 419–20). Rather than leaving us with the image of the chivalric hero rescuing the damsal from the dreaded fate of shame and censure, the hypothetical actually casts Monsieur as a cuckold in full recognition of the fact, further humiliating himself with an unwarranted altruistic gesture. But Monsieur does act more aggressively than we might have expected, more animated than the dazed and tentative Gerrard, whom Monsieur thrusts along with Hippolita and the Parson behind a door for his protection. With Hippolita out of the room, Wycherley seems to encourage the reader to expect further male warfare, but as is his habit, he subverts that expectation, for in come the irrepressible Mrs. Caution and the whirlwinds Flirt and Flounce to inform us that the men will be denied their moment in the arena.

When the others return, we discover that Gerrard and Hippolita have just been married by the Parson. This time-worn convention of off-stage marriages (e.g., Young Bellair and Emilia) seems indeed the easy way out, but we might consider that the revelation adds interesting touches to the matters Wycherley has been concerned with throughout his second comedy. We see that Don Diego and Monsieur are defeated and that Gerrard has won his prize but not without paying a considerable price and certainly not through any skill of his own—his moment of "victory" not even being seen by the audience.[52] Diego and Monsieur now combine forces (and this pattern of two against one has been prevalent from the first act and will be similarly conspicuous in *The Country Wife*) and call on the servants to assault Gerrard. Although the Englishman is "rescued" by the arrival of his acquaintances, the "fiddlers," they merely get in the way rather than battle for their friend. And the Parson in effect joins forces with Gerrard to defeat Monsieur—for the Cleric was brought in to marry Monsieur and Hippolita. The action in this contained environment (a far cry from the expanse of St. James's Park) continues at a frenetic pace, as the characters crowd on each other, some lunging forward, others stepping back—spinning, running, pausing, pushing, and holding. Indeed, one would expect such a play to end within fifty lines or so with the young couple sharing at least some affection, or at least some prediction, regardless of the continuing battle of wits, of future delights—and perhaps a form of reconciliation with the parental or blocking figures. But this is Wycherley; and reflective of the often shifting focus, Monsieur quickly cuts his losses and is willing to take Flirt as a mistress—or so it seems, for one doubts he would actually have any choice in this matter. In so rapidly transferring his "interest" to Flirt, he seeks to mitigate the humiliation stemming from his failure to wed Hippolita. But Flirt shakes him with some frightening prospects: "Nay hold, Sir, two words to the Bargain, first I have ne're a Lawyer here to draw Articles and Settlements."[53] And the "first Article," she informs him, "shall be against Cohabitation; we Mistresses suffer no Cohabitation" (565–72).

Therefore at play's end, we are not concentrating on the married couple but rather on the legalities of the male-female relationship, weighted entirely, that is, to the woman's side: "Then separate Maintenance, in case you shou'd take a Wife, or I a new Friend"; "Then my Coach apart, as well as my Bed apart" (574–81). With each demand, Flirt enfeebles Monsieur further; she will not abide him resting in her bed—lovemaking as well as sleeping we might guess—the effect of these denials being made more severe the more physically attractive one perceives her to be: "Then, that you do not think I will be serv'd by a little dirty Boy in a Bonnet, but a couple of handsom, lusty, cleanly Footmen, fit to serve Ladies of Quality, and do their business as they shou'd do" (593–96). In essence and with enthusiasm she previews his cuckoldry: he will be banished from her bed while she entertains herself with virile playmates—a graphic and distrubing image that he cannot soon forget. Finally, Flirt denies Monsieur the prospects of freedom and power, as well as the comfort of even metaphoric potency, by demanding "advance-money" of "five hundred pound for Pins" and then "a thousand pound a year present maintenance, and but three hundred pound a year separate maintenance for [her] life, when [their] Love grows cold" (612–22). Having so envisaged the ultimate male horror (enhanced by the law so uncategorically serving the woman's interest), Monsieur can only make a feeble stab at humor by lamenting the good old days when a mistress might have been secured for less.

We wonder not only why Wycherley has devoted close to ninety lines to a scene in which secondary characters are the focus but also why he did not give the proviso scene to Hippolita and Gerrard.[54] Other than the playwright's commitment to the unexpected, having Hippolita speak before, after, or instead of Flirt would only be redundant. There can be no doubt that Gerrard is thoroughly under his wife's control; he remains relatively mute from the time he returns after his marriage (he speaks only one complete sentence, one incomplete sentence, and a "so, so"). Gerrard would likely get a not-necessarily-playful nudge or nod from Hippolita after every telling point Flirt makes—in addition to Prue's appropriate giggling, "Hah, ha" (682)—reminding him of how it might well be with them. As for the presumably defeated Don Diego, he tells the others, "I will cheat 'em all; for I will declare I understand the whole Plot and Contrivance, and conniv'd at it" (649–51). For anyone so lacerated, "I knew it all the time" seems the most handy yet most transparent balm: "For do you think I wou'd ever have suffer'd her to marry a *Monsieur*, a *Monsieur Guarda*. Besides, it had been but a beastly incestuous kind of a Match, voto—" (673–74). Other than finding comfort in attacking one of his own sex, Diego's words do touch on an aspect of the truth: he *did* understand *part* of the plot; he did contrive to continue it for his own perverse pleasure—the word "incestuous" he applies to a Monsieur-Hippolita marriage touching on his *own* voyeuristic reveries earlier in the play.

Caution's final words are consistent with the sexual filter through which she has viewed almost everything: "Young-man, you have danc'd a fair Dance for your self royally, and now you may go jig it together till you are both weary; and though you were so eager to have him, Mrs. *Minx,* you'll soon have your belly-full of him, let me tell you, Mistress" (678–81),[55] such an erotic focus making her the irrepressible character she is. And continuing his pattern of "one-upping" his sister (the female), Don Diego contributes his own entendres in addressing Gerrard: "I find you are a brisk man of honour, firm, stiff Spanish honour" (687–88)—Gerrard of course being none of these things on either literal or figurative levels. Quite fittingly, Hippolita has the final words in the play, for she is the ascendant character, mirrored in a more grandiose manner by Flirt, a sort of "primitive" alter ego (who is thereby an appropriate Speaker of the Epilogue): "So, so, now I cou'd give you my blessing, Father, now you are a good complaisant Father, indeed" (704–5). Her victory is total, as her patronizing air indicates; she has overcome even the one person who caused her to fear.[56]

Consensus holds that *The Gentleman Dancing-Master* is the weakest of Wycherley's efforts (a designation not as damaging, of course, when one has written only four plays), difficult to fit into the pattern of the other three.[57] But this work offers much more than its detractors have claimed and "thematically" remains squarely within the context of the other three plays. Being frequently on "the edge of discovery," it teases, frustrates, antagonizes, and captivates the reader—therefore making Hippolita herself as well as the dance perfectly emblematic for the comedy as a whole.[58] Whereas it naturally disappoints those looking for admirable characters, moral guideposts, and even a powerful satiric thrust, Wycherley continues the matters and motifs introduced in *Love in a Wood* but is more controlled in his handling of them—the more constricted environment of Diego's house and compression of characters and plot encouraging the reader's sense of being entrapped along with the men and women, who are stimulated by their fears to act as they do. Only sections of the play are overtly bawdy, but lying slightly below the surface, covered by a thin glaze of indirection, is a tempestuous sexual dynamic that influences every one of the significant characters. In short, then, *The Gentleman Dancing-Master* does not support the weight of one assessment that the playwright "had not yet thought through the psychological forces underlying social affectations."[59]

3
"Plagues and Torments": *The Country Wife*

COMING FRESH FROM A READING OF *THE GENTLEMAN DANCING-MASTER,* one may detect a seamless transition to *The Country Wife.* That is, Wycherley takes us from the courtship phase (Hippolita and Gerrard) to the married state (the Fidgets and Pinchwifes) and displays the male's greatest fear (the loss of manhood) made manifest in Pinchwife's experiences and that of the women (perpetual incarceration) both surmounted in Lady Fidget and realized in Margery Pinchwife.[1] And then there is the continued attention the playwright's gives to ironic notions of male potency—now resting in the paradox of Horner's decision to move from a state of virility to one of "sterility." By assuming the pose of an emasculated male—that ultimate state to which other males, himself included, attempt to push their brothers—Horner cleverly attempts to defuse the explosive possibility of being successfully assailed by others.[2] Horner's gesture is moreover a concession to the fact that in Wycherley's world women are destined for ascendency—that is, those women who have escaped incarceration and have been able to exercise the freedom necessary to display their power. Horner may well realize that such a state of impotence is inevitable, whether it be the immediate aftereffects of a rake's spirited sexual realtions or the indignities of the superannuated "Disabled Debauchee." He simply wishes to subvert the pattern by beginning at the end, with an overt concession to the inevitable. He is perceptive enough to realize that the best way to avoid being peppered in the battle is seemingly to retire from the field as a casualty.

As Horner's only confidant, the Quack believes that he has gone out and "undone" Horner "for ever with the Women" by spreading the word of his sexual debility (I.i.5)—the irony stemming from the town's assumption that a Quack often stages "miracle *cures*" for maladies such as impotence:[3] "Well I have been hired by young Gallants to bely'em t'other way; but you are the first wou'd be thought a Man unfit for Women" (32–33).[4] The Quack fails to perceive that instead of making him less attractive to men and less threatening to women, Horner's status as eunuch will do just the reverse—make him less threatening and thus more attractive to men (who would wish to torment one they can now wholly "trust") but far less pleasing to women because he would have no virility to offer.[5] Horner is typical of those characters in Wycherley who strive for uniqueness and separate themselves as much as they can from the average gamesplayer, while nevertheless being a slave to the game itself. Horner in essence *uses* the unchanging realities of human behavior and motivation, while others—particularly Pinchwife—struggle mightily against them. Although he may be applauded for pushing the ritual in a radical direction, it is ritual still.

Horner's reaction when he hears that "two Ladies and a Gentleman" are coming up is quite telling: "A Pox, some unbelieving Sisters of my former acquaintance, who I am afraid, expect their sense shou'd be satisfy'd of the falsity of the report" (50–52). The reader may immediately recall Gerrard's discomfort at the announcement of Flirt and Flounce; accordingly, an acquaintance with *The Gentleman Dancing-Master* encourages skepticism of Horner's status as successful rake-hero. Although his concerns are somewhat allayed as the "formal Fool" (Sir Jaspar), his wife, and sister arrive, Horner is not immune to the fear of discovery and of the curiosity and power of such women. Sir Jaspar Fidget may well stand for the playwright's more blithe manifestation of the negative male force (Pinchwife the more malicious and therefore more captivating), but even though he is preoccupied with "business," Jaspar clearly delights in another male's humiliation and is more than willing to inflict further pain on the now sexually "helpless" figure before him, punctuating each figurative blow with the laugh of derision: "Hah, hah, hah,; I'll plague him yet" (72). Jaspar is moreover stimulated by the image of the "emasculated" Horner as a Tantalus in Tartarus, reaching vainly for the fruits (Lady Fidget and perhaps Mrs. Dainty Fidget) just without his reach. Warming to new thoughts of his relative potency (publicly, at least, he is the husband of a highly sexual woman) measured against Horner's impotence, Jaspar inadvertently pimps for his own wife—the first indication that here Wycherley will focus more intently on that self-destructive impulse so often characteristic of male relationships. Jaspar is therefore no mere "gull'd gentleman," but rather a man prompted by darker impulses, one who expresses both a sadistic joy in humiliating another male and a fear of his wife's sexual proclivities: "'Tis as much a Husbands prudence to provide innocent diversion for a Wife, as to hinder her unlawful pleasures; and he had better employ her, than let her employ her self" (117–20)—a remark suggesting that he has at least a modicum of common sense and perception.[6]

Horner and Sir Jaspar therefore evaluate males using the same criterion: sexual potency.[7] We have long judged Horner's motivation in the play as the consummation of his lust, but his intitial stimulation seems more the result of the destructive male impulse: "if I can but abuse the Husbands," rather than its complement, "I'll soon disabuse the Wives" (I.i.137–38). Even in a remark of relative "innocence," we find Horner creating a disturbing image of sexual substitution: "I will kiss no Mans Wife, Sir, for him, Sir" (70–71). He is aware that the grandest expression of power over other men, not over women, is in sexual conquest: as a eunuch, he tells his confidant the Quack, he may "be seen in a Ladies Chamber, in a morning as early as her Husband; kiss Virgins before their Parents [particularly the father], or Lovers" (I.i.157–59). Although the males in such instances would be oblivious to Horner's virility, he would eventually and most assuredly encourage a revelation of the truth, providing him the added pleasure of seeing the husbands, lovers, and fathers consciously beaten and their greatest fears realized.

Undoubtedly, Lady Fidget (and to a lesser extent her sister-in-law, Mrs. Dainty Fidget) may be termed a blatant hypocrite, crying "Honour" and "Reputation" while panting for sexual gratification—a fact that has led several generations of critics to call her everything from mildly offensive to completely repulsive, from an object of satire to the one character Wycherley truly hates. I would argue instead that Wycherley finds her an attractive and irresistible character, an even more memorable and "classic" version of Lady Flippant or a mature Hippolita, a woman keenly aware of the need for propriety yet undaunted in her sexual appetite, an energetic presence who is far more appealing than the sterile males in the play. The vigorous disdain she evinces for Horner *once* Sir Jaspar informs her that he is "in fact" a eunuch is prompted not by concerns for her "reputation," but rather by her overt disgust now that he is sexually useless to her. Horner's famous observation—"your Women of Honour, as you call'em, are only chary of their reputations, not their Persons, and 'tis scandal they wou'd avoid, not Men" (I.i.154–56)—seems to place the emphasis squarely on female hypocrisy and to urge our reading Horner as a satiric agent (although the directness of the satiric thrust is blunted by his addressing the remark to the Quack and not to Lady Fidget). But it is evident that he has an incomplete understanding of why avoiding scandal is important to these women. "Reputation" is another of those checks on totally unbridled expressions of pleasure—which the women understand would be detrimental to the health of the individual and to a needed sense of social order.[8] Besides, we might wonder who in society views Lady Fidget as virtuous? Her husband only?

As a volatile sexual creature knowledgeable of Horner's former proficiency, Lady Fidget loathes males who cannot appreciate (physically want) her—a fact Horner accurately perceives: "You do well, Madam [to go], for I have nothing that you came for: I have brought over not so much as a Bawdy Picture, new Postures, nor the second Part of the *Escole de Filles;* Nor—" (86–88). Her aggressive passion demands many forms of satisfaction—from the sex act itself, to metaphoric intercourse and fondling, to representative sexuality in erotic pictures and literature.[9] Surely, Lady Fidget is made uncomfortable by Horner's having brought matters so close to the dreaded truth, but she is also likely aroused by the visual delights he portrays—a form of erotic prelude to sexual activity. At heart, Horner is neither active satiric agent nor misogynist;[10] instead, he is a man intrigued, despite an occasional "severe" riposte, by Lady Fidget's sexual aura, to which he feels compelled to respond.

When Lady Fidget asks Horner—after he has called her "virtue" an affectation—"wou'd you wrong my honour?" he answers, "If I cou'd," a reply that piques her interest, as it suggests the possibility of forthcoming passionate activity.[11] But Sir Jaspar's intrusion (interruption) and assurance that Horner is but a "meer Eunuch" disgusts her again, and this time most seriously: "O filthy French Beast, foh, foh; why do we stay? let's be gone; I can't endure the sight of him" (102–03). Whereas she might admit that Horner's wit is still potent, this quality does not begin to make up for what he lacks. And later, when she is with Mrs. Dainty Fidget and Mrs. Squeamish, the women's rejection of Horner is once more owing to an innate revulsion at his reported weakness: "Stand off"; "Do not approach us.... You are very obliging, Sir, because we wou'd not be troubled with you" (II.i.410–11; 437–38). And in the "China Scene," Jaspar reflects on this point by observing that Horner's "wants make his form contemptible" to women and that Lady Fidget had observed that "a proper handsome Eunuch, was as ridiculous a thing, as a Gigantick Coward" (IV.iii.136–39). Sensing that sexual vitality is both life-sustaining and attractive, the virile man or woman loaths its opposite, a form of sexual death, fearing that such impotence might well be catching.[12]

Of course Horner seems the sophisticated strategist—as he envisages his ploy as a way to "be rid of all [his] old Acquaintances, the most insatiable sorts of Duns"; "And next, to the pleasure of making a New Mistriss, is that of being rid of an old One" (I.i.139–42). But other than an air of rakish irresponsibility, Horner's words reveal an uneasiness at the persistence of those *insatiable* women he has been unable to control and may not have been able to satisfy. Moreover, his claim that his ruse would "rid" himself of old acquaintences is ridiculed by the Fidgets' earlier visit and by the subsequent arrivals of Harcourt and Dorilant, Sparkish, and Pinchwife. Indeed, we never actually see him as a successful lover (although so much criticism assumes his frequent and successful sexual activity), dominating a relationship with an equally

3: "PLAGUES AND TORMENTS" 85

attractive, vibrant, or sophisticated female. He either seduces the easier mark (the country wife) or is swept up by the tide of sexuality begun by a Lady Fidget. He seeks refuge behind the notion and metaphor of gamesmanship, in which indirection is rewarded with self-praise and admiration. Although he comprehends that women have an instinctive desire for sexual expression, whether in mere word or action—"now I can be sure, she that shews an aversion to me loves the sport" (152–53)—even this perception suggests a basic hesitation, the need for a sign before he can act.

Though highly sensitive to the hidden motivations of males, and clever enough to subvert and use them for his own purposes, Horner is not free from the same impulses and fears that plague everyone else—a factor that should prevent us from evaluating his relationship with Harcourt and Dorliant as an example of a healthy fraternity.[13] Rather, it is a curious relationship that says more about the male habit of "bullying" (two or three against one) than it does about the loyalty and comfort of brotherhood. Horner asks upon their arrival if the women have pitied his new condition, to which Harcourt readily answers, "What Ladies? the vizard Masques you know never pitty a Man when all's gone, though in their Service," and Dorlilant adds the following of the "Women in the boxes" whom Horner would not pity "*when* 'twas in [his] power" (emphasis added): "I dare swear, they won't admit you to play at Cards with them, go to Plays with'em, or do the little duties which other Shadows of men, are wont to do for'em" (175–83). Dorilant portrays more graphically the image of the "Shadows of men," that perverse fraternity to which Horner is now reputed to belong: "Ay your old Boyes, old *beaux Garcons*, who like superannuated Stallions are suffer'd to run, feed, and whinney with the Mares as long as they live, though they can do nothing else" (187–89). Not some witty rhetorical commonplace, Dorilant's comment reveals undisguised delight at Horner's "condition" (the admired rival Lothario now seemingly out of commission) and at the image of this particular "Shadow" of a man—both men ignoring the relevance to themselves (time will eventually superannuate them as well) and, like Sir Jaspar, concentrating instead on the pleasurable comparison of their own relative strength with the impotence of such pathetic creatures.[14] What is particularly frightening in this portrait is not merely the prospect of virulent time sapping youth and vitality but of the impotent male exercised, fed, and allowed some expression (by women, the vision implies) though unable to display his virility because he no longer has it—the secret of his humiliation safe from no one.

Neither Harcourt nor Dorilant feels confident that Horner could prosper in their world with anything less than an erect phallus—talk, wit, and drink are insufficient substitues: "Perhaps," Harcourt warns Horner, "you may prove as weak a Brother amongst'em that way, as t'other," to which Dorilant adds that "drinking with Women" is but "a pleasure of decay'd Fornicators, and the basest way of quenching Love" (III.ii.31–35). And Harcourt's words hardly suggest one trying to ease the torment of a man in Horner's reported condition: "Sir, before you go, a little of your advice, an old maim'd General, when unfit for action is fittest for Counsel; I have other designs upon Women, than eating and drinking with them; I am in love with *Sparkish's* Mistriss, whom he is to marry to morrow, now how shall I get her?" (III.ii.45–49). Later, when Sir Jaspar again invites Horner to entertain Lady Fidget, Dorilant wishes that one as virile as he or Harcourt had been given the opportunity to fit Jaspar with a pair of horns—"what a good Cuckold is lost there, for want of a Man to make him one"—and Harcourt replies, again with more glee than sympathy I would argue: "Ay, to poor *Horner* 'tis like coming to an estate at threescore, when a Man can't be the better for't" (III.ii.549–50, 552–53).

Clearly, for every bit of shared "brotherly" advice there are several vivid reminders of Horner's impotence, the allusion to the "Disabled Debauchee" figure only exacerbating Horner's "pain." And Horner too cannot suppress the antifraternal instinct as he informs his "friends," "I converse with [women], as you do with rich Fools, to laugh at'em, and use'em ill" (III.ii.18–20). Here we see the men moving around each other, firing off shot after shot—the ridicule perfectly reflecting the interaction of the male sex. That Harcourt and Sparkish end this scene by vowing their fraternity ("dear Friend") simply puts the proper ironic exclamation mark on the matter (154–64). Even when Harcourt asks Horner for advice on how he might win Alithea, he knows full well that Horner cannot help being reminded of the sexually potent world he no longer inhabits. And Horner's disappointment at the prospects of the Alithea-Sparkish match may only in part be due to his wish that Harcourt have her—"I am sorry for't . . . 'tis for her sake, not yours, and another mans sake that might have hop'd. . . . Poor *Harcourt* I am sorry thou hast mist her" (IV.iii.365–72)—for we should be hesitant in ascribing this reaction to the feelings of a loyal friend.[15] Horner displays little loyalty or sincerity in his dealings with other males, and therefore the likelihood exists that his primary motivation in this matter is not the felicity of Harcourt but the disappointment of both Sparkish and Pinchwife (the latter having orchestrated this incomprehensible match).[16]

To the intelligent Horner, letting Harcourt and Dorilant in on his deceit would only invite betrayal; accordingly, his observation that although he cannot "enjoy" women any longer, he shall enjoy his friends more, for "good fellowship and friendship, are lasting, rational and manly pleasures" (I.i.191–93) is of course a deliberate mockery.[17] Horner tells them that "'tis hard to be a good Fellow, a good Friend, and a Lover of Women, as 'tis to be a good Fellow, a good Friend, and a Lover of Money" (203–5). Even in the witticism, Horner suggests that in matters of sexual conquest masculine "friendship" is of secondary concern. And regarding women, the "friends" next indulge in witty simile, Dorilant adding to Harcourt's disrespectful and telling comment that "Mistresses are like Books" ("if you pore upon them too much, they doze you") his view that "A Mistress shou'd be like a little Country retreat near the Town, not to dwell in constantly, but only for a night and away; to tast the Town the better when a Man returns" (I.i.197, 200–202). (Again, for all such boasting we never see in Wycherley any male assume successfully such a posture before the young woman.) Dorilant's image implies that women are more easily controlled outside the confines of the city, that liberating environment where they are freer to express themselves naturally—in ways with which the males have difficulty coping. The simile is moreover significant in its planting in the reader's mind the connection between the country and masculine stability and power. Dorilant's glib comparison is therefore an effective introduction to Margery Pinchwife, establishing one more reason why Horner would be attracted to her and a primary motivation for her husband's desire to keep her safely in the country.

Sparkish's visit provides further evidence of pervasive masculine antagonisms and the protective aspects of the ego: "he can no more think the Men laugh at him, than that Women jilt him, his opinion of himself is so good" (I.i.223–24). Moreover, Sparkish strives to ascend in company, as Horner tells us, with his "nauseous" attempts at wit. Hardly alone among playwrights, Wycherley implies that false-wit and fastidiousness are "effeminate" qualities, but such men as Dapperwit, Monsieur de Paris, and Sparkish see these "qualities" as something one can escape into, something that cloaks the fear of being emasculated and abused by others. But Sparkish will inevitably break from his rhetorical sanctuary and respond more aggressively in his dealings with his male competitors, although at this point the bantering with the men barely hints at the kind of deeper nastiness of which he is capable. Other than suggesting "Spark" or "Spruce Spark," his name offers a clue that he may be a potentially dangerous commodity, a spark that may at any time ignite into something more deadly.[18] Since the false wits the men revile are males, the creation of males, assailed by males, and emblematic of male weakness, they and the fops serve as signifiers of the internecine nature of masculine relationships. Even in Sparkish's comical defense of the wits, Wycherley embellishes the theme of male conflict and division: "the reason why we are so often lowder, than the Players, is, because we think we speak more wit, and so become the Poets Rivals in his audience: for to tell you the truth, we hate the silly Rogues" (III.ii.84–87).

Men categorize each other, constantly breaking down the fraternity into cliques to be compared with and then found superior to. Groups band together only to attack an individual or another group—ironically making males more vulnerable to the manipulations of women: "Women, Women, that make Men do all foolish things" (93–94). Harcourt reflects further on this matter: "Most Men are contraries to that they wou'd seem; your bully you see, is a Coward with a long Sword; the little humbly fawning Physician with his Ebony cane, is he that destroys Men" (I.i.250–52). Present in both examples is a phallic prop—one to cover the inadequacy, the other to suggest that a destructive power may often lie beneath the veneer of impotence—whether it be Sparkish or Horner. And as another illustration of the larger irony, we find that the more males separate themselves from their brothers, the more they are shown to be alike, regardless of physical appearance, social grace, or public reputation.

Sparkish evinces his malicious side in constant references to Horner's emasculation and the humiliation that comes from public awareness about it: as he said to several ladies, "did you never see Mr. *Horner;* he lodges in *Russel-street,* and he's a sign of a Man, you know, since he came out of *France,* heh, hah, he" (287–89). The women laughed so hard, Sparkish informs Horner, that they "bepiss'd themselves"—certainly a frequent physiological reaction to excessive laughter but moreover a suggested reference, in its scatology, to their total disdain for Horner—their defilement of him. To his mind, Sparkish has scored often and severely on Horner, and the others' attempt to thrust him from the room seems less a gesture of loyalty to Horner than a reflection of anger and discomfort that their supposed inferior could so rise to the occasion. For even though Horner is quite adept at ridiculing Sparkish's manhood: "but hast thou a Mistriss, *Sparkish?* 'tis as hard for me to believe it," Sparkish always repays in kind: "we were some of us beforehand with you to day at the Play: . . . did you not hear us laugh?" (III.ii.74–75, 78–79). As a result, the victorious Sparkish insists that they all dine together—gluttonous for another opportunity to study and disgrace Horner[19]—and even though his offer is rejected, he still manages to score a palpable hit: "I'll go fetch my Mistriss" (I.i.324–25), a final reminder of what he believes Horner lacks and may never have again—all the work of a far more shrewd, subtle, and diabolical creature than his overt demeanor would lead us to believe.[20] Here, then, Horner stands as the baited bear, snapped at by those who torment him with constant reminders of his impotence (Sir Jasper, Harcourt, Dorilant, and Sparkish) and who—while they also turn on each other (Harcourt and Dorilant versus Sparkish and later Pinchwife)—are all in fact united by a common goal of reminding Horner of his debility, and by extension of their own now "exclusive" sexual vigor.

3: "PLAGUES AND TORMENTS"   89

Having established the destructive framework of masculine relationships, Wycherley pushes out Jack Pinchwife, once a cavorter with Horner (so he says and others believe, but to what extent we cannot know) but now apparently a morose and suspicious "country gentleman." The relative neglect or underestimation of Pinchwife in so many critical studies is nothing short of surprising, for he is a character of significance at least equal to Horner.[21] To all appearances he is the stock puritanical boor, a ruffian, misogynist, insufferable fool, insensitive dolt, and jealous cuckold, who indeed gets just what he deserves. But he is moreover an important extension of Wycherley's interest in the instinctive fears and reactions of males, of those who incarcerate out of fear—an extensive fine tuning of Don Diego, now given a wife instead of a daughter, but a wife who seems as much a daughter as a wife. He certainly "pinches" his young Margery—a gesture signifying pain as well as suppression—binding her to him, hoping to nip her vitality and sexual desire. All powerful in the country he believes (we recall Dorilant's simile), Pinchwife feels himself weakening rapidly now that he is in the more emancipating environment of London.[22] In his bluster and penchant for violence, Pinchwife seconds Hobbes's position that the best way one can "secure himself" is through "Anticipation": "that is, by force, or wiles, to master the persons of all men he can, so long, till he see no other power great enough to endanger him."[23]

That late seventeenth-century law, custom, and practice provided the husband with seemingly boundless power over a wife only underscores more emphatically the irony that Pinchwife *fears* having his marriage made known to Horner and the others. Wycherley and his characters appreciate that natural human inclinations do not change nor are instinctive fears allayed because of custom and law.[24] Pinchwife accepts that he will be laughed at by members of his own sex who see the marriage state as a visible signification of *lost* male power, not the increase of it. And although a husband, Pinchwife's age difference with Margery (he is forty-nine; she probably at most eighteen or nineteen) and his aggressive determination to protect her suggest that his function is also that of a father defending his daughter's purity—and thus his own interests. In addition, he serves as father to his sister Alithea (who may be twenty-two to twenty-five), who certainly views him more as an intimidating parent. The darker side of the family relationship Wycherley unveiled through Gripe and Don Diego finds another expression in this play: "I must give *Sparkish* to morrow five thousand pound," Pinchwife tells the others, "to lye with my Sister" (I.i.335–36)—his preoccupation evident in his choice of this tasteless phrase rather than "to wed my sister." Is he simply helping Alithea to the altar—getting her out of his and Margery's way—by making all financial burdens disappear? Or might the presentation of money be a means by which to control his sister, a representative of her sex?

Horner of course relishes the opportunity to harass Pinchwife about his recent marriage: "the next thing that is to be heard, is thou'rt a Cuckold" (I.i.341–42). Surely, the impetus for this remark is destructive, touching as it does the heart of masculine fear.[25] And Horner's subsequent observation, "But I did not expect Marriage from such a Whoremaster as you, one that knew the Town so much, and Women so well" (344–45), speaks little to Pinchwife's former proficiency as a libertine, for without question Horner's comment is heavily sarcastic, a malicious reminder to Pinchwife of what he *could not* be. Horner understands, as do the others, that Pinchwife never *mastered* whores or any other kind of woman, and Horner's articulation of Pinchwife's *knowing* the town and women "so well" also ridicules, because Pinchwife's erotic "knowledge" is restricted to that which stems from contemplation, observation, and fantasy, rather than from experience, as in the proverbial "Biblical sense" of "knowing" a woman—being as well a derisive reference to Pinchwife's pet expression, "I know the town." In an attempt at retaliation, Pinchwife assures Horner that he has married "no *London* wife" (346)—an image personified in the undaunted and sexually demanding Lady Fidget. In arguing for similarities between country and city women, Horner further rattles the foundation of Pinchwife's security—the belief that city and country are antitheses. Distinctions, dichotomies, and contrasts are to Pinchwife like rooms without windows, in which he hopes to hide from what he dreads but cannot, owing to the clear view others have of his fears.

Still, Pinchwife makes the attempt to shut the casements by asserting that country girls are indeed easier to control, voicing the faulty assumption that the woman's power is nothing instinctual but environmental. Remove the woman from the city and she is, like Antaeus off the ground, more easily beaten: "At least we are a little surer of the breed there, know what her keeping has been, whether foyl'd or unsound" (351–52).[26] Metaphor provides Pinchwife another means by which to secure power and control, as here he transforms the vibrant and threatening image of the young woman into a domestic beast, a "breed" country gentlemen have always mastered with minimal effort.[27] And well knowing how a beautiful and sexually eager woman can stimulate and perplex a man, Pinchwife insists on portraying his wife as asexual or almost hermaphoritic, not simply to deter Horner but to assure himself that she could never destroy him: "No, no, she has no beauty, but her youth; no attraction, but her modesty, wholesome, homely, and huswifely, that's all" (357–58). Suggesting his participation in the ritualistic slaughter of the fellow male, Harcourt believes such an awkward wife should be brought to town "to be taught breeding"—the reference continuing Pinchwife's comparison of Margery to something bovine, but now making "breeding" an image disturbing to Pinchwife rather than comforting.

Instinctively "ganging up," Dorilant and Harcourt attempt to turn Pinchwife's pattern of logic on its head: safe in the city, in peril in the country, where there is, as Harcourt tells him, "Open house, every Man's welcome" (374). Dorilant and Harcourt gleefully pepper him by assailing those who have "alwayes coarse, constant, swinging stomachs in the Country"; "Foul Feeders indeed" (370–72)—in this context employing the mid-century military tactic of the "caracole" (each rank riding up, firing their pistols, and then whirling away). (But one should moreover appreciate that in their attempts to bombard Pinchwife with these sexual allusions, they are also—consciously or no—blasting the "incapacitated" Horner as well.) Pinchwife reacts with predictable agitation: "good Wives, and private Souldiers shou'd be ignorant" (363–64). Ostensibly, he means to keep Margery from Horner's private "instructions," but his real concern is that she might come to desire the freedom of sexual expression and the sorority of city women (who would offer her consolation and encouragement) and then to discover an occasion to respond more naturally to any erotic proclivities. Horner's growing interest in the country wife can be attributed in part to the attractive portrait Pinchwife paints despite himself, but actually it is Pinchwife who presents the challenge, not Margery. And we might then ask why Horner does not inform Pinchwife that he is a "eunuch." Does he wish to have Margery in the "conventional" way, or is he aware that, unlike the other males of his acquaintance, Pinchwife would refuse to believe Horner's disclaimers? And if so, would Pinchwife's awareness be the result of a pervasive fear of being cuckolded, or in this case a healthy skepticism the other males do not apparently possess?

More than being insufferably imperious in his repeated efforts to transform Margery into the village idiot—"because she's ugly, she's the likelyer to be my own; and being ill-bred, she'l hate conversation; and since silly and innocent, will not know the difference betwixt a Man of one and twenty, and one of forty" (I.i.381–84)—Pinchwife is so obviously troubled, seeking comfort in these perverse Pygmalionesque fantasies, with his allusions and comparisons de-feminizing his wife (animal, country idiot, homely country waif) and later changing her, with a disguise, into an effeminate male. (And his terms of "endearment" for her—from "Minx" to "Baggage," but never "Margery"—also reveal a wish to reshape her into something he may more easily control, linking him with other "creative" male characters—Don Diego, Horner, and Manly particularly.) But the truth shakes Pinchwife from such reveries, prompting an unexpected and open articulation of his fears: "what is wit in a Wife good for, but to make a Man a Cuckold?";[28] "my Wife shall make me no Cuckold, though she had your help Mr. *Horner;* I understand the Town, Sir" (I.i.391–400). Maliciously more than playfully, Horner sees to it that Pinchwife remains highly vulnerable to meer suggestion: "what is worse [than actually 'clubbing' with another man], if she cannot make her Husband a Cuckold, she'l make him jealous, and pass for one, and then 'tis all one" (395–97).[29]

The exact nature of Pinchwife's sexual relations with Margery is anyone's guess, even though we are sorely tempted to assume that he has been unsatisfactory in the performance of his conjugal duties, which Horner may well consider as he reminds Pinchwife of his "whoring" days. And in good "bullying" fashion Dorilant picks up the cue: "Ay, ay, a Gamester will be a Gamester, whilst his Money lasts; and a Whoremaster, whilst his vigour" (413–14).[30] Should Pinchwife claim, to himself or the others, that he is no longer a whoremaster, he would in effect admit to his impotence. Now he stands as the baited bear, swatting at the curs who come to gnash at his flesh: "you may laugh at me, but you shall never lye with my Wife, I know the Town" (419–20). Yet Pinchwife does break down under the constant badgering and ceaseless disparagement and shockingly admits to his own past failures as a "whoremaster": "A Pox on't, the Jades wou'd jilt me, I cou'd never keep a Whore to my self" (423–24). Although one tends to find this admission amusing— in its corroborating the assumption of Pinchwife's sexual debility—it more importantly depicts a tormented man revealing openly what any other male would fight desperately to keep concealed: the direct admission of sexual failure. But Horner and the others have applied the irons so masterfully that Pinchwife seems unable to control himself and out of duress voices the unthinkable.

Not satisfied with Pinchwife's embarrassing confession, Horner notes that he has indeed seen the "pretty Country-wench" (431). His accomplices (a more apt word than "friends") aid in the identification, and Pinchwife seems emotionally flogged to the point of distraction: "Hell and damnation, I'm undone, since *Horner* has seen her, and they know 'twas she" (440–41). And indeed his inquisitors will allow no escape: "Nay, you shall not go." It is difficult to see how all of this can be characterized as poetic or comic justice, for Wycherley is depicting the more uncomfortable verities about human nature and masculine interaction. Are we to believe that had Pinchwife been more moderate and decorous he would have been less vulnerable or been spared such treatment by these men? Pinchwife will soon understand that only an expression of primitive violence will serve him faithfully against the likes of Horner, Harcourt, and Dorilant, whose motives in this exchange were not to administer justice but to indulge their power and cruelty against the perceived weaker male.[31] The odds being three-to-one only facilitates their efforts by making them more confident and secure from reprisal. And whereas the men earlier rejected Sparkish's (he who had aggravated them with allusions to Horner's weakness) offer to dinner, pushing him out the door, here they wish to deter Pinchwife (who makes them feel superior)—"Come you shall dine with us" (448).

With our first glimpse of the country wife, Wycherley reintroduces the voyueristic motif featured so prominently in *The Gentleman Dancing-Master*, for lurking behind the door, "peeping" in on her, is the husband/father, Pinchwife. Although less formidable than Hippolita, Margery's restless energy is, like the heroine of the earlier play, impossible to suppress.[32] Indeed, Margery's initial words evince her natural desire to escape the kind of sluggish and restricted world Pinchwife has fashioned for her: "Pray, Sister," she says to Alithea, "where are the best Fields and Woods, to walk in in *London?*" (II.i.1–2). Her reference to movement and city delights does not obscure her insecurity, however, in that the fields and woods signify her more familiar environment, something that gives her at least some confidence in exploring the unknown. She intuitively seeks comfort and assistance from Alithea ("will you ask leave for me to go a walking?," [24]), who knows much of the town and the freedom it may provide a married woman. In her own way, then, Pinchwife's sister may be said to "know the town" even better than her brother, and she serves a "sisterly" function by providing Margery with the names of places to visit and by warning her of Pinchwife's possessiveness: "He's afraid you shou'd love another man" (II.i.10). For instance, Alithea teaches Margery a careful bit of propriety after the country wife complains that her husband will not let her go abroad, "for fear of catching the Pox": "Fye, the small Pox you shou'd say" (30–32). She moreover understands a woman's metamorphoses in the country into common animals: "a Country Gentlewomans leasure is the drudgery of a foot-post; and she requires as much airing as her Husbands Horses" (25–27).[33] Pinchwife seeks to defy the natural dynamic by placing restraints on Margery in the liberating city, and we should judge that accordingly his cause is doomed—she will have to be *dragged* back to the country to be adequately controlled.

Margery Pinchwife cannot walk alone; she cannot be too far from her husband; she cannot wear what she wants. Even Pinchwife's taking her to the play (an action with clear self-destructive implications) is a form of suppression, for Margery had to sit "amongst ugly People," not being allowed to "come near the Gentry." But her infectious spirit will not be contained by such restrictive measures, and the city, far from corrupting, only provides her with the opportunity to act on basic inclinations. We note how excited she is by the image, as her husband tells her (again self-destructively), of those "naughty Women" at the playhouse, whom the men "tous'd and mous'd": "but I wou'd have ventur'd [down there] for all that," she tells Alithea (II.i.16–18). That this adventuresome, curious, sexual creature should see London first at the playhouse seems of course most appropriate, not only because the Restoration playhouse was the environment in which women were truly celebrities (as actresses or royal mistresses) but also because within its confines inhibitions were frequently shaken off. To Margery the playhouse was an even more erotic locale in which she too sought the release of her pent- and penned-up spirit: "I was a weary of the Play,[34] but I lik'd hugeously [a plausible entendre] the Actors; they are the goodlyest proper'st Men" (20–21). That Margery is inclined to follow her instincts is nowhere better evident than in her response to Alithea's advice that she "must not like the Actors": "Ay, how shou'd I help it, Sister?" (23). But the Country Wife has yet to appreciate the dangers of open expression in a world that demands indirection and frequent overtures to propriety. She is still to learn that all the world is *not* a stage, even though one must indeed learn to play her part.

Pinchwife reacts to his wife's initial enthusiasms as we would expect, by hurling at her a derisive "You're a Fool," and by lecturing his sister about her influence: "What you wou'd have her as impudent as your self, as errant a Jilflirt, a gadder, a Magpy, and to say all a meer notorious Town-Woman?" (II.i.35–40). His misogynistic conclusions, the misshaping of complex feelings through generalizations and labeling, help Pinchwife stem some of his eroding masculinity, and we note his concern that Margery will become "impudent" and in other ways like a "Town-Woman," through the efforts of his meddling and highly dangerous sister: "Hold, hold, do not teach my Wife, where the Men are to be found; I believe she's the worse for your Town documents already; I bid you keep her in ignorance as I do" (44–45, 55–57).[35] It is clear that Alithea's apparent self-confidence, assertiveness, and protection of her fellow woman are influenced by her residing in London; as Margery notes, Alithea is able to "go every day fluttering about abroad" (III.i.3). Since Pinchwife cannot frighten his sister with threats and demands, he will be forced to consider other methods to keep her, as well as his wife, under control.

Becoming increasingly aware of her surroundings, Margery soon understands the reciprocal requirements of sisterhood—"Indeed be not angry with her Bud" (II.i.58)—and she is able to release both frustration and impatience by admitting that she asks about the town (and men) "a thousand times a day" (59) and by being playfully direct in reply to her husband's question "but thou lik'st none better than me?": "Yes indeed, but I do, the Player Men are finer Folks" (70–71). But she also covers herself by lying boldly: "Dear, I hate *London;* our Place-house in the

Country is worth a thousand of't, wou'd I were there again" (61–62)—and by deliberately fowarding a persona of the innocent and ignorant country girl.[36] She cannot help revealing her exuberance, even while demonstrating a natural duplicity (survival instinct), and she has not learned that in the city that exuberance must always be *publicly* muted. She moreover shows herself adept at hiding behind the half-truth to both rile and confuse: "I did not care for going [to the playhouse]; but when you forbid me, you make me as't were desire it" (92–93). And Alithea picks up on the extension of the reference to sexual activity in the pronoun *it:* "So 'twill be in other things, I warrant" (94). Stimulated by the delicious visions of handsome actors and gallants, Margery further (though thinly) disguises her interests with a whisper of modesty: "What, a homely Country Girl? no Bud, no [actor or gallant] will like me"; "Ay, but if he [Horner] loves me, why shou'd he ruin me? answer me to that: methinks he shou'd not, I wou'd do him no harm" (104–5, 119–20). Perhaps delighting as much from the pleasurable vision as from the momentary control over her husband, Margery exploits Pinchwife's fear that she will indeed end up like those nefarious "Town Women, who only hate their Husbands, and love every Man else, love Plays, Visits, fine Coaches, fine Cloaths, Fidles, Balls, Treates, and so lead a wicked Town-life": "Nay, if to enjoy all these things be a Town-life, *London* is not so bad a place, Dear" (76–80). And Pinchwife's plea *is* almost pitiable: "But you love none better than me?" (72). All that's left to Pinchwife here is the familiar primitive gesture at the arrival of Harcourt and Sparkish: he "Thrusts" his wife into the next room.[37]

The Alithea-Harcourt relationship has been the subject of much analysis to the effect that they represent a romantic or moralistic norm by which to judge the actions of Horner and the others, that they are Wycherley's most positive statement that the world is not throroughly corrupt, and that successful marriage is indeed possible, even in a world of cuckolds and whores.[38] I would argue instead that their relationship reflects none of these views but is rather one more constructed and influenced by fear and insecurity.[39] Initially, Sparkish's motives in foisting Harcourt on Alithea (and vice-versa) stem from a wish to make Harcourt confront intimately what he cannot have intimately—the *beautiful,* not so much the virtuous, Alithea. As a result, we find ourselves uncomfortably on Pinchwife's side as he casts aspersions at Sparkish for his "generosity": "they [other men] shall know her, as well as you your self will, I warrant you ... Praising another Man to his Mistriss!" (II.i.133–34, 154). Here and throughout the play, we often find ourselves uncomfortably confronting Pinchwife, often walking briskly (or running) away from him, but then at other times standing next to him or behind him as a gesture of support. And Sparkish enjoys afflicting Pinchwife—as well as Harcourt[40]—by offering his "trust" and by physically preventing the Country Husband from putting an end to the highly irregular courtship Harcourt has begun: "Nay, you shall not disturb'em" (II.i.209-10). In addition, the creative and theatrical Sparkish participates vicariosuly in the courtly ritual, playing the role of voyeur and director (in the Don Diego mold), teeming with perverse excitement at the prospects of Harcourt's romantic interests: "I am sure you do admire her extreamly, I see't in your eyes.—He does admire you Madam"; "go, go with her into a corner,[41] and trye if she has wit, talk to her any thing, she's bashful before me" (156-58, 196-97). In an attempt to flatter Alithea, yet reflective of his less-than-ideal role in the play, Harcourt admits that he feels comfortable admiring the "whole Sex"—a not-so-subtle reminder to Pinchwife that he is in danger himself from the likes of Harcourt.

Alithea's reaction to this peculiar activity is more intriguing than admirable. Initially, she "looks down" as Sparkish praises her before Harcourt (II.i.139-40). Is this a gesture (one employed by Lucy Crossbite) based on natural shyness or practiced coyness? Genuine embarrassment over being so highly praised? Or discomfort over Sparkish's blatant foolishness or over her immediate warmth for Harcourt—that is, to an awakened sexual stimulation? She naturally doubts Harcourt's motives: "you are an Enemy to Marriage, for that I hear you hate as much as business or bad Wine" (165-67). And such comments as "you look upon a Friend married, as one gone into a Monastery, that is dead to the World" (171-73) testify to her understanding of the male penchant for ridiculing a fellow male and the articulated belief—in male company, where posturing is vital—that a sincere and open commitment to a woman means sacrificing one's masculinity. Sensitive to the restrictions placed upon women by law and custom, Alithea is shrewd, intelligent, humane, assertive, and egotistical—and not above exercising what power she has over men. Her tone in this scene may be morally, though annoyingly, aloof, but it is important to note that it is not consistently so. Her emphases shift constantly, which only keeps her elusive and formidable. She playfully encourages and playfully betrays Harcourt ("your Friend here is very troublesom, and very loving" [236])—wending her way dexterously through Sparkish's vanity and Harcourt's ego. Harcourt might expect (as would we) her easy capitulation to him—seeing the alternative—but this expectation she only frustrates. She provides him openings that quickly close—though not entirely, so that he may at least determine that he has a chance. Harcourt can only strengthen himself through sarcasm: "[She has not] so much [wit] as I thought, and hoped she had" (254)—being left with only the possibility of some physical confrontation with Sparkish to vent his growing frustration. Alithea plays the benign despot to Harcourt, controlling, agitating, and pleasing, without wishing to destroy or humiliate him. Figuratively, Harcourt is on bended knee before her, absolutely no threat in this context to her femininity or liberty—a major contributing factor to her growing more fond of him.

But Alithea's seeming loyalty to Sparkish has served for many as the most vexing aspect of this play. Her "I wou'd not be unjust to him" (II.i.215) sounds simply incredulous, implying a simple-minded, masochistic, or at least insufferably moral character[42]—one who would sacrifice her vibrant "self" to remain faithful to a promise (one she herself had little to do with making—her brother having set up the match). Surely one is more vexed than pleased at her announcement to Harcourt here and later assertions to the effect that she will marry Sparkish because her "honour is engag'd so far to him" and that "if he be true, and what I think him to me, I must be so to him" (III.ii.498–500). But her honorable pronouncements are really a masterful bit of indirection and ambiguity and, as far as she will allow it, an encouragement for the now-suffering Harcourt to continue on his course, needing at this point only a few crumbs to fall from her table. (And, as she assumed, her gloomy qualifying does anything but deter the anxious suitor.)[43]

Harcourt's aggressiveness in refuting Alithea's arguments in favor of honor precipitates the end of their initial conversation; she is obviously too uncomfortable with the truth and instinctively turns from it: "Nay, now you are rude, Sir" (II.i.235)—and she speaks up for Sparkish, although clearly without enthusiasm, as Harcourt attacks him further.[44] On one hand, she is both confrontational and manipulative, encouraging discord between the men, hoping, it appears, for some kind of explosive moment that will clear the air of the unsettling feelings within. And later she quickly turns from "devoted protectress" of Sparkish's reputation to his antagonist, bullying him into clarification: "How's that, do you say matrimonial love is not best?" (III.ii.289). Surely, Alithea controls the scene as might a mythic deity, leading the mortals to the point of confrontation (Sparkish draws, cowardly assuming that he will have Pinchwife's assistance) and then putting a halt to the hostilities, shifting from the voice of honesty to one of deception: "Hold, hold, indeed to tell the truth, the Gentleman said after all, that what he spoke, was but out of friendship to you" (II.i.285–86). It may be that she finds this chaotic moment a happy portent for a marriage—a dolt of a husband, easily outflanked yet encouraging of her effect on other males, and a lover such as Harcourt, one who places her in a clear position of superiority—all this while paying tribute to honor, reputation, and the other necessary components of order—in short, practicing the discourse and behavior of the liberated London wife.

Whereas "Honour" should be both admirable and desirable, especially in an environment that apparently displays little of it, in this *context* it is something more foreign and inimical—something more disturbing than even Lady Fidget's use of the term. But there is no requirement on our part to read Alithea's actions as angelic and as a result unbelievable; we ought instead to consider her motivations and the deep-seated emotions that prompt them. Initially, her keeping the engagement between her and Sparkish paramount in the conversation allows Harcourt to continue his flattery and overtures toward her, for she knows that while her status is indeed a barrier between them, her being engaged still (and ironically) provides the young man the kind of security he would not find if she were as free as Etherege's Harriet. That is, Harcourt's masculinity is spared the ultimate humiliation of being rejected by an *available* woman. She would of course understand that being "taken" increases the confidence of one such as Harcourt, who knows that she could not be physically attracted to the unappetizing Sparkish. And when she tells Sparkish "I hate him because he is your Enemey; and you ought to hate him too, for making love to me, if you love me" (III.ii.195–96), we find that she has cleverly encouraged Sparkish to admit his own (as well as Harcourt's) antifraternal sentiment and masculine weakness while at the same time flattering her pulchritude and virtue: "That he makes love to you, is a sign you are handsome; and that I am not jealous, is a sign you are virtuous, that I think is for your honour" (III.ii.203–5).

It is not difficult to envisage Alithea enjoying the posturing and head-butting (an actress has only to wear a mischievous smile)—as well as the physical tussling between Sparkish and Pinchwife—while Harcourt is courting her. Without question, she consciously stimulates such activity while at the same time keeping her hand disguised with such saccharine replies as, "But 'tis your honour too, I am concerned for" (206). This "Machiavellian" Alithea is quite antithetical to the virtuous and self-effacing character many have praised, but such an Alithea seems more representative of Wycherley's world. And her platitudes about "Love proceed[ing] from esteem," Sparkish's love for her, and the necessity of guarding her reputation (II.i.222–31) seem highly insincere and unpalatable, especially when recalling her comments and advice to Margery earlier in the play—for she truly could not be so naive a logician to accept the conclusion she gives Harcourt: "besides he loves me, or he wou'd not marry me" (223). No doubt the audience and reader share Harcourt's conclusion, "No, if you do marry him, with your pardon, Madam, your reputation suffers in the World, and you wou'd be thought in necessity for a cloak" (232–33).

Rather than unadulterated virtue, Alithea's protestations of loyalty may reflect in part Hobbes's position on vows and oaths: that there is an egotistical glory or pride in keeping and a fear in breaking them—fear from those who might be offended.[45] But more important is the possibility that she would indeed allow herself to marry Sparkish—not out of affection or duty, but out of that pervading fear that marriage to a powerful man will deny a woman freedom and destroy her spirit. She must judge Sparkish (that is, as she perceives him now) as a fool who, in his preoccupation with masculine warfare, flaunts her as a representation of his manhood, paradoxically encouraging her freedom as a way to puff his vanity. Such a husband would be easy to manipulate, thus allowing the kind of freedom she stated as desirable in her initial appearance with Margery, the kind of freedom known to a Lady Fidget, though we assume Alithea would not behave in the same lustful manner. And what would make such a motive paramount in her mind, even as she might struggle with her affections for Harcourt?[46] Quite simply, the example of her brother, who has attempted to control her and to imprison her sister-in-law. She will hear, for example, Pinchwife threaten Margery with something "worse than the Plague, Jealousy" (III.i.50). The platitudes about honor and promises are her way of dealing indirectly with those fears, of transforming the complexities she feels within to something more concrete and comprehensible.[47] Alithea is not simply testing Harcourt's sincerity and stamina, but also Sparkish's claim to be free from the dreaded emotion: "You astonish me, Sir, with your want of jealousie" (III.ii.228)—the point being that if Sparkish cracks and admits that he is *normal* in this regard, she would have just "cause" to discard him, since he would then have failed to live up to the terms of their "contract."

Alithea's somewhat peculiar (or seemingly perverted) sense of decorum and "honor" demands that Sparkish be the one to open the door from which she may escape: "I can't fire him; he's got to resign." As she says to Harcourt, "[Sparkish] only, not you . . . can give me a reason, why I shou'd not marry him" (III.ii.498–99). Because of her fears, Alithea is in a perilous position, and certainly the "finality" of her comments to Harcourt in the scene at the Exchange, "Pray, let me go, Sir, I have said, and suffer'd enough already" and "I will never see you more. . . . Good night, Sir, for ever" (490, 493, 560) might in part be a reaction to Harcourt's physical imposition on her person here, but her words moreover appeal for assistance (as in "I really wish I could be with you, but I don't think I can"). And like a skilled cross-examiner, Alithea uses logic, emotional appeal, and other forms of subtle and direct pressure to trick the witness (Sparkish) into impeaching himself: "I tell you then plainly"; "Do not you understand him yet?"; "Ridiculous!"; "Are you not afraid to loose me?" (III.ii.218, 238, 266, 301). And she knows how to threaten Sparkish with all the power a woman possesses: "Have a care, lest you make me stay too long—" (III.ii.317). Her problem until the end of the play is that this witness's demeanor, with a few exceptions, is implaccable. Truly at one point, Alithea seems, much to her chagrin, convinced that Sparkish is exactly what he claims: "I am satisfied, 'tis impossible for him to be jealous" (IV.i.53). And Sparkish's intransigence prompts even an unadorned emotional response from Alithea: "Monstrous!" (III.ii.232)—interestingly, an epithet she shares with her brother (see III.ii.323).

Moreover, part of Alithea's "immoveable" position is shaped by her own healthy ego: "'tis *Sparkish's* confidence in my truth, that obliges me to be so faithful to him" (IV.i.50–51)—quite a flimsy reason, of course, for sacrificing love. Alithea is tangled in her own promises—her pride forcing her to argue a rational though ludicrous position. Like her brother, she stands baited; but her antagonists are both without (Lucy, Harcourt, and Sparkish) and within (her pride, vanity, and fears). That she is so very wrong about Sparkish's capacity for jealousy only undermines her image as the exalted paragon but at the same time buttresses her standing as a real, complex, and therefore more attractive human being. Such assertions as "I was engag'd to marry, you see, another man, whom my justice will not suffer me to deceive, or injure" (IV.i.17–18) ring as hollow as Wycherley intended them to sound. And in this instance Lucy is correct to call it "rigid honour"—for it is rigid as in "intractable," "stiff," and "death-like" (30). That she does not play well as an "ideal" is all the more reason to argue that she is not as totally open and sincere as her words imply. Besides, who so far in Wycherleys's plays has been?

Because she knows that a woman can maintain a good measure of freedom if she weds one with an unthreatening temperament,[48] Alithea accepts that if Harcourt can prove worthy by showing that he will have no demands on her—that he is respectfully subordinate to her—she would, because she is attracted to him physically, consider marrying him. And certainly at this point, Harcourt has paid proper *court* to her vanity. Yet, she may also rationalize that if Sparkish remains immune from the "green-eyed" horror, he would make a practical, if not ideal, match—one that would not encroach on her freedom but rather encourage it. She tells Lucy, "I own [Sparkish] wants the wit [attractiveness] of *Harcourt,* which I will dispense withal, for another want he has, which is want of jealousie, which men of wit seldom want" (IV.i.43–45). And yet, despite her apparent certitude (part of her public pose), the lioness Alithea paces about waiting for Sparkish to manifest a clear sign of his jealousy so that she may then pounce and be done with him. And always there are the important qualifiers served up as delicious hints to whom she hopes is a perceptive suitor: "but *if* he [Sparkish] be true, and what I *think* him to me" (emphasis added; III.ii.499–500). She understands, as Lucy does not,[49] that her freedom would be curtailed, much as Margery's has been, if she weds one as inclined as her brother toward physical gestures of dominance: "Jealousie in a Husband," she argues in her most important speech, "Heaven defend me from it, it begets a thousand plagues to a poor Woman, the loss of her honour, her quiet, . . . nay, her life sometimes; and what's as bad almost, the loss of this Town, that is, she is sent into the Country, which is the last ill usage of a Husband to a Wife, I think" (IV.i.54–63).[50] Alithea's words are crucial; they must not be interpreted as a simple commonplace assault on making a poor marriage—for they reflect her greatest fears and are the key to understanding her seemingly strange virtue. As does "Cuckold" with her brother, "Jealousie" terrifies and intrigues Alithea; she is fascinated by the possibility that one such as Sparkish could actually be free from its influence. Finally, even Lucy begins to understand: "O do's the wind lye there?" (64).

When Sparkish promises his friendship to the smitten Harcourt, who will be "oblig'd" to his "dear Friend" if he can be "reconcil'd" to Alithea, we find of course both men lying unashamedly—each wishing to destroy the other, each tearing even further at the already ravaged conception of "brotherhood" by dragging the phrase "dear Friend" into this duplicitous exchange. Harcourt resorts several times to a juvenile form of indirection (seeming to talk disparagingly of himself but pointing at Sparkish to make Alithea comprehend his meaning—as if she needed to be so informed), embracing Sparkish Judas-like, the quintessential emblem of a male hostility (III.ii.240–63)—giving life to Corneille's observation "J'embrasse mon rival, mais c'est pour l'e'touffer." And in his striving to control both Harcourt and Alithea, Sparkish pushes them closer and closer together in this Wycherlean perversion of a ménage à trois, secure that he will always be the agent of coitus interruptus: "Come pray, Madam, be friends with him" (319–20).

Pinchwife is once more horrified: "What, invite your Wife to kiss Men? Monstrous, are you not asham'd? I will never forgive you" (323–24). He will not forgive him as a representative of his sex, we might conclude, rather than as the intended of his sister, for Sparkish's so openly pimping for his wife-to-be (as Pinchwife sees it) only raises the Country Husband's greatest fears to the point where they cannot be held silent—forcing him to extend every gesture or hint to its full and horrible potentiality. And to Pinchwife, Sparkish metaphorically places Harcourt under Alithea's sheets, revealing his "wife's" sexual charms to the frustrated and aroused rival: "[Harcourt] is an humble, menial Friend, such as reconciles the differences of the Marriage-bed; you know Man and Wife do not alwayes agree, I design him for that use, therefore wou'd have him well with my Wife" (331–34).[51] If we could have doubted Sparkish's ulterior motives, his answer to Pinchwife's contention—that he "will get a great many menial Friends, by shewing" his wife as he does now—erases any doubt: "I love to be envy'd, and wou'd not marry a Wife, that I alone cou'd love; loving alone is as dull, as eating alone; . . . and to tell you the truth, it may be I love to have Rivals in a Wife, they make her seem to a Man still, but as a kept Mistriss" (342–46). Sparkish's motives are sinister, prompted by his love of inflicting pain and need for ascendency over other males: "What, then, it may be I have a pleasure in't, as I have to shew fine Clothes, at a Play-house the first day, and count money before poor Rogues" (337–39). Here he is undoubtedly the fawning physician with that dangerous cane. But Sparkish will not win at his game, because he underestimates the power, cunning, and apprehensions of Alithea—and is so preoccupied with the image of destruction that he does not feel the noose he has slipped around his own neck. In his fantasy, the now sadistic Sparkish transforms Harcourt into something no more significant than a dildo. He places Harcourt in a Priapian state, never allowed satisaction, taking responsibility for satisfying (or perhaps not) the voraciously sexual wife (whom Sparkish could never satisfy), all to feed the pleasure of the voyeuristic, yet manipulative, husband.

And Sparkish's subsequent appearance only reinforces the danger to Alithea; he tells Pinchwife, "'tis her modesty only I believe, but let women be never so modest the first day, they'l be sure to come to themselves by night, and I shall have enough of her then" (IV.iii.356–59). Sparkish now reveals more blatantly a delusionary sense of his own masculinity (unveiled through some regressive and violent sexual activity) and therefore the kind of harsh restrictions he would hope to impose on his wife. The trusting gentleman—so "oblivious" to Harcourt's designs, so repulsed by the thought of jealousy—would pull off his mask once the laws and customs of marriage made him secure enough to introduce the true man. As for any rivals, Sparkish observes to Horner with further malicious glee, "the time will come, when a Rival will be as good sawce for a married man to a wife, as an Orange to Veale" (379–80). He moreover aims a gratuitous blow at Horner's purported condition: "what pleasure cans't thou have with women now, *Harry?*" (396–97)[52]—and one at Pinchwife's fear of cuckoldry, even in the country: "your stingy country Coxcomb keeps his wife from his friends, as he does his little Firkin of Ale, for his own drinking, and a Gentleman can't get a smack on't, but his servants, when his back is turn'd broach it as their pleasures, and dust it away, ha, ha, ha" (389–92). Commentators have spent precious little time on these remarks, but they are vital to the understanding of Sparkish's crude, menacing, and sexually maladjusted side.

Harcourt's "parson" disguise surely pushes the play into that uncomfortable depth of farce—that is, if one assumes Sparkish actually believes the chaplain is Harcourt's twin brother. But it would be in keeping with the theatrical Sparkish's love of games-playing and his perverse designs to take Harcourt, now in white heat, right to the altar, not only to watch the event that tells him Alithea will not be his but also to have an active part in his own humiliation, even if the marriage would have been a sham. And Alithea need not be seriously peeved or incredulous either. She may well be suppressing smiles or even laughter, playing along in her own way—charmed, really, by Harcourt's child-like attempt at preventing the marriage. To test again his jealousy-free protestations, Alithea confronts Sparkish directly with Harcourt's puerile plot, but of course he chooses not face the truth, advancing instead "trust and belief" to disguise his vanity and pulsing destructive tendencies. Free and capricious with her power, Alithea then turns her "anger" on Harcourt—who has in the ritual given up his identity and perhaps all past associations with mistresses who are like "books"—assuring him that this childish gimmick will not move her: "though you delay our marriage, you shall not hinder it" (IV.i.140).

And even here Wycherley reminds us that Harcourt is no "right-way" character. Lucy says that the parson "Ned" Harcourt "has the Canonical smirk, and the filthy, clammy palm of a Chaplain" (121–22)—which is part of a bawdy joke Sparkish himself had started. What may actually peak Alithea's anger is the fact that Sparkish is *not* showing any jealousy—the requirement of her breaking the match: "Invincible stupidity, I tell you he wou'd marry me, as your Rival, not as your Chaplain" (158–59). When she asks Harcourt at the end of the scene "What can you hope, or design by this?" Alithea knows what the reply will be (her question is not simply rhetorical), but she needs to hear the answer; she needs Harcourt to continue his courtship. By her insults and the "finality" of her protestations—"[L]et us make an end of this troublesome Love, I say"—she has pushed Harcourt to the brink both as a test of his commitment and as an indication of her own and often insufferable pride. And yet she will pull him back to safety with the slightest indication of hope—for example in the pronouncement "Though you delay our marriage, you shall not hinder it" (140); she not only poses the challenge, encouraging him to do exactly that, but also subtly allows Harcourt to read *our* as his and Alithea's own potential nuptials. To be *openly* flattered by Harcourt's persistence would only soften her powerful demeanor, for she knows that power rests in remaining aloof, even if one must eventually capitulate (again, one recalls Etherege's Harriet and Congreve's Millamant). But all must be on *her* terms. Harcourt can only hope to effect a "reprieve" from his doom: "at worst, if she will not take mercy on me, and let me marry her, I have at least the Lovers second pleasure, hindring my Rivals enjoyment, though but for a time" (165–68)—the antifraternal feelings remaining paramount.

One now moves from one intriguing though misjudged woman to

another: Lady Fidget, who arrives (II.i.306) with her ribald cohorts, Mistress Dainty Fidget and Mistress Squeamish.[53] Lady Fidget has come to escort Margery to the theater (in good "sisterly" fashion), to initiate her properly into the sorority of London wives. Pinchwife is understandably dismayed by the prospect and refuses to allow the persistent women to "see" the one he now calls his "Free-hold" (II.i.305)—a rather grim reminder of Margery's fate, the oxymoron suggesting well the tension between the "Free" Margery (her natural spirit) and the "held" Margery (her subjection to her husband and the marriage laws and customs that sustain him). Pinchwife's standing guard in front of the door—again literally "pinched" by adversaries—claiming that Margery has already gone has little effect, for the ladies keep demanding her presence.[54] Sensing that his wife may come to share the undaunted personalities of these irrepressible women, Pinchwife's only recourse is to retreat in the face of insurmountable odds: "Well, there is no being too hard for Women at their own weapon, lying, therefore I'll quit the Field" (333–34).

In the women's discussing the plight of wives, who are "so neglected" by husbands who take up with "little Play-house Creatures" (342–43), we note that the traditional complaint merely provides justification for female sexual freedom. Here the women exercise their power by patronizing the males, employing (appropriating) the same kind of rhetorical and metaphoric abuse males heap on the absent female: "Fye, fye upon'em," Mrs. Dainty Fidget giddily exclaims, "they are come to think cross breeding for themselves best, as well as for their Dogs, and Horses." Lady Fidget completes the figurative association: "They are Dogs, and Horses for't" (357–59), the frustration only intensified by an assumption that their social position does not seem to afford them the same advantage males have in such class-blurring relationships. And what is particularly aggravating to Lady Fidget is the male propensity to cover fear and insecurity with "reports" to "the World" that they have been successful with them: "to report a Man has had a Person, when he has not had a Person, is the greatest wrong in the whole World, that can be done to a person" (364–66). Her repetitive and choppy wording suggests a kind of verbal fidgeting and frenzied amusement the women take in such comments: "Fye, fye, fye, for shame Sister, whither shall we ramble? be continent in your discourse, or I shall hate you" (377–78). Likely punctuating her remarks with a raucous laughter, Lady Fidget's references to discourse and honor offer tribute to propriety, although the women enjoy pushing matters extremely close to the chaotic state: they must bear gifts to Apollo even though their hearts are with Dionysus. Lady Fidget explains to the others that "a woman of honour looses no honour with a private Person"—to which Mrs. Dainty Fidget adds, having picked up on the sexual entendre: "So the little Fellow is grown a private Person" (386–88).

That Sir Jaspar wishes Horner to escort the ladies to the play as a form of public humiliation encourages further our seeing Lady Fidget, especially, and the other women as younger and more sexually appealing than mere farce might want them (the attractive Elizabeth Knepp assayed Lady Fidget in the original cast). Increasingly delighted by thoughts of Horner's impotence, Jaspar portrays as overtly as indirection will allow the sexual act Horner can no longer perform: "Come, come, Man; what avoid the sweet society of Woman-kind? that sweet, soft, gentle, tame, noble Creature Woman, made for Man's Companion" (II.i.452–54). And playing the Philistine to Horner's shorn Samson, Jaspar tells his wife that she should keep him as one of her "droling pack of hombre Players" because he is an "ill Gamester"; he would make a fine addition to the "two old civil Gentlemen" with "stinking breaths" who wait on her: "a Lady shou'd have a supernumerary Gentleman-Usher, as a supernumerary Coach-horse" (470–76)—establishing Horner in a fraternity of impotence. Jaspar next paints into the nightmarish portrait other strokes of humiliation: Horner will be relegated to such effeminate tasks as drinking tea, dealing cards, reading to the women, "picking Fleas" out of their dogs, and "collecting Receipts, New Songs, Women, Pages, and Footmen for 'em" (485–89). But at the height of this reverie of emasculation, and as a likely reaction to it, Horner reasserts himself by beginning a metaphoric lovemaking to Lady Fidget:[55]

Sr. Jas. Heh, he, he, well, win or loose you shall have your liberty with her.
Lad. As he behaves himself; and for your sake I'll give him admittance and freedom.
Hor. All sorts of freedom, Madam?
Sr. Jas. Ay, ay, ay, all sorts of freedom thou cans't take, and so go to her, begin thy new employment; wheedle her, jest with her, and be better acquainted one with another.
Hor. I think I know her already, therefore may venter with her, my secret for hers.—

(507–16)

Clearly, Jaspar reflects that disturbingly voyeuristic intensity shared by Don Diego and Sparkish, as well as offers a self-destructive invitation for Horner to make him a cuckold.

Lady Fidget's reaction to Horner's admission of sexual fitness borders on a missionary's euphoria at the baptism of another heathen: "to suffer your self the greatest shame that cou'd fall upon a Man, that none might fall upon us Women by your conversation; but indeed, Sir, as perfectly, perfectly, the same Man as before your going into *France,* Sir; as perfectly, perfectly, Sir" (528–32). Her repetition of *perfectly* (perfection being to Lady Fidget sexual potencey)[56] and of *dear* in the following speech ("I have so strong a faith in your honour, dear, dear, noble Sir, that I'd forfeit mine for yours at any time, dear Sir") translates these words into sexual entendres, making evident that Horner is the object of *her* lust, not vice-versa; and the exuberance of her reaction gives cause to believe that for once in Wycherley the volatile sexual energy seems destined for uninterrupted release.[57] Horner is indeed sensitive to a woman's fear and accordingly convinces Lady Fidget that she may remain safely behind the protective screen: "the reputation of impotency is as hardly recover'd again in the World, as that of cowardise, dear Madam" (550–52)—an observation that moreover stresses the pleasure males take in the humiliation of another, a pleasure they are not about to relinquish, regardless of the truth. And there is playful though subtle eroticism in her reply: "Nay then, as one may say, you may do your worst, dear, dear, Sir" (553–54), her affectionate words directed primarily at his sexual organ—his "honour."[58] Jaspar's self-destructive prodding is by now superfluous: "get you gone to your business together; go, go, to your business, I say, pleasure, whilst I go to my pleasure, business" (567–68). Therefore, rather than being the master of all he surveys, Horner is now about to enter the service of the domineering Lady Fidget.

The contrast between the exuberant and erotically liberated Lady Fidget of the second act and the "melancholy" and sexually incapacitated Margery Pinchwife at the beginning of the third is striking indeed. The caged bird sings, but only a "sullen" song, as it naturally seeks its freedom to fly. "I confess," Margery tells Alithea, "I was quiet enough, till my Husband told me, what pure lives, the *London* Ladies live abroad, with their dancing, meetings, and junketings, and drest every day in their best gowns" (III.i.9–12). Pinchwife wrongly assumes that his wife has been awakened from a kind of idyllic slumber not so much by the town ("She has been this week in Town, and never desired, till this afternoon, to go abroad") but by the intoxicating delights Alithea has presented to her imagination. After all, it is easier to blame Alithea (or "Mistriss *Flippant,* as he calls her") for his "dreadful apprehensions" than to confront the disturbing implications of Margery's increasingly assertive "Londonness": "Come, pray Bud, let's go abroad before 'tis late; for I will go, that's flat and plain" (35, 83–84).

Interestingly, Pinchwife approaches the horrifying image with some intelligence (although indirectly in an aside to the abstract presence of Horner): "well, if thou Cuckold me, 'twill be my own fault—for Cuckolds and Bastards, are generally makers of their own fortune" (54–55)—and even more openly admits another truth: "I was my self the cause of her going [to the playhouse]" (29–30). And he comprehends, as any discerning person would, that "a Mask makes People but the more inquisitive," for they "have made more Cuckolds, than the best faces that ever were known" (89, 94–95)—an estimation corroborated by his sister: "a Beauty mask'd, like the Sun in Eclipse, gathers together more gazers, than if shin'd out" (105–6)—a bit of wisdom she learns from a *"gentle* Gallant" of hers, wisdom that helps us understand better the masking of her warmth for Harcourt. But Wycherley stresses that an understanding of a problem is no firm defense against its influence, for right in the midst of all this perceptive contemplation, Pinchwife adds, "if we shou'd meet with *Horner,* he wou'd be sure to take acquaintance with us, must wish her joy, kiss her, talk to her, leer upon her, and the Devil and all" (91–93). Completely ignoring his better sense, Pinchwife reaches for what is most handy though most ineffectual: a physical disguise by which to deny his wife's feminine allure.[59]

To the Country Husband, his fellow men are "a swarm of Cuckolds, and Cuckold-makers"—the first to be despised and ridiculed, the second to be feared and avoided. Margery adds the appropriate pinch of anguish by noting that she has not "half [her] belly full of sights yet" (the metaphor being sexual as well as gastric) and points to the "power of brave signs" she observes at the Exchange: "the Bull's-head, the Rams-head, and the Stags-head, Dear"—which Pinchwife rightly determines are the "proper" signification of "every" husband (III.ii.178–83).[60] But more than the allusions to horns and cuckoldry, the three animals (perhaps representing to Pinchwife his tormentors Horner, Harcourt, and Dorilant) are males who batter each other over territory and sexual privilege among the females.[61] And Horner's arrival heightens the sense of interruption and anxiety. He prevents Pinchwife from leaving this pack of "lewd Rakehells" by grabbing and detaining young "Master James"—turning the screws with relish: "[W]ho is this pretty young Gentleman?"; "I never saw any thing so pretty in all my life" (III.ii.380, 383). Pinchwife's civil attempts at disentanglement fail miserably: "Come away, come away"; "How she gazes on him! the Divel; "I am upon a wrack"; "O Heavens! what do I suffer" (396, 401, 418, 451). Dorliant and Harcourt naturally "gang-up" on their adversary by complementing Horner's praise of the young lad's "sister," who "wou'd make all that see her, in love with her" (405–6), and in sending kisses to Margery through her "brother"[62]—and here we see still another "male" (the metamorphosed Little Sir James) adding to Pinchwife's distress. As Horner says, "let us torment this jealous Rogue a little" (424)—the emphasis being on gratuitous affliction more than on appropriate punishment for any unwarranted jealousy. Even Horner's apparent amenity of "Well, then, if she [Margery] be gone to bed, I wish her and you a good night" (435–36) is likely a reminder of Pinchwife's failure between the sheets.

Pinchwife is tied and then baited with visions of three men making love to his wife and the irony of his being guilty of the same kind of merchandising for which he ridiculed Sparkish. His image of "ten thousand ulcers" gnawing away their "lips" is as graphic as it is hyperbolic—the gnawing suggestive of venereal disease, the malady of a promiscuous wife. Can it really be that if the husband were more rational in his actions, less jealous and possessive, Horner and the others would have left him unmolested? Would Margery have warmed to him? The play suggests nothing of the kind.

Margery Pinchwife's satisfaction with her first London sexual experience, as she returns from her tryst with Horner with her hat "full of Oranges and dried fruit," is impossible to disguise (and there was enough time, as Lucy suggests, for more than kissing and fondling: "Their business will be done presently sure, an't please your Worship, it can't be long in doing I'm sure on't" [III.ii.508–9]). A stunned Pinchwife can only stare with horror at seeing the fruit and hearing "The fine Gentleman has given me better things yet" (521).[63] Having immediately surrendered to the metaphor, Pinchwife barks at Horner, "You have only squeez'd my Orange, I suppose, and given it me again" (526–27), the indirection at least helping him cope with the reality of what has likely occurred—a reference Horner puckishly embellishes: "I have only given your little Brother an Orange, Sir" (524).[64] This is the first time in Wycherley that some mutually agreeable sexual activity has actually taken place. There has been a consummation of sorts, even though we do not witness it and must have some doubt as to its exact nature; as in the famous China scene, the sexual activity is funneled through a signifier. But are we to feel anxiety or relief at this consummation? Should we share Margery's satisfaction? Initially, and not on any "moral" grounds, we may answer no, for those trying to prevent the sexual union were the sisters and protectors, Alithea and Lucy, as well as the obsessed Pinchwife. He was foiled, but so were the more altruistic women, who were physically detained to allow for the sexual act to take place—both Harcourt and Dorilant resorting to crude measures to assert their will: "Thou shalt not stir thou robust Creature," Dorilant says to Lucy, "you see I can deal with you, therefore you shou'd stay the rather, and be kind" (503–4). Yet, there is undeniably a sense of pleasure (or relief) now that Margery's natural vivacity has had its release, and perhaps this first mutual and "normal" erotic activity in Wycherley (that is, actual as well as metaphoric) helps make the play more satisfying and exhilarating than *The Plain Dealer*, in which coitus interruptus is more pronounced.

In his interrogation of Margery, Pinchwife demands a contradiction of her stated innocence so that he may find her "false." Considering the pattern of truth avoidance, why else does Pinchwife wish to hear again, as he has already heard almost "an hundred times over," the tale of Horner's kissing his wife also "an hundred times" and putting "the tip of his tongue between [her] lips" (IV.ii.18, 36)?[65] Pinchwife therefore fears the truth but still must prove his suspicions correct, an irony similarly present in his realization that Horner "knew her certainly," while still being thankful for his wife's "simplicity" (27–28). In addition to the husband's "denial" is the wife's excitement in recalling her sexual experience—perhaps coloring it with every retelling, pausing and emphasizing specific words and phrases for carnal effect: "Why, he put ——— ... the tip of his tongue" and "he's a proper, goodly strong man, 'tis hard, let me tell you, to resist him" (34–36, 46–48). True to the self-destructive impulse, Pinchwife, while trying to suppress his wife's natural sexual inquisitiveness, has given her (by demanding the "specifics") a kind of sexual pleasure of which he is otherwise incapable. And Margery is shrewd enough to muffle at least some of the satisfaction she gets in recounting the event,[66] for to tell her husband all would be to transform the sport into something frightening, since he would then resort to a regressive and hostile display to reassert his masculinity, which, as Alithea mentioned earlier when considering jealous husbands, could cost her "her life." And Margery is moreover proficient in shifting the focus of responsibility, for when he asks, "But what you stood very still, when he kiss'd you?," she replies, "Yes I warrant you, wou'd you have had me discover'd my self?" (29–31). Finally, she is not at all averse to reminding her husband that the cuckold-maker waits anxiously below: "he said if you were not within, he wou'd come up to her, meaning me you know, Bud, still" (25–26).

A significant feature of Wycherley's comedies is the manner in which he confronts many of his characters with unrelenting emotional stress until they demonstrate peculiar, absurd, sordid, violent, or otherwise disturbing behaviors. Here Pinchwife articulates a wish to "strangle that little Monster," Love (sexual charm), who "gave women first their craft, their art of deluding" (52–56)—initially threatening the abstract, but soon enough the very object, Margery herself. In his assertion that women were originally "plain, open, silly and fit for slaves," Pinchwife makes clear how easily he can leap from an intelligent assessment into one of the atavistic sanctuaries he has created for himself. He admits, for instance, that women have "more invention in love than men" because "they have more desires, more solliciting passions, more lust, and more of the Devil" (59–61)—a remark that, considering the women in Wycherley's plays, begins as accurate ("more desires, more solliciting passions") but then bounds aggressively toward the primal and misogynistic denial of reality and human complexity.[67] The second part of the characterization also provides a judicial context in which law and custom may justify his increasingly violent responses to his wife's ripening sexuality. Uncontrollable lust and sinful behavior, after all, must be identified, combated, and punished.

We may conclude that Margery's apparent bafflement (after Pinchwife orders her to compose a letter to Horner) over why one in London must write to someone else in London is in part a ruse to keep her husband off balance—but it also reminds him of where he presently is, reinforcing feelings of entrapment in a hostile environment. In the country, which denotes distance and isolation, letter writing is more necessary to communication—whereas the city suggests density, a place where there is no retreat from the madding and cuckolding crowd. Pinchwife is indeed disoriented, fearing at one moment that Margery is purposely deceiving him and assuring himself at the next that "she is innocent enough yet" (IV.ii.85). Her ongoing commentary as she begins to construct the letter and her attempts at altering what he tells her to write diminishes Pinchwife's editorial preeminence and accordingly prompts his most violent expression to this point: "Write as I bid you, or I will write Whore with this Penknife in your Face" (92–93). His floundering manhood requires a violent impetus to put it on firmer ground, and the penknife serves well enough as a menacing phallus[68]—the promise to write on her face suggesting how the phallic symbol threatens that which is most associated with the feminine (youth, beauty, and sexual charm). And the punctuation of his demand is even more gruesome: "Once more write as I'd have you, and question it not, or I will spoil thy writing with this, I will stab out those eyes that cause my mischief" (107–9). Confronted with such violent reinforcement, Margery's survival instinct halts temporarily the manipulation of her husband's emotions: "O Lord, I will," although she cannot help reminding him that Horner will "ne'er believe" she could write "such a Letter" (110, 129–30).[69]

In essence rejecting the view that the city has corrupted her, Margery writes to Horner that she would in the country have ways enough to express herself carnally: "I'm sure if you and I were in the Countrey at cards together,—so—I cou'd not help treading on your Toe under the Table—so—or rubbing knees with you, and staring in your face, 'till you saw me" (IV.ii.158–61). Neither has Pinchwife really forced a chaste and naive Margery into a life of sexual awareness by making it all so attractive to her—in reality, he has only facilitated the prospect despite himself. And after she cleverly exchanges letters with her husband, her desperate husband (noting "I have been detained by a Sparkish Coxcomb, who pretended a visit to me; but I fear 'twas to my Wife" [172–73]), now evaluates his enemies as savage opponents who do not fight by the European rules of open confrontation: "if we do not cheat women, they'll cheat us; and fraud may be justly used with secret enemies, of which a

Wife is the most dangerous; and he that has a handsome one to keep, and a Frontier Town, must provide against treachery, rather than open Force—Now I have secur'd all within, I'll deal with the Foe without with false intelligence" (198–204).

As the scene changes to the enemy's encampment, the Quack (maintaining the emphasis on male antagonisms) asks Horner, "have you not the luck of all your brother Projectors, to deceive only your self at last" (IV.iii.1–2)—in other words, "Have you not failed?" Horner's assurance that he has duped the males and been the beneficiary of the sexual appetites of their "Wives, Sisters and Daughters" (5) is a claim, we might remember, that is unsubstantiated by any clear evidence. Are we wise to believe categorically the assertions of one who takes pride in deceiving others?[70] Regardless, the women he describes here are bawdy, dauntless, and intimidating in their relationships with males—in short, London women, the kind Margery would like to be, the kind Pinchwife fears the most. Horner's "success" is partly, if not mainly, due to his role as eunuch, which not only permits him safe passage but places him in the inferior position the women expect of their lovers.[71] Horner's attack on female hypocrisy may serve to reinforce perceptions of his own masculinity and to reorder the hierarchy of the sexual world, placing himself, in all his "wisdom" and moral censure, above the women who have and will use him physically. And yet for all of his satiric posturing, he has absolutely no chance to dominate the famous scene about to unfold.

Regarding Lady Fidget's concern for her reputation as well as for her intimacy with Horner ("But first, my dear Sir, you must promise to have a care of my dear Honour" [IV.iii.38–39]), as Hobbes assumed, to have reputation and honor (the semblance usually being enough) is also to have power, but in this case the restraints and cautions are self-imposed, *not* externally forced by a husband, brother, or father—an important distinction.[72] Lady Fidget knows as does Horner that such words have a useful, if not required, duality satisfying both the need for propriety and the desire for sexual expression. And Lady Fidget's employment of "Honour" (one notes the polysemic kinship to "Horner," which permits an even easier transference of the concept to sexual activity)[73] allows for the security of indirection. She faces her lover looking slightly off center, using the term as a flimsy garment that both reveals and teases in its "concealment."[74] She is therefore unaffected by Horner's criticism of her concern for "Honour"—his assertiveness in such claims as "I am a *Machiavel* in love Madam"[75] moreover failing to impress. (And Horner's assault on hypocrisy and assertion of virility are more for the Quack's benefit, now listening behind the screen, than Lady Fidget's.) Lady Fidget's desire that Horner never share his "secret" (sexual potence) with those "censorious" acquaintances of hers implies more a delightful sexual avarice than passionate concern for reputation: "A secret is better kept, I hope, by a single person, than a multitude" (68–69). And her use of entendre is both incessant and pleasing: "Ay, but if you shou'd ever let the other women know that *dear secret,* it wou'd *come out*" (emphasis added; 55–56). Once having satisfied the demands of propriety, Lady Fidget is now free to embrace Horner openly, informing him that she will not be a passive partner in their relationship. That the sexual contacts in the play are helped along by either the male or female denying or disguising their true essence (Horner as the eunuch, Margery as Sir James, Lady Fidget as a woman of honor) only underscores Wycherley's belief that men and women must in some way conceal, distort, and decorate their erotic side as a way to control and elevate it from the Dionysian impulse it is and must always be.

Sir Jaspar's intrusion on the lovers is a kind of coitus interruptus—initially disturbing Lady Fidget (discovery diminishing power)—but she is quick to explain that she is only tickling Horner, offering something apparently diversionary but reflective nonetheless: "I love to torment the confounded Toad," she tells her husband (76–77). (And Horner is "tormented" by being temporarily denied sexual gratification.)[76] Though powerful and aggressive, Lady Fidget (like Hippolita) cannot escape her own considerable frustration—or her reliance on entendre—over Horner's so far having "done nothing," adding "Hah, hah, hah, Faith, I can't but laugh however; why d'ye think the unmannerly toad wou'd not come down to me to the Coach, I was fain to come up to fetch him, or go without him, which I was resolved not to do; for he knows China very well, and has himself very good, but will not let me see it, lest I should beg some; but I will find it out, and have what I came for yet" (IV.iii.97–104).[77] As she goes into the next room to await her "Machiavel," Lady Fidget informs us that for a woman of power and intelligence, the locked door can occasionally liberate as well as incarcerate. Lady Fidget leads; Horner follows—the desire to satisfy her sexual desires being far more pronounced here than his. And, annoyed by Sir Jaspar's ridicule, Horner warns him—"though I cannot furnish you [a pair of horns] my self, you are sure, yet I'll find a way" (110–11)—wishing without blowing his cover to assert his manhood and more directly take part in the ritual of destruction. He cannot help predicting Sir Jaspar's fate even though he should avoid such hints that encourage more vigilance from the husband. Finally, even though Horner is smart enough to "take" the "Cue" ("China" as an out); it is Sir Jaspar who provides it: "I thought you had been at the China House?" (79–80).

Horner's linking of women to the animal world ("Oh women, more impertinent, more cunning, and more mischievous than their Monkeys" [117–18]) depicts a shameless creature so graphically associated with licentiousness that we easily sense our arrival at the peak of sexual activity in Wycherley's four plays:

> *Hor.* Stay here a little, I'll ferret her out to you presently, I warrant.
> *Sir Jas.* Wife, my Lady *Fidget,* Wife, he is coming into you the back way.
> *La. Fid.* Let him come, and welcome, which way he will.
> *Sir Jas.* He'll catch you, and use you roughly, and be too strong for you.
> *La. Fid.* Don't you trouble your self, let him if he can.
> (IV.iii.122–30)

Even in his use of lesser animals—the mouse earlier (my interpretation of "mousled") and "ferret" here (one that chases mice and rats)—the playwright encourages our visualizing objects going in and out of orifices. Whether we like it or not, Wycherley places both the audience and reader in a position of the classic voyeur, witnessing the sexual act performed—here through the completely transparent curtain of metaphor. We also detect the female as enthusiastic and undaunted about sex (of any kind), if not more so, than the male. Whereas Horner seems sexually potent in the references to the "back way" and "ferret," we know that it is Lady Fidget who is "throwing [his] things about, and rifling all" he has—encroaching on his privacy and upsetting his valued possessions (the verb *rifling* even suggesting her usurpation of the male's prerogative). We now laugh at the irony in Jaspar's "warning" to his wife that Horner would be "too strong" for her. Horner may go smugly into the room a powerful rake hero, but he returns literally debilitated.

Upon her unexpected arrival, Mrs. Squeamish (very plausibly another fairly attractive as well as sexually stimulated woman[78]) reveals her particular brand of Dionysian agitation by wishing to break down the door ("liberated" London ladies seemingly having little trouble with such barriers) and vowing to "disturb 'em" when she realizes that Horner is giving sexual favors to Lady Fidget—intimating, as Lady Fidget did earlier, that women can be possessive and less sisterly when sexual gratification is concerned. For the moment foiled, Mrs. Squeamish is left to indulge in vicarious sexual release by "staring at the prettyest Pictures," which we can trust are erotic in nature, perhaps something on the lines of Lyly's "Windsor Beauties" or some more blatantly pornographic sketches.[79]

Lady Fidget emerges in postcoital splendor, with the emblem of her sexual activity and triumph—the piece of china (a cylindrical vase, no doubt) in her hand: "I have been toyling and moyling, for the pretti'st piece of China, my Dear." Horner immediately swears to her sexual prowess and concedes his more secondary role: "Nay she has been too hard for me do what I cou'd" (IV.iii.178–79). And Mrs. Squeamish has little difficulty interpreting their allusions, which animates her to the point of *demanding* sex from the now temporarily impotent Horner:

> *Squeam.* Oh Lord I'le have some China too, good Mr. *Horner,* don't think to give other people China, and me none, come in with me too.
> *Hor.* Upon my honour I have none left now.
> *Squeam.* Nay, nay I have known you deny your China before now, but you shan't put me off so, come—
> *Hor.* This Lady had the last there.
> *La. Fid.* Yes indeed Madam, to my certain knowledge he has no more left.
> *Squeam.* O but it may be he may have some you could not find.
> *La. Fid.* What d'y think if he had had any left, I would not have had it too, for we women of quality never think we have China enough.
> (180–92)[80]

All of this memorable banter stresses the near volcanic need for the women to express their unbridled passions and the indispensability of indirection—whether in entendre, euphemism, allusion, metaphor, simile, or any other signifier.[81] In short, the famous China Scene presents Lady Fidget as triumphant—not Horner, who cannot enjoy his experience for long without being set upon by another insatiable woman demanding his services.[82] For the moment reality has become the slave to artifice: he is as helpless now as his disguise assumes, placed inside the carocele as the women in the scene—even Old Lady Squeamish—surround him, firing off expressions of derision and taunting the unarmed and weakened man to engage them in erotic battle.

Horner attempts to mollify the restless Mrs. Squeamish with the assurance that he will have a "Rol-waggon" for her "another time" (194)[83]—his having no choice but to promise future attentions, given his sexual debility now that Mrs. Fidget has left him so well spent. As Old Lady Squeamish observes, "Poor Mr. *Horner,* he has enough to doe to please you all, I see." And whereas Horner's reply, "Ay Madam, you see how they use me" is particularly amusing in its irony and likely mode of delivery, it nonetheless testifies forcefully to the fact that indeed he *is* being used—and to the fact that the women are as merciless as they are powerful: "I could never find pitty," he says to Old Lady Squeamish (she with memory but no participation), "but from such reverend Ladies as you are, the young ones will never spare a man" (203–5). Horner also tells the triumphant Lady Fidget that Mrs. Squeamish "has an innocent, literal understanding" (197–98)—something he does not believe nor should we, its being merely a futile attempt to ward off the anger of his possessive lover. (And even though the sisterhood is seemingly fractured when another man is involved, there is absolutely no gesture of any significance against the other woman—no attempt to destroy her; rather the *male* is the object of the woman's bitchiness.)

As if to punctuate her all-consuming nature, the younger Squeamish pulls Horner by the crevat—"Come come, Beast, [a woman again appropriating the male's favorite derogatory metaphor] and go dine with us, for we shall want a man at Hombre after dinner"; "Come Sloven, I'le lead you to be sure of you" (206–10)[84]—(all reminiscent of Flirt's treatment of Monsieur) and Horner, in answer to the old woman's suggestion that he kiss her granddaughter, again concedes that the aroused woman is a force beyond his control: "No Madam, that Remedy is worse than the Torment, they know I dare suffer any thing rather than do it" (213–14), meaning of course that a sweet kiss would not be enough; it would either lead to more affectionate behavior or cause the woman to laugh at the feeble effort. The image is marvelous: Lady Fidget standing to the side in wicked triumph with her "roll-wagon," Sir Jaspar laughing heartily at Horner, Mrs. Squeamish pulling at the debilitated lover, and Old Lady Squeamish, like Don Diego, in an agitated state, insisting "Alas poor man, how she tuggs him, kiss, kiss her. . . . [P]rythee do" (211–16). Undoubtedly, the china scene *appears* to be Horner's greatest triumph—after all, he has had his cake and beaten Jaspar too, by making him (again?) a cuckold—admirable behavior in a world of libertines, hypocrisy, and aggression. But it is really the women's scene. Even considering his "manly" performance, Horner has been more used by than exploitive of the women. Only the Quack suggests that Horner's actions have been majestic: "I will now believe any thing he tells me" (225). But he is a Quack, one who purports to be what he is not, one who convinces others to believe in half-truths, falsehoods, and exaggerations.

With trepidation, Lady Fidget announces Pinchwife's arrival: "O Lord here's a man, Sir *Jaspar,* my Mask, my Mask, I would not be seen here for the world" (226–27), a remark that lures us into focusing on the commonplace matter of masking and hypocrisy. But the most significant words may be "O Lord here's a man," for only Pinchwife truly represents to women what they dread most—an intimidating and perceptive man, using law, custom, and primitive expression to keep their freedoms and spirits suppressed. He has come to confront Horner, as the only male who could match Horner in battle—a man Pinchwife truly knows "so well"—ridiculing Horner's attempt at rhetorical brotherhood, "But why not, dear *Jack*" (241–43). Horner is unable to manipulate Pinchwife with refurbished language, attempts at flattery, protestations of loyalty or impotence, or any other form of deception. It is only Pinchwife's consuming fear and Margery's undaunted sexual desire that work successfully for Horner.

Pinchwife's delivering the wrong letter (another suggestion of the self-destructive impulse and of Horner's luck rather than skill) indicates that the rake hero can indeed be knocked off balance: "Ha, is this a trick of his or hers?" (269). But not content with what he believes is a missive terminating the relationship, for he knows too well that men like Horner are not easily discouraged, Pinchwife physically threatens his adversary, as he did Margery: "there will be danger in making me a Cuckold"; "I weare a Sword" (IV.iii.299–302). And he is not above admitting to his self-destructive tendencies, for when Horner informs him that his "freedome with [Margery] was your fault, not mine," Pinchwife is compelled to admit to himself, "Faith so 'twas" (314–15). Hardly a mere embodiment of gullibility and peevishness, Pinchwife is the only male character who does not disguise his true feelings to the other males; there is no pretence of virtue, friendship, innocence, or impotence with him.[85] Horner's reply "Thou art mad with jealousie" seems to place him in the role of satirical agent leveling justifiable criticism. Still, even this censure is undercut by the fact that Horner is lying boldly about not having seen, courted, and kissed Margery—and by the fact that Pinchwife has more than good cause to be distrustful of Horner and his wife (296–98). Accordingly, Horner's more adamant assessment, "thou art mad, Man" (304), is only partially correct, for whereas Pinchwife has the *madness* of obsession, he is often keenly perceptive about the motivations of those with whom he interacts (Margery, Horner, and Alithea).

Horner's sudden victory in his memorable reply to Pinchwife's "there will be danger in making me a Cuckold": "Why, wert thou not well cur'd of thy last clap?" (299–301)—is very short-lived as Pinchwife reminds him ("I weare a Sword") that such wit will be of little use should the Country Husband be provoked to violence. Pinchwife's threats against his wife in severe terms ("write whore" with a knife in her face) or ludicrous ones ("pinch me, or kill my Squirrel"—278–79) might be categorized as cowardly if he threatened *only* his wife, but his facility with hostile expression extends to anyone—including the "hero" of the play—making clear that he *is* dangerous. And Pinchwife does not sustain the same kinds of losses both Sir Jaspar and Sparkish receive, for Margery's earlier sexual activity was not entirely the result of his *willingly* pushing her toward Horner (as did the other two men); rather she was "forcibly" taken off stage. To the Quack, Horner professes delight at Margery's letter, but again we see the parasitic character benefitting from the "ingenuity" of Pinchwife's obsession. And even here his revery about the letter is *interrupted* by the return of Pinchwife—this time with Sparkish, another ridiculer of Horner's manhood. Horner must by now wince at the irony of his earlier comment, "I shall be rid of all my old Acquaintances" (I.i.139–40).

We next see the Country Wife in lamentation: "I am sick of my Husband, and for my Gallant" (IV.iv.2).[86] Horner is to her the embodiment of freedom and open sexual expression, and accordingly, when she thinks of him her "hot fit comes" and she is "all in a Feaver" (6).[87] Visions of Pinchwife, however, cause her to "tremble" and break out "in a cold sweat," and "have inclinations to vomit" (4–5)—not so much because of his looks or bland sexuality but because he is the cause of her incarceration and fears. As if on cue, Pinchwife creeps up behind, interrupting his wife's communciation to Horner and preventing her escape: "O Lord Budd, why d'ye fright me so?" (14–17). His reading the letter precludes at least for the moment her required concealment and indirect expression. Now Pinchwife has knowledge of her true thoughts and proof of her "lost" innocence as he reads "if you [love me], you will never suffer me to lye in the arms of another man, whom I loath, nauseate, and detest" (22–24), words—in addition to "sickness," "feaver," "disease," "vomit," "break out," and "tremble"—emphasizing the infirm personal world of the Pinchwifes. One cannot help sensing the desperation in a woman convinced that she is likely doomed to a life of spiritual and sexual barrenness even amid the fruitful arbors, fertile fields, and flowing streams of the country.

Again Pinchwife calls on a primitive response as the only way to control his greatest fear. First he damns the entire sex, equating them with "sensless, indocile animals" and then drawing, not a penknife but something even more potent (as weapon and phallic symbol), a sword, to "make an end" of his wife and "all my plagues together" (37–40)—dangerously shifting his rage from the general (all women) to the particular (Margery). But Sparkish arrives to prevent this violent form of intercourse, a most felicitous manifestation of coitus interruptus, suggestive again of the males' unmitigated ability to frustrate the designs of other men: "What drawn upon your Wife? you shou'd never do that but at night in the dark when you can't hurt her" (44–45), a gleeful allusion to Pinchwife's insufficient phallic sword wielded in the marriage bed.

Pinchwife's retaliatory strike (through a gratuitous outburst against Alithea)—"[She is making] you a Cuckold, 'tis that they all doe, as soon as they can" (50–51)—with its shift back from specific to general misogyny, informs Margery that she is now out of immediate danger: "I am contented my rage shou'd take breath" (64). But Sparkish quickly ends this respite by exploiting Pinchwife's destructive and diseased preoccupations: "we men of wit have amongst us a saying, that Cuckolding like the small Pox comes with a fear, and you may keep your Wife as much as you will out of danger of infection, but if her constitution incline her to't, she'l have it sooner or later by the world" (68–72). And Pinchwife is quick to acknowledge the sagacity of such observations: "What a thing is a Cuckold, that every fool can make him ridiculous" (73–74). His fears now prominent, Pinchwife keeps his hand firmly on the one remaining symbol of his masculinity—telling his wife to continue her latest correspondence to Horner, adding, "if you are false in a tittle, I shall soon perceive it, and punish you with this [the sword] as you deserve" (V.i.3–5). The notion of "punishment" leads Pinchwife (as Othello before him) more deeply into the realm of judicial process—from prosecutor to judge, then to jury, and now edging dangerously close to executioner, as he seeks the final corroborating evidence to justify not only his present treatment of his wife but her ultimate fate. But this time the moment's tragic possibilities are suddenly halted, not by male interruption, but by Margery's signing the letter, "Your slighted *Alithea*" (12). Other than suggesting the Country Wife's awareness (shaped by both instinct and recent experience) that language lies ready to be manipulated and twisted to suit one's needs,[88] Margery's forgery reinforces the power of the sorority to provide aid and protection. That is, although she is not present, "Alithea" does effect Margery's narrow escape. As Pinchwife responds, now that the horrid spectre of cuckoldry has magically vanished, "I am stunn'd, my head turns round" (18).

Unlike other gulls, however, Pinchwife's active intelligence has no room for complacency, and he immediately questions how Alithea could have dictated the letter since Margery was "lock'd" up alone. Desperately needing to deny a pair of horns, Pinchwife comes to rationalize his wife's explanation ("O through the key hole Budd"), but only with considerable skepticism as he measures probablities against possibilities: "This changeling[89] cou'd not invent this lye, but if she cou'd, why shou'd she?" (37–38). And his subsequent resolution, "I'd rather give him my Sister than lend him my Wife, and such an alliance will prevent his pretensions to my Wife sure,—I'le make him of kinn to her, and then he won't care for her" (61–64), testifies to how his fears have pushed this normally perceptive man into bizarre scenarios and ridiculous devices in order to prevent his cuckolding—which, again, may well be a *fait accompli* (the "Orange and dried fruit" scene). Still, Pinchwife feels for the moment calmed—"I'd rather *give* him my Sister"—by the power to dispense a woman as property (V.i.61–62). This vision of his rival married to Alithea and thereby no longer interested in Margery because she would be related is of course utter nonsense and contradicts what Pinchwife has concluded about Horner—a man who would not hesitate, regardless of circumstance, to torment him further. Regardless, Pinchwife's preoccupation with intercourse is striking: "I'd rather fight with Horner for not lying with my Sister, than for lying with my Wife. . . . for we have as much a doe to get people to lye with our Sisters, as to keep 'em from lying with our Wives" (95–103). So shackled is Pinchwife by these elaborate machinations that he is actually *praising* Horner as a man wealthy enough and more sexually attractive than Sparkish—becoming, despite himself, Horner's advocate.

All of this tortured maneuvering sets Pinchwife up for a variation of the bed-trick, in which the increasingly resourceful Margery (likely with some assistance from Lucy) blows out the candle, dresses in Alithea's clothing, and shifts position so that Pinchwife believes he is leading his sister to Horner's lodging. Though undeniably the stuff of farce, Pinchwife's action is still consistent for one who could dress his pretty young wife as a young "Sir James" to throw hot-blooded males off the scent. Here he is so *wanting* his sister to become the agent by which he may escape his fate that he willingly staggers about in the dark, in a gesture of self-destruction—actually leading his wife by the hand to her lover. His speech ebbs and flows from reason back into chaos: he paints a most felicitous image—"Wife and Sister are names which make us expect Love and duty, pleasure and comfort" (V.i.99)—but then defaces the portrait with both threats of violence and betrayal of his own sister to a man he thoroughly despises, a man, given his general distrust of other males, is properly on guard: "let's see her face presently, make her show man, art thou sure I don't know her?" (V.ii.51–52).

"What means the Fool?" Horner wonders, as he is forced to take a bite of his own deceit, evincing the discomfort of one who must now distrust, rather than orchestrate, all language and gesture (68–70). Horner is denied the luxury of uncomplicated sexual conquest; the confusion, distress, and anxiety he has sent flowing toward others has now, in its ebb, returned to him.[90] And when Sir Jaspar arrives and informs Horner that his "Lady and the whole knot of the virtuous gang, as they call themselves, are resolv'd upon a frolick of coming to you to night in Masquerade" (89–91),[91] Horner feels beseiged by those he had earlier abused (the males) or *hoped* to use (the females). The women arrive more unified (as a "virtuous gang") than do the males (Jaspar and Pinchwife "solus"). They come demanding what Horner cannot at present provide—Pinchwife, Jaspar, and the women circling about him in a kind of ritualistic promenade suggestive more of slaughter than of pleasure. In the meantime, as Horner tells the Quack, he is going "to a private feast"—Margery, who waits for him in the next room—again implying that he has simply been the beneficiary of Pinchwife's psychological problems and Margery's sexual hunger.

The play's penultimate scene (in the Piazza of Covent Garden) hardly qualifies as an instance of masculine altruism (in Pinchwife's informing Sparkish of "Alithea's" interest in Horner), for his motive is to remove Sparkish from the picture entirely—one component in the Country Husband's tortured scheme to avoid his greatest fear. Pinchwife also gains the satisfaction of having his earlier warnings to Sparkish come true: "You were for giving and taking liberty, she has taken it only Sir" (V.iii.4–5)—his parting words almost laughable considering Wycherley's negative emphasis on sight throughout his plays: "goe and believe your eyes" (18), for no character in Wycherley ever gains by such advice. Sparkish's reaction, now that *his* greatest fear—humiliation in front of other men—has begun to be realized, is not to seek the truth but to resort to a more vehement expression himself: "Nay I'le to her, and call her as many Crocodiles, Syrens, Harpies, and other heathenish names" (19–20), demonstrating a "normal" reaction to what he has heard. Indeed, we find him decked here in the traditional fool's rainment, his cursing simply rhetorical and harmless—Wycherley's way, perhaps, of showing the rapid deterioration of Sparkish's significance in the play: "unworthy false woman, false as a friend that lends a man money to lose, false as dice, who undoe those that trust all they have to 'em" (34–37). And rather than explaining herself and seeking the motivation for Sparkish's outburst (a forged signature and other epistolary highjinx), Alithea is more than satisfied to allow his childish ranting to collapse the foundation of the "contract": "So I find my Brother would break off the match, and I can consent to't, since I see this Gentleman can be made jealous" (55–56).

We know that her decision is more than mere caprice or a convenient *deus ex machina*—it evolves after all from Alithea's greatest fear and is therefore a culmination of a psychological process, not a revelation or awkward change of heart that serves to extricate the playwright from an intolerable denoument. But for those seeing her as a paragon, it is difficult indeed to justify her rather tepid reasoning: "How was I deceiv'd in a man!" (71)—this rhetorical flourish coming very close to self-parody of her rigid and honorable posturing. Yet even in the throes of comprehension, she fears what might have been: "O *Lucy,* by his rude usage and jealousie, he makes me almost afraid I am married to him, art thou sure 'twas *Harcourt* himself and no Parson that married us" (57–59). And consideration of a near-fatal mistake prompts her warning to the "over-wise woman of the Town, who like me would marry a fool, for fortune, liberty, or title, . . . then if for liberty, that he may send her into the Country under the conduct of some houswifely mother-in-law" (77–82).[92] Her vision of a disastrous marriage is complete with the horror of incarceration in the country under the watchful eye of some powerful and oppressive force, one like her brother. And still she resists accepting the truth of her feelings, protecting herself and her pride with such a transparent remark as "But marry Mr. *Horner,* my brother does not intend it sure; if I thought he did, I would take thy advice, and Mr.

Harcourt for my Husband" (75–77). Surely, Lucy could not be fooled by such a flimsy piece of indirection.

Sparkish's parting words remind us of the indifferent persona he forwarded earlier in the play: "I'le come to your wedding, and resign you with as much joy as I would a stale wench to a new Cully, nay with as much joy as I would after the first night, if I had been married to you" (66–68). But this valediction should not be equated with the magnanimous gesture of many a disappointed fop, such as Congreve's Sir Wilfull Witwould and Cibber's Lord Foppington.[93] First, such a bold admission, if it were honest, would be rare in Wycherley; second, his feelings for Alithea have been clearly subordinated to concerns for his own masculinity and wish to use her to torment other males. In essence, then, this flippant response is a cover for his deep humiliation at exposing himself and thus being known more accurately by others and accordingly rendered powerless. Rather than violence to repair the ripped ego, Sparkish employs a form of "benign" passivity, one that allows him to appear unfazed by Alithea's apparent change of heart. Yet, he does strike Alithea in a vulnerable spot by claiming that he "never had any passion" for her, "till now" (63–64)—for the insult goes to the heart of Alithea's vanity and of course reminds her of what she *needs* in her life—not mere "honor"—but passionate attention from a man *without* debilitating jealousy.

The play's final scene depicts Horner once more anxious over the approach of the formidable group of women headed by Lady Fidget: "A Pox they are come too soon—before I have sent back my new—Mistress, all I have now to do, is to lock her in, that they may not see her—" (V.iv.1–3), the nervousness evident by the flustered hitches in his speech. The desire to isolate Margery from the influence of the others clearly links him to Pinchwife—his words in fact echoing those of his adversary in earlier scenes. Wycherley seems to be hinting that Margery is indeed fated to live her life under lock and key. Because of her natural temperament, her growing proficiency in games of manipulation, and her continuing reliance on primitive expressions (in the female: sexual, not violent) without adequately obscuring them with cloaks of propriety, reputation, and honor, she represents now even to Horner a force that may never cultivate self-control, a young woman disturbing to the conception of order. In any event, the sorority remains strong in that the women do not interrupt Horner's apparent lovemaking to Margery; almost knowingly, they wait until Horner is in that "I have no more left" state—a better environment, of course, in which to frustrate and exercise power over him.

Lady Fidget, Mrs. Dainty Fidget, and Mrs. Squeamish let Horner know that they are more than willing to engage in sexual gamesplaying, especially since their "guardians," Old Lady Squeamish and Sir Jaspar are in argument over backgammon[94]—although Old Lady Squeamish serves her fellow women (consciously or no) by keeping the male at bay (even if Mrs. Squeamish damns "an Old Grandmother" for interfering with a young woman's sexual expression). "Therefore," says Mrs. Squeamish, "let us make use of our time, lest they should chance to interrupt us" (10–11). Unlike Gerrard's in the *Gentleman Dancing-Master*, her employment of the *carpe diem* convention is erotically, not monetarily, oriented. And as a prelude to more amorous activity, Lady Fidget sings a wife's and mistress's anthem, a song of female comaraderie: "Why should our damn'd Tyrants oblige us to live / On the pittance of Pleasure which they only give"—a ditty filled with irony ("damn'd Tyrants"), the obligatory gesture toward propriety ("We must not rejoyce, / With Wine and with noise"), the thinly veiled allusion to enjoyment however gotten ("On the pittance of Pleasure which they only give"; "In vaine we must wake in a dull bed alone"), and male weaknesses and female strength ("Whilst to our warm Rival the Bottle, they're gone"; "'Tis Wine only gives 'em their Courage and Wit"—"Then Sisters lay't on" [27–42]). Metaphor again provides the necessary filter, as we see the bottle in its phallic properties—the glass, with its concave shape also suggesting the female: "Lovely Brimmer," says Mrs. Squeamish, "let me enjoy him first," to which Lady Fidget adds, "No, I never part with a Gallant, till I've try'd him" (46–47).

This teeming Bacchanalian moment (a tableau worthy of Hogarth) releases several of the women's frustrations: "damn a Husband"; "an old keeper"; "And [the younger gallants] rather run the hazard of the vile distemper amongst [common women], than of a denial amongst us" (52–64)[95]—complaints that are *worthy* of the reader's sympathies. Their converting the drink into a "representative of a Husband"—the thing to which men run to enhance self-worth—and then their imbibing the wine suggests as well their all-consuming power.[96] As their aggravation and militancy build—"drink Eunuch"; "Drink thou representative of a Husband" (51–52)—the women further disdain the male's choosing women based on class or "moral" distinctions:

Dayn.   The filthy Toads chuse Mistresses now, as they do Stuffs, for having been fancy'd and worn by others.
Squeam.   For being common and cheap.
La. Fid.   Whilst women of quality, like the richest Stuffs, lye untumbled, and unask'd for. . . . pray tell me beast, when you were a man, why you rather chose to club with a multitude in a common house, for an entertainment, than to be the only guest at a good Table."

(65–69, 77–79)

Horner assumes a secondary place in this energetic scene, coming very close to actually functioning as a eunuch—and even his attempts at spirited insult are overwhelmed by Lady Fidget's exuberance and audacity—which is not averse to the occasional violent image:

Hor.	[P]eople always eat with the best stomach at an ordinary, when every man is snatching for the best bit.
Lady Fid.	Though he get a cut over the fingers. . . . [W]e take freedom from a young person as a sign of good breeding, and a person may be as free as he pleases with us, as frolick, as gamesome, as wild as he will.
Hor.	Han't I heard you all declaim against wild men.
La. Fid.	Yes, but for all that, we think wildness in a man, as desireable a quality, as in a Duck, or Rabbet; a tame man, foh.
Hor.	I know not, but your Reputations frightned me, as much as your Faces invited me.

(81–83, 90–97)

Lady Fidget's casual dismissal of Horner's censure indicates that although much of their complaining reflects genuine concerns and frustrations, still some of it, especially the inflated manner in which it is voiced, is part of the ritual they all take part in, like a daily primping of their curls, in which proper deference is paid to propriety and "honour." And when Horner brings up the matter of "Reputation," Lady Fidget refuses to back away or permit him the pleasure of ascendency: "Our Reputation, Lord! Why should you not think, that we women make use of our Reputation, as you men of yours, only to deceive the world with less suspicion; our virtue is like the State-man's Religion, the Quakers Word, the Gamesters Oath, and the Great Man's Honour, but to cheat those that trust us" (98–103).

Horner sharply feels the vivacious antagonism of the moment—drink and food both serving as sexual metaphors for the women—as they surround Horner (as he, Dorilant, and Harcourt had earlier circled Pinchwife). They tell Horner they do only what men do: "Why should you not think, that we women make use of our Reputation, as you men of yours. . . . Our bashfulness is only the reflection of the Men's" (98–99, 111). Lady Fidget and Mrs. Squeamish thereby neutralize Horner's perceived role as satiric agent, for his blithe assumption that women such as these are the worst hypocrites, mere representations of their sex, has been thrown back in his face and in those of his sex. Horner tries to hold his own with witty retorts, but the women's logic invariably subverts his wit—resulting in Horner's barely being able to keep his nose above the raging rhetorical flood. Lady Fidget cleverly cites examples of male "hypocrisy" that have inflicted far more damage on the nation, fashionable society, and the individual than has any sexually aroused female's protestations to "honour." Horner is denied the satisfaction he believed his condemnation would provide; he finds himself successfully countered at every move. And his major opponent here is a woman that has demanded and received his sexual favors, adding a special flavor to their debate. Lady Fidget puts a stamp on his less-than-heroic status with "Money, foh—you talk like a little fellow now, do such as we expect money?"—thus calling his bluff at not coming to them before. Horner's replies are now even more hesitant: "I was afraid of losing my little money"; "I beg your pardon, Madam, I must confess"; "With your pardon, Ladies, I know, like great men in Offices, you seem to exact flattery and attendance only from your Followers, but you have receivers about you, and such fees to pay, a man is afraid to pass your Grants; besides we must let you win at Cards, or we lose your hearts" (125–39).

This animated exchange is halted by the women's realization that each was not exclusively privy to Horner's "loyalty" and sexual favors. Instead of attacking each other, however, they instinctively band together and turn on the male. As Lady Fidget says, "Well then, there's no remedy, Sister Sharers, let us not fall out, but have a care of our Honour" (162–63). The term "Sister Sharers" informs Horner that he cannot divide and conquer these women as he can the men, nor can he ever assume an ascendency in a relationship with any one of them. Lady Fidget asserts that for women the sisterhood is too important to allow sexual possessiveness to affect it, and she hopes that "Harry Common" (a marvelous term of derision) will "be true to three" (170)—which we may take to mean that he will be expected to satisfy all three in bed.[97] Finally, Lady Fidget's restating her regard for "Honour, the Jewel of most value and use" informs us that this delightful soiree of sexual allusion and female assertiveness ends with the knot of propriety still firmly in place.[98]

Although he has hardly orchestrated events, Horner—as a concession to his ego—believes that he has and therefore attempts to bring all to a satisfactory conclusion. His pulling Margery out of hiding and begging her to leave so that he (as much as she) might escape the wrath of her husband meets with considerable resistence: "he'll now discover all, yet pray my Dearest be perswaded to go home, and leave the rest to my management" (194–96). His pleadings suggest a chaotic unraveling, not a "management," of events, and her reply that she has no plans to leave at all underscores his predicament—not exactly the fate his elaborate scheme promised. His informing her that he will let her down the "back way" (196) also reflects Horner's inability even to control sexual entendre. Here that memorable phrase from the China Scene is now devoid of its figurative appeal—"back way" at present only describing Margery's best method of escape and Horner's best chance to avoid detection and a deadly confrontation with Pinchwife. Margery's reactions to these entreaties are horrifying to Horner: "What care I, d'ye think to frighten me with that? I don't intend to go to him again; you shall be my Husband now"; "every day at *London* here, women leave their first Husbands, and, go, and live with other men as their Wives" (204–10).

Although these rebuttals imply a delightfully innocent country girl who, infatuated with a virile libertine, dreams the fairytale ending of dissolving her marriage with the snap of her finger, such a girl is not Wycherley's Margery. Her actions are more pathetic than childlike; she is aware that in London, ladies have "left" their husbands, but she misconstrues the limits of London freedom and ignores the demands of propriety and its siblings morality and legality. Such a natural expression as she wishes here just cannot be tolerated, and it points to her unfitness for a London life. As a result, this magnificent creature's lot is a sad return to her cage. As for Horner, with both words and wit having failed him, he cannot even communicate with, let alone control, a mere country wife. His assertion to the audience is accordingly as empty as it is superfluous: "Well, a silly Mistriss, is like a weak place, soon got, soon lost, a man has scarce time for plunder; she betrays her Husband, first to her Gallant, and then her Gallant, to her Husband" (214–16).

Pinchwife's arriving with the others and asking Horner if he had indeed brought Alithea to him earlier prompts the rake's desperate attempt, after stalling with asides, to save himself and whatever is left of his crumbling empire: "Then truly, you did bring that Lady to me just now" (235). Critics have defended Horner's lie, explaining that, although he betrays Alithea, he does so to save his mistress. Or, that even though he betrays Alithea he clearly respects and appreciates virtuous women such as she.[99] It appears more evident, however, that his fear of Pinchwife prompts this response—one based primarily on self-preservation. In a moment of anxiety, Horner understandably seeks breathing room in order to contemplate his next move. As for his respecting Alithea—after all, say some, he does not try to seduce her—his impression of and distance from her is more likely predicated on the simple truth that she is just too smart and formidable to be so debauched.[100] And while the men fume and hesitate, the forgotten Lucy comments, "Now cou'd I speak, if I durst, and 'solve the Riddle, who am the Author of it" (244–45)—reminding us that women have power to both agitate *and* resolve.

As the play speeds to its end, Alithea is furious, Pinchwife impatient to marry her to Horner, and Horner still unable to effect a satisfactory resolution. Alithea then precipitates the long-anticipated move by telling Harcourt that now she fears only *his* "censure." Having been prompted to make clear his willingness to be subordinate, Harcourt seizes the opportunity and assures Alithea that "'tis possible for me to love too, without being jealous"—those utterly magic words that allow her to accept him wholeheartedly, allaying her greatest fears and making Harcourt the "perfect" husband (250–51).[101] Harcourt (actually Alithea) therefore solves one problem, and Horner's words to Pinchwife, "I have resign'd your Sister to him, he has my consent" (268–69) merely accompany Harcourt's solution, not initiate it. Besides, Horner's gesture has no effect on soothing the Country Husband, who quickly deposes Horner's authority: "But he has not mine Sir, . . . and you shall marry her presently, or, ———" (270–73), as he lays his hand on his sword. And here the apparently innocuous presence of the real Parson adds one further male to surround and plague Horner at play's end.

It is left of course to Margery to catapult matters to their conclusion, first saving Horner from masculine aggression (at the hands of Pinchwife and Harcourt) and then asserting openly her own needs: "he shan't marry her, whilest I stand by, and look on, I'll not lose my second Husband so"; "don't quarrel about finding work for the Parson, he shall marry me to Mr. *Horner*" (274–81). With her public courage remains a commitment to the sorority, for Margery is quick with an apology to Alithea: "Pray Sister, pardon me for telling so many lyes of you" (284). Having again confronted the inescapable conclusion that his greatest fear has been realized, Pinchwife can only resort to a vestigial expression to help salvage what is left of his manhood: he "Offers to draw" on both Margery and Horner: "I will never hear woman again, but make 'em all silent, thus—" (287–88). But as we have come to expect, other males thwart his efforts: Harcourt, who physically grabs him, and Sir Jaspar, who leads the entourage of ladies into the room, flooding the scene with characters, effectively blocking Pinchwife's violent expression.

It is appropriate that Pinchwife informs Sir Jaspar that he has been abused—thus bringing the motif of internecine warfare to a fitting conclusion: "I tell you again, he has whor'd my Wife, and yours too, if he knows her, and all the women he comes near" (301–2). Pinchwife has obviously given Horner too much credit, ignoring for the moment the women's desire for being so "whor'd"; but his sharing this information with Jaspar at least provides him the satisfaction of being right all along—and it is important to remember that he *is* right—pulling another man into the thickening morass of cuckoldry with him.[102] And while the men continue to shape their separate fictions, Lucy steps forward to aid her fellow sisters, assuring the disordered Horner that she will save him and the situation, to which the rake can only respond, "Canst thou? I'll give thee—" (317).[103] That she begins speaking before he can complete his sentence suggests either (or both) that she needs no money to assist her fellow women (not so much to aid Horner) or that *she,* and not Horner, will be the one to determine the cost of her assistance (one might assume sexual favors later on).[104] Whereas Lucy confesses to Pinchwife what appears to be the truth—"your Wife is innocent, I only culpable; for I put her upon telling you all these lyes, concerning my Mistress, in order to the breaking off the match, between Mr. *Sparkish* and her" (318–22)—even here the indirection is conspicuous, that is, in Lucy's leaving out the details regarding Margery's sophistication in matters of deception and Lucy's own vicarious delight in steering Alithea toward the promise of romantic gratification. Although it is Pinchwife who is kneeled to, Pinchwife who is begged of, Pinchwife who all others stand around and fear—whereas Horner has only a secondary role in this climactic moment[105]—Margery refuses to allow a smooth return to order and propriety, demonstrating how unfit she is for London life by failing to silence her natural and untamed spirit: "Hold, I told lyes for you, but you shall tell none for me, for I do love Mr. *Horner* with all my soul, and no body shall say me nay" (329–31).[106] Although she pulls off her and Horner's masks, Wycherley's other characters instinctively refuse to look, and her frantic lover can only blurt out, "Peace, Dear Ideot," a plea that moves the subversive female not a whit: "Nay, I will not peace" (333–34).[107]

The Quack's arrival offers Horner his one hope of survival: "you may have brought me a reprieve, or else I had died for a crime, I never committed" (341–42). Still, he cannot finish his thoughts, being unnerved by the sight of a menacing Pinchwife and an insatiable Margery, and he whispers to the Quack to convince the doubtful that he is indeed impotent. Again, Horner needs help in effecting a resolution[108]—requiring the assistance of one of society's most illegitimate figures. To Pinchwife's credit, although he will accept Lucy's confession as a way to escape horrid implications and to salvage his manhood, he will not condone the ridiculous assumption that Horner is sexually harmless: "An Eunuch! pray no fooling with me" (352).[109] He remains throughout the one male character who is above accepting the Quack's diagnosis of Horner's condition,[110] even though he is sorely tempted to do so and thus ease his distress: "Well, if this were true, but my Wife—" (380). That he finally (tacitly) accepts what Lucy and Alithea tell him proves only that he must at all costs avoid the public perception (despite what he truly believes) of his cuckoldry: "For my own sake fain I wou'd all believe / Cuckolds like Lovers shou'd themselves deceive" (410–11).[111] The company's stunned reaction to the country wife's contradiction of the Quack's diagnosis—"'Tis false Sir, you shall not disparage poor Mr. *Horner,* for to my certain knowledge—"(369–70)—makes clear that the lonely warrior Margery Pinchwife will be unable ever to breach such impenetrable defenses with such an impotent weapon as literal truth.

As the curtain begins to close, Alithea warns her brother that he should avoid "too strong an imagination"—meaning of course any attempts at analyzing or plotting against his wife—and she offers a platitude as an antidote to male possessiveness: "Women and Fortune are truest still to those that trust 'em" (382, 384), which seems more her effort to solidify her own gains than the playwright's desire to conclude on any moralistic or educative note.[112] These points are made for Harcourt's benefit, of course, and they establish the conditions for his marriage to Alithea. Lucy follows with another commonplace, although one that speaks well to the female ascendency at play's end: "And any wild thing grows but the more fierce and hungry for being kept up, and more dangerous to the Keeper" (385–86). Dorilant, Sparkish, and Horner reject these visions of "London" husbands as a way to escape the image of such female potential; but Harcourt, showing that he is truly a suitable mate for Alithea, accepts the reality and acquiesces willingly to her demands. After she cues him, "There's doctrine for all Husbands Mr. *Harcourt*," he speaks up properly and docilely, "I edifie Madam so much, that I am impatient till I am one" (387–88). On the other hand, with much bitterness, Pinchwife adds, "But I must be one—against my will to a Country-Wife, with a Country-murrain to me" (392–93)—his particular way of acknowledging the verity of what Alithea and Lucy have stated but at the same time signaling his determination to fight against that truth and continue to suppress his fears. And his phrase *against my will* accurately reflects the furtive compromise that makes the worst kind of personal existence in Wycherley's world.

Pinchwife will force himself to believe that the "wild animal" Lucy alluded to may indeed be tamed or at worst made to forfeit its natural aggressiveness and instincts after long periods of incarceration. And as if to corroborate her husband's implied promise, Margery, having accepted that acting upon her natural inclinations has failed to move, resigns herself to her fate: "And I must be a Country Wife still too I find, for I can't like a City one, be rid of my musty Husband and doe what I list" (394–96). Those who find the conclusion lighthearted or otherwise an affirmation of the joys of sexuality fail to appreciate the disappointment and depression expressed in Margery's capitulation. Lucy again tries to protect her "sister": "what she has said to your face of her love for Mr. *Horner* was but the usual innocent revenge on a Husbands jealousie" (403–5). But her assessment (a protective lie) offers little comfort to one who has begun to feel the loss of her natural exuberance and hope for freedom: "Since you'l have me tell more lyes—Yes indeed Budd" (407–9)—a response marked by exhaustion and growing despair. This Persephone, now at the conclusion of her fertile period, awaits a return with her Dis to the uninviting underworld that is the country.

3: "PLAGUES AND TORMENTS"

Horner speaks the last two couplets of the play as a dance of the cuckolds begins around him.[113] His positioning in the dance has encouraged some to portray him as a phallic symbol amid the ritual,[114] and his having the final word implies that he has indeed been the center of the comedy. But although he steps forward to deliver the concluding lines, he has not ruled as a comic or satiric monarch, nor has all been resolved satisfactorily—and thus rings very hollow his aside to the Quack, "[W]ell, Doctor is not this a good design that carryes a man on unsuspected, and brings him off safe" (378–79), for Horner had to be *brought off* safe by others whose concerns, fears, and machinations effected both his successes and his rescue. There has been neither peace nor victory here; rather all returns to *status quo ante bellum*—an empty and frustrating cessation of hostilities. Horner's speaking the final lines amid the dance of the cuckolds is ironically most appropriate, for he too has been cuckolded in that his manhood has been subtly undercut throughout the play by men and women (and the playwright) alike[115]—the irony being that his desire to reverse the pattern by going from cuckold to sexual potentate has been subverted, leaving him only where he began[116]— completely surrounded by all these "old Acquaintances" he had hoped to be rid of. That *The Country Wife* has no delightful resolution punctuates the playwright's belief that life is ambiguous, incongruous, frustrating, deceptive, and filled with fear: after all, often what emerges from chaos is only chaos.[117] Finally, Jocelyn Powell may provide the most effectively succinct estimation of the play by noting that it is not a mirror of life so much as it is "a commentary on the workings of the human animal."[118] Indeed, Wycherley's brilliance in *The Country Wife* is more than farcical and comic; it is engagingly psychological.

4
"Surrounded with so many fears and griefs": *The Plain-Dealer*

IN *THE PLAIN-DEALER*, WYCHERLEY PUSHES ON TOWARD A RESOLUTION of his comic vision[1]—one seemingly reflected in the play's vigorous cynicism, the natural result of constant exposure to what one fears most and cannot control. The step from Pinchwife to Manly, then, may be deemed an easy one; in many respects the men are as close as brothers. However, in his last play, Wycherley reveals that the instinctive need for human companionship and interaction, no matter what the risk, cannot be suppressed, even though Manly will try to reject that unalterable fact, attempting to control himself and others through dismissal, escape, and fantasy—narrowing his world and all its complexities to a constrictive simplicity.[2] Despite the traditional emphasis on the play's unmitigated social condemnation, Wycherley in fact leaves us with an uplifting conclusion—that faithfulness and sincerity are possible, though they must always be temporary, occasionally *in*sincere, and anachronistic.

Although the Dedication to Lady Bennet[3] presents a familiar exterior constructed out of the materials of dramatic convention, visible underneath is something far more substantial. That is, whereas Wycherley's dedication to this "famous strumpet" is filled with allusions to bawdiness, cuckoldling, feminine hypocrisy, concerns for social reputation, and masking, it also makes pertinent reference to the instinctive and often daunting sexual drive of women; the inability of males, customs, and laws to control that impulse; the dread of a direct confrontation with the truth; and the fear of emasculation and female domination: "[women] must have a blind easie Fool, whom they can lead by the Nose, and as the *Scythian* Women of old, must baffle a Man, and put out his Eyes, ere they will lye with him, and then too, like Thieves, when they have plunder'd and stript a Man, leave him" (137–40). To counter (more than complement) Manly's cynicism, the reader is encouraged to exercise a healthy *skepticism* that looks for more than the obvious—as suggested in his advice to Lady Bennet—"And, Madam, tho you have not seen this Play, I hope . . . you will the rather read it" (46–47).[4]

4: "SURROUNDED WITH SO MANY FEARS AND GRIEFS"

Manly demonstrates immediately an intense need to avoid confronting that which threatens to upset the precarious balance he has established for himself—the evidence at once failing to support Virginia Birdsall's assertion that Manly is "a man of courage, unrestrained by fear."[5] His misanthropic pose—actually a kind of neurotic self-centeredness—is mainly a defensive and emotional reaction (that is, he is not really embracing from any deep philosophical considerations an *odium humanis generis*), a device by which he may protect himself from the perceived hostility of his environment. The pose is also a kind of indolence that spares him from tolerating his own weaknesses and those of his fellow men and women. He enters "surlily"; his first words, addressed to Plausible, are "Tell me not"; his first evaluation of others is disdainful yet well reflective of himself: "your little Tricks, which you the Spaniels of the World, do daily over and over, for, and to one another; not out of love or duty, but your servile fear" (I.i.3–5). In addition, he establishes quickly the use of one of his favorite verbs: "I *hate* a Harness," and his claims of independence from the "Arts" and "Rules" of "the prudent World" are immediate and emphatic: "I'll have no Leading-strings, I can walk alone" (9–10).[6] This vigorous cyncism should strike us, as it does Plausible, as being too severe, even considering the imperfect and often despicable state of things. We begin this early to wonder if such a posture as Manly's, if it is meant to combat or even to correct the way of the world, can in any way be effective.[7] And then there is the Hobbesian definition: "CONTEMPT being nothing else but an immobility, or contumacy of the Heart, in resisting the action of certain things."[8]

Wycherley therefore begins the play from Manly's asserted position of radical skepticism (cynicism), from which the only movement possible is that toward acceptance, if not altruism and sincerity, however slight. If Manly is to survive in the world he must make an accommodation. "What, will you be singular then, like no Body?" asks Plausible (12)—a question that marks a major motif of the play: heroic individuality. Manly mistakenly perceives human nature as something tangible from which one can escape, either physically or imaginatively.[9] He claims independence, but we see early on that he does not have it. His selecting only one man (Vernish) and one woman (Olivia) to constitute his heroic universe cannot obscure his connection to and need for human relationships. The question for us as well as Manly is not one of absolutes but one of degrees. Even though he seems to indict the entire race, Manly will let slip such qualifying phrases as "the few good men in the World"; "I speak ill of most men"; "If I ever speak well of people, (which is very seldom indeed) it shou'd be sure to be behind their backs" (I.i.32–45)—the qualifying only serving to undercut his stated philosophy.

Plausible in effect prepares Manly and the audience for the appearance of Fidelia by punctuating his conversation in the initial scene with "i'faith, i'faith," "no, faith," or "Your most faithful"—meaning that, whereas his saccharine optimism and profession of trust may be easily parried by Manly's references to fools, knaves, sycophants, flatterers, "common Whores and Pickpockets" (21), the more unobtrusive allusion to *faith* (and by extension, sincerity) introduces Manly to his major adversary—that most noble quality in women and men, though often weakened and concealed by avarice and pettiness, a ready antidote to all-incompassing despair and cynicism. Manly of course fights vigorously against any such implication: "I wou'd justle a proud, strutting, over-looking Coxcomb, at the head of his Sycophants, rather than put out my tongue at him" and "laugh at Fools aloud, before their Mistresses" (46–54). His antagonisms are no less unpalatable because he promises to be open about his disgust; and Manly appears here a *miles gloriosus,* one who talks a good game but who we trust might not perform half as well in combat, whose boasts more often disguise fears and insecurities than reflect prescience and fortitude. His railing, no matter how energetic and often justified is just too, too easy.

Plausible's apparent immunity to the power of Manly's words bears witness to their ineffectiveness—a point, I believe, not lost on Manly himself, who now in frustration seeks his sanctuary: "[I stir] Only to see you out of doors, that I may shut'em, against more welcomes" (81–82)—relying on more primitive measures to impose his will, as he thrusts the physically weaker Plausible through the door. Whereas in Wycherley's first play the door is a sanctuary from direction and in the second and third a means for the male to incarcerate and control women and to assail other males, in *The Plain-Dealer* the door is also a way for the male to keep himself protected and separated from a world he despises—and dreads. By being so plain in his condemnations, Manly goes over the bounds of indirection to which the reader has grown accustomed. And, still, many of Manly's outbursts are inescapably trite, even if accurate, complaints that have very little effect on either changing or "revealing" the way men and women behave and interact with each other. There may be something to the fly stinging the stately horse, but Manly will influence absolutely no one by his railing, regardless of how much force he puts behind his sting. What good is plain dealing, one might then ask, if it becomes the sibling of distrust and fear, negating a healthier kind of human interaction? Therefore, to rush to Manly's side would be to find ourselves neatly entrapped by the playwright; we need to step more cautiously as we traverse through the labyrinth of this play.[10]

From the sailors, we learn of Manly's loss of "five or six thousand pound" with which he would have gone to "live and bask himself on the sunny side of the Globe" and of his sinking his own ship to avoid the dis-

4: "SURROUNDED WITH SO MANY FEARS AND GRIEFS"   133

grace of losing it to the Dutch (I.i.108–20). Although Manly has displayed courage by participating in the war, the sinking of the ship points as well to a most hollow kind of "victory"—not a victory, really, though semantically not a complete and humiliating loss either—a sort of middle ground between two degrees, in which one may escape the reality of a defeat.[11] Manly's delight was evident only when he was destroying others and asserting his individuality—"I never saw him pleas'd but in the Fight" (124). And when his men[12] made him confront feelings of gratitude and dependence, Manly responded with aggressive disdain, which saved him from a more human response: "remember after we had tug'd hard the old leaky Long-boat, to save his Life, when I welcom'd him ashore, he gave me a box on the ear, and call'd me fawning Water-dog?" (131–34). They moreover depict, albeit in an "irresponsible" manner, their refreshing commitment to life as opposed to Manly's diseased and isolated view of sex: "Indeed, an't like your Honour, 'twill be hard for us to deny a Woman any thing, since we are so newly come on shore" (155–56). This gruff rejection of his men makes most problematic the notion that Manly's bitterness stems entirely from his view of the hypocritical *social* world. And aware that he had been at least momentarily helpless and in need of assistance, Manly's egocentricism (not really his soured though accurate opinion of the world) does not allow any act of genuine brotherhood to upset his narrowly conceived and ordered universe—in which he is beholden to only *one* man and *one* woman. He must protect himself (and ironically have others protect him) from any agent that would prompt a reevaluation of his "order." He accordingly assails his men for allowing Plausible to sneak through the defenses and insists that they be more vigilant, using violence if necessary to protect his splendid isolation (143–45).

In Freeman we have perhaps Wycherley's key or "ideal" character in the scheme of all four of his plays. Initially we might consider what's in the name. One thinks first of *carefree,* as is evident in his backhanded estimation of marriage and many of his observations to Manly, such as "the pleasure which Fops afford, is like that of Drinking, only good when 'tis shar'd" (I.i.168–69). Freeman: a man free of what? Care? Responsibility? Serious contemplation? A *L'Allegro* to Manly's *Il Penseroso?* An "adversarius" to Manly's satirist?[13] At a more significant level, Freeman is free from the psychological ills that afflict Manly and almost all of Wycherley's male characters. Although he is quick to cast aspersions at other males, he is free from the truly destructive tendencies that define male relationships—and as a result does not lead himself to the altar of self-destruction. He is moreover free from the debilitating manifestations of violence, anger, distrust, and blithe optimism—the "qualities" that cover fears and insecurities.

This is not to say that Freeman is completely free from primal impulses, nor that he is admirable in any traditional sense: "cou'd you think I was a Friend to all those I hugg'd, kiss'd, flatter'd, bow'd to? Hah, ha. . . . but, when their backs were turn'd, did I not tell you they were Rogues, Villains, Rascals, whom I despis'd, and hated?" (I.i.232–36). But we sense that not one of his victims is damaged by Freeman's flippant attitude and insincere flattery. (And the possibility exists that Freeman exaggerates his cavalier machiavelism here as a way to keep Manly's interest in the discussion.) In the political atmosphere of Whitehall, as in the corridors of modern-day state houses, such flattery is generally expected, with the understanding by all involved that less kindly things are said in private. When Freeman exercises his "aggression," it is without the malice we have seen elsewhere in Wycherley and particularly from Manly in this play:[14] his is a different kind of attack—more like a pillow fight than a duel with swords—both expending roughly the same energy but with far different effects. In addition, Freeman is free of the sexual aspects of the male destructive impulse that add the tinge of bitterness to the struggle. Freeman has channeled the destructive urge in a healthier direction, never allowing a preoccupation with sexual virility to influence his course—one reason why it is more appopriate he marry a Widow Blackacre rather than an Eliza. Freeman has learned that freedom means an *acceptance* of things as they are and a willingness to exist contentedly within the boundaries one cannot change—those established by the laws of human nature. Even so, his concession that males as a group cannot be brothers does not prevent him from aiding the individual, in this case Manly. And he *includes* others even while having his fun: "for the pleasure which Fops afford, is like that of Drinking, only good when 'tis *shar'd* (emphasis added; 168–69). Freeman would agree with Swift's position that discord marks the species but that one may "hartily love John, Peter, Thomas and so forth." To be liberated, Freeman realizes, one must understand that paradoxically he can never be free from the ways of the world, including its more unseemly vicissitudes. Freeman represents a healthy reality (not moral perfectability), whereas Fidelia will suggest a necessary though limited spiritualism and faith—both necessary to a secure life, both attempting to save Manly from total and enervating cynicism.

Freeman stimulates Manly with his refreshing exuberance and continually chastises him for his obvious shortcomings. And when the captain again shouts at his men for their "inappropriate" wit and levity, Freeman informs him that laughter must be allowed to dilute the bitter flavor of reality: "Nay, let the poor Rogues have their Forecastle jests; they cannot help 'em in a Fight, scarce when a Ship's sinking" (192–93). And Manly's ridicule of Freeman's appreciating another man's wealth or title as opposed to "intrinsick worth" ("I weigh the man, not his title," Manly tells him) is comic, if not insufferable. He holds that a rugged wisdom separates him from those who are either weak or slow-witted, and he damns Plausible, we might recall, for no other reason but that he encroaches on Manly's "inviolable" sanctuary—as a result, all his talk here about considering "intrinsic worth" over "counterfeit Honour" is shallow if not meaningless (175). Manly is much like the iconoclast who, while appearing to be courageous in assailing what others hold dear and deem necessary, is actually shoring up a fragile ego by elevating himself above the many "fools" who cannot see things his way. We observe as well that Manly demonstrates both a shaky resolve and a distorted view of human kind when he admits, "I have but one [friend], and he, I hear, is not in Town; nay, can have but one Friend, for a true heart admits but of one friendship, as of one love" (197–99).[15] Manly may claim that Vernish is the only one who has his ear and heart, yet Freeman and soon Fidelia will be his more constant companions—allowed to keep Manly company with the minimum of protest from the "foul weather" captain. In short, Manly is Freeman's reclamation project, that sunken ship loaded still with riches and therefore worthy of salvage.

In Manly's praise of Vernish we discover a fascinating self-portrait, for *this* Vernish (not the real Vernish) is a figment of Manly's imagination, a construction that mirrors Manly's perception of himself: "he has the courage of men in despair, yet the diffidency and caution of Cowards; the secresie of the Revengeful, and the constancy of Martyrs: one fit to advise, to keep a secret: to fight and dye for his Friend" (200–203). Courage, despair, fear, suppression, violence, resolve, self-destruction—all are stated or implied here, all emotions Manly has churning within, confusing and disturbing him, and annoying those without. By trusting Olivia to this "creation" called Vernish (subconsciously himself), Manly narrows the distance even further between himself and his love interest.[16] But Freeman wakes Manly from his fantasy with a demand for something rare in Wycherley—direct discourse: "pray, what d'ye think of me, for a Friend?" (207). As often noted, the following discussion regarding friendship is "indebted" to Molière, but, other than giving vent to his spleen, Manly's words more importantly reveal further evidence of his insecurity—the ostensible validity and heroic tenor of the words failing to disguise the troubled man. He cannot be a friend, Manly says, because Freeman sides "with all Mankind, but wilt suffer for none" (a plainly false assertion) and because he, Manly, refuses to take part in the "ceremony" of friendship, that is, the paying court to "Pimps, Flatterers, Detractors, and Cowards, stiff nodding Knaves, and supple pliant kissing Fools" (I.i.209–11, 226–27). As exhilarating as such condemnations may be, we detect in this one Manly's dread of numbers—"all

Mankind"—and of the groups, rather than the individuals, he cites with contempt. He illogically assumes that if he is friend to Freeman, he would necessarily have to be friend to all Freeman's friends and so on. Manly imagines being overwhelmed by others—and several times punctuates his fear with a horrifying image of intimacy: "I . . . will not tug on in a Faction, kissing my Leader behind, that another Slave may do the like to me. . . . I cannot wish well to . . . supple pliant Kissing Fools" (I.i.9–11, 225–27). The more persons Manly perceives in this daymare, the less control he feels he has—and he battles mightily against the image of his being merely one person indistinct from hundreds or thousands. With an ego despising the plural, Manly wishes to bring the numbers down to the bare minimum—one friend, one love, and himself.

Freeman plays the antagonist as a way of forcing Manly out of his sanctuary, wishing to anger the captain first into self-incrimination: "there is hardly such a thing as an honest Hyprocrite, who professes himself to be worse than he is, unless it be your self; for, though I cou'd never get you to say you were my Friend, I know you'll prove so" (215–18). He wants Manly to see plain dealing for what it is—a mask to cover anxiety: "Wou'd you have a man speak truth to his ruine?"; "And you wou'd have me tell the holy Lady too, she lies with her Chaplain[?]" (241–42, 262–63), challenging Manly's obdurate position on brutal honesty and forcing the surly captain to support his hard-line misanthropy in the face of the reality and common sense of Freeman's questions. True to form, Manly attempts to subvert the interrogation by offering a far-fetched scenario of a world totally committed to plain dealing (270–82), to which an incredulous Freeman can only reply with "Well, Doctors differ. You are for *Plain-dealing,* I find; but against your particular Notions, I have the practice of the whole World" (283–85)—a world, as Manly then states, he does not "understand" (296–97). Rather than a rhetorical parry, Manly's reply accurately defines his limitations: he *does not* understand that healthy accommodation with the world is a better response than unmitigated "plain dealing." Freeman accentuates his refutation of Manly's position with sincere speech—the like of which we rarely find between men in Wycherley's plays: "But, Sir, pray believe the Friendship I promise you, real, whatsoever I have profest to others: try me, at least" (298–99)—a statement that stands out majestically as proof of the playwright's muted optimism in regard to human relationships. It is Freeman who provides the positive light—or the "right way"—not characters like Valentine and Christina or Harcourt and Alithea. Yet, Manly's incorrigibility dismisses the proofs Freeman offers of his friendship: his willingness to fight for Manly, to lend him money, to speak well of him before his enemies, and to prevent anyone from talking about him behind his back. As Manly says, such *would* indeed show him a friend, "but it were unreasonable to expect it from thee, as the World goes now" (312–13). Manly's dependence on the comfort of his generalizations remains strong; he will have no one disprove him and make the world more complex. But we must be aware that he again subverts his own philosophy, as he continues to entertain such protestations from Freeman. Perhaps like the coy mistress, Manly's heart may not always be in the rejection of his suitor.

Manly's idealistic view of a society altered by plain dealing speaks to some kind of prelapsarian existence, something artistically anachronistic given the realities of "the World [as it] goes now." Accordingly, I would argue that Fidelia's antiquated character makes her more appealing to Manly, who from the first has affection for the "little Voluntier" (316). Few of the period's stage characters have presented critics with as many headaches as has Fidelia. What is this apparent Renaissance and romance heroine doing in the more unsightly environs of a Restoration comedy?[17] Surely, her disguise is consistent with Wycherley's use of the device in *The Country Wife* (and yes, it did provide another "breeches" role for Betty Boutell), and perhaps she does serve to culminate the disguise motif. But why would Wycherley borrow so heavily from Fletcher and especially from Shakespeare's *Twelfth Night,* changing Viola to Fidelia and even keeping a character named Olivia placed in a similar dramatic configuration?

Wycherley likely knew first of all that Fidelia would in fact be perceived by his audience as a product of a by-gone era, a romantic heroine thrust violently into a harsher world—as Fidelia is catipulted initially into a dangerous life at sea and now in the even more precarious environment of London society. But Manly too sees her as anachronistic (if not prelapsarian) and as a result less of a threat to him and his imagined paradise free from the demands of social life. Although the recipient of his general wrath, she (or *he* as Manly judges Fidelia) is such a delicate creature, effeminate in action and language, that the Captain cannot place "him" into the categories he has shaped to define London's men and women—thereby representing a "gender" protected from Manly's generalizations. Fidelia is a spiritual force—faith and sincerity being necessary to human beings if there is to be any hope for them—and if she is totally rejected we may determine that the playwright's vision of life is as bleak as a number of commentators have claimed. Unlike his parallel character in *Twelfth Night,* Manly does not call his "little Voluntier" another name, as Orsino addressed Viola as "Cesario," therefore keeping her symbolic role more firmly in place; and it will be only when Manly is more responsive to matters of faith and sincerity that he may learn her real name—Fidelia Gray, a name suggesting complexity, shades other than black or white, the two colors (mainly the former) that comprise Manly's prism. Whereas Fidelia seems anachronistic merely because of her Elizabethan roots,[18] she is furthermore antiquated by her allegorical function, which is evident in her speech—so often seasoned with abstractions and personifications: "As well as you do Truth, or Honour, Sir"; "Fame, the old Lyar, is believ'd"; "but the want of Love, Faith, and Duty" (I.i.320–36).[19] Part of the play's success, then, is in Wycherley's combining basic allegory with deeper psychological insight.[20]

Manly appears to ridicule Fidelia's devotion and friendship by chastizing her for "Flattering and Lying" (I.i.322), but clearly evident are the rays of light that have now shot into his darkened perspective, even as he continues to reject anything counter to his own rigid estimations of human action and motivation. Manly is more humorous and playful around Fidelia, teasing the young "man" about his cowardice on the open seas, at the same time owning to "hate thy Flattery worse than thy Cowardise, nay, than thy Bragging" (342–43). Fidelia's tears and oaths of loyalty, no matter how much Manly seems to disdain them, cannot help moving him and eliciting his affections because he senses, as does Freeman, that "he [Fidelia] seems to speak truth with [his eyes]" and that a rare commodity, sincerity, accompanies the tears and protestations. Fidelia has latched unto Manly like a barnacle to a ship's hull, and he will be powerless to separate himself from her, even though he tries vigorously to scrub her off with insults: "no more, you little Milk-sop"; with bribery (he offers her gold—a substitute for human commitment); and with the threat of force: "Be gone, go, I must be cruel to thee" (351–77). Although he blows a tempest here, the gentle breeze of positive human interaction brushes lightly against Fidelia, further weakening the image of the monolithic misanthrope Manly has pushed between himself and his world.[21]

Fidelia's jealousy, evident in her estimation of Olivia, is perhaps her most realistic human quality—but even allegorically such possessiveness fits the motif of the good angel Fidelia pulling hard to keep Everyman on her side. And her first soliloquy—given in good anachronistic Elizabethan blank verse—tells us, in Fidelia's discussion about placing herself among the "sooty *Indians*" in the West Indies, that her vision is again a totally foreign one (531–48). Fidelia conjures a place few women or men would find appealing, thereby intimating that pure faith (and sincerity) simply cannot be expected of human beings; it has to be mixed with the more aggressive and sexually oriented instincts characteristic of the world from which Manly wishes to flee. Faith is thus a tempering element, but it must not expect a warm welcome; it must, like Fidelia, move cautiously, disguising itself and suffering considerable frustration. That Faith must blend with the more sordid and violent aspects of life

4: "SURROUNDED WITH SO MANY FEARS AND GRIEFS" 139

to have any influence will help us understand better Fidelia's later involvement in the squalid scheme to punish Olivia.

Manly's quixotic quest for privacy and isolation is further violated by the appearance of the Widow Blackacre and her son Jerry. The Widow is a force none have been able to control; she is a Medusa "with a Mantle, and a green Bag" whose power as a woman is enhanced by her marriage to the law, that aspect of propriety through which men have controlled women and destroyed other men. Whereas Wycherley's female characters have nourished and maintained their power through overt and subtle sexual expression, the Widow Blackacre *appears* asexual, all the more apart from other women because of the legal world in which she moves. Like Fidelia she strikes us as alien. But as her imposing presence suggests (Manly calls her "implacable"—a "Fiend" like "a Baud in disguise"), she channels her own volatile sexual energy into the law (she learned well, it appears, from her father, "the great Attorney"). Like some mythological hybrid-beast, she "breeds her Son" (God only knows what killed his father), exacting tribute through society's most emphatic extension of propriety, the Law—that often distasteful and intimidating force much welcome because it harnesses the forces that might otherwise lead to chaos but also much feared because it inhibits natural expression and threatens the loss of freedom and security.[22] And because he is the one person who accepts the hostile and complex world for what it is, Freeman shows an interest in the Widow as a prospective wife: "they say she has Fifteen hundred pounds a Year Jointure" (I.i.395–96). Exploitation? Without doubt, but not simply wishing to seduce an innocent young daughter of a wealthy citizen, Freeman accepts the widow for the formidable person she is, measures the challenge ahead, and decides to pursue her and his fortune in the spirit of a healthy joust—on her turf, but under his rules. The Widow is furthermore a refreshing contrast to Manly—although both have warped perspectives—for while he wishes to incarcerate himself from the world, she chooses to take it to court.

Manly's "discussion" with the Widow, as amusing as it is, points to the tension and antagonism that marks so much of the conversation in Wycherley's plays. Manly is preoccupied and so is the Widow Blackacre—which frustrates communication—but Manly is more distressed because he seeks information from her about the Widow's "Kinswoman," Olivia.[23] As the pattern continues, he reaches out to yet another human being for assistance while at the same time rejecting disdainfully the possibility of his being dependent on someone else. He has required the help of his crew to survive; he has entrusted his money to Olivia and her safety to Vernish; and he has needed, regardless of his denials, the interaction with Freeman and Fidelia. And Manly is compelled by the law to serve as a witness for the Widow Blackacre's suit—forcing him in another way to assist and communicate. Although in this exchange about lawyers and lovers, Manly and the Widow seem to match each other blow for blow (the number of words they speak is about even), we notice that in fact the Widow has the best of it, if only because she talks about activity and influence, whereas Manly seeks passivity and cessation of speech and action. In short, he is all powder and little ball. For example, the Widow argues, "if I ever visit, 'tis only the *Chancery-lane* Ladies, Ladies towards the Law; and not any of your lazy, good-for-nothing Flirts, who cannot read Law-French," whereas Manly counters, "Dam these impertinent, vexatious people of Business, of all Sexes; they are still troubling the World with the tedious recitals of their Law-Suits: and one can no more stop their mouths" (427–34). His continuing verbal assault, "Dam *Pere, Mere* and *Fitz,* Sir" (I.i.466), and his contemptuous tossing away of his subopoena are Manly's ineffective and petulant attempts to remain free from the demands of the world, rather than any admirable gestures of contempt for it.[24] As for the Widow, she informs us that she is a woman with little use for the sisterhood, and by immersing herself in the male world she undoubtedly seeks to be independent and unique, although she is still subject to the more instinctual expressions of Wycherley's other female characters. And like the others (Manly and Olivia especially) who deliberately divorce themselves from the group, the Widow Blackacre will be sorely vexed for her "heroic individuality."

Freeman is correct to assume that the Widow Blackacre will eventually comprehend the sexual entendres in such remarks as "I wou'd beg you to hear me a little, a little of my business" (486–87), for she makes clear that the way to arouse her passions is indeed through the law—a natural progression since her energies are channelled in that (in)direction. Instead of trinkets and love poems, Freeman throws before her feet visions of satchels and law briefs:

> *Wid.* Yours wou'd be some sweet business, I warrant: What, 'tis no *Westminster-Hall* business? Wou'd you have my advice?
> *Free.* No, faith, 'tis a little *Westminster-Abby* business: I wou'd have your consent.
> *Wid.* O fie, fie, Sir; to me such discourse, before my dear Minor there!
> (490–95)

The clever movement from Westminster Hall, the hot bed of law activity, to Westminster Abbey, where marriage ceremonies take place, hints to the Widow that she may possibly remain ensconced in her world even in a relationship with Freeman, who at least seems willing to utter

4: "SURROUNDED WITH SO MANY FEARS AND GRIEFS"   141

words pleasing to her ear. And at Westminster Abbey, as the Widow would know, were the coronations of England's queens, Mary and Elizabeth, as well as the tombs of Elizabeth, Mary Queen of Scots, and other powerful women who had made a significant mark on a man's world.[25] As for Westminster Hall, the Widow (and older members of Wycherley's audience) would have recalled the agitation by groups of women in the 1640s (at times numbering in the thousands) demanding a stimulation of the economy, detaining members of Parliament, and even assaulting some of them.[26] Freeman, she likely perceives, has some appreciation of a woman's power, and accordingly she pays no mind to her son's warnings that the man is only after her cash. That we see Jerry "haling away his Mother" only gives us a visual confirmation of her interest in Freeman. Because he will be open (his direction here testifying again to his relative freedom from the normal restraints of Wycherley's characters) and honest enough not to disguise his designs for her money, she will at least be able to predict his behavior and, with her understanding of the law, feel more secure in entertaining his advances:

> *Free.* Here is one that wou'd be your kind Relation, Madam.
> *Wid.* What mean you, Sir?
> *Free.* Why, faith (to be short) to marry you, Widow.
> (II.i.774–76)

Yet, Freeman is well aware that sweet are the uses of propriety, especially when it comes to sexual allusion (here more for the Widow's benefit than his own): "But you have no business anights, Widow; and I'll make you pleasanter business than any you have: for anights, I assure you, I am a Man of great business"; "Try me but, Widow, and employ me as you find my abilities, and industry" (786–91). We should accept that the Widow delights in such talk and judges Freeman astute in his belief that being "impudent and baudy" (796) is the only way to penetrate the barrier she has established between her world and her instinctive sexuality—one constructed with legal precedents and reinforced with green bags and pounds of legal documents.[27] It is, after all, the Widow Blackacre who says, "You think with us Widows, 'tis no more than up, and ride" (798–99). Freeman moreover knows that she will brook no love suit that does not resemble a law suit.

In the Widow's response to Freeman's insistence that "she must love and marry" only him, we sense her defenses eroding as her replies become less reliant on legal terminology: "now adayes, every idle, young, hectoring, roaring Companion, with a pair of turn'd red Breeches, and a broad Back, thinks to carry away any Widow, of the best degree; but I'd have you know, Sir, all Widows are not got, like places at Court, by

Impudence and Importunity only" (II.i.800–804). However, the "only" at the end of her speech is intended to encourage Freeman to make a counter offer, intimating that she is going to be both judge and advocate of the love suit. Major Oldfox (cagy but superannuated) will play the role of prosecutor, insisting that Freeman is too young for the mature Widow, who insists on demonstrating her own vitality by claiming an age younger than what she is (812–13). But her realization that she is older than Freeman (likely by twelve to twenty years),[28] as well as the younger man's open admission of his aims and his "lowly" status, gives her enough security to deem such a match attractive, for, like Hippolita and Alithea, she demands independence within marriage and a guarantee of maintaining the ground she has so far gained through her immersion into the law.

Well aware of this woman's need to be ascendant, Freeman cleverly pays homage to the goddesss of "legal" propriety: "because I have nothing to keep me after her death, I am the likelier to take care of her life, And, for my being twenty Years younger than her, and having a sufficient stock of Impudence, I leave it to her whether they will be valid exceptions to me, in her Widow's Law or Equity" (823–27). Flattered, aroused, assured, but still angered at being pushed by the males toward a decision, the Widow reminds them, by savaging Major Oldfox, of her considerable reservoirs of strength: "Thou wither'd, hobling, distorted Cripple"; "Thou sensless, impertinent, quibling, driveling, feeble, paralytic, impotent, fumbling, frigid Nicompoop" (846–52). Although Freeman is not above delighting in the more combative aspects of masculine interaction: "I told you I shou'd be thought the fitter Man, Major" (860), his reaction again reflects no deep-seated anxieties or malice: "because you are no dangerous Rival, I'll give thee counsel" (952–53).

The Widow Blackacre refuses to be taken without a struggle; she turns on her younger suitor and levels a string of "insults" which testifies to the sexual force that is buried under the piles of legal paperwork: "Thou art a foul-mouth'd Boaster of thy Lust, a meer Bragadochio of thy strength for Wine and Women"; "I mean, you wou'd have me keep you, that you might turn Keeper; for poor Widows are only us'd like Bauds by you; you go to Church with us, but to get other Women to lie with" (II.i.893–908). She of course seeks assurance from Freeman that he is none of these things, especially one who would take such women to Church but not to bed. Perceptive as always, Freeman begs on bended knee to be believed—"But, dear Widow, hear me. I value you only, not your Jointure" (926–27)—for the moment risking injury to his masculinity, as Jerry stands over him, peppering him with accusations. The Widow Blackacre understands that Freeman is not truthful in regard to his motives—the transparent nature of his claim could fool no one—but still he has assumed the posture of virile supplicant, which for now is good enough to sustain her interest. But she will be the one to dictate when and if a judgment on his suit will be rendered, and she throws out one more allusion to her consuming fear of being sexually ignored: "a Widow, a little stricken in Years, with a good Jointure, is like an old Mansion-house in a good Purchase, never valu'd; but take one, take t'other: And perhaps, when you are in possession, you'd neglect it, let it drop to the ground, for want of necessary repairs, or expenses upon't" (929–33). Freeman's answer is perfect—the sexual image daring, yet, matching her lead, masked adequately enough by the property metaphor: "No, Widow, one wou'd be sure to keep all tight, when one is to forfeit one's Lease by dilapidation" (934–35)—a response that both startles and stimulates the Widow Blackacre enough to realize that she should stay no longer, lest she give herself away and lose her advantage: "Fie, fie, I neglect my Business, with this foolish discourse of love" (936–37). Being adaptable and feeling confident that his points were effectively made, Freeman will bravely follow into her own domain: "I'll be industrious too, and make a business on't, and get her by Law, Wrangling, and Contests" (950–52).

Manly's discussion with Freeman, which praises Olivia's "Virtue and Conduct" as well as her beauty, emphasizes his own artistic function by calling her "so perfect a Beauty, that Art cou'd not better it" (I.i.554–55). That is, Art cannot better the portrait he himself has painted—one that reflects his self-image: "She is all truth, and hates the lying, masking, daubing World, *as I do*" (emphasis added; 557–58). The heroic artist is determined to keep his portrait in pristine condition—Olivia "is not (I tell you) like other Women" (568)—and he entrusts her with his fortune as a measure of her (and his) heroic individuality and the epic scenario he has created for himself. But the money designates insecurity more than confidence; as Freeman says, Manly is "fain to bribe [her truth and constancy] with Money" (580–81). Nothing deters Manly from rising to full heroic stature and issuing an Olympian dissertation that, despite its general validity, nevertheless reveals a predominate fear of being besieged by superior forces and a desire to keep the enemy before him in plain sight—or simply to run from that enemy altogether: "generally, no Man can be a great Enemy, but under the name of Friend; and if you are a Cuckold, it is your Friend only that makes you so; for your Enemy is not admitted to your house: if you are cheated in your Fortune, 'tis your Friend that does it; for your Enemy is not made your Trustee.... Therefore I rather choose to go where honest, downright Barbarity is profest; where men devour one another like generous hungry Lyons and Tygers, not like Crocodiles; where they think the Devil white, of our complexion, and I am already so far an *Indian*" (588–98).[29] And like Pinchwife, Manly raises the most disturbing of all spectres: "thou wilt find her so handsom, that thou, who art so much my Friend, wilt have a mind to lie with her" (600–602). In Manly's vision is both a volatile and a sordid sexuality. He is prepared to leave England not so much because of general disgust but from his own apprehensions over being devoured in the dark or attacked from behind. We see here a most fearful, man, looking always over his shoulder, reflecting in his "heroic" demeanor the instinctual urge to exercise destructive tendencies toward other men—not just in voicing and demonstrating contempt to those he meets in London but also in imagining combat even in the primitive world of the Indies.

On first blush, the "paragon" Olivia seems indeed the perfect mate for Manly: "Ah, Cousin, what a World 'tis we live in! I am so weary of it"; as Eliza is for Freeman: "Truly, Cousin, I can find no fault with it, but that we cannot always live in't; for I can never be weary of it" (II.i.1–4). However, we should be as suspicious of Olivia's professions of weariness as we are of Manly's praise of her virtue. As Eliza says, "You cannot be in earnest sure, when you say you dislike [the world]" (7–8). Although never the play's significant interest, Eliza represents the best of Wycherley's women—realistic, energetic, undaunted—aware of the compexities of life and accepting of the *concordia discours* of human relationships. Unlike Manly, who believes that his is an admirable kind of plain dealing, Eliza understands the futility of hurling aspersions at the world: "Railing now is so common, that 'tis no more Malice, but the fashion" (73–74). Neither can Olivia's "weariness" inhibit the exuberance of Eliza and Lettice nor make less desirable the smorgasbord of worldy pleasures they depict—Balls, Plays, Masquerades, Hyde Park, the Court, "a rich young Husband," and a "liberal, handsome young Lover"—all enjoyments that epitomize feminine power and freedom, but which to Olivia are all her "aversion." Unlike Lady Fidget's "honour," Olivia's tag word truly rankles because, although it disguises both as well and as ineffectively as Lady Fidget's, it strikes a more serious chord. It does not, as does "honour," reflect the inevitable concession to propriety but rather pays court to what is at the heart of Manly's philosophy: the rejection of life. Every time Olivia matches or echoes Manly's attacks on society or any individual (eliciting our disapproval), the more she in effect mocks what he says, diluting in another way the power of his censure. By rejecting openly such pleasures, Olivia stives for her own heroic stature apart from her sex. Eliza and Lettice attempt (as does Freeman with Manly) to flush Olivia out to confront her hypocrisy, forcing her to accept a place *among,* not above, her sisters. Given Wycherley's emphases, Olivia is distasteful as much for her denial of her own sex as she is for the betrayal of Manly; she more than justifies Eliza's treating her more roughly than women normally treat each other in Wycherley's comedies.

Eliza easily counters Olivia's unfertile viewpoint first by conjuring something horrifying indeed: "but methinks we ought to leave off dissembling, since 'tis grown of no use to us; for all wide observers understand us now adayes, as they do Dreams, Almanacks, and *Dutch Gazets*, by the contrary" (II.i.90–93). Eliza cannot be completely serious here, for she is too intelligent to believe that women would ever relinquish their reliance on indirection. Instead, what Eliza employs is a form of shock therapy, in which a dreaded image is graphically presented so that the patient will awaken from her malaise, phobia, or "madness." And Olivia reacts predictably: "O filthy, hideous! Peace, Cousin, or your discourse will be my Aversion" (96–97). But Eliza rides hard on the fleeing Olivia: "Yes; for, if any thing be a Womans Aversion, 'tis *Plain-dealing* from another Woman: and perhaps that's your quarrel to the World" (98–100). This is Olivia's greatest fear—being exposed and known—and accordingly she seeks her immediate escape: "Talk not of me sure; for what Men do I converse with? what Visits do I admit?" (101–02). Therefore, whereas the announcement of Novel is unquestionably amusing in its "exposure" of Olivia's hypocrisy, his appearance does save her from confronting the truth about her anxieties. That she and Manly seem so similar in their personalities and their fears might suggest an approval of their match; but to join them (at this point Manly is moving toward an enlightenment through the efforts of Freeman and Fidelia) would be a negation of life, a nihilistic union consumed in its own lassitude and dread. And related to Manly's praise of plain dealing, we might look again at what Eliza says to Olivia about this "virtue"—that what she fears is a plain dealing from another that has a viable *purpose* behind it—that is, to reveal something to the *individual* for the sake of betterment or correction, rather than, in Manly's case, the indiscriminate blasting of plain dealing at a group who hears it not. The first is the utility, the latter the futility, of plain dealing.[30]

We note as well that whereas Manly's visitors come to him *despite* his wishes, Olivia's come *because* of hers, making evident that she cannot suppress her natural inclinations to interact with men: with Novel she is comfortable and able to satisfy her appetite for destructive talk and ego gratification. Novel seems another of those fops oblivious to insult, covering his failure to measure up with ornate masks of vanity, condescension, and tinkling talk. Clearly, Novel desires to be perceived like Manly and Olivia, something apart from his group—striving for "heroic foppery" by doing everything with stark originality in mind. As ludicrous as Manly's, his quest demonstrates not only an unrestrained ego but also a debilitating insecurity. His frequent asking for assurance, "d'ye think my way new?" equates to a childlike want of recognition, and like Sparkish, who risked being thought a fool because another impulse predominated, Novel cares little about the trivial nature of his uniqueness as long as he may think himself superior in any way to his rivals—all men, but especially the wits.

Olivia and Novel easily find the common ground because each enjoys attacking both men and women (and if Olivia were at one with the sorority, she would never tolerate a male's assault of her sex). So in sync are the two character assassins that Olivia interrupts and then completes Novel's thoughts before he can articulate something original[31] (to Novel a form of coitus interruptus we may assume) and exercises her quicker intellect while he suffers the indignation (and figurative emasculation) of hearing her refer obliquely to him: "but as the Fool is never more provoking than when he aims at Wit, the ill-favor'd of our Sex are never more nauseous than when they wou'd be Beauties" (II.i.207–9). And every aspersion they cast helps further diminish the effectiveness of Manly's censure, even if we view his as more justifiable, because we simply come to be fatigued by the constant haranguing in itself—evident here by Eliza's frustrated response to Olivia's "portraits," which she observes are "much uglier" than the overly flattering sittings painted by Peter Lyly: "you are the first of the profession of Picture-drawing I ever knew without flattery" (214–15). The allusion to art reinforces the perception of these characters' creative natures and their shaping and distorting of reality (Olivia now an artist as well as the artist's [Manly's] subject), yet oddly, Eliza's criticism would be taken as a welcome compliment ("you are the *first* of the profession"), for such a designation gives Olivia the sense of uniqueness she craves.

In his efforts to shine, Novel turns one division of his army over to Olivia in the hope of distinguishing himself in another part of the field: "but, now I think on't, the Women ought to be your Province, as the Men are mine" (220–21). He finds, though, that Olivia's troops have beaten him to the site, as is clear in her interrupting him once more—the coitus interruptus motif joined by one of coitus reservatus—as the increasingly irritated Novel finds that there is to be no satisfactory release for him.[32] Olivia continually proves Novel's impotence by thwarting his every effort to shine, and if all this were not painful enough, the poor fop finds Eliza intruding as well: "What," he says in exasperation, "interruption from this side too!" (243). There can be no question as to the women's dominance; Olivia physically "holds him" as he attempts to leave the scene of his humiliation, for she has not yet delivered the *coup de grâce*. She refuses his request for the barrage to stop and projects him forward to fight for his manhood—only to find the field empty of any foe:

"Mr. *Novel*, stay; and, tho' you shou'd rail at me, I wou'd hear you with patience: pr'ythee who else was there with you?" to which the vanquished man can only admit, "We had no Body else" (262–64, 267). The scene is undeniably a tantalizing visual treat, with Novel jumping into the conversation, occasionally scoring a palpable hit—"There I was once beforehand with you, Madam" (374–75)—but more often knocked away before he can even unsheath his sword. Far from being a vain hypocrite who unconsciously acts like those she condemns, Olivia seems very aware of what she is doing to Novel, jerking him about with her proficiency in malicious talk and hammering him down by the rapidity of her excoriations. To avoid undue concern with character improbability later on, we should see her as evolving quickly from a silly to a more deadly kind of character. With each veil she takes off, another more intriguing and frightening lies underneath.

Novel's "rival" Plausible is allowed into Olivia's world because he too appears to know his place: "Madam, I am your eternal Slave, and kiss your fair hands" (288–89). His inflated praise of Sir John Current and Sir Richard Court-Title, two more of Olivia's "suitors," seems to corroborate Eliza's view that he "speaks ill of all people a different way, and Libels every body with dull praise" (304–5). But more significant is that Plausible's ridiculous cordiality to other men makes him somewhat unique in that he appears segregated from his sex, apart from those who seek to humiliate and destroy each other.[33] Plausible's choice of phrasing—"such pattern of Heroick Virtue!" and "the glory of our Age"—again speaks to the mythic and heroic fiction several of the characters (Manly, Olivia, Fidelia, Widow Blackacre, Novel) have imposed between themselves and the real world, the one epitomized by Freeman and Eliza.[34]

The characters' assessment of Wycherley's own *Country Wife*, prompted by Molière's example in *La Critique de L'École des femmes*, exploits contemporary reaction to the play and affirms the playwright's delight in self-deprecation. But we might also consider that Wycherley here suppresses every author's greatest fear—rejection or condemnation of his work—by humorously expressing it through Olivia (hardly a critic we would respect) and then defending it through Eliza (one we would)—much as Horner "accepts" the state he would fear most (impotence). At any rate, Olivia's condemnation of this "filthy Play" is simply her way of revealing and releasing her sexual volatility. For example, she admits to blushing when she speaks of the *The Country Wife*, but the redness on her cheeks results more from arousal than from any theatrical, let alone genuine, attempt at modesty or disgust: "O horrid! does it not give you the rank conception, or image of a Goat, a Town-bull, or a Satyr? nay, what is yet a filthier image than all the rest, that of an Eunuch?"

(414–16)—each of these beasts personalizing the lascivious and animalistic urges frequently mimicked by men and women, with the references to "Eunuch" sounding much like Lady Fidget's reaction upon hearing of Horner's "condition." Likely intending to prompt a more honest reaction from Olivia, Eliza says that she can "think of a Goat, a Bull, or Satyr, without any hurt" (417–18)—and Olivia's response, I would argue, should be uttered in the heat of increasing sexual passion, rather than in mock disgust: "I, but, Cousin, one cannot stop there" (419). Indeed, she proceeds (and the "proceeding" only proves her fascination) to the act itself: "O no; for when you have those filthy creatures in your head once, the next thing you think, is what they do; as their defiling of honest Mens Beds and Couches, Rapes upon sleeping and waking Countrey Virgins, under Hedges, and on Haycocks: nay, farther—" (421–25). Sensing that her cousin may become too direct even for her ears, Eliza feels compelled to interrupt: "Nay, no farther, Cousin, we have enough of your Coment on the Play, which will make me more asham'd than the Play it self" (426–27).

This vision of figurative intercourse and accompanying orgasm is by now predictably followed by a return to propriety, and Olivia uses the unforgettable post-coital moment from the *Country Wife* (Lady Fidget's emergence with the china in her hand) as a way to regain order, even though her passions are hardly extinguished in the attempt: "I say, the lewdest, flithiest thing, is his *China;* nay, I will never forgive the beastly Author his *China:* he has quite taken away the reputation of poor *China* it self, and sully'd the most inncocent and pretty Furniture of a Ladies Chamber; insomuch that I was fain to break all my defil'd Vessels. You see I have none left; nor you, I hope" (433–38). This marvelous passage gives us much: a playful reference to Wycherley's own manhood and virility (china having been earlier equated to sex and the male sex organ), the need to condemn in order to disguise interest, the loss of Olivia's sexual innocence (whenever that was), her hope that Eliza has not distinguished herself by remaining a virgin ("You see I have none left, nor you, I hope"), and her indication that verbally and figuratively she has reached a point of sexual satiety (Horner's signaling his own sexual exhaustion, we recall, with the words, "I have none left now"). Yet, regardless of its humor, Olivia's condemnation of china and of the play itself is unwholesome and illegitimate, prompted by the need to remain "undetected" and "unique"—even while her sexual preoccupations continue to belie her censure (as did Mrs. Caution's): "'tis now as unfit an ornament for a Ladies Chamber, as the Pictures that come from *Italy,* and other hot Countries, as appears by their nudities, which I always cover, or scratch out, wheresoe're I find 'em. But *China!* out upon't, flithy *China,* nasty, debauch'd *China!*" (441–45). Despite her attraction to these pieces of sexual art, she must "cover, or scratch out"—concealment and violent passion marking her contradictory attitude about sex. Such an "attack," however, does not alter Eliza's more healthy perspective: "All this will not put me out of conceit with *China,* nor the Play" (446–47).[35] Olivia then panics when Eliza announces she is off to see the play—jealousy wishing to stop pleasure (especially since Olivia would then be left in the company of two sexually uninteresting males, who in their estimations of the *Country Wife* fail to detect the play's active sexuality), further violating the unspoken code of sisterhood. Still, it is Wycherley's own *Country Wife* that awakens Olivia's dormant eroticism, which will come to dominate her actions from this point on.[36]

As he and Freeman arrive with Fidelia, Manly holds back, watching and listening, exposing his insecurity and fear of being proved wrong in his estimation of Olivia. His threat to Fidelia after she advises distrust of Olivia—"You lye, Sir, and hold your peace, that I may not be provok'd to give you a worse reply" (II.i.485–86)—reminds us that the primitive measures are always available to one in need of protecting his manhood. (We note as well Fidelia's more allegorical function as the "good angel" as opposed to Olivia's "bad angel"—the simplicity of interpretation being hers as well as the reader's.) Manly naturally has difficulty understanding what Olivia might see in Plausible or Novel; he obviously fears being replaced. Again, it is *not* really a matter of Manly's unsuitability for society because he is the only person who sees matters *correctly.* He is simply so very often so completely *wrong*—as moreover evident in his happy rationalization of Novel and Plausible's presence in Olivia's chamber: "perhaps they are admitted now here but for their news of me" (489–90). Olivia and her "mate" Novel not only emasculate Manly—"I always lov'd his Brutal courage, because it made me hope it might rid me of his more Brutal love" (493–95)—but they dismember him as well: Novel says that "the Rogue has been these two years pretending to a wooden Leg, which he wou'd take from Fortune" and that "he has no use of his Arms, but to set 'em on Kimbow" (498–508). No aspect of Manly escapes her censure, even his scent: "Foh! I hate a Lover that smells like *Thames-street!*" (521).

Manly's need to redeem and assert his masculine presence compels him to shove Novel and Plausible and to challenge the former by standing toe-to-toe. He tells Olivia, "You have fitted me, for believing you cou'd not be fickle, tho' you were young; cou'd not dissemble Love, tho' 'twas your interest" (533–35).[37] But the captain leaves himself vulnerable because he displays more jealousy of Novel than shock at his being so dreadfully wrong about Olivia's virtue. In his unwillingness to confront the dreadful reality, he retreats from that which would destroy the heroic fiction he has created with himself, Olivia, and Vernish as the exceptions to the corrupt world. In his asking (rather than demanding or assailing) "But, Madam, tell me, pray, what was't, about this spark, cou'd take you?" (560–61), Manly redirects his anxiety to what is handy, though highly improbable—Olivia's physical attraction to Novel. And Novel aids in the diversion by turning everyone's attention to clothing and other superficial nonsense. Amused and encouraged by her power, Olivia gleefully mocks Manly by ridiculing the fantasy he has constructed: "No, noble Captain, you cannot sure think any thing cou'd take me more than that heroick Title of yours, Captain; for you know we Women love honour[38] inordinately" (585–87). Reveling in another male's distress, Novel punctuates Olivia's remarks: "Hah, ha! faith I can't hold from laughing" (594), prompting in Manly the now habitual retort: "Nor shall I from kicking anon" (595). Manly is so determined to protect his myth that he orders Novel and Plausible to hold their tongues, "for I will only suffer now this Lady to be witty and merry" (608–9), in essence accepting ridicule from the one who can do him the most damage while silencing those who can do the least.

In the midst of this malicious reverie, Plausible's uniqueness begins to be consumed by the more natural behavior pattern of males. That is, whereas he asked Olivia and Novel at first—"O, be not so severe to him" (512)—he now joins in the merriment: "And i'faith, dear Captain, I beg your pardon, and leave to laugh at you too, tho' I protest I mean you no hurt; but, when a Lady Raillies, a stander by must be complaisant, and do her reason in laughing: Hah, ha" (618–21). Although Manly forcibly ejects Novel and Plausible from the room, he has hardly shown himself a man in front of Olivia. And, in all her imperious splendor, Olivia challenges the captain to assert himself while giving him absolutely no hope of controlling her. Manly responds with justifiable anger, pointing to her "ingratitude, falshood and disdain" and vowing to henceforth "despise, contemn, hate, loath, and detest [her], most faithfully" (II.i.653–56). But as "manly" as this attack appears, it is nevertheless feeble because Olivia *demanded* that he be rough on her and even more so because his condemnation will have no effect on improving her conduct—in short, these words, filled with sound and fury, signify not much of anything. And Olivia's reply, "Get the Hombre Cards ready in the next Room, *Lettice,*" informs Manly just how impotent his assault has been.[39]

Whereas Manly seems little inspired by her encouragement to maintain his resolve ("And you'll be sure to keep your word, I hope, Sir"), Fidelia's effeminate demeanor does stimulate Olivia, who, having considered *The Country Wife,* is now more interested in matters of the flesh—her body likely still tingling from thoughts of "china." She is attracted to Fidelia because she sees another "male" she might control,

4: "SURROUNDED WITH SO MANY FEARS AND GRIEFS"

one who is so unlike Novel and Plausible: "A Gentleman, so well made as you are, may be confident—us easie Women cou'd not deny you any thing you ask, if 'twere for your self" (681–83). Although Olivia's attraction to Viola in *Twelfth Night* may be viewed as a reflection of a grieving sister's discomfort with more traditional masculinity and the need to return cautiously (through an effeminate "male") to an active life, the intentions of Wycherley's Olivia are furtive, and one cannot rule out the possibility that her initial motivation is to torment Manly further by seducing one of the captain's men, one he finds effeminate—the very antithesis of his heroic self-image.[40]

It is at this point that Wycherley delivers the big shock: Olivia informs Manly that she has given his jewels and money to her *husband* (as yet unnamed). Reminded that we are still groping about in the labyrinth, we are left uneasy by Olivia's answer to Manly's pained question, "Why, did you love him too?": "Most passionately; nay, love him now, tho' I have marry'd him, and he me: which mutual love, I hope you are too good, too generous a Man to disturb, by any future claim, or visits to me" (704–7). Is this profession of loyalty simply tailored to her love of deception, her habit of speaking in contrarities? Or is it embellished with the intention of adding considerable pain and humiliation, as Manly hears her speak of an ideal marriage and "mutual love"—having her create *without him* a kind of heroic relationship with another mate? But this is her method, as it is Manly's, of raising herself above the mundane, above the expected—even if in imagination more than fact. Prompted by her words, "if you wou'd have me thrive, Curse me; for that you'll do heartily, I suppose" (731–32), Manly "discovers" the intensity of his love with an ejaculation of curses having, again, no effect on his smiling adversary. Pleased that she has so easily led him about, Olivia offers a patronizing observation that quickly shifts the blame to him but which also reminds him of his helplessness: "May the Curse of loving me still, fall upon your proud hard heart, that cou'd be so cruel to me in these horrid Curses: but Heaven forgive you" (743–45). Her earlier superficial and hypocritical bantering with Novel hardly prepares us for the sophistication of her cruelty. Manly's only recourse is to grope desperately for a familiar image. Turning from Olivia and upon learning of Widow Blackacre's arrival, he announces, "D'ye hear that? let us be gone, before she comes; for hence forward I'll avoid the whole damn'd Sex for ever, and Woman as a sinking Ship" (761–63). At this point the surly captain is truly in danger of going down with his vessel; he still has not learned that escape and self-quarantine are not the answer.

Moving reluctantly to his other "hostile world" ("I Hate this place [Westminster Hall], worse than a Man that has inherited a *Chancery* Suit: I wish I were well out on't again"), Manly cannot avoid his predominant fears, regardless of the many insults he hurls to cover his exposed flank: "Well, a Plague, and a Purse Famine, light on the Law" (III.i.1–2, 23–24). Once more the healthier Freeman provides the counter perspective: "Why, you need not be afraid of this place; for a Man without Money, needs no more fear a croud of Lawyers, than a croud of Pick-pockets" (3–5). Freeman can be undaunted and witty because he understands that failure, disgrace, and frustration are all inevitabilities of the human experience; he cuts easily through the imaginative cobwebs Manly has spun and sees Westminster simply as a playground of fools. As his brief soliloquy here suggests and despite his vigorous protestations to the contrary, Manly is indeed part of a larger group, an admission that reveals some positive movement and refreshing self-revelation: "How hard it is to be an Hyprocrite! / At least to me, who am but newly so" (26–27). This anachronistic blank verse appropriately signals the entrance of Fidelia, and fulfilling her allegorical function she assures her captain that she will remain faithful and always "share" his "miseries": "I shall be afraid of your anger more than danger, and so turn valiant out of fear" (47–48).[41] Like a brass ring, Fidelia and all she embodies is there for Manly's taking if he will only make the effort. He must come to reject his heroic egotism and accept what she represents as sincere and genuine qualities even if they can have little influence in changing the world.

Manly's decision to share his emotional anguish with Fidelia ("he [Fidelia] shall know it—he shall—but then I must never leave him, for they are such secrets, that make Parasites and Pimps Lords of their Masters" [III.i.70–72]) is a crucial moment in the play, for it depicts him moving purposely toward an acceptance of a life *dependent* on others. He now allows some kindness to mix with his harsher pronouncements, apparent in such oxymorons as "kind Impertinence, leave me" (36). Still, Manly continues to fear losing control and being consumed by a hostile force; his distance remains his security—as he makes clear to Fidelia: "And do not discover it [my secret], by too much fear of discovering it" (81–82). By employing Fidelia as a messenger, as Shakespeare's Orsino so used Cesario (Viola), Manly hopes to spare his frail masculinity from any direct hearing of Olivia's ridicule: "Go flatter, lie, kneel, promise, any thing to get her for me: I cannot live, unless I have her" (103–4). Clearly, for all his ruggedly inclusive and sweeping condemnations, Manly's problems stem not from the realities of a sordid world but rather from his highly frustrated personal affairs. Manly rejects in one moment Fidelia's caution—"And wou'd you have me contribute to the loss of [your honor]?"—forwarding instead a despicable scheme as the only way to repair the considerable damage done to his ego: "No, I will not forget it, but think of revenge: I will lie with her, out of revenge" (107, 113–14).

4: "SURROUNDED WITH SO MANY FEARS AND GRIEFS"   153

Assuming that as a cuckold he is no better than thousands of fools who have suffered similar disgrace, Manly conceives of rape as a satisfactory and justifiable expression of his rage, one that achieves dominion over one whom he has been unable to budge with appeals to logic and fidelity. As creator of the composition "Olivia," he believes he has every right to mar what is now the imperfect portrait. And, as further indication of his disordered state, he shifts quickly from Jacobean avenger to Elizabethan lover: "Be gone, I say, and bring me love or compliance back, or hopes at least" (119–20). The question is whether he will eventually be like Freeman—a Restoration compromiser.

In the often confusing and bitter world of Restoration law, that "parental" institution that often fails to nurture its dependents, we find the Widow Blackacre exercising her tyranny over males no less ardently than does Olivia. She assails one of the lawyers, prods Serjeant Ploddon on, demands her minutes of Jerry, and commands Quaint and Blunder to talk for her in Chancery: "Go, go," she tells them all. She is the center of all action—the monarch regally bedecked in robes of law, issuing proclamations, expecting total compliance, acting more as one coronated in Westminster Abbey than one whose simple business lies in Westminster Hall. Such counsels of legal war stimulate the Widow's sexual instincts; and she holds out interesting possibilities for the warrior who does her bidding: "Go, weary our Adversaries Counsel, and the Court," she tells Quaint, and "I shall make thy Wife jealous of me: if you can but court the Court into a Decree for us" (III.i.174–77)[42]—then whispering to him either a threat or more likely an erotic promise to encourage his efforts: Elizabeth with her Essexes. And later she says to the two Knights of the Post whom she has lured into the room at the Cork on Bow Street: "You are safe enough, Gentlemen, for I have been private in this house ere now, upon other occasions, when I was something younger" (V.ii.375–77). Even her sound estimations of others' motives take their form through graphic sexual imagery only microscopically coated by legal diction: "for every body wou'd be riding a Widow, as they say, and breaking into her Jointure: they think marrying a Widow an easie business, like leaping the Hedge, where another has gone over before; a Widow is a meer gap, a gap with them" (413–16).

But Petulant, yet another character who wishes to be thought unique, refuses to act as one of her champions should: "what know I? what care I?"; "Perhaps I do, perhaps I don't, and perhaps 'tis time enough" (III.i.190–91, 198). And his refusal to stir and his rebellious gesture of flinging her "Breviate" at the Widow without returning his fee prompts the kind of violent response that is meant to emasculate as well as to vent spleen: "Gadsbodikins, you puny Upstart in the Law, to use me so, you Green Bag Carrier, you Murderer of unfortunate Causes, the Clerks

Ink is scarce off of your fingers, you that newly come from Lamblacking the Judges shooes, and are not fit to wipe mine; you call me impertinent and ignorant! I wou'd give thee a Cuff on the ear, sitting the Courts, if I were ignorant" (220–26). The humiliation at being so reminded of his "boyish" standing in the law and the intimidating reverberations of the Widow's speech preclude any effective response by Petulant, who leaves appropriately in silence. In the male universe of the law, then, the widow has assimilated that masculine taste for aggression, and knows well where to aim her blows.

Major Oldfox complains that Jerry Blackacre wishes to peruse *St. George for England* and *The Seven Champions of Christendom* instead of Oldfox's own treatise, *The Art Military*. The Widow does not wish her son to read about "Rambling, and Fighting, and studying Military Discipline, and wearing red Breeches" (as in Oldfox's treatise) but thinks that *The Young Clerk's Guide* would better suit Jerry's temperament and, more importantly, her intentions to keep him under control. And the short scene between the Widow and the Major later in the play provides an engaging contrast between the "law" and "art," as Oldfox forwards his writings to win the Widow, while she wards him off with references to her own litigious papers—a kind of ritualistic seduction in which the participants use the papers as symbols of their bodies. For example, Oldfox admits that his best "parts," which he wishes the Widow to know, may be found in the "overflowings of [his] fancy and Pen." The superannuated Major has nothing left to display his virility but his wretched and impotent lines, and in exasperation voices again the play's omnipresent motif: "O Lady, Lady, all interruption, and no sence between us" (IV.i.242).

As always, delivering his blows more in the spirit of contest than in the throes of malice and insecurity, Freeman subtly assaults Jerry's manhood by reminding him that others his age and even younger have "kept" women, had "half a dozen Claps, and lost as many thousand pounds at Play" (III.i.338–40). Implying that sex is more powerful than even the law, Freeman advises young Blackacre that he "make false Love to some Lawyer's daughter [an interesting transference of the Oedipal sexual associations with his mother, the daughter of a lawyer herself], whose Father, upon the hopes of thy marrying her, shall lend thee Money, and Law, to preserve thy Estate and Trees" (361–64). And Jerry *is* fearful of his mother's marrying, for she would then "cut down" his tree. Fully capitalizing on the lad's inadequacy, Freeman offers his "support" but also the accepted extension of male potency—money, which Jerry's mother, understanding the virility of a full purse, never allowed him, not even "six-pence in one's Pocket, to see a Motion, or the Dancing of the Ropes" (373–74). Freeman always moves comfortably in a world of limited possibilities, one in which fear plays so large a role, cultivating an attitude and an understanding that allow for optimum success. He therefore stays far removed from the alluring though destructive "heroic" world that emphasizes the individual, the fictive, and the unique. But Freeman's subsequent arming Jerry with trinkets prompts an assurance from the Widow that she is not *that* preoccupied by the law: "What, Sir, d'ye think to get the Mother, by giving the Child a Rattle?" (424–25). She quickly learns that Freeman has made a surreptitious foray on her arsenal and stolen important legal papers: "I'm undone; they are all that concern my Estate, my Jointure, my Husband's Deed of Gift, my Evidences for all my Suits now depending! What will become of them?" (434–37). A superb strategist and field commander, Freeman realizes that the Widow must be attacked at her weakest flank, at the point where her energies—sexual as well as legal—lie most exposed.

Manly's depiction of the Widow Blackacre includes the concave symbols of femininity and his own anxiety at the thought of being enclosed and entrapped: "But canst thou in earnest marry this Harpy,[43] this Volume of shriveld blur'd Parchments and Law, this Attornies Desk?"; "wilt thou commit thy self to a noisom Dungeon for thy life?"; "I tell thee again, he that is the Slave in the Mine, has the least propriety in the Ore" (444–60). Freeman's response shows no trepidation but only acceptance of what the relationship would demand; he would gain financial security; she the satisfaction of her physical needs: "Why, d'ye think I shan't deserve Wages? I'll drudge faithfully" (457–58)—a remark that again nudges us toward seeing the Widow as at least somewhat sexually appealing, thereby mitigating the "sacrifice" Freeman would make if she indeed looked like an incensed Medusa. And to his credit, Manly comprehends that such women are nobody's fools; they can be as manipulative as the younger males who pursue them: "if thou wou'dst have her Money, rather yet to be her Trustee, than her Husband; for a true Widow will make over her Estate to any Body, and cheat her self, rather than be cheated by her Children, or a second Husband" (460–64). And what may be the most important aspect of this scene is Manly's apparent concern for Freeman, his *sharing* of advice, his admonishing, his warning—all serving, again, to undercut his heroic misanthropy.

Even though the loss of her "Writings" has left the Widow without an Excalibur, she makes clear that she has weapons enough to continue the fight: "if there be Law; and my Minor and Writings are not forthcoming, I'll bring my Action of Detinue or Trover" (485–87). Nor can Manly feel confident that she is relatively harmless without her papers; for when he asks, "If you have lost your Evidence, I hope your Causes cannot go on, and I may be gone?" she replies, "O no, stay but a making Water while, (as one may say) and I'll be with you again" (489–92). This scatalogical expression informs the men that the universe of the Widow's discourse extends from city law court to city shore ditch and that severing her from the law would not in itself make her totally helpless or pliant. And when a maternal appeal fails to move her son—"if thou wilt go home with me again, and be a good Child"—she impulsively chooses as would any male (Manly included) a characteristic form of violent response: "Why, thou Villain," she tells Freeman, "Rob me of my Child and my Writings! but thou shalt find there's Law" (IV.i.287–94).

Freeman moves forward to announce his terms at the moment when the Widow seems most assailable—that is, when she begins to weep. Freeman has played rough, yet still with that broad smile on his face, ascendent for the moment but unwilling to presume a total victory; besides, he knows that the marriage will give the Widow plenty of opportunity to exact any revenge: "if I cannot get you, I'll keep him, who is less coy you find; but, if you wou'd have your Son again, you must take me too. Peace, or War? Love, or Law?" (IV.i.310–12). His overconfidence has perhaps betrayed him here, because he should know that to the Widow "Love" and "Law" are not mutually exclusive terms. In any event, the Widow displays her renewed combative spirit as she refuses Freeman's offer of marriage and warns of repercussions: "I'd have you to know, Sir, I shall be hard enough for you both yet, without marrying you" (316–17). Jerry denies her request that he return to her sphere of influence by ridiculing all "Lawyering, and Pettifogging" (328–29)—a serious error because the highly insulted Widow is now forced to strike with even more fury in order to reassert the power she lost by her weeping: "thou wert not born in Wedlock"; "Thou art but my base Child; and according to the Law, canst not inherit it: nay, thou art not so much as Bastard eigne" (337–46). In another of Wycherley's "shocks," the vengeful Widow Blackacre cruelly snips young Jerry's budding masculinity (cultivated by Freeman) by informing him that he is not even the bastard son of her deceased husband, giving him no sense of a masculine lineage, making him an orphan—an object of complete derision.[44] The implications regarding the Widow's sexual past are of course not lost on Jerry, Freeman, or Major Oldfox, but her natural desire for ascendancy, combined with the "masculine" techniques she has embraced, overrules any initial concern for propriety. Again invigorated for having won the field, she heads to "the Prerogative Court" for a celebration, assured that she can overcome any problems caused by the admission of previous sexual indiscretions: "Pshaw! I can prove any thing; and for my Reputation, know, Major, a wise Woman will no more value her Reputation in disinheriting a Rebellious Son, of a good Estate; than she wou'd in getting him, to inherit an Estate" (IV.i.369–72).

Oldfox's having the Widow Blackacre bound and gagged ("you shall be acquainted with my parts, Lady, you shall") again brings to the surface her volcanic preoccupations: "Acquainted with your parts! A Rape, a Rape—What, will you ravish me?" (V.ii.418–25). Here the pattern of sexual indirection is turned on its head as Oldfox employs a more overt sexual language as a filter for something far less erotic: "Yes, Lady, I will ravish you; but it shall be through the ear, Lady, the ear onely, with my well-pen'd Acrostics" (426–27). Wycherley draws out the sexual possibilities as long as he can—albeit "in the ear" being a startling point of entry—the pen once more serving as the phallus, one as limp as the acrostics they create. Even so, Oldfox does rely on the kind of primitive expression typical of the males in these plays (and previews Manly's shoddy plot against Olivia) when logic or reason cannot protect them from facing their shortcomings. As we could have predicted, even this "sexual" activity is interrupted, a male again frustrating another male's pleasure. "What," says Oldfox, "shall I never read my things undisturb'd again?" (428). Freeman's untying the Widow is without question significant, for whereas he puts her in his debt (as does the writ he has taken out against her), she appreciates that he has rescued her from a kind of incarceration and sexual predicament—real or overtly metaphoric—permitting her to maintain dignity and escape defilement. Freeman plays Perseus to her Andromeda, freeing her from the monster of acrostics, dispatching him not with Medusa's head but with something else that turns men to stone—references to the law: "Nay," says Oldfox, "then I'll be gone, for fear of being Bayl, and paying her Debts, without being her Husband" (434–35).[45]

The defeat at the hands of the law (Freeman's writ) and reliance on the generosity of the younger male again strip the Widow Blackacre of her defenses: "Undone, undone then! no Man was ever too hard for me, till now" (443–44). And when offered the choice of matrimony or jail, the Widow understandably laments the vulnerability of the married woman: "Matrimony, to a Woman, worse than Excommunication, in depriving her of the benefit of the Law: and I wou'd rather be depriv'd of life" (459–61). This observation, very reminiscent of Alithea's musings on jealousy, suggests how different she is from many other women in the period's drama who contemplate marriage, for she sees matrimony not so much as putting a woman under the thumb of the law (which gives power to the husbands) but rather that being married she might be *separated* from the law, which would suppress the symbol of her womanhood, the source of her power. But Wycherley's female characters are always resiliant, and she begins once more to reassert herself in a way that satisfies both her sexual interests and her need for propriety and the protective aspects of the law, tenaciously holding on to her sense of mystery as she flings legalities at Freeman: "But hark you, Sir, I am contented you shou'd hold and enjoy my person by Lease or Patent; but not by the spiritual Patent, call'd a License; that is, to have the priviledges of a Husband without the dominion; that is, *Durante beneplacito:* in consideration of which, I will, out of my Jointure, secure you an Annuity of Three hundred pounds a Year, and pay your debts" (461–66). Freeman's satisfaction with the agreement proves acceptance of what the Widow wants most, what Wycherley's female characters want most—her liberty as well her law—and his willingness to adopt a subordinate position even though he has won significant concessions.[46]

The deal Freeman seeks for Jerry comes not in an overt demand but rather in a request of the judiciary, which the Widow *grants* as a beneficent personage rather than concedes as a beaten adversary.[47] Accordingly, she does not remain helpless for long, but rather like the legal Antaeus gets her strength from recontact with juristic terminology. Even Freeman's suggested alteration of the arrangement—"Four hundred pounds a year"—and the payment of his debts, "not above a thousand pounds" (really a concession on his part, from her offering to pay "all" his debts) again emphasizes that he plays the game in the spirit of compromise without malice or desire to fight against the inevitable—here the Widow's passion for control and ascendency. He accepts that she will always do battle for her freedom, so he concedes it immediately—"I'll bate you your person, to dispose of as you please" (484–85)—although she would prefer still another "consideration" to make the agreement binding: "Well, a Widow, I see, is a kind of a *sine cure,* by custom of which the unconscionable Incumbent enjoyes the profits, without any duty, but does that still elsewhere" (491–93). Given the realities of life, a healthy accommodation has been reached, one that gains for one party without damaging what is important to the other—a kind of workable compromise of which Manly has been incapable, the kind of philosophy that allows Freeman to move so freely in the world.[48] The Widow's exuberant personality is not destroyed or even significantly altered by her "loss" to Freeman; she has been invigorated by his attentions and has turned what seemed a total defeat into a draw, if not a form of victory for her as well.

But the law's connection to male aggression remains always conspicuous, as apparent in Manly's telling Freeman that since he has been at Westminster Hall he has incurred "three Quarrels, and two Law-Suits" (III.i.503). Here the battle rages between those who are armed with the law and those who know only physical solutions to disagreements—the "civilized" versus the primitive, it seems—but in both cases the instinct is the same. Manly evinces an enervating phobia, not a rugged and invigorating contempt: "I'll assure you, then, their business is to persecute me" (398). And in one moment of cruel retaliation he gives "sincere Ad-

4: "SURROUNDED WITH SO MANY FEARS AND GRIEFS"   159

vice, to a handsom, well-drest, young Fellow (who ask'd it too) not to marry a Wench, that he lov'd, and I had lay'n with" (526–28). His railing suggests one besieged by troops on all fronts, enemies who "pluck" him aside, "sputter" in his face, "put" him "a long Law-Case," and "keep a Man half an hour in the croud with a bow'd body." All is acted upon him; he can do nothing but wish them "hang'd out of [his] way" (400–410). More specifically, the lawyer whose ears Manly had boxed calls on witnesses who approach the nervous misanthrope, and they call more witnesses, after Manly has verbally assaulted them, who also come upon the isolated captain and ineffective railer, who can only utter the familiar refrain "I see more Quarrels crouding upon me: let's be gone, and avoid 'em" (531–32). Quite perceptively, Freeman comments on Manly's compelling need for security and his unfitness for life: "you are too curst to be let loose in the World; you shou'd be ty'd up again, in your Sea-kennel, call'd a Ship" (504–5).[49]

But an enemy in the uniform of a fop arrives before Manly can leave the suffocating atmosphere of Westminster Hall, and Novel's presence brings out the captain's anxiety and near panic at being so crowded: "Pr'ythee let me be rid of thee, I must be rid of thee" (544). Successfully shedding Novel, Manly then finds his way blocked by the arrival of Oldfox. Whether he looks in front or behind, to the right or to the left, Manly beholds others riding hard upon him, leaving no exit, no surcease from the reality of the world, no opportunity to live out the heroic fantasy he has created for himself. Oldfox's protestations of friendship—"What, you are modest I see! therefore too, I love thee" (565)—are no less repulsive to Manly, not because he sees them as hypocritical but because they demand an answer, a response, a legitimate kind of human interaction. We would be wrong to view Manly as correct and Oldfox as unworthy of Manly's attention; for it is Manly's problem with life that is at issue. He attacks the Major's manhood by making light of his military prowess during the English Civil War (this from one who was left to cut his losses in the Thames), but Oldfox returns the blow by reminding Manly of the captain's inability to escape the clutches of his latest enemies: "I consider thou art peevish, and fretting at some ill success at Law" (578–79). Every time Oldfox tells Manly that he "loves" him, the more he sees Manly wince in pain: "I love thee more and more; and shall I tell thee what made me love thee first?" (582–84).

Even when Manly is finally able to dispose of Oldfox, another lawyer comes toward him, once more preventing his escape from Westminster Hall and forcing him to interact with still others, such as the Alderman, who does his part to remind Manly of social obligations: "Why shou'd you avoid your old Friends?" (653–54). And when the Alderman asks to know who might be ripe for financial picking, offering Manly "a snip" of the action, Manly grabs him by the nose and levels a barrage ignited by moral indignation: "Then go lay it upon a Hospital, and take a Mortgage of Heaven, according to your City custom; . . . do, I say, and keep the Poor you've made, by taking forfeitures, that Heaven may not take yours" (677–81). Certainly this seems a moment in which the playwright's disgust rises to full expression in the mouth of the satiric agent, perhaps justifying, at least in part, Manly's soured attitude toward life. However, whereas Manly may feel he is simply assailing hypocrisy and corruption, he comes very close to embracing figuratively a group of fellow human beings (the poor and infirm), again subverting his heroic decision to forgo the ways of men. And the Alderman, certainly no fool though he may be despicable, diffuses to a considerable extent Manly's explosive strictures by reminding him that such men as the captain, in their glorification and exercise of war, have filled the hospitals with "Cripples," which is Wycherley's superb way of suggesting how weak any unqualified principle or moralistic pronouncement may be, thereby placing one more obstacle in the path of the reader.

Even though the Widow Blackacre's scenes are more significant than often perceived,[50] our primary interest remains with the Manly-Olivia-Fidelia plot. Without hesitation, Fidelia informs Manly that Olivia finds him "offensive" and "nauseous," something worse than a "debauch'd Hector" and a "finical baffled Coward"—in short, "her aversion": "she wou'd sooner take a Bedfellow out of an Hospital, and Diseases, into her Arms, than you" (IV.i.21–30). Fidelia forces him to associate the relationship with weakness, disease, impotence, and worse (likely embellishing Olivia's words for maximum effect): "she had the baseness, the injustice, to call you Coward, Sir, Coward, Coward, Sir"; "I've done. Coward, Sir" (41–46). As some child awaiting a treat his guardian cannot afford to give, Manly asks, "Did not you say she was kinder than I cou'd wish her?"; "but, at last, you prevail'd it seems: did you not?"; "You prevail'd for me, at last, you say?" In another way he is the incompetent general aware that he is losing the field, almost demanding that his subordinates inform him of an impossible sudden reversal of fortune: "So then, let's know that only"; "No more of your fooling, Sir; it will not agree with my impatience, or temper" (47–64).

And the hardly reluctant Fidelia saves the most devastating evidence for last—Olivia's interest in Manly's "dear Voluntier": "Her tongue, I confess, was silent; but her speaking Eyes gloted such things, more immodest, and lascivious, than Ravishers can act, or Women under a confinement think" (80–82). Demonstrating his continued refusal to accept any reality failing to support his brutal generalizations, Manly heroically fights on: such "vain young Fellows" as his volunteer often misread a woman's look as sexual when it must have only been cosmetic (83–87).

As long as Olivia gave only looks, Manly can rationalize her actions as less romantically demonstrative than Fidelia assures him they were. But Fidelia is quick to destroy this comforting fantasy as well: Olivia "threw her twisting arms about my neck, and smother'd me with a thousand tastless Kisses" (95–97).[51] Manly's reaction to this image is especially revealing: "But she was false to me before, she told me so her self, and yet I cou'd not quite believe it; but she was, so that her second falseness is a favor to me, not an injury, in revenging me upon the Man that wrong'd me first of her Love. Her Love!—a Whores, a Witches Love!— But, what, did she not kiss well, Sir? I'm sure I thought her Lips—but I must not think of 'em more—but yet they are such I cou'd still kiss,— grow to—and then tear off with my teeth, grind 'em into mammocks, and spit 'em into her Cuckolds face" (108–16). Manly's speech moves quickly and tempestuously from pathos and self-pity to distasteful and graphic violence, covering the range of his complex emotions and indicating that with him there will be no moderate acceptance of truth— any alteration of his myth will be accompanied by desperate and savage measures meant somehow to shore up his damaged ego and to punish severely whoever caused him to face his philosophical (as well as sexual) inadequacies.[52]

We are witness to another variation of the coitus interruptus motif as Fidelia recounts the welcomed intrusion of a visitor at the moment Olivia was strengthening her demands for sexual gratification. Regardless, Manly is now fully committed to the reassertion of his supposed sexual prerogative; by concocting his own variation of the bed trick, he may not only take his revenge on Olivia but he can cuckold—and thus destroy—his male rival. Ironically now, Manly accepts the truth as an ally in mischief and justice: "there is some satisfaction in being quite out of doubt: because 'tis that alone with-holds us from the pleasure of Revenge" (175–76). Freeman's appearance then *interrupts* Manly's contemplation of this vengeful sexual intercourse, keeping the play vibrating with feelings of agitation and frustration.[53]

We return at last to Olivia's lodgings, highly curious by this point to see more of her. But the playwright disappoints our expectations by keeping her out of sight for close to one hundred lines. We are left instead in the company of the interlopers, Plausible and Novel, who have both been given letters from Olivia, which each believes will demonstrate to the other the futility of seeking her hand. The hostilities commence with name-calling, followed by the projection of heroic scenarios in which neither is equipped to participate successfully: "Well," says Novel, "you shall find me in Bed, with this Lady, one of these dayes" (IV.ii.27–28). The two popinjays circle each other, repeating the flatteries Olivia has given both of them in her letters; each seeks to further his self-image—

one marked by aggressive virility, the other by self-satisfied effeminacy. But Wycherley reverses his pattern by having virility interrupt sterility: a titillated Olivia can barely contain her excitement over the impending tryst with Fidelia: "my new Lover . . . has his Lesson, and cannot miss me here, tho' in the dark: which I have purposely design'd, as a remedy against my blushing Gallant's modesty; for young Lovers, like game Cocks, are made bolder, by being kept without light" (106–10). Of course, this tantalizing vision is suspended by Vernish, whom Olivia mistakenly greets with passionate kisses and sweet but contrived words. We observe how cleverly she escapes discovery, turning her husband's attention to Manly, amusing him with tales of the Captain's earlier abuse. And Vernish's delight rivals that of Iago: "in the mean time, I'll lead the easie honest Fool by the Nose, as I us'd to do; and, whil'st he stays, rail with him at thee; and, when he's gone, laugh with thee at him" (146–49). Vernish's gaiety is matched by his wife's heightened passion for Fidelia and her increasing agitation at getting Vernish out of the way: "To morrow! O do not stay till to morrow: go to night, immediately"; "go, dearest, I am impatient till you are gone—" (162–68). Olivia's optimism after showing her husband out—"now all interruptions of the last are remov'd" (171)—fails to comfort, for this is not *The Country Wife;* we have assumed by now that some manifestation of coitus interruptus (literal or figurative) will continue to plague the characters right to the end.

Upon Fidelia's arrival (with Manly in hiding), Olivia lunges after her timid and elusive prey: "Nay, you are a Coward; what are you afraid of the fierceness of my Love?" (189–90). The energy in this scene matches that anywhere else in Wycherley's plays—the movement constant, the tension pronounced, the frustration agonizing. Just Fidelia's mentioning of Manly's name, however, halts temporarily Olivia's Dionysian frenzy: "O! name not his Name; for in a time of stol'n joys, as this is, the filthy name of Husband were not a more alaying sound" (194–95). We find ourselves, perhaps against our conscious wishes, somewhat annoyed and impatient with Fidelia as she encourages Olivia to talk of Manly, forcing from the Restoration Maenad her true estimation of the "Surly, untractable, snarling Brute!" (212). (And much of the sexual tension here stems from our periodically forgetting that Fidelia is not in fact a young male.) The struggle between Olivia, who condemns and was unfaithful to Manly, and Fidelia, who defends and would be faithful to him, is clearly in the allegorical framework of the good-angel/bad-angel tug of war for the soul of Everyman(ly). We even find Olivia *pulling* at Fidelia—evil consuming and seducing faith—and Fidelia *pulling* at Manly—faith saving Everyman. All of this tussling is consistent with Fidelia's character and function, but we might also note in a more literal sense that

4: "SURROUNDED WITH SO MANY FEARS AND GRIEFS" 163

Olivia is *correct* in much of her estimation: Manly does, after all, rail "at all Mankind," and he does display cowardice (to face life) and some cruelty. In fact, part of Fidelia's defense—for example, that he is a "Man of that sence, nice discerning, and diffidency"—is impossible to accept; and other than Manly's courage, though not success, at sea, Fidelia primarily finds Manly's physical features his most impressive asset as a man. Fidelia's perspective colors her observations as strongly as do Olivia's, and therefore neither estimation of the captain can be taken as wholly satisfactory.

Olivia understandably grows impatient with such talk, which she sees is an intrusive prelude to the romantic business at hand: "Come hither, come; yet stay, till I have lock'd a door in the other Room, that might chance let us in some interruption" (245–46). Her wish, as we should know by now, is hopeless. Again Wycherley has thoroughly foiled our expectations for Olivia's character based on her initial appearance with Novel. Labeling her as either hypocrite or "witwould" does not account for her complexity and, yes, even her appeal.[54] As for Manly, defenders of his "satiric vision" earlier in the play must contend with his fervent commitment to a sexual form of revenge, one that is mated to the most violent expression in Wycherley's four plays: should Fidelia give him away, he tells her, "I'll cut [Olivia's] Throat first, and if you love her, you will not venture her life; nay, then I'll cut your Throat too"—punctuated by "Not a word more, lest I begin my Revenge on her, by killing you" (266–71). That Manly has directed this outburt to a woman absent and to his effeminate and cowardly "Voluntier" is really unimportant, for just the meer exercise of his aggression demonstrates how necessary is his reliance on primal (not intellectual or satirical) expression to maintain control and redeem his manhood.

Fidelia restates her anachronistic function with another soliloquy in blank verse—twelve lines of unadulterated self-pity: "for when a Lover's hopes / Are dead, and gone, life is unmerciful" (288–89). Coming, it seems, from Olivia's bedroom (or somewhere near), Manly intrudes on Fidelia's weeping, informing us quietly that he has "thought better" of his plans to "discover [him] self now" (290–91).[55] Whether he refused to act because he lacked a witness or the courage to go forward (or whether he had a bout of conscience) is unclear, but he continues to depend on Fidelia for a successful execution of the bed-trick: "No disputing, Sir, you must; 'tis necessary to my design, of coming again to morrow night" (298–99). That he needs assistance once more undercuts the heroic posture he had assumed for himself—the increasing reliance on Fidelia (despite the disreputable context) showing a movement toward accepting sincerity and faith as valid human qualities. Still, he remains wedded to his barbaric promise, even now his only security: "do this faithfully, and I promise you here, you shall run my Fortune still, and we will never part as long as we live; but, if you do not do it, expect not to live" (303–6).

Olivia's subsequent encouragement of Fidelia with sweet words seems uncharacteristic of such a passionate and explosive temperament. But her "tame" demeanor is mainly attributable to the comfort she feels around such a gentle and effeminate "male," even though such words aid in the transition from propriety to raw sexual expression. She wishes to pull Fidelia into a fertile and womb-like feminine environment: "let us go in again; we may be surpriz'd in this Room"; "we shall be secure enough within: Come, come—" (314–18). But Fidelia's resistance only triggers less gentle responses: she pulls Fidelia, "Come, come, . . . you must not go yet: Come, pr'ythee" (323, 327). Postponing the amor with the transparent excuse that she has the "Falling-sickness," Fidelia tantalizes as well as frustrates Olivia with the prospect of drawing out the seduction, giving her further evidence of the young "man's" helplessness and inferiority: "These young Lovers, with their fears and modesty, make themselves as bad as old ones to us" (339–40). However, Fidelia's escape is interrupted by Vernish, the one man who gives Olivia caution—for his being her husband, sustained by law and custom, makes him more formidable to her than an angry and indignant Manly. Vernish's believing he is about to be cuckolded prompts the expected response—a drawn sword to save his threatened manhood.

But rather than disarming him, Fidelia's admission of her true gender stimulates Vernish's aggressiveness—not only is she an apppealing female but, by having to reveal the truth without disguise or indirection, she is moreover defenseless. Vernish "feels her breasts," pulls her about, and closes her in another room: "Stay there, my Prisoner; you have a short Reprieve" (413)—a compression of what Wycherley's women fear most: helplessness, debasement, and incarceration. Yet ironically, in this play Fidelia may be so jeopardized because only she is an alien. She is not the sexual, undaunted creature her fellow sisters are; she is a symbol of fragile, vulnerable faith—a quality frequently in fear of its life.[56] As for Vernish, he has a rare opportunity to enjoy the moment: he knows his wife is fearful of discovery; that his manhood has not at all been threatened by a rival (even though he is still discomforted by Olivia's vigorous sexuality); and that he has before him the fearful *and* defenseless woman ("Help, oh—"), physically attractive but not to the extent that she may manipulate the male through her charms. Vernish becomes at this point the main figure in a sadistic reverie (linking him to Gripe as well as to Manly): "Come, there is a Bed within, the proper Rack for Lovers; and if you are a Woman, there you can keep no secrets, you'll tell me there all unask'd"; "I'll show you; but 'tis vain to cry out:

no one dares help you, for I am Lord here" (380–85). Of course, Vernish's sordid fantasy is interrupted by a visitor coming to discuss finance, that frequent signifier of virility: "I'll fetch the Gold, and that she can't resist; / For with a full hand 'tis we Ravish best" (414–15).

At the commencement of the final act, Olivia seems to lapse into the superficial and misanthropic comic figure we initially found conversing with Novel and Eliza. She again talks of the "wicked World" and her fear of losing her good name. But surely something else is at work here. Eliza reads the indictment: "you know your self most guilty, you impeach your Fellow Criminals first, to clear your self"; "you pretend an aversion to all Mankind"; "That you condemn the obscenity of modern Plays, only that you may not be censur'd for never missing the most obscene of the old ones" (V.i.10–24). We know all of this—we knew it early on—and we can only wonder why Wycherley gives it to us again. We might first recall that Eliza, as smart as she is, sees Olivia only from the perspective of the satirist who identifies hypocrisy and sham and then attempts to expose it. But this moment in the play is a rather weak one, especially considering what we have seen that Eliza has not. Concerned with other matters, Eliza has failed to discern the more significant aspects of Olivia's character. She has missed the depth by focusing on the superficialities, and for all her likeability and common sense, Eliza's assessments here do not reflect Wycherley's primary concerns in the play—one reason why her character does not measure up to its promise.

Still, for all her criticism, Eliza remains influenced by notions of sisterhood; she is not out to destroy Olivia regardless of her "hypocrisie": "[T]his last deceit of your Husband was lawful, since in your own defence"; "No, you need not fear yet, I'll keep your secret" (107–8, 137). But wishing still to remain separated from her fellow women, Olivia is reluctant to accept Eliza's altruism: "I'd have you to know, I have no need of Confidents"; and then seeks to use Eliza, as males use other males, to enforce her authority and protect her mystery: "I'll quarrel with her, that people may never believe I was in her power; but take for malice all the truth she may speak against me" (138–45). Therefore, Olivia has severed the natural bond between women in the vain hope of moving in a more fictive rather than realistic sphere. She is the only women in Wycherley who so articulates the desire to remain apart from her sisters. By contrast, even though Eliza quite justifiably accepts a termination of their relationship and believes Olivia will be "damn'd enough already, by [her] Oaths"—her instincts prompt one final bit of advice, which she phrases as a question (one not completely rhetorical) so that the dialogue and her attempts at assistance might perhaps continue: "Yet take this advice with you, in this Plain-dealing Age, to leave off forswearing your self; for when people hardly think the better of a Woman for her real modesty, why shou'd you put that great constraint upon your self to feign it?" (154–59).[57]

When an amused Vernish tells Olivia that she has actually had a passion for a "Woman in Mans cloaths" (V.i.37), her initial reaction is concern only for her dominion: "he dissembles, only to get me into his power" (39–40), but then likely refusing to consider that her feminine instincts could have been so in error, she, like Manly, seeks any explanation that would prevent her having to confront such a disturbing reality: "Or has my dear Friend made him believe he was a Woman? My Husband may be deceiv'd by him, but I'm sure I was not" (40–42). Feeling his oats, Vernish informs Olivia that he "might have known" Fidelia better had not he been "interrupted" by the goldsmith and had she not escaped by sliding down some torn window curtains to the street. Being a Wycherlean character, however, Vernish must salvage the image of propriety (as well as keep Olivia off balance): "for, you must know, I jested with her, and made her believe I'd ravish her; which she apprehended, it seems, in earnest" (56–58). The effect of this admission on Olivia (who now must entertain the possibility that her lover *was* a woman) is to his advantage as she evinces doubt, jealousy, anger, and anxiety over his words: "but how dar'st you go so far, as to make her believe you wou'd ravish her? let me understand that, Sir. What! there's guilt in your face, you blush too: nay, then you did ravish her, you did, you base Fellow" (64–67)—the second false assumption of a rape or ravishment, I would argue.

But typical of her sex, Olivia is as resiliant as she is resourceful, and her fury at the insult to her femininity propels her forward to regain the ground she has lost by being so openly jealous: "What, ravish a Woman in the first Month of our Marriage! . . . wrong my Bed already, Villain! I cou'd tear out those false Eyes, barbarous unworthy Wretch" (67–70). The delight Vernish experienced at having his virility so strongly acknowledged is consumed now by Olivia's general ferocity, which pushes him in his retreat back over the terrain he believed he had just secured: "Pr'thee hear, my Dear"; "I swear—pr'ythee hear me" (72–74). And warming to her growing advantage, Olivia rides hard upon her fleeing adversary: "I have heard already too many of your false Oaths and Vows, especially your last in the Church. O wicked Man!" (75–76). Not satisfied with wielding these hard-edged weapons, Olivia also draws out the maudlin bow, which sends its powerful arrow accurately to its target: "And wretched Woman that I was! I wish I had then sunk down into a Grave, rather than to have given you my hand, to be led to your loathsom Bed. Oh-oh- [Seems to weep]" (76–79). Like the Widow Blackacre earlier, Olivia remains ascendant, quickly shoring her defenses after the masculine assault, leaving her opponent again weakened and frustrated at having lost the field. Now Vernish can only plead for her forgiveness and affections, offering his sexual performance, two hundred "Guineys," and further ridicule of Manly as inducements. Looking about after Vernish has retired, we wonder what happened to that lascivious and sadistic character—a man who is now beaten, docile, and obsequious. Once more, as our perspectives again shift, we are reminded that Wycherley continues to toy with us in the labyrinth.

Manly's interrogation of Fidelia (another connection to *The Country Wife*) suggests that he will make no sudden conversion, for he insists that his revenge plot go forward despite the protestations of his reluctant accomplice: "No disputing, or advice, Sir; you have reason to know I am unalterable" (V.ii.15–16). Manly's desire that Freeman bring others in to witness Olivia's "infamy" would of course embellish his revenge, as he admits (V.ii.363), but more importantly he needs witnesses not only of her infamy but also of his own heroic reemergence. Although the reaffirmation of his promise to "defend" and not to "part" with Fidelia if she is faithful presages at least a modification of the mythic ideal of singular opposition to the world, his annoyance at Freeman's subsequent appearance at the Cock in Bow-Street continues to speak to his fears. Freeman pushes Manly to reach out to those who would be the least risk: "Pshaw! but most of 'em are your Relations; Men of great Fortune, and Honour" (V.i.50–51). Yet Manly fights on, rigidly committed to his "heroic" posture (as it precludes the vulnerability that comes from placing oneself in another's debt): "damn 'em, now I'm poor, I'll anticipate their contempt, and disown them" (55–56). Outmaneuvered on that flank, Freeman relocates his attack: "But you have many a Female acquaintance, whom you have been liberal to, who may have a heart to refund to you a little, if you wou'd ask it: they are not all *Olivia*'s" (57–59). (And each revelation about Manly's past and present relationships further erodes his "uniqueness.") The Captain's response, "a Wench is like a Box in an Ordinary, receives all peoples Money easily; but there's no getting, nay shaking any out again: and he that fills it, is surest never to keep the Key" (62–64),[58] may be interpreted beyond its casual misanthropic parameters to suggest his fear of the feminine, the image of the womb-like enclosure, which has drawn him in and made him helpless to escape—the entendres attacking the image of the all-consuming female.

It is now very difficult to see Manly's insufferable and stale observations as much more than a contrivance allowing him to transfer the realization of his own insecurity and weakness to an *ad nauseam* attack on society. Freeman is as immune to Manly's criticism as Manly is to Freeman's insistence that he sees things less cynically. Manly *does* move toward a state of reluctant acceptance—but the movement is slight and quiet, hardly matching the aggressive and vociferous attempts by each man to make his point. Accordingly, when Manly claims that he can always return to his sanctuary on the sea, Freeman, now incredulous, replies, "Give you a Ship! why, you will not solicit it," to which Manly answers, "If I have not solicited it by my services, I know no other way" (V.ii.84–86). Initially, Manly seems blind to the fact that the sea provides little sanctuary, given that his ship has sunk. And his "independence" in refusing to ask for a vessel because his past service deserves its reward is again undercut because he *expects* human interaction from others based on loyalty and gratitude—two qualities he refuses to accept as part of the human lot.[59]

The intrusion of Novel and Plausible's ongoing debate aggravates as well as entertains those who remain intrigued by the darker implications of the revenge motif, but their presence does provide Manly another occasion to spout *his* philosophy and condemnations, which by now are as intolerable as that of his two visitors: "Yes, a Fool, like a Coward, is the more to be fear'd behind a Man's back, more than a witty Man: for, as a Coward is more bloody than a brave Man, a Fool is more malicious than a Man of Wit" (V.ii.177–79)—a remark in its circuitous construction and logic illustrating the stasis connected with Manly and his general perspective. He criticizes Novel's incessant verbiage: "thou art always talking, roaring, or making a noise" (183–84), failing to appreciate both that Novel's way is matched by his own bellowing and that Novel's way is at least more dynamic—action and stimulation (although negative) marking his performance—a clear contrast to Manly's desire for silence and retreat. Novels' energy ("Talking is like Fencing, the quicker the better" [188]) sweeps us along and represents the inevitability of life's rapidity and flux regardless of those like Manly who wish to simplify and suppress it, forcing it to a halt. And Manly also faults Novel for always talking "without thinking" (192)—suggesting that the deep "thinker" (Manly) often refuses to live because all action must be subordinated to a carefully conceived philosophy—a kind of contemplation that breeds the stagnant perfectionism that will not budge until all conditions are met. And Manly's "I have nothing to say to you" (266)—as he pushes everyone out of the room—contrasts sharply with Novel's final words to Oldfox: "you Fools have never any occasion of laughing at us Wits, but when we quarrel; therefore let us be Friends, *Oldfox*" (257–59)—the former statement signifying the covert, surreptitious, and blackened nature of Manly's vision; the latter, the enthusiasm for battle and lack of cloying residue in the mind of one who moves and acts, accepting the combative nature of human relationships. Manly is thus appropriately a sailor—one who delivers broadsides—one who navigates

4: "SURROUNDED WITH SO MANY FEARS AND GRIEFS"   169

away from shore and often away from battle as quickly as he entered into it.

Manly's embracing his one "friend," Vernish, completes the portrayal of his ludicrous heroic sensibility. And Manly's "affection" for Vernish is based not on any sincerity but on desperation, in order to save at least part of the heroic triad of which Manly boasted earlier. Vernish is quite adept at attacking his friend's virility, covering with a "varnish" of praise severe commentary on Manly's failures: "he that is in your arms, is secure from all fears whatever; nay, our Nation is secure by your defeat at Sea, and the *Dutch* that fought against you, have prov'd enemies to themselves only, in bringing you back to us" (V.ii.92–95). Vernish enjoys playing Manly's confidant, especially in hearing him complain of Olivia's betrayal. Having the rare occasion through indirection both to satisfy his desire for destroying Manly and attacking Olivia, she who vanquished him earlier, Vernish finds, to his distress, that his manhood is threatened by Manly's admission of his own ineptitude and abuse: "Ay, a Mercenary Whore indeed; for she made me pay her, before I lay with her" (122–23). Manly of course wishes to construct a scenario in which his ego may be salvaged, although in the same breath he casts aspersions at it: in his desire to assault Olivia, he has tranformed her into a "Mercenary Whore" who lessens that very revenge by making Manly pay[60] (again, for something he did not actually do). And there is the ever-present interruption as Manly is about to share with an increasingly agitated Vernish ("a confounded Whore indeed!") the details of his sexual "success" with Olivia (149–50) but is prevented from doing so by Freeman and the other males who are pressing in to see Manly and demand his interaction.

After being told that Olivia has no intentions of giving him his money—Vernish gleefully adding that she would spare not a shilling to "save you from starving, or hanging, or what you wou'd think worse, begging or flattering; and rails so at you, one wou'd not think you had lay'n with her" (268–71)—Manly advises that Vernish "never trust, for that matter, a Womans railing; for she is no less a dissembler in her hatred, than her love" (272–73)—such aspersions cast at another railer of course undercutting the impact of his own frequent railing.[61] Nor does Wycherley ignore the matter of antifraternalism as his last play comes to a close. After informing Manly that he cannot procure for him any funds, Vernish says under his breath, "Yet wou'd rather end your wants, by cutting your throat" (294–95)—the violent allusion making the two men, for once, truly "brothers." Even Manly's embrace of Vernish is encroached upon by Novel who "looks in, and retires again": "these Fools, you see, will interrupt us" (303). Manly calls Olivia's "cuckold" a fool who could not tell the difference between his young "voluntier" and a young women, forcing Vernish to ponder his own conception of reality: "I cou'd not be deceiv'd in that long Womans hair ty'd up behind; nor [in] those infallible proofs, her pouting, swelling breasts: I have handled too many sure not to know 'em" (311–13). Vernish is left, then, to ponder the significance of his being vulnerable to another male: "Perhaps, [Olivia] is his Wench, of an old date, and I am his Cully, whil'st I think him mine; . . . if he has but lately lay'n with her, he must needs discover, by her, my treachery to him; which I'm sure he will revenge with my death, and which I must prevent with his, if it were only but for fear of his too just reproaches" (349–55).

It is most fitting that the last scene in Wycherley's canon is set near the bed—in the darkness—in an anticipation of some erotic activity, for a sexual dynamic (in many guises) has marked almost every moment of his four plays. Olivia's preoccupation with satisfying her passions recalls Othello's obsession with meeting out justice to Desdemona; both blow out candles, Olivia in the hope that finally the act may be consummated and her frustrations alleviated: "my Husband is gone; and go thou out too, thou next interrupter of Love" (V.iii.2–3).[62] The "Kind darkness" casts comforting shadows on the brilliant and agonizing light of truth. Amorously, Olivia attempts to deter any second thoughts from her "timorous young" lover: "I hope, my Dear, you won't have [a fit] to night; and, that you may not, I'll lock the door, tho' there be no need of it, but to lock out your Fits" (9–11)—the gender reversal of incarcerating the pliable male suggesting her more masculine and thus unnatural ways. Still, Olivia hopes as well to lock out interruption, her true "aversion," and revel in the safety she finds in the darkness and closed confines—in the fertile and feminine environment.

Manly strives mightily to break free of Olivia's hold on his emotions, but to no avail: "Well, thou hast impudence enough to give me Fits too, and make Revenge it self impotent, hinder me from making thee yet more infamous, if it can be" (13–15).[63] Fidelia stalls with an allusion to patience—a virtue as anachronistic in Wycherley's world as blind faith—and Olivia's response displays the intense agitation that is more characteristic of authentic human behavior: "How! time enough! True Lovers can no more think they ever have time enough, than love enough: You shall stay with me all night; but that is but a Lover's moment. Come. . . . I'm resolv'd not to be interrupted" (18–20, 29–30). The disappointment experienced in another example of coitus interruptus rises in proportion to the increasingly louder knocking on the door; Olivia's idyllic grotto of pleasure is now under attack by Vernish and Manly—each attempting to reassert his masculinity in all its primitive unmajesty. With some regret, I would argue, we listen to a resigned Olivia lament, "Then here is the happiest minute lost" (39).

As in his other three plays, the physical activity is pronounced as the play comes to its end—entering, exiting, reentering, breaking in, running forward with sword, fencing, stopping, starting, embracing, pulling, and pounding. Olivia moreover finds that she has been locked in by her husband—the more typical pattern of female incarceration. In addition to the characters themselves, Wycherley's major motifs make their final appearance: we see the forced entry of others to interrupt the pleasures of the flesh, the light (the torches being held by the sailors) from which the characters naturally turn, the destructive nature of male relationships, and the horror of discovery. And it takes a literal kicking down of the door to prepare for the shock of revelation. Olivia's tying together two curtains to make a rope for her escape signifies her trying to keep order and control while all around her is fragmenting rapidly, best represented, perhaps, not by the men fighting in the room but by Fidelia's peruke falling off and her long hair tumbling down. And Olivia reveals once more the self-sequestration from her sex as she metaphorically hangs herself with her own cords: "What?—*Manly!* And have I been thus concern'd for him, embracing him? And has he his Jewels again too? What means this? O 'tis too sure, as well as my shame! which I'll go hide for ever" (67–69). Wycherley demonstrates that a woman who severs herself from her sex or *attempts* to act differently must pay a price no less severe than that paid by Pinchwife or the other males.

The confrontation in the darkness between Manly and Vernish depicts two men fighting more overtly than any of Wycherley's other male characters, who only reach a point of drawing. We witness as well Fidelia's running "at Vernish behind"—an active gesture but one with no effect on her stronger opponent. This blithe symbol of faithfulness and sincerity does have vitality, but it cannot be expected to affect much on its own—it is not strong enough to challenge successfully the brute strength of human instinct, the fierce nature of life. To be linked as she is to a potential rape shows also her qualities are impure; they must be mixed with the vulgar, animalistic, and violent; they cannot remain pristine and angelic. Fidelia's suffering a wound in her arm and fighting against fainting is her rite of passage into the real world, which helps prepare our acceptance of her marriage to Manly. Faith must get itself dirty and bloody if it is to be successful; like sincerity, it will be found as imperfect as is Freeman (Fidelia will likely wear a scar for the rest of her life) and somewhat inconstant, but it can be a part of human interaction, tempering—if only slightly—the other rougher human desires, fears, and behaviors that nothing, not even vigorous satire, can alter.

Manly's discovery of the truth about Olivia and Vernish—indirectly of course since no one tells it to his face—stuns him, seemingly justifying his commitment to misanthropy. But he is quickly softened upon learning that his "little Volunteer" is a woman. Whereas she has "deceiv'd" him, he learns that deception may at times be altruistic and not simply malignant. In his realization, Manly places himself below Fidelia, offering the kind of homage he earlier extended to Olivia and an appropriate "apology": "the sense of my rough, hard, and ill usage of you, (tho' chiefly your own fault) gives me more pain now 'tis over, than you had, when you suffer'd it" (101–3). Although he fights on with his qualifications ("tho' chiefly your own fault"), he is now willing to accept the termination of his mythic fantasy (heroes don't apologize), his language reflecting a sincerity of its own, a gentleness that marks the slight though important change in his perspective: "Then, take for ever my heart, and this with it; [Gives her the Cabinet] for 'twas given to you before, and my heart was before your due" (113–15).[64]

After the Widow Blackacre offers to help her fellow woman through the law, Olivia leaves voicing revenge, a device we recall most memorably perhaps in Shakespeare' Malvolio, Etherege's Loveit, and Congreve's Fainall.[65] We have no idyllic conclusion, with Olivia apologizing or converting, mainly because Wycherley's tempestuous world does not lend itself to such pleasing denouments. But although exposed and thus with her greatest fears realized and her power abated because she is known, we trust that Olivia will survive her loss and eventually claim other victories, using her beauty, dominating personality, and sexual aggressiveness to her advantage.[66] Even though the play evinces little poetic justice, Wycherley evidently found no reason to tie up everything neatly: he gave us open-ended, indeterminate possibilities at the end of his first three plays, and this one is no different. The triumph of sincerity and faith is not total or in any way grand, but it does alter Manly's demeanor (he even offers consoling words to the "Rascal" Vernish as he dispatches him), but it cannot alter the *world*—Olivia, Vernish, Novel, Plausible, the Widow Blackacre, and Freeman will go on as usual. The "justice" lies primarily in the showing of Manly's philosophy as wrong, as unhealthy, no matter how hard he tries to assert its validity. That he receives the benefits of sincerity and faithfulness (Freeman and Fidelia) actually substantiates his error—the futility of his philosophy—and therefore they are just *punishments* by being rewards.[67]

Fidelia demonstrates her tenacity and newly-gained ascendency as she *pulls* Manly "from the company" and reveals to him the riches he has won by accepting her openly. Fidelia "Gray," an embodiment of faithfulness is an "onely Child"—a solitary wanderer, rich and determined, yet whose wealth and power must remain latent until she is openly acccepted. Her last name, as often noted, suggests an ambiguity—neither black nor white; but it also implies that she is no longer pure (in her being an accomplice to the rape plot, being assaulted by Vernish, seduced by Olivia, and cut in the fight between Manly and Vernish). As Manly's words suggest, sincerity and harsher reality are not a perfect blend but are more satisfying than a rejection of life: "I was going to tell you, that for your sake onely, I wou'd quit the unknown pleasure of a retirement; and rather stay in this ill World of ours still, tho' odious to me, than give you more frights again at Sea, and make again too great a venture there, in you alone" (152–56).[68]

Manly then embraces Freeman as a friend and concedes that "there are now in the World / Good-natur'd Friends, who are not Prostitutes, / And handsom Women worthy to be Friends" (167–69). With more than a little irony, then, Manly ends where he began: with one woman, one male friend[69] and with a general hostility to the world as he sees it, thus preventing him from ever being as free and healthy as Freeman. But whereas he continues to resist human nature and the immutable state of things, this one-woman/one-friend construct is now mainly stripped of the grandiose isolation Manly had conceived with Olivia and Vernish. The "heroic" qualities they represented are now replaced by the persistent influence of faithfulness and sincerity, which may yet shape Manly into a less vitupertaive and insufferable man. The ending is a proper conclusion to a realistic play that does not take upon itself the task of showing how the world may be corrected but rather how a small victory may be won for the individual in the midst of often hostile reality.[70] Even so, the acceptance of sincerity and faith will always seem anachronistic, out of place, and incongruous (as Freeman's marriage to the Widow Blackacre rather than to his seemingly more natural mate, Eliza). And Fidelia, demonstrating *her* acceptance of reality, has encouraged Manly to embrace her with enticing visions of financial gain as well as of a loyal and affectionate wife. With the words "Yet, for my sake, let no one e're confide," Manly ends the play still fearful of losing control and seeming vulnerable. That is, although through his acceptance of Freeman and Fidelia he has achieved some security and comfort; he is still a man with instinctive anxieties that will probably never be completely eradicated. Perhaps at best we have witnessed only a movement from cynicism (if not nihilism) to a healthier skepticism.

If there is any clear message at the end of *The Plain-Dealer,* it may be that one cannot always live by uncompromised principles or philosophy—or a fervant desire to correct the world. One must live by accommodating and adapting, much as Freeman does. To claim Freeman as Wycherley's one ideal character risks almost universal disagreement because his actions are not morally or ethically pure. Nor is he as scintillating a figure as Horner, as psychologically interesting as Pinchwife or Manly. It is what Freeman stands for that is ideal in Wycherley—the acceptance of what is inevitable, an accommodation with the truths of human behavior and motivation, which allow for faithfulness and sincerity. The most compelling irony in *The Plain-Dealer* is perhaps that in resisting the heroic individualism important to Manly, Freeman is so very unique among Wycherley's male characters by being so very fit for the world.

5
Conclusions: "More Fears, Plagues and Torments Yet in Store!"*

THE PLAYS OF WILLIAM WYCHERLEY MAY BE SAID TO REFLECT THE VIEW of later psychoanalysis—that the purpose of investigation is not to eradicate a series of evils but rather to understand the elemental instincts, which are neither good or bad in themselves. Yet, these comedies do not advocate Rochester's sentiment, "Such natural freedoms are but just: / There's something generous in mere lust"[1]—for much of Wycherley's point has been to show that *free* expression is impossible (and dangerous) in the real world. The characters' frequent cloaking of sexual meaning in "acceptable" speech therefore reflects Foucault's belief that until Freud, especially from the mid-seventeenth century on, there were established "procedures meant to evade the unbearable, too hazardous truth of sex."[2] Patricia Meyer Spacks adds of the "female struggle between sexual passion and moral control": "It is specifically sexuality that, women fear, cannot be regulated or contained."[3] The reshaping and rechanneling of the volatile Dionysian urges and preoccupations mark almost every one of Wycherley's characters—the males consigning their frustrations, fears, and deficiencies to others and funneling their anxieties into aggressive behavior against fellow males, with the women reminding them always of their weakness, to which the males invariably respond with threatening language and gesture. Despite being recalled for posterity as "Manly" or "Brawny" Wycherley, this playwright never hesitates in showing just how fragile is the very concept of masculinity.

Felicity Nussbaum observes in her study of misogynistic literature that "it would require another and very different study to trace the history of antifeminist thought in Restoration comedy and domestic tragedy."[4] If it were done, it should refuse to indict Wycherley. And I do not mean to push forward a Christina or Alithea as saving exceptions to the antifeminist Juvenalian stereotypes. We find that Lady Flippant, Flirt and Flounce, Mrs. Caution, Lady Fidget, Mrs. Squeamish, the Widow Blackacre, and Olivia—whom the playwright supposedly despised or attacked with purpose and relish—all respond to the basic desires for free expression, for sexual activity of actual and figurative kinds, for ascendency and dominance, and for survival—fearing restriction in any form and avoiding debilitating inhibitions and the spiritual death fated for Margery Pinchwife. These women possess a vitality that charms, invigorates, troubles, torments, and allures. More than simply sexually charged; they are intelligent, resourceful, ingenious, undaunted, altruistic, and powerful.[5] In short, they are all *alive,* serving as graphic contrast to many of the males who, in their various states of fear, represent a kind of living death—all pointing toward some kind of destructive end. And in opposition to the male's regressive tendency to attack and destroy one of his own sex, we have the woman's inclination to aid, comfort, and protect her sister. Accordingly, Wycherley shared the Hobbesian position: "And whereas some have attributed the Dominion to the Man onely, as being of the more excellent Sex; they misreckon in it. For there is not always that difference of strength, or prudence between the man and the woman, as that the right can be determined without War."[6]

The most popular road taken to a more simplified understanding of Wycherley is, of course, that marked "Satire." Many strong and respected voices from Dryden to Zimbardo (and since) have examined and praised the satirical and corrective nature of Wycherley's plays, especially his last. I have suggested throughout this study that satire, in general, is to Wycherley something more incidental than designed. After all, anyone who writes about the frailties of men and women cannot help including what we would term satire, but I disagree with the assertion that Wycherley "can *only* be understood as a master of a distinct generic form, moral satire" (my emphasis).[7] Whereas one may argue that Wycherley displays the "social and moral standards from which the noble class has fallen," we still have to ask just where in the plays do we see those standards upheld or revealed? Are we merely to assume them? Moreover, *The Plain Dealer* poses several problems for the critic, and even Rose Zimbardo agrees that one purpose of the play is "to satirize satire itself."[8] And others have considered conscious and unconscious motivations of seventeenth-century satirists, concluding that satire of the period does not necessarily have to be corrective in intent. Yet when all the critical dust settles, I still do not find Wycherley's plays as mainly or even largely satirical—in either the common or generic sense of the term.[9] Perhaps Northrop Frye's handy definition may help: "Sheer invective or name-calling ('flyting') is satire in which there is relatively little irony: on the other hand, whenever a reader is not sure what the author's attitude is or what his own is supposed to be, we have irony with relatively little satire."[10]

Without question, the clothing of the satirist can be tailored to fit

5: CONCLUSIONS

William Wycherley; however, it seems to me an uncomfortable fit—with the playwright always straining at his collar. Wycherley wears better the scientist's frock, examining (not attacking) the weaknesses and obsessions of human beings—more interested in observing that very art of assailing. Yet the preponderance of criticism portrays him as the aggressor: he "attacks," "ridicules," "despises," "condemns"; and certainly an emphasis on his "observing," "revealing," and "studying" is far less muscular or glamorous in its seeming passivity than the virile satirist of traditional criticism. But commentators have also found some problems in the consistency of Wycherley's satire and have had to contend with such questions as "Is Horner both satiric agent and object?" As Fredric Bogel points out, there has also been a "charade of moralistic apology in which critics of satire have been encouraged to engage: justifying a writer's satiric attacks by arguing that such attacks serve moral ends and that the satirist may thus escape charges of negativism or superiority or attraction to the debased and repellent."[11]

Eliza says to Olivia, "Well, but Railing now is so common, that 'tis no more Malice, but the fashion; and the absent think they are no more the worse for being rail'd at, than the present think they are the better for being flatter'd" (*PD,* II.i.73–76). That such attacks on superficiality and hypocrisy are commonplace only dilutes the effect of *anyone's* vigorously offering familiar strictures on the world. Even Eliza is a physician who cannot heal herself, for whereas hers is a more altruistic kind of correction (unlike Manly's malicious and egotistical railing), such sober criticism has no effect on Olivia's thoughts and actions. The satirist (for argument's sake Eliza's role here) may hold up a mirror for the sinner to peer into but the natural inclination, in Wycherley at any rate, is to turn from that reflection. As Hippolita notes of Monsieur de Paris, "This Fool, I see, is as apt as an ill Poet to mistake the contempt and scorn of people for applause and admiration" (*GDM,* III.i.32–33). One may argue that, even though Horner's criticism of female hypocrisy has no effect on Lady Fidget, it might well strike home to a woman who sees or reads the play. But then again, one need only recall Olivia's reaction to *The Country Wife.* She certainly did not learn to temper her apparent superficiality by seeing the play; she simply saw what she wanted to and no more—her ego, like everone else's, being fully able to block out the negative image of self. Manly's incessant broadsides have no influence on others, on society—not even on himself, as we find him acting more and more like those he professes to despise. His satirical voice is one crying out in a wilderness, all right—a place where people just do not live.

Novel makes a cogent observation when he tells Oldfox, "So much for talking; which I think I have prov'd a mark of Wit; and so is Railing,

Roaring, and making a noise: for Railing is Satyr, you know; and Roaring, and making a noise, Humor" (V.ii.206–09). In Wycherley, "satire" serves to release the frustrations of insecure and fearful human beings; yet, such a release satisfies only temporarily, and then only the one who makes the outburst. As Novel tells Oldfox, in the end "You rail, and no body hangs himself" (V.ii.249). If we need further evidence, we might look to Freeman's last words in the play: "I think most of our quarrels to the World, are just as we have to a handsom Woman: only because we cannot enjoy her, as we wou'd do" (V.iii.161–63). Some seventy years later, Joseph Warton was to comment in his satire "Ranelagh House" (in the "Manner" of Le Sage) on one young satirist's topic, "Reasons for entering Bedlam": "Yet he himself deserves a place among his own madmen for thinking, as he does, that the follies and vices of mankind are to be reform'd by satire and ridicule."[12]

A study of these plays moreover encourages a consideration of the critical latitude allowed in an analysis of works originally meant for stage production. Because Wycherley's plays are "stage pieces," W. R. Chadwick reminds us, we ought to avoid those vehicles assembled to travel "down the road of interpretation"—and yet Chadwick too climbs into his own critical set of wheels and rolls forth on the journey. He mentions further that writing with particular actors in mind "implies an interesting declaration of intent as regards the type of play Wycherley wrote."[13] Whereas such evidence suggests a certain kind of intent, it has little to do with the finished product—the printed text that survives long after the bodies of Mohun, Hart, Nokes, Boutell, and Knepp have turned to dust. Without question it is (or ought to be) historically interesting and relevant to recall that Shakespeare wrote with Armin; Otway with Barry; Congreve with Bracegirdle; and Cibber with Oldfield in mind. But these facts should in no way restrict one's assessment of the *result* of dramatic *literature*.

Besides, did Shakespeare's expectations regarding how Burbage was to act Richard III or Hamlet limit Garrick's, Kean's, Gielgud's, Olivier's, and more recently Branagh's "interpretations" of these characters? What of televised or filmed Shakespeare as opposed to Shakespeare on the stage of the Globe, at Blackfriars, at Drury-Lane, or in Central Park? That one can interpret more creatively with camera close should not be frowned upon because the plays were not written with cameras in mind. And then the theatrical interpretations of Wycherley's comedies (mainly *The Country Wife*) and the audience reactions to them have hardly been uniform. B. Eugene McCarthy's bibliography of Wycherley studies, for example, provides us with a glimpse of the critical divergence among theater critics in the twentieth century—suggesting the power directors and actors have (and have always had) on the shaping of one's assessment of the play. (That is, whatever "solid" intentions Wycherley had when writing *The Country Wife* did not seem to pass on with subsequent performances.) And several of these responses also speak to the double-sided world of the viewed and the read Wycherley. Edward Shanks (1924) noted that he was "nauseous" when he read *The Country Wife,* but impressed when he saw it; Ivor Brown (1934) was surprised to find no "moral rage" after seeing the play; Ashton Leigh (1936) was angered at the audience's delight at the play's indecency; and the *Times* (1950) wrote of *The Gentleman Dancing-Master* that is "was more amusing to read" and of a BBC radio presentation of *Love in a Wood:* "hard to weld coherently together on stage" but comes together well in the "mind's eye" on radio. We also find A. C. Ward (1958) commenting that plays such as *The Country Wife* are boring and objectionable if not done *well* on stage; and Gerald Weales (1958) adding that the play was funny but not as "angrily funny" as Wycherley should be done—and later (1973) complaining that modern productions do not understand *The Country Wife* well at all.[14] As Robert Hume concludes, "If twentieth-century audiences can respond in radically different ways to the same play, ... then why should a seventeenth-century audience not respond just as variously."[15]

And can we really doubt that some of the more intelligent and sophisticated members of Wycherley's audience thought maturely about what they had recently seen on stage—realizing something significant in private about what they merely laughed at in public? "In the world of make-believe," John Harold Wilson points out, "the husband whose wife was unfaithful was usually presented as a comic figure, to be laughed at for his jealousy, his stupidity, or his credulity. In reality, the seventeenth-century cuckold was a pitiable fellow."[16] This is not to say that Pinchwife is a "pitiable fellow," but Wilson's observation rightly assumes that an audience was entirely capable of viewing such a character in both the worlds of theatrical make-believe and the one its members actually inhabited. There are some who would argue, as Arthur Scouten has done, that the plays are "static"—that by and large they ought to be seen and not read; yet others, such as David Vieth, can appreciate the "almost mystical ambiguity" of Wycherley's dramatic efforts. Some, such as Katharine Rogers, have observed that drama "cannot be fully effective when one's attitude toward the characters is made to fluctuate"; whereas others, myself included, find such fluctuation and indeterminacy a truer reflection of life and a mark of engaging drama.[17]

We might also consider other factors that make production a shaky basis for restricting evaluation of Wycherley's plays. What liberties were taken with the script/text that Wycherley handed to the producer and actors? What was cut to save time or to highlight something more comically effective? What of an actor's looks, hints, gestures? Such mannerisms can go a long way toward twisting meaning far from so-called authorial intent. And what were the physical attributes that guided the actor's interpretation and the audience's reaction? "None of the actors possessed copies of the whole text," Jocelyn Powell informs us; "[t]hey had their 'parts' carefully written out by the prompter, with cue-lines only added." And performing a part on stage did not preclude a variety of interpretations: the role of Pinchwife "gives Mohun a series of fascinating opportunities to suggest emotional depths in ironical contexts."[18] Surely, Harriet Hawkins has it right: "there should be a limit to how much any critic can use verifiable evidence about how the 'original audience' might have responded to deny our own right to respond, fully and naturally to the play itself."[19] In addition, we have the determination of the theater historian Peter Holland: "In each case, indeed in every part" of *The Plain-Dealer*, audience "expectations were thwarted, turned back on them"; the play demonstrates an "ever increasing group of preconceptions overturned, of patterns unfulfilled."[20] Finally, Dryden observed that "In a playhouse, *everything* contributes to impose upon the judgment.... But as 'tis my intent to please my audience, so 'tis my ambition to be read: that I am sure is the more lasting and nobler design" (emphasis added).[21]

A critic/historian no less erudite and influential than Robert Hume finds *The Country Wife* a farce above all else, and no one need to see it beyond that—in fact interpretations that do so need to be discouraged. But the neatly bundling of a play in a generic straight-jacket (or in a historical binder) is most unfortunate. If the play is no more than a farce, then the critic's scalpel will find nothing but air as it cuts through. That so much more has been discovered in the play is not simply evidence of the critic's ingenuity—no matter how off the wall—but rather a testament to the value of *The Country Wife* as effective dramatic *literature*. To Hume and Judith Milhous, all interpretations must be measured against their producibility on stage. They point to the "fact" that "the efforts of some fifty critics [writing on *The Country Wife*] add up to total confusion" and that because certain interpretations do not seem "communicable in performance" they are therefore illegitimate. Again, although it is of historical importance (and of much interest) to determine which possibilities would have been the most stageable in 1675, it seems unnecessarily limiting to dismiss any and all of the "unproducible" interpretations, which include in the main "tortuous (and unproducible) subtleties"—or to lump all "nonproducible" intepretations into the now obese "Critical Muddle." Even so, Milhous and Hume admit to the difficulty of staging Wycherley's plays then or now: the playwright "does not specify"; "Our best guess is"; "the essential openness of the script Wycherley has given us"; and the "astonishing latitude Wycherley leaves his performers makes the exact constitution of any one actual production unusually arbitrary."[22]

We may look as well to prologues and epilogues, which reveal, albeit often comically, the playwright's disappointment at the audience's inability to comprehend or appreciate what they are about to see or have just seen. And contemporary evidence clearly testifies to the difficulty and ambiguity of some stage performances—for example, Dennis's comment on *The Plain-Dealer* that the town "appeard Doubtfull what Judgment to Form of it."[23] What good does it do to claim, as John Harwood does, that "Messrs. Hart, Mohun, Lydal, and others could only present one interpretation at a time"[24] when it is evident that not every perceptive member of the audience would have agreed on what that interpretation was—or whether it was the "correct" one. Should we really limit ourselves to those approaches that see these plays merely as scrapbooks of Restoration performances? Obviously, the reader of the play, regardless of any inclination to read it as performed action, has the opportunity an audience does not have of pausing to absorb a significant passage, going back and read again an earlier section bearing heavily on another one, and dwelling on character, motivation, symbol, structure, and language. Rereading the play demands a far different approach to *The Country Wife* than viewing it would. And what of those who see the play for the second or third time? The "concentrations" of the second or third viewing are considerably different than the first—where following the plot is the primary concern. Nor can I accept the validity of Kenneth Muir's assertion that "we never feel . . . we need to read *[The Country Wife]* in order to extract the full favour."[25] A tantalizing flavor one may indeed get from *only* seeing (or visualizing) it staged, but the *full* flavor?

Although I agree with Robert Hume that the plays should not be simplified to one handy or operative theme, I question the way he dismisses a large number of interpretations: "All fine and dandy—but how do we prove it?" But what is there to *prove* irrefutably? How much of literary criticism can be *proved*? Hume has every right, of course, to call for more hard scholarship on the theatrical history of Wycherley's plays and of Restoration drama in general—and who would not welcome such studies and read them with considerable attention?—but to claim that other kinds of work are shallow because they are done "with a paperback text, a pad of paper, and inspiration" too easily and certainly unfairly (even though wittily) dismisses a good deal of penetrating criticism.[26] And along with Milhous, Hume takes arms against an ocean of critics, against the "chaotic state of Wycherley criticism" and strikes a heavy retaliatory blow: "to imagine that there is a single 'valid' interpretation is madness."[27] The hyperbole aside, does a critic actually believe he or she is offering the one and only way to look at *The Country Wife?* I doubt this very seriously. One offers *another* view—one the critic feels is correct or more correct than others—but one not necessarily mutually exclusive of others (or parts of others). I find much healthier the spirit implied in Samuel Johnson's observation that "Truth like beauty varies its fashion, and is best recommended by different dresses to different minds."[28] That Shakespeare wrote a particular kind of tragedy, history, or comedy because the form was especially popular with his audiences has never really limited critical response to his plays—nor should it have. It seems, however, that Restoration scholarship must guard against becoming too protective of its valuable historical gains in recent years. And finally, in response to Rose Zimbardo's uncategorical position that "Neither Manly nor Freeman, nor indeed any other character in any of Wycherley's plays, has interiority or 'psychology,'" one offers a polite "What?"[29]

Frank Kermode, among others, has helped to clarify our thinking about multiple interpretations, especially of those "canonical texts" such as *Hamlet* (and we could add on a lesser scale *The Country Wife* and *The Plain-Dealer*): "that however a particular epoch or a particular community may define a proper mode of attention or a licit area of interest, there will always be something else to say.... There can be no simple and perpetual consensus as to the proper way to join the shadow of comment to the substance of the play." And Kermode suggests that such indeterminacy and flexibility is reflective of the play's worth as dramatic literature: "in short, the only role common to all interpretation games, the sole family resemblance between them, is that the canonical work, so endlessly discussed, must be assumed to have permanent value and, which is really the same thing, perpetual modernity."[30] And this seems to me one important reason why Wycherley endures—why he has been the subject of considerable literary criticism as well as historical interest. A muddle? Hardly.

To John Harwood, some ambitious critics "suggest an unconscious projection of several modern prejudices into the comedies, and their theories require them to distort considerably some plays."[31] The question is "distorting according to what?" Text? Authorial intent? Stage production possibilities? I see nothing wrong with such projecting if the play will bear it or if the play *encourages* it—for after all, the critical emphases on satire and moral purpose may be projecting a variety of "modern" and personal prejudices onto Wycherley's plays as well. I do not agree with all of Anthony Kaufman's reading of *The Country Wife,* but I find it an intriguing analysis of Horner—one the play encourages— one that should be considered and then accepted, amended, or rejected. I cannot dismiss it simply as a piece of antihistorical eccentric criticism.

And the limits of the closed-shop attitude is reflected best, I think, in Hume's assertion that "Delightfully bawdy and funny *The Country Wife* is; profound it is not, and only a prude, a hypocrite, or a stuffy academician would have it otherwise."[32] Again, I prefer the conclusions of Harriet Hawkins: "In fact, the drama itself demonstrates that seventeenth-century playwrights felt perfectly free to bless some very unconventional, passionate, idiosyncratic, perhaps truly moral, perhaps completely immoral, characters with the unanswerable arguments of poetry and truth to human experience." "If the drama is going to hold a mirror up to human nature at all," she adds, "the mirror is bound to reflect—above all—human individuality. And thus it is going to reflect human passion, wickedness, idiosyncrasy, courage, and isolation.... So often the seventeenth-century drama seems much braver than some twentieth-century criticism of it."[33]

Perceptive critics have appreciated the period's complexity and indeterminacy, qualities that make Wycherley's plays attractive to modern readers. David Vieth argues that the period often "suspends judgment; it questions, though it does not doubt; it wishes to believe, but is not sure it can." Jean Hagstrum sees the period's events working against assumptions of uniformity and encouraging conflict of thought: "England too had known fire and disease, which produced abundant opportunities to feel terror and tenderness, to say nothing of the tensions that came in the wake of the Civil War and must often have produced an intolerable psychological strain." Lawrence Stone moreover posits one theory worth contemplating—the "constant tension between the natural desire for freedom of the individual will and the pressing need for social order"—a tension I find most conspicuous in Wycherley's plays.[34] I believe that more intelligent members of Wycherley's audience could not always check such realities at the playhouse door; sheer escapism Wycherley's plays were not. "Much as men enjoyed and indulged the pleasures of life," Jocelyn Powell reminds us, "they also needed to comprehend and analyse them, making the very act of living one of fascinating self-consciousness"; the "brilliance of the period was rooted in paradox."[35]

Although painting and architecture in the 1670s were evolving away from the baroque forms of earlier in the century, in several respects we can look upon Wycherley's plays as indicative of the Baroque style—in which we find light and shadow so expertly contrasted and blended, restless forms in perpetual contest, the eye unable to rest on any one place. In general, Baroque art saw the significance of displaying the innermost character of the person portrayed—that which survives superficial and transient appearances. We find in such paintings as Vermeer's "Artist in His Studio," Rubens's "The Toilet of Venus," and several of the works of Georges de la Tour eyes looking away, backs turned, figures looking at us indirectly through mirrors, light screened by shadow and object—all suggesting the indeterminate and obfuscatory nature of life. Psychological depth meant something to these artists—as I think it did to William Wycherley. And although other dramatists, Otway for example, evinced a strong interest in the darker aspects of human nature, Wycherley is able to depict what he sees as the disturbing truths of human motivation and behavior without losing the exuberance that he felt also marked much of life.

Unlike his splendid contemporary Etherege and successor Congreve, who divert and engage their readers with the magic and sparkle of their art, Wycherley puts his hands roughly on the readers' shoulders to detain them. We do not leave Wycherley feeling so much relieved or really delighted as somewhat fatigued—yet still more intrigued by the experience of having read him. In Wycherley's comedy of fear there is an unmistakeable pleasure and exhilaration in revealing what the fears and weaknesses are; there is no sense of his turning away from them with disgust. His appeal is in the way he deals with these basic instincts and impulses and articulates and analyzes them in the controllable form of comic drama—its own kind of propriety to which the playwright must pay his court. We are drawn to Wycherley in large part, then, because he tells us something about ourselves; he titillates our imagination. In his plays Wycherley lures the reader into a labyrinth, from which there is no easy exit. We are frequently led to believe or expect one thing based on familiar patterns on dramatic convention and then find that our expectations have been all or at least in part incorrect. Always, we must think, question, and doubt as we consider the vastly fascinating aspects of human nature. By confronting and engaging the reader, Wycherley involves one in a way not duplicated in Etherege, Dryden, Vanbrugh, and Congreve. And Manly's words to Fidelia near the end of *The Plain-Dealer* say so much regarding our engagement with their author: "I desir'd you to bring me out of confusion, and you have given me more" (V.ii.99–100). For this reason, above all others, he must be judged not the most polished or most witty, but easily the most engaging of all the Restoration comic dramatists.

Notes

INTRODUCTION

The quotation from the introduction title is from *Love in a Wood*, III.iii.132.

1. Collier's *A Short View of the Immorality and Profaneness of the English Stage* (1698) and Macaulay in "Comic Dramatists of the Restoration," *Edinburgh Review* 72 (1841): 490–528. Situated between Collier and Macaulay, Joseph Warton was less severe in his estimation, although he still felt compelled to shake his finger at the "wicked triumverate" of Wycherley, Congreve, and Vanbrugh. See Warton, *Adventurer* 105 (6 November 1753). A particularly helpful introduction to the traditions and attitudes toward the period's comedy is John T. Harwood's *Critics, Values, and Restoration Comedy* (Carbondale and Edwardsville: Southern Illinois University Press, 1982). For an overview of Wycherley criticism, see Robert D. Hume, "William Wycherley: Text, Life, Interpretation," *Modern Philology* 78 (1981): 399–415; and B. Eugene McCarthy, *William Wycherley: A Reference Guide* (Boston: G.K. Hall, 1985). An antidote to simplistic and outdated perceptions of the period's drama would be Hume's "Content and Meaning in the Drama," in Hume, *The Rakish Stage: Studies in English Drama, 1660–1800* (Carbondale and Edwardsville: Southern Illinois University Press, 1983), pp. 1–45.

2. Virginia Birdsall and Thomas Fujimura have tempered the emphasis on Wycherley as vigorous satirist, however—the former finding that at the very least Wycherley seemed "torn between the tolerant comic view and the angry satiric one," with the latter concluding that, whereas he is sometimes a satirist, the evidence is "against treating him as a fierce satirist." Still, Rose Zimbardo holds to the view that, regardless of those who would think otherwise, Wycherley *was* a satirist and perceived himself as one and that if "we want to understand the satire of this elusive joker, we have to look to his plays, not to critical speculations about them"—although one assumes that these "speculations" (including her own) so emerged after careful "looks" at the four plays. Virginia Ogden Birdsall, *Wild Civility: The English Comic Spirit on the Restoration Stage* (Bloomington: Indiana University Press, 1970), p. 108; Thomas Fujimura, *The Restoration Comedy of Wit* (Princeton: Princeton University Press, 1952), p. 119; Katharine M. Rogers, *William Wycherley* (New York: Twayne Publishers, 1972), preface and pp. 87, 90; Rose Zimbardo, *Wycherley's Drama: A Link in the Development of English Satire* (New Haven: Yale University Press, 1965), pp. 2, 16, 18—views restated in Zimbardo's entry "William Wycherley" in Paula R. Backscheider, ed., *Restoration and Eighteenth-Century Dramatists, First Series* (Detroit: Bruccoli Clark Layman, 1989), pp. 263–300 [see p. 271]; P. F. Vernon, *William Wycherley* (London: Longmans, Green, 1965), p. 12; John Harold Wilson, *A Preface to Restoration Drama* (Cambridge: Harvard University Press, 1968), pp. 155, 165; Bonamy Dobrée, *Restoration Comedy, 1660–1720* (Oxford: Clarendon

Press, 1924), p. 86; William Freedman, "Impotence and Self-Destruction in *The Country Wife,*" *English Studies* 53 (1972): 421; W. R. Chadwick, *The Four Plays of William Wycherley* (The Hague: Mouton, 1975), p. 179; John E. Cunningham, *Restoration Drama* (London: Evans Brothers, 1966), p. 77; Donald Bruce, *Topics of Restoration Comedy* (London: Victor Gollancz, 1974), p. 128; Zimbardo, "Wycherley: The Restoration's Juvenal," *Forum* 17 (1979): 22.

3. Although he writes specifically of the *The Country Wife,* Richard Steiger makes a telling point when he asserts that Wycherley "neither supports nor satirizes the hypocrisy of Restoration society; he merely presents it as the inevitable context within which the individual must survive." And more recently Peter Hynes has concluded that Wycherley reveals in his plays an affinity for "neopragmatism." Steiger, "'Wit in a Corner': Hypocrisy in *The Country Wife,*" *Tennessee Studies in Literature* 24 (1979): 68; Hynes, "Against Theory?: Knowledge and Action in Wycherley's Plays," *Modern Philology* 94 (1996): 188.

4. Hume, "William Wycherley: Text, Life, Interpretation," p. 411; Zimbardo, "William Wycherley," p. 283.

5. Rogers, *William Wycherley,* p. 97; Thompson, *Language in Wycherley's Plays* (University: University of Alabama Press, 1984), p. 4; Powell, *Restoration Theatre Production* (London: Routledge & Kegan Paul, 1984), p. 144; Friedson, "Wycherley and Molière: Satirical Point of View in *The Plain Dealer,*" *Modern Philology* 64 (1967): 195.

6. See particularly Derek Hughes, "*The Plain-Dealer:* A Reappraisal," *Modern Language Quarterly* 43 (1982): 315–36; Anthony Kaufman, "Wycherley's *The Country Wife* and the Don Juan Character," *Eighteenth-Century Studies* 9 (1975): 216–31; Kaufman, "Idealization, Disillusion, and Narcissistic Rage in Wycherley's 'The Plain Dealer,'" *Criticism* 21 (1979): 119–33; David Vieth, "Wycherley's *The Country Wife:* An Anatomy of Masculinity," *Papers on Language and Literature* 2 (1966): 335–50; W. Gerald Marshall, "Wycherley's Drama of Madness: *The Plain Dealer,*" *Philological Quarterly* 59 (1980): 26–37—views restated in Marshall, *A Great Stage of Fools: Theatricality and Madness in the Plays of William Wycherley* (New York: AMS Press, 1993); and Freedman, "Impotence and Self-Destruction in *The Country Wife.*" David Vieth, for instance, concludes that *The Country Wife* is "remarkable for the individuality of its characterizations and the depth of its treatment of them" (p. 335).

7. Kaufman, "Wycherley's *The Country Wife* and the Don Juan Character," p. 222. Skura, *The Literary Use of the Psychoanalytic Process* (New Haven: Yale University Press, 1981), p. 4. Skura writes that character analysis "provides a vital meeting place for psychoanalysis and literature, where problems in interpretation arise with particular force and clarity" (p. 33).

8. Sutherland, *English Literature of the Late Seventeenth Century* (Oxford: Clarendon Press, 1969), p. 115.

9. Rose Zimbardo is certainly correct to note that in a literary study "Wycherley the man is of no consequence; it is Wycherley the poet who concerns us." I would add that neither should Wycherley "the inheritor of stage or literary tradition" in any way limit our approach to his plays. Zimbardo, *Wycherley's Drama,* p. 78.

10. Kenneth Muir provides another reality to consider: "One says 'reader' rather than 'spectator' because there have been no professional performances of *[The Plain-Dealer]* in recent years." (Although revivals of the play have occurred since Muir's study—for example, the London production of 1989.) Muir, *The Comedy of Manners* (London: Hutchinson, 1970), p. 82.

11. I know something of what I speak, for I staged a production of *The Country Wife* in 1990, in which the interpretation of Wycherley's play was affected not only by my own critical beliefs but also by the particular strengths and limitations of the actors cast, the restrictions of the limited stage space, and an understanding of and concession to the audience's level of sophistication. (The same is true of my productions of Goldsmith's *She Stoops to Conquer* in 1988, Sheridan's *The Rivals* in 1997, and Sheridan's *The School for Scandal* in 1999.)

12. McMillin, ed., *Restoration and Eighteenth-Century Comedy* (New York: W. W. Norton, 1973), p. vii.

13. Rochester, *A Satyr against Reason and Mankind* (II.139–56) in David M. Vieth, ed., *The Complete Poems of John Wilmot, Earl of Rochester* (New Haven and London: Yale University Press, 1968). For more on Hobbes and the drama, see Derek Hughes, *English Drama, 1660–1700* (Oxford: Clarendon Press, 1996), pp. 12–17.

14. Specifically, Wycherley uses "fear," "fears," "fear" (as verb), "feared," "fearful," "afraid," "fright," "frighten," "frightened," "dread," and "terrify'd" *at least* (I may have missed a couple) forty-five times in *Love in a Wood*, forty times in *Gentleman Dancing-Master*, thirty-three times in *The Country Wife*, and fifty-one times in *The Plain-Dealer*.

15. Commentary from Hobbes to Freud has of course informed us that laughter is often the reflection of some fear or anxiety—laughter at the relief over having been saved from that which distresses us. See Hobbes, "On Laughter" and Freud, *Jokes and Their Relation to the Unconscious* (1905) in *The Standard Edition of the Complete Psychological Works of Sigmund Freud*, vol. 8 (London: The Hogarth Press, 1953).

16. The omission of Wycherley's poems is not meant as a comment regarding their worth to modern readers. My concentration is rather on that relatively small body of dramatic work that has earned Wycherley his reputation—and will be responsible for keeping it in the future.

Chapter 1: Into the Labyrinth

1. Such as Calderón's *Mañanas de abril y mayo*. See John Loftis, *The Spanish Plays of Neoclassical England* (New Haven: Yale University Press, 1973), pp. 121–25; P. F. Vernon, "Wycherley's First Comedy and Its Spanish Source," *Comparative Literature* 18 (1966): 132–44; and J. U. Rundle, "Wycherley and Calderón: A Source for *Love in a Wood*," *PMLA* 64 (1949): 701–7. Rundle complained that "no other Restoration play . . . assimilated Spanish material so poorly as does *Love in a Wood*" (p. 707). Just why this should be a valid complaint seems unclear. Vernon defends Wycherley by noting that the playwright "borrowed with discrimination and that his revisions of his source reveal a consistent awareness of the play's total meaning" (p. 133). Derek Hughes believes that here we see Wycherley involved "with the Anglicization of Spanish drama, though in ways which took it well away from the old intrigue pattern." Hughes, *English Drama*, p. 122.

2. Rose Zimbardo detects borrowings from Jonson and especially Fletcher: the play is a "pastoral romance," she argues, the first step in Wycherley's progress from "pastoral to satire." Robert Hume is quick to remind us that "double-plot plays were not uncommon earlier in the century: *Much Ado About Nothing* is structurally quite a close parallel," and he argues that what the play "says about

cits, rakes, love, and avarice ... does not transcend the commonplace." Eric S. Rump and Derek Cohen have evaluated the play's farcical construction, and W. Gerald Marshall has found the low, middle, and high plots united and delineated through the concept of "providential order," in which the characters "receive a retributive justice that is meted out with uncanny precision." Another structural approach is that of John Bowman: "Think of the play as a great masked ball in which partners are constantly changing partners." Zimbardo, *Wycherley's Drama,* pp. 24–33; Hume, "Diversity and Development in Restoration Comedy, 1660–1679," *Eighteenth-Century Studies* 5 (1972): 376, 393, and also "Content and Meaning in the Drama," in *The Rakish Stage,* p. 29; Rump, "Theme and Structure in Wycherley's *Love in a Wood," English Studies* 54 (1973), 326–33; Cohen, "The Farce Pattern of Wycherley's *Love in a Wood," English Studies in Canada* 3 (1977), 267–77; Marshall, "Wycherley's *Love in a Wood* and the Designs of Providence," *Restoration* 3 (1979), 8–16; Bowman, "Dance, Chant and Mask in the Plays of Wycherley," *Drama Survey* 3 (1963): 184.

3. James Thompson writes that *Love in a Wood* is "a relatively straight-forward and conventional intrigue comedy, where we know whom to approve and whom to disapprove," with Rose Zimbardo concluding that the "geography" is "Fletcherian in its heights and Jonsonian in its depths." W. Gerald Marshall has moreover reinforced the handy critical separation of low, middle, and high plots in his study of theatricality in Wycherley's plays. Thompson, "Ideology and Dramatic Form: The Case of Wycherley" in Carl R. Kropf, ed., *Reader Entrapment in Eighteenth-Century Literature* (New York: AMS Press, 1992), p. 166—a reprint of the essay's first appearance in *Studies in the Literary Imagination* 17 (1984), 49–62; Zimbardo, "William Wycherley," p. 275; Marshall, *A Great Stage of Fools,* pp. 19–44. Brian Corman also notes the "three distinct levels of courtship intrigue" but appreciates the way Wycherley "links" the three worlds. Corman, *Genre and Generic Change in English Comedy* (Toronto: University of Toronto Press, 1993), p. 28.

4. My estimation is not shared by most commentators. For instance, Kenneth Muir quickly dismisses Lady Flippant by noting that she "is ridiculed because of the contrast between her words and her deeds"—or, as J. Douglas Canfield succinctly puts it, because she is "a sexual hypocrite." T. W. Craik finds that "her grotesque style and her grotesque actions ... combine to make her character too unreal to have any satirical effectiveness"—a position seconded by Rose Zimbardo: Flippant has the "indiscriminate appetite of the nymphomaniac." Here we find, as we frequently do in Wycherley, an assessment unfortunately hampered by the assumption that the overall vision of the play is moral or satirical. Muir, *The Comedy of Manners,* pp. 67–68; Canfield, *Tricksters & Estates: On the Ideology of Restoration Comedy* (Lexington: University Press of Kentucky, 1997), p. 101; Craik, "Some Aspects of Satire in Wycherley's Plays," *English Studies* 41 (1960): 169; Zimbardo, *Wycherley's Drama,* p. 35; and "Wycherley: The Restoration's Juvenal," p. 20.

5. All quotations are from *The Plays of William Wycherley,* ed. Arthur Friedman (Oxford: Clarendon Press, 1979). Other editions include *The Plays of William Wycherley,* ed. Peter Holland (Cambridge: Cambridge University Press, 1981); *The Complete Plays of William Wycherley,* ed. Gerald Weales (New York: New York University Press, 1967); and the recent handy paperback publication of the four comedies edited by Peter Dixon (Oxford: Oxford University Press, 1996).

6. Although I do not share his emphasis, Robert Markley at least treats the

matter with more sophistication: "Lady Flippant's 'honour' may begin as unambiguous deceit but becomes more complicated and self-deceiving as she repeatedly invokes it. She has not merely perverted 'honour' into a sign for dishonour but so corrupted the word's moral and lexical significance that she has no way of restoring it to a 'normal,' pristine state." And Derek Hughes rightly points out that Lady Flippant "introduces the sense of chaotic flux that is to run through the play." She is the "personification of social dislocation." Markley, *Two-Edg'd Weapons: Style and Ideology in the Comedies of Etherege, Wycherley, and Congreve* (Oxford: Clarendon Press, 1988), p. 147; Hughes, *English Drama*, pp. 122–23.

7. And a more overtly sexual reference might be detected as well: as Roger Thompson reminds us, "copulation in risky, improbable places"—such as "in a lottery booth at Tonbridge, in the playhouse and in coaches"—was "popular" in seventeenth-century pornography. Thompson, *Unfit for Modest Ears* (Totowa: Rowman and Littlefield, 1979), p. 122.

8. See also John Tatham's *The Rump*, Abraham Cowley's *Cutter of Coleman Street*, John Wilson's *The Cheats*, and John Lacy's *The Old Troop*, all of the early 1660s. John Loftis comments, "The savagery with which Gripe is depicted . . . provides a reminder that *Love in a Wood* is a Cavalier's play, bristling with the remembered resentments of the Civil Wars." On the other hand, A. N. Kaul thinks that the playwrights missed an opportunity to make more of the "bourgeois culture" than they did: "Restoration comedy has no true Malvolios. Its Puritans and citizens, if given a voice at all, are not given the slightest semblance of a case. Often, like Alderman Gripe, they are shown as rakes too—middle-class rakes, motivated as exclusively by pleasure-seeking as the courtly rake and lacking only the courtier's savoir faire." Without question, Kaul is correct to blur the lines of distinction between men like Gripe and the more acceptable rake figures. Loftis, *The Spanish Plays of Neoclassical England*, p. 122; Kaul, *The Action of English Comedy* (New Haven: Yale University Press, 1970), pp. 107–8. For more on the playwrights' treatment of the Puritan characters, see Ben Ross Schneider, Jr., *The Ethos of Restoration Comedy* (Urbana: University of Illinois Press, 1971), pp. 37–71.

9. That these characters are comfortable with graphic double entendre is quite evident later when Mrs. Joyner warns Mrs. Crossbite, "I say beware, the sweet bits you swallow, will make your daughters belly swell, Mistress; and after all your Junkets, there will be a bone for you to pick, Mistress" (III.i.41–43).

10. For more on the perversity of the old Puritan figure see Thompson, *Unfit for Modest Ears*, pp. 50–54.

11. More particularly, critics have pointed to the Hobbesian "sudden glory" theory of conflict and laughter that speaks to one's sense of superiority (for audience and reader as well as character) over the person laughed at or ridiculed. Virginia Birdsall finds the "Hobbesian spirit of the time" conducive to good comedy, since the Hobbesian "appetite"—in its vital and unintimidated qualities—smacks into "the teeth of social repression." Conversely, Ben Ross Schneider questions such Hobbesian emphases in the plays, observing that "generosity" and "courage" are parts of the dramatic ethos. We often see fighting among males, he writes, because the society values "physical courage." I believe Birdsall is closer to the mark. Birdsall, *Wild Civility*, p. 37; Schneider, *The Ethos of Restoration Comedy*, pp. 58, 72, 81.

12. *Leviathan*, Everyman Edition (London: J. M. Dent & Sons, 1973), p. 50.

13. Besides, he adds, he will "throw off" Dapperwit when he marries—the

implication being that his "friend" will suffer the supreme humiliation of being let go in favor of a woman he wants but cannot have. And yet, despite Addleplot's fanciful estimation of his own virility and power (he will "court" both Lady Flippant and Martha—the "two strings" to be played by his phallic "one Bow"), he will be reminded by Joyner that it is the female who actually plays upon the instrument. She of course takes his money, for which she will promise him a woman his own personality cannot possibly win.

14. The characters reflect well Hobbes's position that speech may "signifie" what men and women "desire, feare, or have any other passion for" (*Leviathan*, p. 13.) Critics have long noted the richness and significance of Wycherley's language, but not to the extent that James Thompson has done: "language [in Wycherley's comedies] is a glass that exposes the innermost man, by means of a consistent coincidence of stylistic and ethical qualities, a parallelism of moral and verbal conduct." *Language in Wycherley's Plays,* p. 5. Robert Markley offers another perspective: "Wycherley relentlessly sets words against actions to undermine comforting notions of linguistic stability." Markley, *Two-Edg'd Weapons,* p. 139.

15. Robert Markley comments, "For Dapperwit and Vincent, wit is a form of detraction, a verbal rendering of basic antagonisms between men of the same class who frequent the same company." I would counter only that this antagonism has little to do with class similarity. Markley, *Two-Edg'd Weapons,* p. 142.

16. Joceyln Powell writes that "the actor's job was to build a proper image of his character, to physicalise it in descriptive gesture that was exciting in its aptness, so that the character was as perspicuous in the visual design of the entertainment as it was in the structure of the text—*if necessary more so*" (my emphasis). Powell, *Restoration Theatre Production,* p. 105.

17. Later, Dapperwit will say of Lucy Crossbite that after she makes herself up and "warrant[s] her breath with some Lemmon Peil," the "dore flies off of the hindges, and she into my arms." The sexual entendre ("dore flies off of the hindges") aside, Dapperwit clearly depicts an aggressive female giving full vent to her sexual exuberance (III.ii.80–82).

18. The sexual allusion should not be missed. Men having standing intercourse in London then and later was not uncommon. A famous instance would be Boswell's dalliance with a London prostitute during his stay in 1762–63: "She allowed me entrance. But the miscreant refused me performance. I was much stronger than her, and *volens nolens* pushed her up against the wall. She however gave a sudden spring from me; and screaming out, a parcel of more whores and soldiers came to her relief" (4 June 1763). *Boswell's London Journal, 1762–1763,* ed. Frederick A. Pottle (New York: McGraw-Hill, 1950), pp. 272–73. Earlier, Shakespeare had his Sampson tell Gregory, "I will push Montague's men from the wall and thrust his maids to the wall" (*Romeo & Juliet,* I.i.15–16)—quickly followed by a friendly (and thinly veiled) discussion of lost maidenheads and flaccid penises.

19. Her name, in later seventeenth-century usage, meant something a little different than the modern *flippant:* "marked by disrespectful levity or indifference." Instead, we find the word conveying such associations as "nimble," "moving lightly or alertly," "talkative," "sparkling," "sportive," "playful," "*une coquette*" *(OED).*

20. And Ranger himself announces his "[i]ntending a Ramble to St. *James*'s Park to night, upon some probable hopes of some fresh Game" (I.ii.81–82). Boswell would make clear that little had changed in the passage of a century: "I felt

carnal inclinations raging through my frame. I determined to gratify them. I went to St. James's Park, and, like Sir John Brute, picked up a whore." London Journal, p. 227. Roy Porter adds that in the eighteenth century "Sex in public was quite acceptable. Prostitutes and their clients copulated in St. James's Park." Porter, "Mixed Feelings: the Enlightenment and Sexuality in Eighteenth-Century Britain" in Paul-Gabriel Boucé, ed., *Sexuality in Eighteenth-Century Britain* (Manchester: Manchester University Press, 1982), p. 9.

21. Rochester writes of the long history of sexual activity and sexual frustration associated with the place:

> When ancient Pict began to whore,
> Deluded of his assignation
> (Jilting, it seems, was then in fashion),
> Poor pensive lover, in this place
> Would frig upon his mother's face. . . .

Nature too succumbed to the sexual fever:

> Whence rows of mandrakes tall did rise
> Whose lewd tops fucked the very skies.
> Each imitative branch does twine
> In some loved fold of Aretine,
> And nightly now beneath their shade
> Are buggeries, rapes, and incests made.
> (ll.14–24)

Rochester, *A Ramble in St. James's Park* in Vieth, *Poems,* pp. 40–47. Vieth dates the poem to "Before 20 March 1672/3." Obviously, Hazlitt did not have Rochester's poem (or even Wycherley's play) in mind when he wrote, "Happy thoughtless age, when kings and nobles led purely ornamental lives; when the utmost stretch of a morning's study went no farther than the choice of a sword-knot, or the adjustment of a side curl; when the soul spoke out in all the pleasing eloquence of dress; and beaux and belles, enamoured of themselves in one another's follies, fluttered like gilded butterflies, in giddy mazes, through the walks of St. James's Park!" *The Complete Works of William Hazlitt,* ed., P. P. Howe, 21 vols. (London: Dent, 1930–34), 6:70.

22. Norman Holland is right to assert that "for Wycherley, the country stands for a place where one's inner nature is very close to the surface." However, it would be wrong to think that it may not be equally so in town. One requires only the sense of enclosure (security) in book-lined chambers or in tree-lined parks to shed imposed or self-imposed inhibitions. Holland, *The First Modern Comedies: The Significance of Etherege, Wycherley, and Congreve* (Cambridge: Harvard University Press, 1959), p. 43.

23. James Sutherland comments, "Since comedy is traditionally a Dionysiac revel, expressing the unrestrained and unregenerate nature of man, it might be expected that from its first beginnings Restoration comedy would show that libertine spirit which was to become so characteristic of it." Here, though, I see "Dionysian" meaning "intense" or "frenzied" as well as "unrestrained." Mark Morford and Robert Lenardon ask, "Was the celebration of [Dionysus's] worship a cry for release from the restraints of civilized society and a return to the mystic purity and abounding freedom of nature, or was it merely a deceptive excuse for self-indulgence in an orgy of undisciplined passion?" W. R. Chadwick believes

that, in the subtitle, Wycherley may also be using "in a wood" (normally meaning "confused" or "perplexed") in its other sense of being mad or in a frenzy. Sutherland, *English Literature of the Late Seventeenth Century,* p. 89; Morford and Lenardon, *Classical Mythology* (New York: David McKay, 1971), p. 188; Chadwick, *The Four Plays of William Wycherley,* p. 25. For more on the spirit of permissiveness, see Dale Underwood, *Etherege and the Seventeenth-Century Comedy of Manners* (New Haven: Yale University Press, 1957), esp. chap. 2, "The Fertile Ground."

24. Northrop Frye adds that "Ritual is not only a recurrent act, but an act expressive of a dialectic of desire and repugnance: desire for fertility or victory, repugnance to drought or to enemies." *Anatomy of Criticism: Four Essays* (Princeton: Princeton University Press, 1957), p. 106. My emphasis in this scene is therefore more on sexual agitation and posturing than is John Bowman's: "The expressive effect of such stagecraft must be a conscious one, and although the whole play is not constructed in such an involved pattern, there still exists enough movement throughout to project a continuous effect of a masked ball." Bowman, "Dance, Chant and Mask in the Plays of Wycherley," p. 184.

25. On the level of entendre, "I was never put to't yet" cannot really suggest Flippant's sexual inexperience (a highly unlikely possibility), but rather either her lack of success with this group of men or with men in general since she began actively seeking male acquaintance—*or* perhaps her admission that she has always been the *active* partner in her relations with men ("putting to" rather than "being put to"). As Lawrence Stone writes, the common view in the seventeenth century was that suitors of widows were expected to come up with "aggressive sexual advances." We may trust that Lady Flippant was quite familiar with the old adage, "He that wooeth a widow must go stiff before." Stone, *The Family, Sex and Marriage in England, 1500–1800* (New York: Harper and Row, 1977), p. 281. And later, when she complains that no "Satyr," "no Burgundy man, or drunken Scourer" has found his way to her, even though she "left the Herd on purpose to be chas'd" (V.i.168–71), it appears that it is her forwardness, not an aged or otherwise unsightly appearance, that is frightening to the men she seeks to attract. Custom had after all dictated that a woman must do her hunting more subtly.

26. It is therefore intriguing that Lady Flippant and Gripe are of the same blood, not because of any similarities but because of their stark differences: the one reflective of the diseased and cloying, the other of the vibrant and delightful aspects of human motivation and interaction.

27. Foucault concludes that, beginning with the seventeenth century, "Calling sex by its name" became "more difficult and more costly": "As if in order to gain mastery over it in reality, it had first been necessary to subjugate it at the level of language, control its free circulation in speech, expunge it from the things that were said, and extinguish the words that rendered it too visibly present." Michel Foucault, *The History of Sexuality,* trans. by Robert Hurley (New York: Random House, 1976; trans. 1978), 1:17. In this vein, Lady Flippant announces, "I abominate honourable Love, upon my Honour" (II.i.77–78), which does not imply smuttiness as much as it signifies a stimulating kind of virility—"honourable Love" connoting platonic and "boring" kinds of affection.

28. Addleplot observes out loud to a masked Flippant that the woman who "stray'd" from him earlier is "bow-legg'd," "hopper-hipp'd," and toothless, with the complexion like "Holland Cheese" and the breath of the foulist kind (152–54). A literal description?—or more likely a kind of misogynistic release of his

anger and frustration at one who had tormented him? It is unclear when Elizabeth (Mary) Knepp (Wycherley's Lady Flippant, Lady Fidget, and Eliza) was born, but an educated guess based on the evidence (a 1664 reference to her as an actress, for example) would be a birthdate between 1644 and 1647, putting her in her mid to late twenties when she performed in the premiere of *Love in a Wood*. Knepp captivated Pepys with her voice and vivacious stage presence and apparently allowed him, probably on more than one occasion, to "tocar her corps all over and besar sans fin her"; "but did not offer algo mas," he added on 23 April 1668. Thomas Fujimura provides a refreshing exception to the prevailing view: he calls Flippant the "most original and entertaining character in the play," a "naturalistic creature, anticonventional and sexual." Brian Corman adds that she, along with Gripe, Addleplot, and Dapperwit are "the most effective characters" in the play. Robert Latham and William Matthews, eds., *The Diary of Samuel Pepys,* 11 vols. (Berkeley: University of California Press, 1970–83), 9:172; Philip H. Highfill, Jr., Kalman A. Burnim, and Edward A. Langhans, *A Biographical Dictionary of Actors, Actresses, Musicians, Dancers, Managers, and Other Stage Personnel in London, 1660–1800* (Carbondale: Southern Illinois University Press, 1973–), 9:53–57; Fujimura, *The Restoration Comedy of Wit,* p. 128; and Corman, *Genre & Generic Change,* p. 30.

29. Writing in general terms about Restoration comedy, Thomas Fujimura observes that there is "pleasure in skeptical, malicious, and sexual wit because our repressed tendencies are satisfied by the short cut provided by wit; and such relief from restraint is conducive to mental health." *The Restoration Comedy of Wit,* p. 65.

30. Earlier that evening Lady Flippant had "eat up" Addleplot's "meat, and drank her two bottles" and then run off leaving him "alone"—i.e., sexually checkmated. Foucault writes of a kind of sexual power that asserts itself "in the pleasure of showing off, scandalizing, or resisting." *History of Sexuality,* p. 45.

31. *The Country Wife* and even *The Plain-Dealer* show us that Wycherley expected his audience to accept that in staged drama time moves far more rapidly in the bedroom than in any other part of the house. Therefore, we cannot doubt Addleplot simply on the grounds that not enough time had elapsed for him to do to Lady Flippant what he here claims.

32. Interestingly, an anagram of Addleplot's alias *Jonas* is *Jason*—he who met the quintessentially irresistible force in Medea. Perhaps, then, even Sir Simon's alias is addled.

33. Some might gloss "to squeek" in a more innocent context—such as simply to cry out in anger. However, given Wycherley's predilections, the sound certainly reverberates with good sexual acoustics. Not surprisingly, Boswell again assists in the identification: "She wondered at my size, and said if I ever took a girl's maidenhead, I would make her squeak." *London Journal,* pp. 49–50.

34. Christina has vigorous support among critics—many of whom have embraced her as one of the few "moral" characters in this or in any of Wycherley's plays. For example, Rose Zimbardo takes the "faithful Shepherdess" designation literally, noting that Christina, with her "high plot ideals," serves Wycherley's satirical ends by being a sharp contrast the the "low" behavior and goals of Gripe, Mrs. Crossbite, Lucy, and Addleplot—an endorsement seconded by Norman Holland, who believes that Christina "establishes the ideal against which the other people are measured," and by W. Gerald Marshall, who finds that she is "intended" by Wycherley as "the positive embodiment of virtue." James Thompson adds that her honor "is a matter of internal worth, rather than

reputation": she "rises in our estimation." On the other hand, P. F. Vernon contends that "It is difficult to take even the suffering of the innocent Christina very seriously, since her solemnity is undercut by the witty, and not unwholly unjustified, mockery of her maid Isabella." Robert Markley characterizes her as "the worthy woman attached to the worthless or uncaring man," but carefully points to her rhetorical shortcomings: her language is "a redaction of Fletcherian sentiment: passionate, histrionic, and excessive.... Her language, like Ranger's wit, allows her only to choose her fetters, not to escape them." Finally, Katharine Rogers finds Christina reflective of the playwright's failure at this stage to understand that "sentimental heroics" do not belong in a Comedy of Manners. This of course assumes that Wycherley *intended* Christina to be seen as a paragon— a conclusion with which I cannot agree. Zimbardo, "Wycherley: The Restoration's Juvenal," p. 22; Holland, *The First Modern Comedies,* p. 42; Marshall, *A Great Stage of Fools,* p. 44; Thompson, *Language in Wycherley's Plays,* p. 52; Vernon, "Wycherley's First Comedy and Its Spanish Source," p. 134; Markley, *Two-Edg'd Weapons,* pp. 148–49; Rogers, *William Wycherley,* p. 37.

35. Wycherley will make most use of *Twelfth Night* in his *Plain-Dealer,* but even here we can detect still another parallel. Christina informs Lydia, "I have made a resolution to see the face of no man, till an unfortunate Friend of mine, now out of the Kingdom, return" (II.ii.87–88). Matters of devotion aside, Christina's vow is reminiscent of Olivia's determination to reject living for ostensibly nobler reasons. Shakespeare's Olivia, owing to the death of her brother, "hath abjur'd the sight / And company of men." Both Olivia and Christina might profit from the wisdom of Sir Toby's philosophy, "I am sure care's an enemy to life." *Twelfth Night,* I.ii.40–41; I.iii.2.

36. From Christina we also hear, "you mistook me for another"; "I never saw your face before"; "this is the first time you ever saw me?"; "when did you see me last ...?"; and "lest you should be seen go hence"—to which Ranger replies, "I was resolv'd to see you"; "since I have seen you"; "my Cousin is but a tolerable woman to a man that had not seen you"; "'tis not the hundreth time I have seen you; for since the time I saw you first"; "but I saw you"; "it was my business to watch"; and "I am in Love I see"—all in the space of some seventy lines (105–77). Later, Christina tells Isabella, "we will pass it by, lest the people of our lodging shou'd watch us" (IV.ii.65–66).

37. The reference to Penelope calls to mind that exemplar of marital fidelity and patience, but mythological allusions in Wycherley may follow the pattern of his plays and go beyond the common perception. Penelope's story also recalls the attempt of Icarius, her father, to control her life, his desire to keep her confined to his world, his active involvement in her marriage to Odysseus, his feelings of betrayal and impotence when she chose her husband over him, the constant attention of suitors while Odysseus was away, and Odysseus's killing of the suitors upon his return—many of Wycherley's dramatic concerns being present in the mythological reference. Regarding the familiar question, although it is certainly impossible to know if we are faced with an allusion (or extension of an allusion) *intended* by the author, one cannot pronounce with certainty either that the better educated and imaginative of Wycherley's early readers would not have pondered the implications of a reference to Penelope.

38. Zimbardo, "Wycherley: The Restoration's Juvenal," p. 24. Other commentators, such as James Thompson, see Valentine as representative of the "noble idealism" that contrasts with "rakish expediency" (Ranger). Departing considerably from the consensus view of Christina and Valentine, Cynthia Matlack

argues that their relationship "parodies the love-honor conflicts in heroic plays," and she reminds us that both Betty Boutell (Christina) and Edward Kynaston (Valentine) had already performed in heroic drama, the former as Benzayda, the latter as Boabdelin in Dryden's *Conquest of Granada*. I cannot agree that Wycherley provided a deliberate parody of the heroic genre (that actors played both roles seems interesting though here thematically insignificant), but Matlack's belief that Christina may be more subject to "ridicule" than deserving of admiration (to Marshall she is "the new Eve, the shepherdess who can lead us into a restored Eden") appears to me right on target. Even A. N. Kaul's depiction of the Christina-Valentine relationship as "wholly Platonic and wooden" does not go far enough in divorcing it from the realm of the ideal, although Robert Markley's characterization of Valentine—with his language of "self-flagellating certainty"—as "the first of Wycherley's neurotics" certainly does. Finally, Brian Corman finds Valentine more a Jonsonian "humours" character, with Wycherley's being "heir to Jonson's comic mantle." Thompson, "Ideology and Dramatic Form," p. 55; Marshall, *A Great Stage of Fools,* p. 44; Matlack, "Parody and Burlesque of Heroic Ideals in Wycherley's Comedies: A Critical Reinterpretation of Contemporary Evidence," *Papers on Language and Literature* 8 (1972): 276–78; Kaul, *The Action of English Comedy,* p. 110; Markley, *Two-Edg'd Weapons,* p. 148; Corman, *Genre & Generic Change,* p. 30.

39. One might argue that Vincent approaches the *honnête homme* character not really common, as Robert Hume reminds us, until the 1690s but anticipated by several early examples, such as Worthy and Lovetruth in *The Country Gentlemen* (1669). Thomas Fujimura adds that Vincent "seems to represent a middle ground of common sense and honesty, as opposed to the extremism of the others"—a man "characterized by sound judgment." I would say, however, that his judgment is not always sound in regard to human behavior and that Wycherley can only be ironic, if he intends, as Norman Holland suggests, Vincent's name to mean *vincere* ("to conquer"), for in truth he rides at the head of an army of shadows. Hume, "The Myth of the Rake in 'Restoration Comedy'" in Hume, *The Rakish Stage,* p. 158; Fujimura, *The Restoration Comedy of Wit,* p. 130; Holland, *The First Modern Comedies,* p. 39.

40. Susan Staves, among others, has enlarged our perspective of the fops, who do much "more than display the evils of superficiality and selfishness." Staves, "A Few Kind Words for the Fop," *Studies in English Literature* 22 (1982): 395-428.

41. Later, Martha will fail to budge Dapperwit from his poetic reverie about "what a Wit without vanity is like": "he is like—he is like—a Picture without shadows, or, or—a Face without Patches—or a Diamond without a Foyl; these are new thoughts now, these are new" (V.i.100–103)—another instance of a character's straining for originality and uniqueness.

42. Even Dapperwit's demanding Ranger's comb to run through his wig suggests another attempt to dominate and usurp, more than it might common vanity (93). After Lucy peppers Dapperwit's masculinity with her rejection, Ranger feels free of course to lend sarcastic assistance: "Here, will you have my Comb again, *Dapperwit?*" (196).

43. In his modernized edition, Peter Holland includes an exclamation mark after "honeysuckle" and inserts the direction "Kisses her" after "thus and thus and thus." Friedman's, on the other hand, has no exclamation mark and places the "Kisses her" after Gripe's speech ends, after "Mrs. *Joyner,* prethee go fetch our Treat now." I prefer the implications of Friedman's old spelling text, for, in

Holland's, Gripe may come off as an aroused though harmless old fool, having each *thus* stand for an old man's feeble kiss, whereas in Friedman's Gripe is able to punctuate each *thus* with an explicit gesture or facial expression far more sinister than comic. The lack of exclamation also allows for a more deliberate contemplation of the sexual and sadistic fantasy—a more diabolical than enthusiastic response. See Holland, *The Plays of William Wycherley,* p. 64; Friedman, p. 69.

44. Perhaps the Puritan knew something of Nicholas Chorier's notorious *Tullia and Octavia,* a.k.a. *Satyra Sotadica* (the original Latin edition appearing initially around 1660), with its advocacy of "Lesbian love, sodomy, seduction of the young and innocent, multiple copulation, flagellation and more subtle forms of sadism." See David Foxon, *Libertine Literature in England, 1660–1745* (New York: University Books, 1965), p. 48. Roger Thompson elaborates on this erotic (pornographic) work of "instruction": "Octavia gives a graphic account of how her mother took her, before her wedding, to a holy man, Father Theodore, who gave her a penance of whipping. He told them that it was perfectly decent for women to strip before him as an act of piety and repentance. Then he flogs Sempronia first heavily, then lightening the blows, then fiercely again, for an hour, which the torn and welted Sempronia calls 'sport, not suffering'. Then he turns his attentions to the neophyte and beats her till the lash drips with blood while she flagellates her own clitoris. Her mother explains that this will increase the voluptuousness of her wedding night. Sempronia comes seven times with Giocondo after this holy disciplining" (*Unfit for Modest Ears,* p. 30). The parallels to the Gripe-Lucy scene are intriguing. Thompson adds that the "seducing minister" and "flagellant" were popular figures in the Restoration (p. 51). Moreover, Roy Porter observes of the eighteenth century (but, I believe, with relevance to the late seventeenth as well), "it was commonly admitted that the widespread practice of beating (e.g., in schools) was sexual in nature—an association repressed and buried in Victorian times." Porter, "Mixed Feelings," p. 12.

45. To the others who have come with her into the room, Mrs. Crossbite says, "see there the wicked Engine of the filthy execution" (403–4). The bracketed stage direction notes that she is "Pointing to the Chair" Gripe has set against the door—or to be used as a "bed." But might we also consider that the "wicked Engine of the filthy execution" to which she points is a part of his anatomy? After all, Gripe has by then apparently grabbed Lucy and attempted to commence his "lovemaking" (385–89).

46. And Mrs. Joyner's "betrayal" of Lucy ("that Treacherous false Woman, my God-mother, who has betray'd me, sold me to his lust" [397–98]) is qualified of course by its being intended as a "set-up"—with Lucy's strictly following the script: "I wish he had murder'd me, oh, oh—" (391). Mrs. Joyner's comments to Lucy before Gripe locks and bars the door, "The Gentleman will not hurt you," may be viewed as a bawd's refusal—for the sake of financial gain—to consider the vile and dangerous prospects of the sexual arrangement, but she very likely knows that all will be interrupted before any real harm can come to Lucy.

47. Wycherley may have found one inspiration for Gripe's predicament in John Wilson's popular and rough play *The Cheats* (1663), in which Alderman Whitebroth falls into the blackmailer's trap after fornicating with Mrs. Double Diligence.

48. "Discourse transmits and produces power; it reinforces it, but also undermines and exposes it, renders it fragile and makes it possible to thwart it." Michel Foucault, *The History of Sexuality,* p. 101.

NOTES TO CHAPTER 1

49. Even her subsequent remark about Ranger, "he is as impudent a dissembler as the widow *Flippant,* who is making her importunate addresses [to Dapperwit], in vain, for ought I see" (50–51), is likely more bemused than critical. Once again, our need to find satirical correction in Wycherley makes difficult extending the contextual possibilities.

50. A clear contrast to masculine discord is the kind of sorority reflective in Leonore's sound advice to Lydia that Ranger "is not worth the looking after" (V.i.270–71)—which of course has no effect on Lydia, who seems to epitomize the play's sense of unfufillment. (Lady Flippant shares that feeling, although her exuberance does not invite our sorrow or concern.) And yet, Leonore suggests, there may be comfort in comparing Lydia's empty feelings with those of other women; she advises that they find and then talk to those who have been similarly disappointed, so that they may at least share each other's misfortunes.

51. Earlier, Isabel had noted Christina's capability of expressing normal "fear and apprehensions" (IV.ii.78).

52. Aided of course by the manipulative Lucy who, in her attempt to lure the old Puritan, assures him that if "the rooms be full, we'l have an arbor ... come along" (155, 159, 166–67). Whether her ends are questionable or appropriate, Lucy's sexual assertiveness is again typical of Wycherley's female characters—and there is no need to condemn or dismiss it as immoral. In this Dionysian, rather than Appolonian, world, the arbor provides Lucy with a palpable context of power—Artemis (Diana) being her inspiration—an association punctuated by, who else, Lady Flippant, who notes the "slim pickins" among the trees: "the Park affords not so much as a Satyr for me" (169–70).

53. Valentine observes, "I had rather, indeed, he shou'd satisfie my doubts, then my revenge" (339–40)—the words *doubts* and *revenge* being important designations of masculine motivation in all four of Wycherley's plays.

54. That is, in the sense of luring, assaulting, perplexing, and irritating the reader, who expects a more familiar response. David Vieth is most responsible for defining the concept. See Vieth, "Introduction" and "Prospectus" in the special issue, "Entrapment in Restoration and Early Eighteenth-Century English Literature," *Papers on Language and Literature* 18 (1982): 227–33.

55. This behavior makes most difficult seconding A. N. Kaul's assessment that Ranger "finally stands converted at the end of Act IV." Likewise, P. F. Vernon's sympathetic treatment of Ranger—"Ranger is often ridiculous, but since he is open to change, even he is more sympathetic than his opposite number [Hipolito] in the Spanish play"—too easily passes over Ranger's actions in this scene. Vernon adds that Ranger attempts to rape "Christina" only "to revenge himself on her for having, as he imagines, separated him from Lydia." And although finding Wycherley's handling of the "reformation" somewhat weak, W. R. Chadwick pronounces with certainty that the reformation is "heartfelt as its form and tone indicate." Kaul, *The Action of English Comedy,* p. 110; Vernon, "Wycherley's First Play and Its Spanish Source," pp. 137, 138; Chadwick, *The Four Plays of William Wycherley,* p. 30.

56. W. Gerald Marshall argues that Lydia "also receives the punishment she deserves" because she has been engaged in such secret plotting. Such a conclusion as this seems once more the unfortunate result of seeing Wycherley as a playwright whose design is to mete out proper reward and punishment. Marshall, "Wycherley's *Love in a Wood* and the Designs of Providence, p. 10.

57. Blot: "*In Backgammon:* An exposed piece or 'man' liable to be taken or forfeited; also, the action of so exposing a piece" (Friedman, *Plays,* p. 110).

58. I believe, then, that Kenneth Muir's summary misses much: "It is the sincere and faithful characters who are presented for our admiration, and it is marriage rather than extra-marital adventures which seems to be regarded as the proper aim. The faithful Christina is united to her Valentine; and his friend Ranger, after some ranging, is converted at the end, so that he objects to Lydia's ironical description of 'the insupportable bondage of matrimony.'" Eric Rump also sees the conclusion as rosy: Christina and Valentine, "the heroic lovers of the play, are finally united once Valentine's jealous doubts have been dispelled" and Ranger "gives up 'Intrigues, honourable or dishonourable, and all sorts of rambling' . . . in order to devote himself to Lydia." Again, I have to wonder what it is that is so "heroic" about Valentine. Muir, *The Comedy of Manners*, p. 68; Rump, "Theme and Structure in Wycherley's *Love in a Wood*," p. 331.

59. Mrs. Joyner therefore provides an uncomfortable "bedfellow" for those concerned with "justice": "You need not fear it, like the Lawyers, while my Clients endeavour to cheat one another; I in justice cheat 'em both" (V.ii.16–17).

60. As Pepys relates, in November of 1667 Nell Gwyn and Rebecca Marshall (whom he believed, incorrectly, to be the daughter of the notorious Puritan Stephen Marshall) got into a verbal skirmish over each other's morality. Nellie said that whereas she was "whore" to only one man, Bec was "whore to three or four, though a Presbyter's praying daughter!" *The Diary of Samuel Pepys*, 8:503. Several commentators have preferred to see this revelation as pointing to the play's "retributive" designs, Gripe's being clearly deserving of having his daughter pregnant out of wedlock. But his reaction following Martha's announcement—in which he reasserts his aggressiveness—works counter to such assumptions. See W. Gerald Marshall, "Wycherley's *Love in a Wood* and the Designs of Providence," p. 9. Katharine Rogers likewise finds Wycherley reforming and punishing "selfish and heartless behavior." *William Wycherley*, p. 41.

61. A la Shakespeare's Shylock: "My daughter! O my ducats! O my daughter! O my Christian ducats!" (*Merchant of Venice*, II.viii.15–16).

62. Critics have been quick to note that the play's "use of formal devices is often awkward and its satiric point is more superficial. Above all it lacks compression"—and that in the play "the craft of comedy is whirling too fast." P. F. Vernon, "Wycherley's First Comedy and Its Spanish Source," p. 143; John Bowman, "Dance, Chant and Mask in the Plays of Wycherley," p. 193. See also, Virginia Birdsall, *Wild Civility*, p. 111; Kenneth Muir, *The Comedy of Manners*, p. 69. Yet, while noting Wycherley's inability always to maintain a "balance between the comic and the ideal," W. R. Chadwick does add that the playwright shows himself to be a "serious" dramatist—a view seconded by James Thompson, who writes that for all its faults it is "still impressive for a first play." Chadwick, *The Four Plays of William Wycherley*, pp. 43–45; Thompson, *Language in Wycherley's Plays*, p. 37.

63. *Leviathan*, p. 63.

Chapter 2: On the Edge of Discovery

1. Chesterfield's letters to his son, Johnson observed, "teach the morals of a whore, and the manners of a dancing master"—whores and dancing masters being linked without apology. Claude Rawson notes the oxymoronic effect of the term "Gentleman Dancing-Master": a "necessary part of a 'genteel education,'" dancing was taught to gentlemen by men who were not considered of the gen-

teel class, even though "the dancing-master must have acquired pretensions of gentility which exacerbated the situation." Rawson rightly assumes, then, that the title of Wycherley's play "must have derived much piquancy from this whole situation." *The Diary of Samuel Pepys,* 4:140, 158. Boswell's *Life of Samuel Johnson, LL.D.,* ed. George Birkbeck Hill, rev. by L. F. Powell, 6 vols. (Oxford: Clarendon Press, 1934–64), 1:266. Rawson, *Henry Fielding and the Augustan Ideal under Stress* (London: Routledge and Kegan Paul, 1972), pp. 27–28.

    2.   Faine would I go both up and downe, up and downe, up and downe
               No child is fonder of the gig
               Than I to dance a merry Jig
               Faine woulde I try how I could frig
               Up and downe, up and downe, up and downe,
               Faine would I try how I could caper.

See E. L. Burford, ed., *Bawdy Verse: A Pleasant Collection* (Harmondsworth: Penguin Books, 1982), pp. 64–65. Even that famous "metaphysician" Soame Jenyns suggested the inescapable link between dancing and sexual attraction. In his *The Art of Dancing* (1729), he portrays dancers of both sexes flushed with anticipation: "Each youthful breast with gen'rous warmth inspire: / Fraught with all joys, the blissful moments fly, / Whilst music melts the ear, and beauty charms the eye." He recalls Edward III's loosening the strings of a dancer's garters: "The gallant King catch'd up the lovely prize, / Whilst crimson blushes o'er her cheeks arise"; and of Herod's lust for the dancing Herodia: "Where-e'er she moved, his heart and eyes pursued." The point is impossible to miss:

> Nor think, ye fair, that any native charm
> Can e'er our eyes attract, or bosoms warm,
> Unless you learn the rules these lines impart,
> The useful precepts of the dancing Art.
> . . . .
> But when the finished dance you once have done,
> And with applause thro' ev'ry couple run,
> There rest awhile:—There snatch the fleeting bliss,
> The tender whisper, and the balmy kiss;
> Each secret wish, each softer hope confess,
> And with your hand her panting bubbies press;
> With smiles the fair shall hear your warm desires,
> While music softens, and while dancing fires.

Jenyns, *The Art of Dancing: A Poem in Three Cantos* (1729), ed., Anne Cottis (London: Dance Books, 1978), pp. 20, 28, 42, 43, 46.

    3. Juvenal continues: "If your wife has musical tastes, she'll make the professional / Singers come when she wants. She's forever handling / Their instruments, her bejewelled fingers sparkle / Over the lute." See *Juvenal: The Sixteen Satires,* trans. Peter Green (Harmondsworth, Middlesex: Penguin Books, 1974), pp. 129, 142. Wycherley would have had available to him Robert Stapylton's 1644 English translation of *Juvenal.* (Barton Holyday's was not published until 1673.) Consult Felicity Nussbaum, *The Brink of All We Hate: English Satires on Women* (Lexington: University Press of Kentucky, 1984), pp. 77–93, for the period's translations of Juvenal's *Sixth Satire.* Norman Holland sees dancing as a double entendre in the play but he makes little of it (*The First Modern Comedies,* p. 65). For a more traditional perspective consult John Bowman's "Dance, Chant and Mask in the Plays of Wycherley": "If *Love in a Wood* is a masked ball,

then *The Gentleman Dancing-Master* is an antic two-step, a bravura performance on a tightrope" (p. 185). W. Gerald Marshall believes that the comedy is immersed in the *commedia dell'arte* tradition, with constant dancing being one of its customs. Marshall, "The Idea of Theatre in Wycherley's *The Gentleman Dancing-Master*," *Restoration* 6 (1982), 1–10.

4. Karen Woods discusses the reactions to dance up to the eighteenth century in her dissertation, "Dance in England through a Study of Selected Eighteenth-Century Texts" (University of Georgia, 1995). Woods cites the work of Eric Stanley, "Dance, Dancers, and Dancing in Anglo-Saxon England," *Dance Research* 9 (Autumn 1991): 18–31; of Alessandro Arcangeli, "Dance and Punishment," *Dance Research* 10 (Autumn 1992): 30–42; and of Curt Sachs, *World History of The Dance;* Trans. Bessie Schonberg (New York: W. W. Norton, 1937), p. 282. See also Nickie Roberts, *Whores in History: Prostitution in Western Society* (London: Harper Collins, 1992).

5. I agree with W. R. Chadwick, who calls Hippolita "an archetype of the eternal Female whose drive to manipulate and dominate others in order to achieve the security she desires is common to her sex." Similarly, Virginia Birdsall finds that the play "comes close to sounding at times like a tract in defense of the emancipated woman." Chadwick, *The Four Plays of William Wycherley*, p. 61; Birdsall, *Wild Civility*, p. 122. James Thompson suggests that Wycherley may have wanted his audience to recall the Hippolita from Fletcher and Massinger's *The Sea Company*, a young woman who has been kept apart from men (*Language in Wycherley's Plays*, p. 132, n. 21). We might also consider, though, the more likely association of the name suggested by Edward Howard's *The Women's Conquest* (1671), a play that includes the intervention of the Amazons. Plays such as these and William Cartwright's *The Lady Errant* (1635–38), the anonymous *Female Rebellion* (ca. 1659), Joseph Weston's *The Amazon Queen* (1667), and Howard's *The Six Days Adventure* (1671) opt for a male-controlled society, as did Fletcher's *Rule a Wife and Have a Wife* (1624), and often show the Amazon "succumbing" to her lover. But such will not be the case with Wycherley's Hippolita. See Felicity Nussbaum, *The Brink of All We Hate*, pp. 43–56; and Jean Gagen, *The New Woman: Her Emergence in English Drama, 1600–1730* (New York: Twayne, 1954).

6. See Friedman, *Plays*, pp. 128–29, n. 1.

7. We can assume, then, that she is more than "a romance heroine" or simply Wycherley's "embodiment of his conception of 'natural innocency.'" Zimbardo, *Wycherley's Drama*, pp. 51–52; Birdsall, *Wild Civility*, p. 125. Other views of Hippolita would include the estimation of Yvonne Shafer, "Hippolita has a freshness and charm which keep her from seeming lewd or unpleasantly aggressive"; that of W. Gerald Marshall, who finds Hippolita the improviser of her own "play-world"; and that of Robert Markley: "Hippolita seems a projection of her society's casual misogyny," an "adolescent horror," who "combines Lady Flippant's libidinal energy with Olivia's machiavellism. But unlike Wycherley's female grotesques, Hippolita is pre-social rather than hypocritical." Markley believes therefore that she has a "lack of artifice," whereas Marshall finds that she is "creating her own 'plays'-within-the-play," which "allows her to act the role of a woman before actually assuming it in everyday life." Shafer, "Restoration Heroines: Reflections of Social Change," *Restoration and Eighteenth-Century Theatre Research*, second series, 12, no. 1 (1987): 45; Marshall, "The Idea of Theatre," pp. 2–4, and *Great Stage of Fools*, pp. 46, 50; Markley, *Two-Edg'd Weapons*, p. 151. The number of judicious responses has easily drowned out Bonamy Do-

brée's howl of protest, "underlying all there is a hatred Wycherley has for Hippolita because she has the desires natural to an animal"—although Dobrée was correct to detect the animalism in her character and to reject any idealistic identifications. T. W. Craik counters with the view that "the whole play demonstrates Wycherley's approval of her." Dobrée, *Restoration Comedy,* p. 85; Craik, "Some Aspects of Satire in Wycherley's Plays," p. 172.

8. Nor are we surprised by Lawrence Stone's observation that many a child of the seventeenth century "grew up with a fear and even hatred" of the parent, but it might be helpful to remember—when considering the sexuality of a fourteen-year-old—that beatings and other forms of abuse were "mitigated by much physical caressing and fondling, including genital play." Stone, *The Family, Sex and Marriage in England,* pp. 168–69, 507–12. Foucault has written that, as the century wore on, "the boisterous laughter that had accompanied the precocious sexuality of children for so long" was "gradually stifled." Foucault, *The History of Sexuality,* p. 27.

9. She tells Monsieur, "do not spare him a jot"; "railly him soundly"—the latter command she repeats four times (I.i.197–209). Prue informs us that Hippolita had occasion to learn about the ways of males and females when she attended the "*Hackney*-school," but, now that she has arrived at the threshold of womanhood, she probably learns more from Prue's advice and her own natural inclinations than from her experience at the school. Virginia Birdsall rightly observes that Prue "keeps reminding us of both her own and everyone else's basic nature." *Wild Civility,* p. 129. For more on what Hippolita might have learned at the Hackney School, see Shafer, "Restoration Heroines," p. 39.

10. Other than the influence of Calderón's *El Maestro de danazar,* Friedman mentions the similarity of Hippolita's scheme to lure Gerrard to John Marston's *Parasitaster, or, The Fawne* and Ben Jonson's *The Diuell is an Asse.* As for the specific borrowings from Calderón's play, John Loftis reminds us that they are not "verbal or consecutive"; they are rather "situational." Loftis, *The Spanish Plays of Neoclassical England,* pp. 127–28. Serious scholars have moreover been suspicious of Wycherley's "claim" that he wrote the play at age twenty-one (1662), his major source not having appeared until 1664. See Friedman, Plays, pp. xiii–xvi.

11. She would likely endorse what Monsieur subsequently tells Prue, "Ne're fear it, dreams go by the contraries" (IV.i.281; Friedman, *Plays,* p. 200, n. 1), yet taking little comfort in the commonplace. Hobbes wrote that "In summe, our Dreams are the reverse of our waking Imaginations," but he noted as well the debate at the schools over dreams: some say "Imaginations rise of themselves, and have no cause: Others that they rise most commonly from the Will" (*Leviathan,* pp. 7, 8). There was moreover the sentiment of the seventeenth-century Jesuit Paolo Segneri (1624–94), who advised, "Examine even unto your dreams, to know if, once awakened, you did not give them your consent." Quoted in Foucault, *The History of Sexuality,* p. 20. Hobbes comments further: "For . . . Dreams be naturally but the fancies remaining in sleep, after the impressions our Senses had formerly received waking" (*Leviathan,* p. 159). Finally, Roger Thompson cites the sexually oriented dreams of Simon Foreman in the early seventeeth-century: "The widespread use of supernatural aids in problems of love and lust recorded in his diary argues a deeply superstitious and trammelled attitude toward sexuality among his contemporaries." *Unfit for Modest Ears,* pp. 10–11.

12. What Patricia Meyer Spacks writes in regard to later eighteenth-century

women is also relevant here: "Not only does the mind by its very nature sometimes demand continuing attention to the impermissible, but it also finds, often, outside stimuli for dangerous fantasy.... Some women, for example, have innate strong passions. Natural virtue cannot save them from their feelings; they need all the resources of religion and social morality." On a more practical level, Hobbes advised that one be adequately covered in bed: "lying cold breedeth Dreams of Feare, and raiseth the thought and Image of some fearfull object." Spacks, "'Ev'ry Woman Is at Heart a Rake,'" *Eighteenth-Century Studies* 8 (1974–75): 39, 41; Hobbes, *Leviathan,* p. 6

13. Thomas Fujimura detects the connection between Mrs. Caution and sexuality but does not take it far enough: "she expresses detestation of sex as a filthy thing, and yet constantly suggests sexual ideas to her young charge.... This question of sexual wit and modesty must have been of some concern to Wycherley." Fujimura, *The Restoration Comedy of Wit,* pp. 136, 137.

14. And yet, an even closer affinity still exists between them. Caution tells Don Diego, "I am sure my Husband never kept me up.... you *Spaniards* are too censorious, Brother" (II.i.10–11, 14)—suggesting her own natural aggressiveness and resistance to male authority and incarceration—qualities often and vigorously demonstrated by her niece.

15. And female masturbation by hand or with the assistance of "Signior Dildo" was a feature in much bawdy poetry of the seventeenth century. See, for example, Thomas Nashe's "Dildo" Ballad (ante 1601), "Dildoides" in Butler's *Hudibras* (1672), and Rochester's *Signior Dildo* (1673): "This signior is sound, safe, ready and dumb / As ever was a candle, carrot, or thumb." There was also Rochester's "Fair Chloris in a Pigsty Lay" (sometime before 1672), with its depiction of more "normal" masturbation techniques:

> Frighted she wakes, and waking frigs,
> Nature thus kindly eased
> In dreams raised by her murmuring pigs
> And her own thumb between her legs,
> She's innocent and pleased.
> (Vieth, *Poems,* pp. 28, 59)

The increasing public and private anxiety over masturbation seems not to have become fully evident until the beginning of the eighteenth century. See Stone, *Family, Sex and Marriage in England,* p. 516. As Roy Porter concludes, "The Enlightenment's toleration of sexuality was drawn to exclude ... the young. From early in the [eighteenth] century there was a growing torrent of medical and moral opposition to masturbation, directed primarily against young people." "Mixed Feelings," pp. 16–17.

16. The tenor of the conversation, and that to follow, makes playfully ironic Mrs. Caution's parting words in the scene: "We may go to bed" now (321–22).

17. James Thompson has counted eighty-six uses of "fool" in the play. *Language in Wycherley's Play,* p. 64.

18. Zimbardo, *Wycherley's Drama,* p. 53; and "William Wycherley," p. 276. And Gerrard hardly lacks for other supporters. Norman Holland finds that Monsieur is the "real dancing master (the outside of a gentleman)," whereas "Gerrard is the real gentleman." Anne Righter calls him "a young man of wit and sense"; T. W. Craik, "an honourably-intentioned *jeune premier.*" And Kenneth Muir believes we should admire him because he is "sincere and faithful." Holland, *The First Modern Comedies,* p. 66; Righter, "William Wycherley" in *Restoration*

Dramatists, ed. Earl Miner (Englewood Cliffs: Prentice-Hall, 1966), p. 107; Craik, "Some Aspects of Satire in Wycherley's Plays," p. 174; Muir, *The Comedy of Manners,* p. 68. Morever, Thomas Fujimura deems both Hippolita and Gerrard "Truewits," although there "is nothing very complicated or ambiguous about [Gerrard's] character." *Restoration Comedy of Wit,* p. 133.

19. Considering the play's lack of "satiric import," Rose Zimbardo concludes that the comedy might have been "intended as a propaganda piece extolling everything that is good, old-fashioned, and English and despising whatever is foreign; and it may have been inspired by the general patriotic enthusiasm that prevailed in preparation for the impending Third Dutch War." "William Wycherley," p. 277.

20. That they eat "vigorously" is apparent in what they order: "young Partridge," "Some Ruffes," "young Pheasants," and "young Rabits"; and in what the waiter says of them: "[T]hey bring such good stomachs from St. *James's* Park or rambling about in the streets, that we poor Waiters have not a bit left" (170–72, 273–81). However, one factor arguing against obesity or even corpulence needs mentioning: they have burned many a calorie in St. James's Park, we can be sure. Other than their energetic metabolisms, the association of eating and lovemaking here (and in *The Country Wife*) emphasizes sexual appetite as opposed to simply a lust for food stuff. Metaphorically, they *devour* all in their path. Their appetites for men, sex, life—as well as rabbits—are insatiable. In addition, their taste for *young* pheasants, partridges, and rabbits suggests an interest in young (and therefore both more virile and more pliant) males as sexual partners—as Millwood so articulated hers in Lillo's *London Merchant.*

21. Antonia Fraser's study of seventeenth-century women offers important commentary on Wycherley's female characters here and throughout his four plays. Regarding the mid-century specifically, Fraser writes that the "new liberty enjoyed by women in the Civil War and Commonwealth period was frequently associated with two phenomena dreaded by sober citizens of whatever politics. The first of these was sexual licence. . . . Some of the women among those sectaries known as the Ranters were unbalanced and hysterical. . . . Some of the women surrounding [James Naylor] were very wild in their behaviour, such as a couple known merely as Mildred and Judy. . . . The second dreaded phenomenon was that of the 'Amazonian' all-female mob." Fraser, *The Weaker Vessel* (New York: Alfred A. Knopf, 1984), pp. 224–25.

22. Gerrard's bantering with Flirt and Flounce might suggest a traditional masculine presence—but his "wit" has *no* effect on them—the movement of the scene implies that he is backing up as he offers such lines as "you are come a little too early for me, for I am not drunk yet." In short, he appears, as I will argue, as does Horner in the drinking scene near the end of *The Country Wife.*

23. Later, Monsieur tells Hippolita, "[my] Company . . . keep me up so late I cou'd not rise in dè morning" (III.i.14–15). The double entendre here is more than irresistible; in Wycherley it is just about incontrovertible.

24. That she will never again use the expression in the play suggests not Gerrard's salutary effect on her speech but her refusal to demonstrate further something about herself he believes he understands and can predict.

25. *Man of Mode,* III.iii.75–76; *Way of the World,* IV.i.348–50.

26. I believe, then, that the scene and the relationship go well beyond what Yvonne Shafer concludes: "Hippolita is delighted with Gerrard when she meets him and determines she will marry him. But there are two types of tests to undergo: first, the test of wit to see if she can continue to bring him into the house

under the nose of her father and with the fiancé's [Monsieur's] assistance, and second, to determine the extent of Gerrard's feelings for her." "Restoration Heroines," p. 44. Moreover, Rose Zimbardo calls them "the ideal woman and man," who are marked by "honesty and simplicity"; Norman Holland finds them "witty lovers who know what they are doing": the play "pictures two decent people surrounded by a world of folly"; and James Thompson believes they are "honest, honorable, and good intentioned," a couple whose understanding makes them "models of correct conduct for gentleman and gentlewoman." Zimbardo, *Wycherley's Drama*, p. 53; Holland, *The First Modern Comedies*, pp. 66, 69; Thompson, *Language in Wycherley's Plays*, pp. 62, 69. Regardless, Hippolita's comments do not suggest to me a gushing young Miss trying hard not to give away her enthusiasm for her suitor. A more aloof and mature Hippolita, I might add, is easily producible on stage.

27. Quoted in Nussbaum, *The Brink of All We Hate*, p. 29. Monkeys likewise served as sexual substitues in erotic seventeenth-century poetry. In *The Four Legg'd Elder* (1647), attributed to Sir John Birkenhead, we find, in addition to the Elder's discovery of his maid's fornication with his dog Swash, the warning,

> Take heed all Christian Virgins now,
> The *Dog-Star* now prevails:
> Ladies! beware your *Monkeys* too
> For Monkeys have long Tails.
>   (*Bawdy Verse*, pp. 114–15)

28. Patricia Meyer Spacks writes of women in the eighteenth century (again relevant, I would argue, to those in the latter half of the seventeenth century), "women were also aware of the artfulness of innocence—aware of it in their own experience, and conscious of its usefulness as a fictional device. Innocence might provide a valuable screen to hide behind." Spacks, "'Ev'ry Woman Is at Heart a Rake,'" p. 32. In his effort to demonstrate the playwright's "unsympathetic" treatment of Hippolita, Sam Terry points to a contrast between her "intrinsic qualities and her assumed role," with her being referred to as "innocent" (or a variation of the term) "some twenty times" in the play: "Ironically each time Hippolita is described as innocent, her immediate action reveals her as anything [but] innocent." True enough, although not surprising, and I fail to see why Wycherley necessarily *frowns* upon her employment of that "innocence." The play does not lend itself satisfactorily to the kind of moral reading Terry gives it, although his assumptions about Gerrard's negative qualities are a welcome corrective to the more idealistic or otherwise positive readings of his character. To Terry, Gerrard is "a courtly gentleman who is an utter fool." Terry, "The Comic Standard in Wycherley's *The Gentleman Dancing-Master*," *Enlightenment Essays* 6 (Spring 1975): 5, 10.

29. At the end of the first scene, Hippolita had said to herself, "if [Gerrard] has wit he will come, and if he has none he wou'd not be welcome" (I.i.325–26). The latter part of her comment explains much of her treatment of him, I would argue.

30. Robert Markley rightly notes Gerrard's "inability to get the point": Gerrard "is a victim of his conventional expectations about women; he is unable to tell the difference between Hippolita and the idealized 'sweetest' and 'Dearest' creature of popular romance.... Gerrard fills the role of truewit without demonstrating his suitability for it." *Two-Edg'd Weapons*, p. 153.

31. W. R. Chadwick is one of the few who have commented on Gerrard's apparent dullness, in comparision to Hippolita, but he considers this a fault of the playwright's, for Hippolita should not be seen as Gerrard's superior. Again, I fail to see this as a fault. A Restoration comedy that shows a woman ascendant need not be criticized for doing so. Chadwick, *The Four Plays of William Wycherley*, pp. 72–73.

32. The Restoration audience would likely have recalled the comical Diego from Samuel Tuke's *The Adventures of Five Hours* (1663), but they would have been wrong to dismiss Wycherley's character by assuming too close an affinity. W. Gerald Marshall more accurately perceives that both Monsieur's and Don Diego's "obsessions and concomitant perpetual aberrations lead them into bizarre play-worlds in which the external and 'real' world is imaginatively reconstructed in terms of their own obsessive and mad view of it": "Whereas the humors character is involved in eccentric *action*," Monsieur and Don Diego are "involved in eccentric *perception* of self and others." Marshall, "The Idea of Theatricality in Wycherley's *The Gentleman Dancing-Master*," pp. 5, 8; and *Stage of Fools*, pp. 55–57. Seeing him as far less significant, Markley observes that Diego is a "theatrical caricature," who "may be simply Wycherley's excuse for poking fun at the conventions of 'Spanish' plays that enjoyed a vogue in the 1660s." *Two-Edg'd Weapons*, p. 155.

33. Similar to the characters in *Love in a Wood*, Diego's speech is often punctuated by the verbal tag "Look you" and by rapid repetition of the verb "to see": "well, has she *seen* my Cousin? . . . And she has *seen* him, has she? I was contented he should *see* her. . . . but she has *seen* no body else . . . ? Where is her Chamber? pray let me *see* her. . . . I long to *see* her"—all these *see's* within the space of only ten lines (II.i.44–54).

34. When one male in Wycherley's comedies is threatened by a loss of self-esteem or power, other males are perceived more overtly as enemies; and no man, regardless of occupation, is immune from censure. As Diego remarks about clergymen, "No, we are bold enough in trusting them with our Souls, I'le never trust 'em with the body of my Daughter. . . . trust a Coward with your honour, a Fool with your secret, a Gamester with your purse, as soon as a Priest with your Wife or Daughter" (II.i.23–29).

35. In the third book of *The Courtier*, the Magnifico makes clear that the woman should never be "too forceful and energetic" in dance: "So when she is about to dance or make music of any kind, she should first have to be coaxed a little, and should begin with a certain shyness. . . ." Castiglione, *The Book of the Courtier* (Harmondsworth: Penguin Books, 1976), p. 215. See Woods, "Dance in England . . . ," p. 31.

36. W. Gerald Marshall asserts that in "her theatrical environment, Hippolita is able to move beyond adolescence and to 'act' the role of a woman for the first time: she dances with a man; flirts with him; tests his true feelings for her." Hippolita "separates from her father, undergoes a transitional stage in her play-world, and finally is incorporated into adult society" (*Great Stage of Fools*, pp. 48, 50). Still, I fail to see her, to any considerable extent, going (to borrow from a 1950s hit tune) from "bobbysox to stockings." Wycherley depicts a mature young woman from the beginning—a female who at once manipulates intinctively and naturally. There is really nothing she "grows into."

37. Foucault describes two degrees of pleasure that commonly stemmed from concerns for family and societal controls: first is the "pleasure that comes of exercising a power that questions, monitors, watches, spies, searches out, palpates,

brings to light" [Don Diego]; the second is "the pleasure that kindles at having to evade this power, flee from it, fool it, or travesty it" [Hippolita]. Foucault, *The History of Sexuality,* p. 45. Some forty years after the performance and publication of Wycherley's play, Jane Barker—whose book "Exilius," as Patricia Meyer Spacks informs us, "is a rich repository of sexual fantasy"—provided a tale of near incest: "A wicked father tries to seduce his daughter, after first attempting to marry her to his bastard son. Virtuous Clarinthia refuses, so her father abducts and attempts to rape her." See Spacks, "'Ev'ry Woman Is at Heart a Rake,'" pp. 45–46. Barker's "Exilius" (1715) in *Entertaining Novels of Mrs. Jane Barker,* 3rd. ed., 2 vols. (London, 1736). Lawrence Stone points out that at least in the previous century the laws against incest were "surprisingly lenient"—sodomy and bestiality being seen as more repugnant—and in crowded houses, especially, with adolescent children living at home, the occurrences of incest were likely "common." Stone, *The Family, Sex and Marriage in England,* p. 491.

38. Robert Markley also points out that "the associations between foreign dress and corrupt English makes it tempting to see this scene as an ironic comment on the 'clothing language' metaphors popular during the period." *Two-Edg'd Weapons,* p. 157.

39. Virginia Birdsall is one who sees Wycherley's emphasis on the sexual nature of the dancing: Hippolita's is "the 'shameless dance' in the Garden—the dance of creative life." And I would take issue only with the first part of her view that "If Gerrard is Hippolita's teacher in the art of seduction, it is she who instructs him in the art of intrigue and deception," for she instructs him in all areas. Birdsall, *Wild Civility,* pp. 130, 131.

40. The association of the palm with sexual virility or sterility had of course been well-established by Wycherley's day.

41. Her parting words (IV.i.448–50) allude to Cassandra, the one who would not be believed. Caution mentions how Troy was "taken, rumag'd, and ransak'd"—the sexual connotations being fairly obvious—and her liking herself to the "Troth-telling *Trojan* Gentlewoman of old" is most apt in other ways as well. Cassandra was beautiful, frustrated in her hopes for a husband, and punished for her "caution" in responding to Apollo's advances. Before speaking her prophecy, she would fall into a trance, causing her family to believe her mad. Appropriately, Don Diego finds occasion to call his sister "mad" (III.i.391).

42. And Gerrard's holding to the image of an innocent Hippolita helps him avoid confronting her true and more intimidating essence—his posing as "experienced" to the "innocent" young woman placing him, in his mind, in the superior position. As a gloss on these matters, we might recall the conclusions of Patricia Meyer Spacks: "Female innocence, then, is male oppression: the terms are modern, but the perception was quite available to the women of the eighteenth century"—and, again, of the late seventeenth century, we may confidently add. Spacks, "'Ev'ry Woman Is at Heart a Rake,'" p. 31. Hippolita's apparent excitement over riding off in the coach-and-six reminds us that indeed that she is but fourteen, inexperienced in the pleasures of city life and more than anxious to enjoy them. But one may wonder if she is not being playfully deceptive in her enthusiasm for such stylish travel: "'tis not in the power of fourteen year old to resist it" (III.i.513). To be so giddy like a young country maid would be totally inconsistent with the character Wycherley has so far portrayed. More probable is that with her affected juvenile response she is keeping Gerrard off balance and unaware (two major sources of her power over him now and later, should

they marry), while at the same time showing us that Gerrard himself is not the prime attraction in leaving her father's house. Gerrard is more aroused by her money (suggesting the invalid's transferrence of sexual energy); she by her freedom (a more healthy egocentricism).

43. Although Wycherley's era would not have been as quickly responsive to the sexual entendre "to come," here the active verb form at least accelerates the Dionysian motion prompted by Diego and Caution. In the space of only thirty-eight lines, Diego uses "come" *fourteen* times—the other characters adding three other uses of the verb.

44. Although our emphases are different, I find valuable W. Gerald Marshall's concentration on "madness" in this play: Diego is "an insane father who is lost in his own *drama of madness.*" In the play "we find a fascinating treatment of the mind's ability to create various illusions, all of which helps to generate the fundamental madness which emerges" in Don Diego (*Great Stage of Fools*, pp. 11–12). Marshall is correct to remind us that "Restoration psychology is varied and complex" and that "madness can be, in many cases, the *direct* result of an *obsessed imagination*" (pp. 51–52). I would only disagree with the implication that Diego (or any other of Wycherley's characters Marshall deems "mad") is outside the norm.

45. Her complaint that the mistresses "ne're think of the poor watchful Chamber-maid" implies a conscious slight—a violation of the sorority—but it could only be benign neglect, for there is simply very little evidence of division among women in Wycherley's plays.

46. Once more, there is no need, even with the allusion to the wax and grease, to visualize Prue as homely, slovenly, or obese. The dynamics of the scene are better enhanced the more attractive she is. Here then is yet another way in which casting can affect or destroy a viable critical perspective. In addition, whenever such a woman is portrayed as undesirable, the male comes off ultimately "wise" in his refusal to satisfy her. But if she is appealing in any way, then he must appear slow-witted and impotent. Even though one may feel more comfortable with the former, the latter depiction better fits the realities of this play.

47. Virginia Birdsall finds Hippolita's delaying tactics problematic, "as simply another move in the game of power," but she concludes that psychologically it is the "young girl's sudden loss of nerve at the moment of decision." (Birdsall's first inclination, I would argue, is the proper one.) She goes on to note that the entire "*carpe diem* emphasis has been violated in her unexpected recalcitrance": "we can only finally conclude that it is Wycherley himself who has lost his nerve." Hardly, for I think the playwright has matters well in hand at this point. Birdsall, *Wild Civility,* p. 132.

48. In such a context, I have difficulty endorsing Katharine Rogers's assertion that the basis for the couple's relationship is "purely romantic" and that Hippolita delays merely to "extend basic comic situations and to complicate the general confusion." Rose Zimbardo explains such behavior by arguing that these "perfect romantic lovers [are] forced to strange expedients by a corrupt age." I would counter that the "corrupt age" is simply a red-herring that dismisses far too easily such "imperfect" and "non-romantic" behavior on the part of Gerrard and Hippolita. Rogers, *William Wycherley,* p. 50; Zimbardo, *Wycherley's Drama,* p. 54.

49. A bit earlier, Caution had used that most basic of all sexual entendres *(it)* to speak of the sex act: "That slippery Fellow will do't . . . Indeed he will do't,

royally he will" (IV.i.436, 438). (One is very tempted to see the reference to "royalty" as an allusion to the reigning monarch and noted lover, Charles II.) Wycherley continues his use of the same entendre in the following exchange:

> *Ger.* Your daughter does not desire it.
> *Don.* Come, come, Baggage, you shall desire it of him....
> *Hip.* My Father will have me desire it of you, it seems.
> (702–05)

50. At least here he acknowledges Hippolita's status as a "Woman" rather than as a silly girl

51. Virginia Birdsall argues that we now "look in vain" for "the early, delightfully youthful and spontaneous Hippolita" and that because of the heroine's "inconsistency" Wycherley has "come close to betraying his comic vision." Whereas Birdsall is correct to see her outside a pristine and idealistic context, there is no need to lament her "lost" innocence and spontaneity. She is little different, really, than she was at the beginning of the play. On the other hand, Kenneth Muir believes that Hippolita's "charm and innocence convert Gerrard from a Restoration gallant to a bashful lover." This is a most generous way to characterize their relationship, seeing that under that "charm and innocence" are sexual attractiveness and aggression, and under Gerrard's bashfulness lie his insecurity and his incompetence. Birdsall, *Wild Civility,* p. 133; Muir, *The Comedy of Manners,* p. 72.

52. Accordingly, I would disagree with Thomas Fujimura's contention that in effect "Hippolita tells Gerrard that marriage between Truewits must be based on equality and trust" and W. R. Chadwick's belief that here Wycherley is "proposing a concept of marriage which is based on interdependence and mutual respect." However, I find more perceptive and convincing Chadwick's observation that the play is "a serious attempt" to "analyze in some depth female motivation and behaviour when faced with the uncertain business of marriage." Fujimura, *The Restoration Comedy of Wit,* p. 135; Chadwick, *The Four Plays of William Wycherley,* p. 72.

53. As Robert Hume comments, "Only a marriage settlement could guarantee a wife an income of her own from her own property—though if the husband failed to pay it the woman had difficulty enforcing the contract ... In short, the subjugation of the woman was just about total. Like the American slave in the nineteenth century, a wife might be lucky in her owner but more likely might not, in which case she was essentially helpless." These points are irrefutable as far as law and custom went, but unlike the American slave, the seventeenth-century woman could by the force of her personality and pulchritude or by her husband's sexual insecurity or passive temperament make conditions far more to her advantage—*but* always with the realization that an assertive male could marshall almost unstoppable forces. See Hume, "Marital Discord in English Comedy from Dryden to Fielding" in *The Rakish Stage,* p. 180.

54. Chadwick, for one, finds this part of the action a "weakness" in the play, especially so near the denouement. Others have moreover wondered if Wycherley wished to give James Nokes (Monsieur) more to do at the end of the play. Chadwick, *The Four Plays of William Wycherley,* pp. 79–81.

55. Friedman advises that we read "belly-full" in its proverbial sense of "to have a sufficiency or one's fill," but surely Caution sees the term in the more sexual sense of having one's vagina filled by the male organ and then having a "belly-full" of child.

56. Hippolita's final words are the proper end to the play, not the silly couplet that follows: "When Children marry, Parents shou'd obey, / Since Love claims more Obedience far than they" These lines have about as much to do with Wycherley's concerns as do Bellmour's moralistic couplets at the end of *Jane Shore*. The demands of the theater can only explain this nonsense. The play has not supported the view that here "as in all [Wycherley's] plays, the ideal is romantic love" or that in the love scenes the playwright is "at his most charming; the mood of tenderness is enhanced by gentle humour and good sense." Zimbardo, *Wycherley's Drama*, p. 49; Vernon, *William Wycherley*, p. 22.

57. It is Wycherley's "most tiresome play"; there is "insipidity of the plot"; it is "perhaps the most ingenuous and innocuous comedy of the period"; there is a "failure of inventiveness"; "[N]o wit is needed to see [Wycherley's] points; they are too laboured." Gerald Weales, ed., *The Complete Plays of William Wycherley*, p. xix; Rogers, *William Wycherley*, p. 50; Holland, *The First Modern Comedies*, p. 64; Birdsall, *Wild Civility*, p. 121; Dobrée, *Restoration Comedy*, p. 83. James Thompson writes that whereas *Love in a Wood* was "extremely popular," *The Gentleman Dancing-Master* was a "disaster"; and Rose Zimbardo adds that it is a "trifle of a play"—with the characters being "simple, stock comic figures"—and believes that in his choice of epigraph (Horace's "It is not enough to make your reader laugh, though there is something ever in that") Wycherley was apologizing for writing "so flimsy a play as *The Gentleman Dancing-master*, acknowledging that it is not worthy work for a satirist." For different reasons I agree with Zimbardo that it isn't worthy of the satirist. I much prefer the tenor of W. Gerald Marshall's analysis: a play "rich in both theme and artistry," *The Gentleman Dancing-master* may be termed "one of the most fascinating works to emerge from the Restoration stage." Thompson, "Ideology and Dramatic Form," pp. 163–64; Zimbardo, William Wycherley" *(DLB)*, pp. 275, 276; Marshall, *Great Stage of Fools*, pp. 45, 62.

58. John Playford's *The English Dancing Master* (London: Thomas Harper, 1650) describes a number of dances that effectively comment on much that has gone on in Wycherley's play. The playwright might well have smiled—as would some contemporary readers—when recalling such dances as "The Spanish Jeepsie," "The Spanyard," "All a Mode de France," "The Beggar Boy," "Goddesses," "Daphne," "Confesse," "Faine I Would," "Dissembling Love," "The Punks Delight," "Dull Sir John," and "Have at Thy Coat Old Woman."

59. Rogers, *William Wycherley*, p. 54.

Chapter 3: "Plagues and Torments"

1. Critics have traditionally noted similarities only between *The Country Wife* and *Love in a Wood* (eg., Ranger as a preview of Horner, Christina and Valentine an early version of Alithea and Harcourt). A good critical overview is provided by Judith Milhous and Robert D. Hume in *Producible Interpretations: Eight English Plays, 1675–1707* (Carbondale and Edwardsville: Southern Illinois University Press, 1985), pp. 73–106. We need to keep in mind that perhaps only two years or so elapsed between the writing of *The Gentleman Dancing-Master* and *The Country Wife*. The implication has always been that Wycherley's first two plays were his juvenalia, written a considerable time earlier than his "mature" plays. Although criticism has come a long way from John Palmer's observation early in the century that *The Country Wife* is the "most perfect farce" in

English drama, Robert Hume encourages our seeing it in roughly the same terms: "an immensely enjoyable play in which we take almost nothing seriously. . . . The gross character exaggerations are characteristic of farce, more than comedy." Palmer, *The Comedy of Manners* (London: G. Bell and Sons, 1913); Hume, *The Development of English Comedy in the Late Seventeenth Century* (Oxford: Clarendon Press, 1976), p. 104.

2. Bonamy Dobrée's memorable assessment of Horner as a "grim, nightmare" figure has been countered most dramatically, perhaps, by Virginia Birdsall: Horner is "a wholly positive and creative comic hero" on the side of "health, of freedom, and most controversial of all, of honesty." Rose Zimbardo observes that Horner is "not sufficiently detached from the scene to be the satirist's persona. . . . [L]ess a character than an emblem," Horner is "in himself a graphic declaration of the satiric thesis." W. R. Chadwick also defends Horner against some of the earlier criticism: if he is a "monomaniac," so are other heroes of sex comedies; he has "ideals"; he is a "picaresque hero" neither "admirable [n]or reprehensible." Peter Holland comments: "The name *is* a symbol; it connects with other patterns of meaning and makes them relevant to the use of the word in the play. Horner *is* . . . a satyr in his cynical analysis of society, as well as his sensuality." Anthony Kaufman argues that Horner cannot be considered a hero because of his "diseased" view of the world and his "sterility of emotion." W. Gerald Marshall writes that Horner, "essentially . . . a negative creator, an antidramatist," continually "sets stages upon which he invites those around him to forget about spiritual love." Douglas Ford believes that Horner "serves as Wycherley's self-reflexive device," a "symbol of authorial anxiety" affirming the "poet's [own] power to create." Finally, Brian Corman asserts that Horner is "an attractive and clever character who, though no moral paragon himself, tends to apply his skills and talents only to those worse than he is." Dobrée, *Restoration Comedy,* p. 94; Birdsall, *Wild Civility,* p. 136; Zimbardo, *Wycherley's Drama,* p. 90; "William Wycherley," pp. 279, 280; Chadwick, *The Four Plays of William Wycherley,* pp. 117–19; Holland, *The Ornament of Action: Text and Performance in Restoration Comedy* (Cambridge: Cambridge University Press, 1979), p. 194; Kaufman, "Wycherley's *The Country Wife* and the Don Juan Character," pp. 220–21; Marshall, *Great Stage of Fools,* p. 80—views that first appeared in "Wycherley's 'Great Stage of Fools': Madness and Theatricality in *The Country Wife,*" *Studies in English Literature* 29 (1989), 409–29; Ford, "*The Country Wife:* Rake Hero as Artist," *Restoration* 17 (1993), 77–78; and Corman, *Genre and Generic Change,* p. 34.

3. Quacks moreover "specialized" in "renewing maidenheads" (with alum usually). The frequent damage done to the vaginal wall caused pimps to assault the quacks, who would hasten to the Netherlands or France, from where they had come. Several years before the first perfomance of *The Country Wife,* Dutch quacks "were attacked in the famous petition of the Whores to the Prentices in 1668 after the Shrove Tuesday riots" that so upset Charles II and Lady Castlemaine. Burford, *Bawdy Verse,* p. 145.

4. Horner's "confiding" to the Quack cannot, of course, be construed as evidence of masculine trust, for the Quack is not a participant here but rather a kind of perverse chorus, overseer, and voyeur. Besides, Horner's initial words in the play (in an aside), "A Quack is as fit for a Pimp, as a Midwife for a Bawd," suggests the distrust and separation of the males. What is significant, however, is that by having Horner's trust, the Quack is placed in the position of authority, the familiar role for any kind of confessor, over the one who confides—and

Horner willingly establishes this relationship. (The next person Horner so informs is Lady Fidget, who also maintains dominance over him in her particular way.) Foucault discusses the nature of power in the relationship between penitent and confessor in *History of Sexuality,* pp. 59–67. David D. Mann sees the Quack "set[ting] up the thematic oppositions of seeming and being": "we become him: we are all quacks and frauds; merely by accepting him, we have made ourselves accomplices in the action." My point is, though, that we should *not* accept him; we should be dubious of him and Horner's confiding only in him. Mann, "The Function of the Quack in *The Country Wife,*" *Restoration* 7 (1983): 19, 21.

5. I cannot then support Anthony Kaufman's contention that, given the parameters of the "Don Juan" character, Horner's "disguise of impotence" requires our seeing a "latent impulse" of male homosexuality. William Freedman views the impotence as symbolic of "the Restoration society as Wycherley presents it." Kaufman, "Wycherley's *The Country Wife* and the Don Juan Character," p. 223; Freedman, "Impotence and Self-Destruction in *The Country Wife,*" p. 422. Freedman's essay says much about the nature of impotence and self-destruction with which I concur, but his applying these concepts to Restoration society as a whole (Horner's "injury" is "meant to comment on one prevalent insufficiency in the Restoration world: the inadequacy, in effect the impotency, of its males") takes matters far beyond where I believe they should rest. For more on these issues see Giles Slade, "The Two Backed Beast: Eunuchus and Priapus in *The Country Wife,*" *Restoration and Eighteenth-Century Theatre Research,* second series, 7, no. 1 (1992), 23–34.

6. Anthony Kaufman believes that in Jaspar we see "a deliberate neglect of women as he foists off his wife unto the supposedly 'safe' Horner in order to absorb himself entirely in his business affairs." I see his motives much differently. "Wycherley's *The Country Wife* and the Don Juan Character," p. 226.

7. Roger Thompson is quite succinct: "Masculine impotence or at least inadequacy was a seventeenth-century obsession" *Unfit for Modest Ears,* p. 105. And Derek Cohen adds that this "world of men is a world of continuous sexual contestation." Cohen, "*The Country Wife* and Social Danger," *Restoration & Eighteenth-Century Theatre Research,* second series, 10, no. 1 (1995), 2.

8. Dale Underwood has examined several aspects of Restoration libertinism, noting the conflict between individual expression and the desired social order. Underwood, *Etherege and the Seventeenth-Century Comedy of Manners,* pp. 18–20. For further discussion of the dichotomy, see Richard Stieger, "'Wit in a Corner': Hypocrisy in *The Country Wife.*"

9. Jean Hagstrum refers to "the notion that profoundly suggestive pictures can be socially or morally acceptable substitutes for forbidden feelings or wishes." Hagstrum, "Pictures to the Heart: The Psychological Picturesque in Ann Radcliffe's *The Mystery of Udolpho*" in Paul J. Korshin and Robert R. Allen, eds., *Greene Centennial Studies* (Charlottesville: University Press of Virginia, 1984), p. 439. Horner's reference to *L'Escole des filles, ou la philosophie des dames* (1655) is to one of the most notorious "pornographic" works of the day; even Pepys vowed to burn it—that is, after reading it (*The Diary of Samuel Pepys,* 9:58). In 1675, the year of Wycherley's play, several young dons at All Souls College were found using the Oxford University presses to run off copies of Giulio Romano's engravings from Aretino's *Postures*—the period's famous sex manual. Stone, *The Family, Sex and Marriage in England,* pp. 539–40. See Roger Thompson for more on erotic literature and iconography of the time. *Unfit for Modest Ears,* pp. 4–5, 28.

10. My argument in this chapter runs counter to Anthony Kaufman's major contention that Horner demonstrates an "abnormal hostility towards women," whom he "compulsively exploits." Kaufman adds that Horner's "successful but unsatisfying seductions are a gesture of hatred towards women, a desire to revenge himself on them, for the initial erotic attachment to the mother, inevitably betrayed, may lead to the hostile charge that all women are fickle." I contend that Horner is manipulated and often dominated by them—and he evinces the natural defensive posture (born from insecurity) of a severe critic. "Fear of" seems more accurate to me than "abnormal hostility towards" women. Kaufman, "Wycherley's *The Country Wife* and the Don Juan Character," pp. 220–21, 224. Kaufman's views are reiterated in "The Shadow of the Burlador: Don Juan on the Continent and in England" in A. R. Braunmuller and J. C. Bulman, eds., *Comedy from Shakespeare to Sheridan* (Newark: University of Delaware Press, 1986), pp. 239–43. At the other end of the rope, Harold Weber feels that Horner "insists throughout the play on a just appreciation of women." *The Restoration Rake Hero* (Madison: University of Wisconsin Press, 1986), p. 54.

11. As for the play's frequent use of "honour," Rose Zimbardo concludes that the term is a "double entendre that reveals how far [Horner's and Lady Fidget's] behavior falls below the [social and] moral standard to which their words allude." But Wycherley never gives us a sense of anyone's falling from a higher social or moral status. There are no characters representing that ethereal world of a proper and moral society. (See my later assesssment of Harcourt and Alithea.) Zimbardo, "Wycherley: The Restoration's Juvenal," p. 21. James Thompson has counted seventy-six uses of *honour*, correctly noting that often the reader "must perform a lexical substitution, 'translate' from the obviously literal meaning to some distant, different, private meaning." *Language in Wycherley's Plays*, pp. 75–78, 81. We might also detect Wycherley's tempting us, with so many uses of *Honour*, to consider its linguistic cousins *Horner* and *horror*.

12. Although we move in opposite directions, I strongly agree with Peggy Thompson, who argues that the women are "exhausting sexual creatures"—"essentially and aggressively sexual" and that Wycherley sensed that women had become "the literary embodiment of all kinds of conflicting desires and fears." Thompson, "The Limits of Parody in *The Country Wife*," *Studies in Philology* 89 (1992): 102–4, 113–14.

13. W. R. Chadwick contends that the men are "quite clearly friends in the best sense"; and Thomas Fujimura notes that they treat Horner "amiably at all times, despite a supposed infirmity that would soon expose a lesser man to ridicule." Eve Kosofsky Sedgwick points to the "bond of cuckoldry" and argues that "Given that the object of man's existence is to cuckold men, Horner is a master. . . . If he gives up the friendship and admiration of other men, it is only in order to come into a more intimate and secret relation to them—a relation over which his cognitive mastery is so complete that they will not even know that such a bond exists." Anticipating Sedgwick's interest in male "homosociality," W. H. Matalene wrote that at times Horner "betrays his panic at the prospect of losing his London friends" and that "blinded by the physiological magic of copulation," he "overlooks the homosocial pleasure he has taken from having his admired male companions look upon him as a great copulator." Ronald Berman also discusses the concept of friendship (both male and female): part of Wycherley's "intention," he concludes, "is to demonstrate" Bacon's view that without true friends "the world is but a wilderness." Chadwick, *The Four Plays of William Wycherley*, p. 117; Fujimura, *The Restoration Comedy of Wit*,

p. 140; Sedgwick, "Sexualism and the Citizen of the World: Wycherley, Sterne, and Male Homosocial Desire," *Critical Inquiry* 11 (1984): 228, 231–32; Matalene, "What Happens in *The Country Wife*," *Studies in English Literature* 22 (1982): 402–3; Berman, "The Ethic of *The Country Wife*," *Texas Studies in Language and Literature* 9 (1967): 50.

14. Later, Harcourt says to Horner, "Now your Sting is gone, you look'd in the Box amongst all those Women, like a drone in the hive, all upon you; shov'd and ill-us'd by'em all, and thrust from one side to t'other" (III.ii.10–12)—a graphic metaphor likely voiced with far more satisfaction than good-natured pity. And Dorilant implies that Horner disgraces himself and his sex by submitting to such humiliation: "Yet he must be buzzing amongst'em still, like other old beetle-headed, lycorish drones; avoid'em, and hate'm as they hate you" (III.ii.13–14). For more on the issue of male friendship, see Peggy Thompson, "The Limits of Parody in *The Country Wife*," pp. 106–9.

15. J. Peter Verdurmen believes Horner's words are "delivered in an emotional aside, . . . presumably based upon a just estimation of the couple's intrinsic worth and the consequent desirability of their marriage." Verdurmen, "Grasping for Permanence: Ideal Couples in *The Country Wife* and *Aureng-Zebe*," *Huntington Library Quarterly* 42 (1979): 344.

16. And how are these comments spoken? With troubled sincerity or sardonic ridicule at Sparkish's expense? Horner may also sense that Pinchwife would suspect Horner's own interest in Alithea, another "property" of Pinchwife's to spoil (and Pinchwife *is* concerned at Horner's disappointment in hearing of the match). Horner is furthermore perplexed that one such as Sparkish could attract such an appealing and independent woman as Alithea, for he expected Sparkish to secure only some old "stale Maid" who "has liv'd to despaire of a husband" or a young one who has failed to stimulate a "Gallant" (IV.iii.361–62).

17. In addition, Lawrence Stone points to the frequent application of "friends" in the seventeenth century as meaning "no more than 'my advisors, associates and backers.'" *The Family, Sex and Marriage in England*, p. 97.

18. I believe Sparkish's character offers more than Robert Markley's description implies: "Sparkish is not a fop but a caricature of aristocratic presumption. He represents the failure of wit and carriage as measures of social value." I moreover find misleading conclusions such as Alan Roper's that Sparkish "is impervious to the assault of events": he is "so self-regarding as to be almost solipsistic, incapable of rational communication with others." David Vieth points to the destructive aspects of the three plots headed by the "husband" figures: "the Pinchwife plot represents the country, the Fidget plot the 'city' or commerical district of London, and the Sparkish plot the 'town' or fashionable world on the fringes of Court." However, Vieth adds that despite "superficial differences" among these worlds, the "fundamental implication is that the same 'nature' underlies them all." Markley, *Two-Edg'd Weapons*, p. 169; Roper, "Sir Harbottle Grimstone and *The Country Wife*," *Studies in the Literary Imagination* 10 (1977): 115; Vieth, "Wycherley's *The Country Wife*: An Anatomy of Masculinity," p. 338.

19. Sparkish offers three alternative places to meet: at *"Chateline's,"* the *"Cock,"* or at the *"Dog* and *Partridg"* (I.i.316–20). Other than recalling *"chatelain"* as meaning Lord of a manor (Sparkish would like Horner to realize that he can no longer be lord of even his own sexual desire), the person with a good ear for French might also think of *"châtier"* (to punish, to flog) and, more appropriately, *"châtrer"* (to emasculate or castrate, or in noun form, a eunuch)—

all of which Sparkish would most fervently wish Horner to consider. The "Cock" certainly had a number of masculine associations, but Horner and some of the members of Wycherley's audience and reading public might have been reminded as well that in classical times the cock was often castrated, the only bird to be so mutilated. The eunuch priests of Cybele, one of the oriental cults brought to Rome, were called the Galli (the "cut offs") because of the cock's (gallus) more debilitating and disgusting associations. See C. T. Onions, ed., *The Oxford Dictionary of English Etymologies* (New York: Oxford University Press, 1966); N. G. L. Hammmond and H. H. Sculland, eds., *The Oxford Classical Dictionary,* 2nd. ed. (Oxford: Clarendon Press, 1970); and T. H. White, *The Bestiary: A Book of Beasts, Being a Translation from a Latin Bestiary of the Twelfth Century* (New York: G. P. Putnam's Sons, 1960). In addition, the Partridge's perverse sexual habits had also been long noted—the male occasionally mounting the male; the female stealing eggs of another female. And the Partridge was excellent at camouflaging its identity: "Frequent intercourse tires them out. The males fight each other for their mate, and it is believed that the conquered male submits to venery like a female" (White, *The Bestiary,* pp. 136–37). Although the scientifically minded mid-seventeenth century, as William J. Farrell reminds us, began to criticize and replace "the old habit of collecting anecdotes and analogies about animals, insects, and plants from the books of the past," nevertheless, "the old dependence on the lore of the library still persist[ed]." Farrell, "The Role of Mandeville's Bee Analogy in 'The Grumbling Hive,'" *Studies in English Literature* 25 (1985): 524. George Farquhar wrote that the "Nature of Comedy . . . bears so great a Resemblance to the Philosophical *Mythology* of the Ancients, that old *Aesop* must wear the Bays as the first and original Author." Farquhar, "Discourse upon Comedy" in *The Complete Works of George Farquhar,* ed., Charles Stonehill (London: Nonsuch Press, 1930), 2:336–37.

20. Sparkish may also be cognizant of Hobbes's position that the more often observed "the lesse uncertain is the Signe" (*Leviathan,* p. 11). Although William Freedman is certainly right to note that Sparkish's self-destructive impulse evolves from his insecurity, I would not agree that he "is dependent for satisfaction entirely on the supposed esteem of others" and that "everything he does is designed to win their praise and avoid their contempt"—for I see his satisfaction coming from destroying, not pleasing, others. Freedman, "Impotence and Self-Destruction in *The Country Wife,*" p. 429.

21. Virginia Birdsall labels him one of the "blind fools" and "moralizing hypocrite[s]." Although W. R. Chadwick finds him more important than do most critics, noting that his role is as long as Horner's, he views him only in the most negative terms: "every facet of his character provokes disgust"; he is an "evil man" at times "close to the villain of melodrama"—even though he does provide the "darker colouring" necessary to understanding Wycherley's view of the world. Whereas he fails to develop his point, John Cunningham sees as I do that in the play "the more interesting thing is really the treatment of Pinchwife"—a "study of jealousy and possessiveness, as serious, in a way, as Othello." Birdsall, *Wild Civility,* pp. 137, 147; Chadwick, *The Four Plays of William Wycherley,* pp. 114–16; Cunningham, *Restoration Drama,* pp. 86, 87.

22. As Maximillian Novak writes, in another play of 1675—John Crowne's *The Country Wit*—the implication is "that people live in the country not because they prefer a rural existence but because they simply do not have the intelligence to cope with the ways of the city." In Pinchwife's case, however, he lacks more the inner security rather than the intelligence to survive in London. Novak,

"Margery Pinchwife's 'London Disease': Restoration Comedy and the Libertine Offensive of the 1670s," *Studies in the Literary Imagination* 10 (1977): 13.

23. *Leviathan,* p. 64. Freud would later write, "A man's attitude in sexual things has the force of a model to which the rest of his reactions tend to conform." *The Complete Psychological Works of Sigmund Freud,* 10:241. Charles Hallet has explained the play in Hobbesian terms but concludes far differently than I that Wycherley is attacking "the Hobbist society from which ... hypocrisy stems"—not the *Leviathan* or Hobbesian philosophy per se but rather the *influence* and application of that philosophy (mainly its concentration on self-interest). Again, I find Wycherley *reflecting* an agreement with much of Hobbesian thought, not attacking it or its influence. Hobbes's philosophy held the mirror to, not redirected or influenced, human behavior and thought. Hallet, "The Hobbesian Substructure of *The Country Wife*," *PLL* 9 (1973): 380. Douglas Duncan also finds Hobbesian parody in the play. See "Mythic Parody in *The Country Wife*," *Essays in Criticism* 31 (1981): esp. 308–12.

24. Lawrence Stone offers a succinct and most sensible reminder regarding the marriage laws and customs that could suppress women: "But it would, of course, be absurd to claim that the private reality fully matched the public rhetoric." Women had "useful potential levers of power within the home." *The Family, Sex and Marriage in England,* p. 199.

25. James Thompson observes that Pinchwife "fears the power of the word" and that Horner is "more quick, more ingenious, more audacious than the others" in his use of language. *Language in Wycherley's Plays,* pp. 83, 85. J. Peter Verdurmen suggests slight oedipal overtones in the relationship between Horner and Pinchwife—although Pinchwife is "a rather sorry father figure." (Seeing Horner as in his mid-twenties would at least provide the proper age difference.) Verdurmen, "Grasping for Permanence: Ideal Couples in *The Country Wife* and *Aureng-Zebe*," p. 332, n. 9. For more on the Freudian implications in the play, see Antony Kaufman's "Wycherley's *The Country Wife* and the Don Juan Character"; and, especially for a perspective on Horner's and the play's use of jests, Carol L. Hee, "'The Sign of a Jest': Freudian Jokes in Wycherley's *The Country Wife*," *Literature and Psychology* 30 (1980): 8–17.

26. In his colloquy "Marriage," Erasmus tells of a man who married an "innocent" of seventeen, who had never been outside her parents' house. The husband believed she would be more easily trained to fit his taste, but she rebelled and the frustrated spouse took her back to her mother and father. The bride's father advised the new husband to give his wife a good beating as a way to control her. The young man was reluctant, so the father threatened to perform the beating himself. The girl then went to her knees and begged forgiveness of both her father and her new husband—and thus became the perfect wife. Such a vision (including the suppositions of the old Roman *patria potestas*), would tend to remain fixed in the mind of a man like Pinchwife, influencing his disturbed perspective of his wife and the country. For the belief that Erasmus was describing Thomas More and his first wife, Jane Colt, see Richard Marius, *Thomas More* (New York: Alfred A. Knopf, 1984), pp. 39–41.

27. As David Vieth concludes, "Pinchwife's speeches about women reflect fear, hostility, and a debased physical version of sex" "Wycherley's *The Country Wife*: An Anatomy of Masculinity," p. 339.

28. As Friedman reminds us, commentators have long recognized the similarity of Pinchwife's words here to the speeches of Arnolphe in Molière's *L'École des femmes*. But Friedman rightly draws a distinction between Molière's character

and Pinchwife in the severity of the responses. Friedman, *Plays,* p. 262, n. 2. Douglas Ford feels that Pinchwife's disturbing nature is "seemingly incongruent with the light nature of the play." But I would argue that he is perfectly reflective of what is the *truer* nature of the play. Ford, *"The Country Wife:* Rake Hero as Artist," p. 80.

29. A generation later Mrs. Fainall asks Marwood, "You would not make [a husband] a cuckold?" "No; but I'd make him believe I did, and that's as bad" (*Way of the World,* II.i.61–63).

30. As Freud noted, "Generally speaking, a tendentious joke calls for three people [here four]: in addition to the one who makes the joke [Horner], there must be a second who is taken as the object of the hostile or sexual aggressiveness [Pinchwife], and a third [Dorilant and Harcourt] in whom the joke's aim of producing pleasure is fulfilled." Quoted in Hee, "The Sign of a Jest: Freudian Jokes in Wycherley's *The Country Wife,"* p. 10.

31. Hobbes wrote that "much Laughter at the defects of others, is a signe of Pusillanimity," which he had also defined as "fear of things that are but of little hindrance" (*Leviathan,* pp. 26, 27). Wallace Jackson is one critic who concedes that Pinchwife is at least "a far more dangerous and *knowing* adversary than Sir Jasper." Jackson, *"The Country Wife:* The Premises of Love and Lust," *South Atlantic Quarterly* 72 (1973): 543–44.

32. As W. R. Chadwick says, she is "a splendid female animal, amoral, clever, sensual, who follows her natural instincts," adding that because she is "consistently naive and artless," the audience must feel "compassion for her." *The Four Plays of William Wycherley,* pp. 112–13. To some, most notably Thomas Fujimura, Margery Pinchwife is simply "a pleasure-loving and unaffected girl from the country . . . simply a pawn in this witty plot." *The Restoration Comedy of Wit,* p. 143.

33. As Patricia Meyer Spacks writes, women insisted that their "sheltered lives, limited opportunities, nurture the seeds of their destruction. Men, of course, are ultimately the shelterers." Spacks, "'Ev'ry Woman Is at Heart a Rake,'" p. 31. Wycherley's audience would have soon determined that Margery was no Ariana or Gatty (in Etherege's *She Wou'd If She Cou'd*), blowing into London in search of amusement.

34. Although not the focus of this study, Wycherley's self-effacing humor (wonderful slights of his craft and dramatic milieu) stands for me as one of his most delightful and noteworthy qualities. As for the play's more telling allusions to the theater, Joseph Candido argues that they are there to "remind us at certain prescribed moments of the deliberately contrived nature of the spectacle before us." Candido, "Theatricality and Satire in *The Country Wife," Essays in Literature* 4 (1977): 35.

35. One of those places where men may be found is "St. *James's* Park." Alithea's admission "Though I take the innocent liberty of the Town" (42–43) and Margery's interest in the theater were anticipated in *The Gentleman Dancing-Master:* "And [I] would take all the innocent liberty of the Town to tattle to your men under a Vizard in the Play-houses, and meet 'em at night in Masquerade" (Hippolita to Mrs. Caution; I.i.296–98). Alithea's pride in having kept her freedom without any tinge of ill-repute—"who boasts of any intrigue with me? what Lampoon has made my name notorious?" (46–47)—suggests as well that she, like Lady Fidget, is highly sensitive to the necessity of a guarded reputation. And the fact that she has entertained male suitors—"wou'd you not have me

NOTES TO CHAPTER 3

civil?" (52)—should inform us that Alithea is more socially lively than her honorable and oft-admired pose suggests.

36. We might keep in mind that Margery's longings and experiences in the country may have been more than virginal: when her husband informs her that a "lewd" fellow was in love with her, she responds, "Was it any *Hampshire* Gallant, any of our Neighbours?" (113). Such a comment would only stimulate further Pinchwife's suspicion about his wife's interests and at least momentarily take away his comforting association of the country with any power and serenity. I am therefore unwilling to accept the implication of Brian Corman's assertion that Pinchwife "corrupts Margery by mistreating her." *Genre & Generic Change,* p. 31.

37. Pinchwife's punctuation "In baggage, in" (127) squares well—in diction and sentiment—with Lord John Vaughn's description of a wife: "The clog of all Pleasure, the luggage of Life, her portion but small, and her C——t very wide." Thompson, *Unfit for Modest Ears,* p. 120.

38. Rose Zimbardo calls them "the twin virtues," Alithea representing the "truth that opposes hypocrisy" and Harcourt a "romantic love that stands against lust." James Thompson believes they are the only ones in the play who "strive to be what they would seem, or to be as good as their word": at the end of the play they stand alone as examples of "decent behavior in a mass of corruption"—although he adds that the couple is "too dull and weak to support" the view that they represent "the Horatian mean, the locus of value." David Morris sees the relationship as "essential to Wycherley's moral purpose"; at the beginning, however, Alithea (Greek for "truth") is "literally betrothed to Folly (Sparkish)." Peggy Thompson considers Alithea an "angelic virgin," a status that "removes her from the powerful physical forces animating the other women." David Vieth is less willing to see them as ideal but admits that they "achieve a modest sort of proportion and wholeness in their relationship," although the "price of wholeness" is "imperfection." Finally, Brian Corman says that they suffer from "a mild case of what might be called Celia-Bonario syndrome, the dullness—even unattractiveness—that good characters suffer from contact with especially effective and vital rogues." The couple seems to be "a remnant, greatly devolved, of the elevated high plot still found in *Love in a Wood.*" Zimbardo, *Wycherley's Drama,* p. 161; "William Wycherley," p. 281; Thompson, *Language in Wycherley's Plays,* pp. 73, 91; "Ideology and Dramatic Form: The Case of Wycherley," p. 170; Morris, "Language and Honor in 'The Country Wife,'" *South Atlantic Bulletin* 37, no. 4 (1972): 9; Thompson, "The Comic Parody in *The Country Wife,* p. 104; Vieth, "Wycherley's *The Country Wife:* An Anatomy of Masculinity," p. 344; Corman, *Genre & Generic Change,* pp. 34–35.

39. Cynthia Matlack finds the "difficulty encountered by Alithea and Harcourt in their courtship" a parody of the love-honor conflict in the period's heroic plays. She is right to resist viewing Alithea's honor as ideal, but I cannot see Wycherley's consciously providing parody of the heroic genre. Matlack, "Parody and Burlesque of Heroic Ideals in Wycherley's Comedies," p. 279. Her essay thus provides a contrast to J. Peter Verdurmen's "Grasping for Permanence: The Ideal Couple in *The Country Wife* and *Aureng-Zebe.*" Derek Hughes notes that "Epistemologically, it is hard to distinguish Harcourt's noble faith from Sir Jaspar's foolish credulity." *English Drama,* p. 138.

40. And Sparkish's torment of Harcourt includes the former's insistence that he is a "frank" person in a "frank age" (III.ii.327–28, 343–44)—"Frank," of course,

being Harcourt's Christian name—and thus "Sparkish" is trumping and consuming "Frank."

41. Sparkish likely realizes that to "go into a corner" is often the street prostitute's suggestion to her prospective customer—and thereby one more method of afflicting Harcourt.

42. D. R. M. Wilkinson writes that Alithea's "loyalty to Sparkish is quite improbable from a lady of quality, or at least from a lady of any precipience—both by Restoration and by twentieth century standards." Chadwick counters by pointing to the restrictions put on women by marriage laws and customs and suggesting that Alithea later hopes love might grow from the match, as Lord Halifax implied in his *Advice to a Daughter,* 1688: "In other words, her stand is the stand that any sensible honourable woman of her time and class would take. And this is precisely Wycherley's point, for it is the sickness of the whole marital system, a sickness that infects not only the bad but also the good, that is the main thesis of *The Country Wife.*" Richard Steiger is forced to conclude that if Alithea "does, as her name suggests, represent 'truth,' it is a severely compromised version." Wilkinson, *The Comedy of Habit: An Essay on the Use of Courtesy Literature in a Study of Restoration Comic Drama* (Leiden: University Press, 1964), p. 135; Chadwick, *The Four Plays of William Wycherley,* p. 110; Steiger, "'Wit in a Corner': Hypocrisy in *The Country Wife,*" p. 66.

43. Derek Hughes writes that "Alithea thus ultimately discredits the expectations that her name initially arouses, although her name [Gr.—"truth"] is one which peculiarly insists upon its own veracity, and she thereby demonstrates the difficulty of encompassing the totality of the self within the public world and the signs by which it coheres." Hughes, "Naming and Entitlement in Wycherley, Etherege, and Dryden," *Comparative Literature* 21 (1987): 266—restated in *English Drama,* p. 142.

44. Again, one must consider the many possibilities for facial expression and line delivery here. Sarcastic or serious? Troubled or playful?

45. *Leviathan,* p. 73. Charles Hallet argues that based on the true spirit of "contract," Alithea "is perfectly correct in refusing to treat the marriage contract lightly"; she is "the one woman in the play who does not act out of self-interest." My argument is that she, as much as anyone else, does act out of both self-interest and self-preservation. Hallet, "The Hobbesian Substructure of *The Country Wife,*" p. 391.

46. Eventually, she will plainly admit to Lucy (and herself): "I love him" (IV.i.13).

47. Robert Markley is one of the few who has seen such a motivation for Alithea's "loyalty" to Sparkish. *Two-Edg'd Weapons,* p. 176.

48. Again, as Lawrence Stone reminds us, "In any familial relationship . . . the distribution of power over decision-making will, in the last resort, depend on the personal characters of the husband and the wife." *The Family, Sex and Marriage in England,* p. 217.

49. Chiding her mistress for preparing herself for "a stinking second-hand grave"—Sparkish's bed—Lucy proves that she has a vivacity of her own as well as a loyalty to a fellow women, which finds intolerable the thought of a lifeless match without sexual gratification. But she does not at first comprehend Alithea's deep-seated fears, which makes impossible her acceptance of her mistress's perplexing behavior and reliance on "honor." As she says about Alithea's marrying such a fool as Sparkish, "you intend to be honest don't you? then that husbandly virtue, credulity, is thrown away upon you" (IV.i.46–48). Thomas Fu-

jimura believes that Wycherley "is to blame, perhaps, for making Lucy wittier than her mistress, but the fault is not so much that Lucy is too witty as that Alithea is not witty enough." But an understanding of Alithea's complex reasons for behaving as she does makes insignificant the division of wit between her and Lucy. Fujimura, *The Restoration Comedy of Wit,* p. 144.

50. Lucy's subsequent words on the horror of the country suggest also that Wycherley's title is meant to convey more fear than amusement. For a discussion of the debate over City and Country comedies of the 1670s, see Maximillian Novak's "Margery Pinchwife's 'London Disease.'" (Stone examines the tradition of slander, marital discord, and petty spying in the villages during the sixteenth and seventeenth centuries. *The Family, Sex and Marriage in England,* pp. 99, 144–45.) The nature of Alithea's concerns is therefore unlike that suggested by Honour's maid Rose in Henry Neville Payne's *The Morning Ramble* (1673): "Well is not that better than to be troubl'd with a formal fopp of bus'ness who lodges his wife in the Country, to prescribe for the Ague, then scratches his empty Noddle [and] cryes, I protest I must post to London." Quoted in Novak, p. 7.

51. Wycherley's so often and effectively pushing us toward sexual double meaning permits our imagining Harcourt doing Sparkish's conjugal business in the "Marriage-bed."

52. His remarks here find use for the fruit metaphor Horner had earlier claimed as his own (in the scene with "Little Sir James" at the Exchange): "I have only given your Brother and Orange, Sir"—Horner says to Pinchwife (III.ii.524). It is no wonder, then, that Horner reacts with anger here: "O thou damn'd Rogue, thou hast set my teeth on edge with thy orange" (IV.iii.381–82).

53. Kenneth Muir finds that "the main force of Wycherley's satire is directed against female hypocrisy" and that the hypocrisy of these women "is anything but endearing"—a point with which I cannot concur owing to what I see as Wycherley's point about the necessity for the verbal safeguards, the exuberance with which he portrays these women, and his consistent interest in the nature of indirection. Once more, where do we see the "norm" by which to judge the hypocrisy? P. F. Vernon argues that although the "satire on the affectation of Lady Fidget and her companions is a real tour de force," the playwright does look upon them "quite sympathetically," believing that they are "not ultimately responsible for their behavior." Susan Staves also takes a softer, and I think more accurate, line: the women are "presented as hypocrites, but as reasonably conscious hypocrites who are aware of the difference between the universe of reputation and the universe of fact." Finally, Richard Steiger sees no difference in the three women: they are "more or less indistinguishable from one another." But such a conclusion fails to appreciate that Lady Fidget is far more sexual and powerful than the other two and that Mrs. Squeamish's part in the action is of more consequence than Mrs. Dainty Fidget's. Muir, *The Comedy of Manners,* p. 76; Vernon, *William Wycherley,* pp. 28–30; Staves, *Players' Scepters: Fictions of Authority in the Restoration* (Lincoln: University of Nebraska Press, 1979), p. 161; Steiger, "'Wit in a Corner': Hypocrisy in *The Country Wife,* p. 56.

54. And his attempt to flank them only enhances the pervading theme of "fear": "Well it must out then, to tell you the truth, Ladies, which I was afraid to let you know before, least it might endanger your lives, my wife has just now the Small Pox come out upon her, do not be frighten'd; but pray, be gone Ladies, you shall not stay here in danger of your lives; pray get you gone Ladies" (322–27).

55. Another manner in which Horner asserts himself is in the familiar antimale outburst—in this case as an analogue to the "hypocritical" women who

stand before him: "Why, these are pretenders to honour, as criticks to wit, only by censuring others; and as every raw peevish, out-of-humour'd, affected, dull, Tea-drinking, Arithmetical Fop sets up for a wit, by railing at men of sence, so these for honour, by railing at the Court, and Ladies of as great honour, as quality" (II.i.417–21)—a motif wonderfully punctuated by Dorilant, who tells Sir Jaspar, "Nay, if [Horner] wo'not, I am ready to wait upon the Ladies; and I think I am the fitter Man" (440–41). As his sex (and the play) almost dictates, Jaspar returns the blow: "no pray withdraw, Sir, for as I take it, the virtuous Ladies have no business with you" (445), which shows us that often in Wycherley characters offer sexual entendres despite their intentions. The characters all serve the teeming world Wycherley creates—unwillingly or no.

56. This usage may also be seen as an ironic twist of Jaspar's earlier employment, "Hah, hah, hah, he hates women perfectly I find" (I.i.91).

57. Derek Cohen is one of the few critics to give Lady Fidget her due: although "her morals are repellent," she "possesses a rare intelligence which, combined with her viciousness, makes her a formidable character whose strength even Horner seems to have underestimated"; she is "honest and forthright, frankly using the power of hypocrisy to help her overcome the obstacles that society and nature have put in her way." Cohen, "The Revengers' Comedy: A Reading of *The Country Wife*," *Durham University Journal* 76 (1983): 33.

58. In one notorious Restoration treatment, we can find

> Did she not clap her Leggs about thy Back,
> Her Porthole ope; Damn'd P——ck what dis't Lack?
> Henceforth stand stiff, and gain thy *Honour* lost,
> Or I'le ne're draw thee but against a Post.
>   Thompson, *Unfit for Modest Ears*, p. 122 (emphasis added)

59. Again a contemporary audience would have been easily cognizant of the fact that Margery is no Florimel (Dryden's *Secret Love*, 1667), no Hilaria (Ravenscroft's *The Careless Lovers*, 1673), no Betty Goodfield (the anonymous *The Woman Turn'd Bully*, 1675)—all women who *choose* to don male garb to manipulate and trick. For a discussion of the attractiveness of such gender shifting on the stage, see Pat Rogers, "The Breeches Part" in Boucé, pp. 244–58.

60. Margery's allusions to sight are also conspicuous: "I like to look upon the Player-men, and wou'd *see*, if I cou'd, the Gallant you say loves me" and "I wou'd *see* first some *sights*"; "did the Gentleman come hither to *see* me indeed?"; "[S]hall we go? the *Exchange* will be shut, and I have a mind to *see* that" (III.i.60–61, 68, 75–76, 97–98)—hammering home the fear Pinchwife equates with the visual. Accordingly, he attempts to put an end to his anxiety with the simple remedy, "Sister, how shall we do, that she may not be *seen?*" (87).

61. For more on "signs" throughout the play, see Michael Neill, "Horned Beasts and China Oranges: Reading the Signs in *The Country Wife*," *Eighteenth-Century Life*, n.s. 12 (1988): 3–17; and Deborah C. Payne, "Reading the Signs in *The Country Wife*," *SEL* 26 (1986): 403–19. Unlike Payne, I do not see Wycherley seemingly to "long for that world of perfect interpretation: a language beyond words, looks, and sighs; an act beyond conventional gesture" (pp. 416–17). Derek Hughes observes that as "Pinchwife's fear of being entitled a cuckold shows, names have genuine power to become the objects of fear and desire." Margery moreover "matures by gaining control of the art of signification." Hughes, *English Drama*, pp. 140–41.

62. To Charles O. McDonald, the scene takes on a far different sexual connotation than other critics (myself included) are willing to give it: "Horner seems, though I could not prove this in less than some pages, thoroughly duped by Margery's disguise as a page—the humor of the scene is entirely homosexual." McDonald, "Restoration Comedy as Drama of Satire: An Investigation into Seventeenth Century Aesthetics," *Studies in Philology* 61 (1964), 543.

63. Richard Steiger observes that the fruit "functions dramatically by virtue of its consistency with the play's ubiquitous imagery equating sex and food." Steiger, "'Wit in a Corner': Hypocrisy in *The Country Wife*," p. 69, n. 8. In addition to the employment of fruit in other plays of the period, relevant anecdotes from outside the theater would include that of the "famous libertine" Henry Killigrew, who in the 1660s confronted Frances Jennings disguised as an orange wench. Seeing her with the less attractive (and also masquerading) Mrs. Price, Killigrew, when asked by the women if he would like some oranges, replied, "Not just now but if you like to bring me this little girl tomorrow [Jennings], it shall be worth all the oranges in the shops to you." His hand then strayed to Frances's bosom. Antonia Fraser, *The Weaker Vessel,* p. 412.

64. Oranges may of course be seen as breasts, buttocks, or testicles. The dried fruit Margery holds offers such possibilities as prunes, apricots, or dates, the kind of dried fruit that may look suspiciously like the female sexual organ—or the state of the male sex organ after coitus—and certainly a playwright such as Wycherley encourages our looking for such things. (Later, Horner will make a more traditional equation of fruit and sex when he tells Sir Jaspar that he will not be one "that wou'd be nibling at your forbidden fruit" [IV.iii.86–87]). I believe in addition that Wycherley expected his audience to recall Peter Lyly's series of portraits titled "The Windsor Beauties" (done in the early 1660s), which as Jean Hagstrum reminds us portray sensual women with "glowingly white skin, partially exposed breasts, full and sensual lips pursed as though to invite a kiss, and languishing and flirtatious eyes. The actions in which they are engaged partially fulfill the amorous promise of their countenances, as they accept grapes from a kneeling Indian boy, hold their skirts up for a gift of fruit. . . ." The portrait of Lady Jane Needham (Mrs. Middleton), for example, features her looking most provocatively while holding close a collection of fruit. Hagstrum, *Sex and Sensibility: Ideal and Erotic Love from Milton to Mozart* (Chicago: University of Chicago Press, 1980), pp. 105–6, plate 4. And Wycherley refers to Lely in *The Plain-Dealer,* Prologue and play. Peter McNamara sees the oranges as emblematic of Margery and the dried fruit as reflective of Pinchwife. McNamara, "The Witty Company: Wycherley's *The Country Wife*," *A Review of International English Literature* 7 (1976): 65. Finally, Michael Neill calls attention to Shakespeare's *Much Ado About Nothing:* "Give not this rotten orange to your friend, / She's but the sign and semblance of her honour" (IV.i.30–31). Neill, "Horned Beasts and China Oranges," p. 16, n. 16.

65. Margery adds that Horner "so musl'd" her (Friedman's text). Holland's modernized edition has "mousled," as does Fujimura's Regent's Edition of the play—both defining it as "rumpled." (Peter Dixon's 1996 text has "muzzled.") The *OED* defines "mousle" as "to pull about roughly." Friedman adds that "muzzle" means, as Johnson's *Dictionary* has it, "To fondle with the mouth close. A low word" (Friedman, *Plays,* p. 311, n. 1). The meaning is problematic, however, in that Horner's putting the "tip of his tongue between [her] lips" does not suggest that Margery has been muzzled, pulled about, or roughed up. Another image is likely conveyed by "mousled": that of Horner's tongue (here the substitute penis)

poking about as a mouse does in and out of a hole or crack. The publication of *The Wandering Whore* (in several numbers, 1660–63) included this description of the whore's technique: "They kiss with their mouths open, and put their tongues in his mouth and suck it." Thompson, *Unfit for Modest Ears,* p. 67.

66. One detail she adds is that the "Gentlewoman of this house" came into the room—another "sister" who, despite the ambiguity of her title, assists in Margery's liberation—at the very least by *not* interrupting Horner's affectionate advances (IV.ii.15).

67. It is Peggy Thompson's contention that *The Country Wife* actually "conforms to the myth of a sexual fall and its assumptions about women as sexual beings" in presenting lust as an "intimidating, overpowering force and women as carnal, devious, and demanding Eves whose sexual urges the male characters take seriously, even if the women are themselves ludicrous creatures." "The Limits of Parody in *The Country Wife,*" p. 106.

68. As William Freedman writes, "while Wycherley read no Freud he knew something of sexual symbolization." Freedman, "Impotence and Self-Destruction in *The Country Wife,*" p. 426. G. Douglas Atkins also reminds us of Freud's impression that the writing process takes on "the significance of copulation." Margery's writing of the letter rather than her husband may be therefore construed as another way in which Pinchwife's masculinity is menaced, even though he still dictates what she is to pen. Atkins, *Reading Deconstruction, Deconstructive Reading* (Lexington: University Press of Kentucky, 1983), p. 132.

69. Jon Lance Bacon adds, "In a century when few women were able to sign their own names, writing had an obvious relevance to feminine identity. A woman's signature carried considerable significance in terms of political self-assertion. Several times during the Interregnum, groups of women petitioned Parliament." More to the point, Bacon argues, "The manner of his portrayal indicates Wycherley's approval of Margery's subversiveness." "Wives, Widows, and Writings in Restoration Comedy," *Studies in English Literature* 31 (1991), 433–34. Implying again the connection to and evolution from the last play, Hippolita did not share Margery Pinchwife's ability to write.

70. Robert Markley for one believes that "Horner accumulates mistresses so quickly that by the time of the China Scene he has more women than he can sexually satisfy." *Two-Edg'd Weapons,* p. 165. However, we only know for sure that he has sexual experiences with four women in the play—enough, without doubt—but not enough to encourage any hyperbole.

71. To Virginia Birdsall, Horner stands as a kind of "phallic symbol incarnate," a view seconded by Kenneth Muir: Horner "is more a phallic symbol than a man." Birdsall, *Wild Civility,* p. 156; Muir, *The Comedy of Manners,* p. 72. Much seventeenth-century bawdy verse features the relationship of a woman to her dildo—that object which frustrates males in its ability to satisfy the woman more ably but to the woman poses no threat, nor places any restriction on her sovereignty. See, again, Rochester's *Signior Dildo* (1673), Butler's "Dildoides" in *Hudibras* (1672), and much earlier Thomas Nashe's "Dildo Ballad" (ante 1601). For another perspective, consult Harold Weber, *The Restoration Rake Hero:* "Like Rochester, the rake is too complex and enigmatic a figure to be reduced to a sexual machine" (p. 3).

72. Patricia Meyer Spacks writes that "Seldom indeed, even in fiction, was a woman allowed to enjoy sexual satisfaction without concern for her dignity, honor, or innocence." Foucault has moreover commented on the "advent of the great prohibitions" in the seventeenth century: "the imperatives of decency."

Virginia Birdsall's criticism of Lady Fidget and her friends—they "are scarcely even willing to admit to having natural inclinations"—therefore misses an important point. Nor can I agree with Harold Weber's conclusion that Lady Fidget's "affected disdain for pleasure and her incongruous attempts to reconcile her lust with her 'dear, dear Honour' reveal an individual ashamed of, and afraid to admit, her natural passions." Given Wycherley's world, Lady Fidget's approach hardly suggests one ashamed of her natural passions. One need only recall her earlier conversation with Horner and her subsequent one (in the fifth act) with Mrs. Squeamish and Mrs. Dainty Fidget. Spacks, "'Ev'ry Woman Is at Heart a Rake,'" p. 35; Foucault, *The History of Sexuality,* p. 115; Birdsall, *Wild Civility,* p. 144. Weber, "Horner and His 'Women of Honour': The Dinner Party in *The Country Wife,*" *Modern Language Quarterly* 43 (1982): 112. For a further view on the fear of public disclosure, see Katherine Zapantis Keller, "Re-reading and Re-playing: An Approach to Restoration Comedy," *Restoration* 6 (1982): 64–71. Keller believes that "everyone" in *The Country Wife* is a "satirist" attempting to destroy the facades of others, while keeping their own in place.

73. To Robert Markley, "The ironic coupling 'Horner/honour' offers paradoxical standards of pretence and honesty, each term defining itself by the satiric corruption of the other." *Two-Edg'd Weapons,* p. 159.

74. One further use of *Honour* needs mentioning. In later seventeenth-century card playing, *Honour* (or more chiefly *Honours*) was a term in whist to denote the four trump cards—those powerful weapons that frequently gave women victory on the playing field. (See Horner's remarks about letting women win at cards [V.iv.138–39].) Here then may be another variation of the code word Lady Fidget expects Horner to understand—*Honour* standing not only for propriety and sex but also for female ascendency.

75. For more on the Machiavellian aspects of the play, see Gorman Beauchamp, "The Amorous Machiavellism of *The Country Wife,*" *Comparative Drama* 11 (1977–78): 316–30. "Sex is in *The Country Wife,*" Beauchamp writes, "what power is in *The Prince:* the energizing force, the motive for action" (p. 318).

76. Peter McNamara points out that "symbolically the toad is the inverse of the frog, which images fecundity; hence 'Toad' refers jocularly or demeaningly, depending on a lady's current estimate or underestimation, to Horner's sexuality." McNamara, "The Witty Company: Wycherley's *The Country Wife,*" p. 70.

77. Although china is less effective than fruit as a sexual signifier, it does offer interesting interpretive possibilities. As Friedman points out, china houses were often "used as places of assignation," and others have seen china as refined and decorated earth; "a vehicle for obscenity"; something that "completely hides its earthy origin"; a vessel for food, suggesting sex as mere appetite; a "fitting emblem for honor itself—since honor, like china, is at once precious, attractive, and frail; in short, a "euphemism for everything from Horner's sex organ to the sex act itself." I would add that china is also a commodity that is frequently exhibited, then sold, protected, often dropped and broken and then replaced, something coveted yet fragile—as is sex and one's reputation or actual proficiency in it—something common but claimed to be rare—something that all can possess in name, but few in quality. And, as Aubrey Williams has written, in the period there was a "growing passion for fine China among women." Friedman, p. 318, n. 1; Rogers, *William Wycherley,* p. 59; Chadwick, *The Four Plays of William Wycherley,* p. 99; Holland, *The First Modern Comedies,* p. 77; David Morris, "Language and Honor in 'The Country Wife,'" p. 7; Carol Hee, "The Sign of a Jest: Freudian Jokes in Wycherley's *The Country Wife,*" p. 13;

Williams, "The 'Fall' of China and *The Rape of the Lock*," *Philological Quarterly* 41 (1962): 415.

78. As for her calling Horner "this Woman-hater, this Toad, this ugly, greasie, dirty sloven"—Richard Steiger points out that the "speech is a tip to the audience that [Mrs. Squeamish] knows the truth about Horner, for, as Horner has said earlier, 'she that shews an aversion to me loves the sport.'" Steiger, "'Wit in a Corner': Hypocrisy in *The Country Wife*," p. 69, n. 6.

79. She expresses her appreciation of art to her grandmother Old Lady Squeamish, who is hardly the typical senex figure; she is more related to Wycherley's own Mrs. Caution. The older woman takes delight in conjuring an image of Horner as a "Snake without his teeth"—an allusion having the component of both castration and impotence.

80. Katharine Rogers believes that this scene and much of the play emphasizes Wycherley's attack on the "selfishness which pervaded sexual relationships in his society." But I cannot find here or elsewhere Wycherley's looking severely on the sexual activity of his age—the exuberance of the moment making most difficult such moralistic or satirical conclusions. Harold Weber contends that the "success" of the China Scene proceeds mainly "from the joy which Horner takes in revealing the hypocrisy of Lady Fidget and the stupidity of her husband." I can agree with the latter half of his statement, but to whom is Lady Fidget exposed? Not to her husband certainly. The audience? To Roy Porter, "These naturalistic and hedonistic assumptions—that Nature had made men [and Wycherley's women] to follow pleasure, that sex was pleasurable, and that it was natural to follow one's sexual urges—underpinned much Enlightenment thought about sexuality." Rogers, *William Wycherley*, p. 59; Weber, "The Rake Hero in Wycherley and Congreve," *Philological Quarterly* 61 (1982): 146; and *The Restoration Rake Hero*, p. 53; Porter, "Mixed Feelings" in Boucé, p. 4.

81. C. D. Cecil finds the "whole point" of the China Scene "is to display the skill with which a brilliant rake and a few obliging 'right' women can conduct *un discours licentieux* without disconcerting one another or discovering themselves to a suspicious intruder." Foucault has written that "Sexuality is not the most intractable element in power relations, but rather one of those endowed with the greatest instrumentality: useful for the greatest number of maneuvers." Cecil, "Delicate and Indelicate Puns in Restoration Comedy," *Modern Language Review* 61 (1966): 576; Foucault, *The History of Sexuality*, p. 103.

82. Rochester's "The Imperfect Enjoyment," which David Vieth dates to the 1672–1673 period, speaks well to the issue. "Is there then no more?" his lover cries. The male's attempts at reviving his potency fail him—the once proud thunderbolt now dwindled to a "dead cinder." Vieth, *Poems*, p. 38.

83. Yes, a "roll-wagon" is a also cart, as Thomas Fujimura notes in his 1965 edition of the play—but by now we shouldn't be squeamish about glossing it as a "cylindrical vase"—the shape being the point of Horner's reference, of course.

84. That Horner has had sex with Lady Squeamish may be inferred from Old Lady Squeamish's remark that he had "admir'd" her granddaughter's picture "so last night" (215–16).

85. His telling Horner that Margery is an "innocent creature" with no "dissembling in her" is of course deliberately deceptive, but it is a gesture of self-preservation—not an element in a scheme or game (328–29).

86. Antonia Fraser considers the period's interesting parallel between notions of sickness and notions of sexual pleasure: "Jane Sharp, the midwife [whose book was published in 1671], writing for popular consumption, agreed with Lord

Monmouth that the 'Green Sickness' which occurred in unmarried girls would be cured by the physical delights of marriage." What Lord Monmouth had written was a joyous endorsement of sexual pleasure: to the newly-married Philadelphia Cary he suggests that she tell her ill sister "that such an ingredient as you have had of late would do her more good than any physick she can take. But she is too good and too handsome to lack it long if she have a mind to it; and therefore she may thank herself if she continue to be ill.'" *Weaker Vessel,* p. 51.

87. She has "the London disease they call Love." As Maximillain Novak observes, "I cannot find a passage in the play that suggests there is anything wrong with sensuality." "Margery Pinchwife's 'London Disease': Restoration Comedy and the Libertine Offensive of the 1670s," p. 19. I would only add that neither do I find the playwright consciously *advocating* openly unrestricted or at least freer sexual license.

88. James Thompson argues, however, that *ultimately* Wycherley is concerned with a "certitude of language" and with incorruptible "standards for right speech." In Wycherley's plays, "Correct and honest speech is rewarded with trust, while incorrect and dishonest speech is punished with distrust." *Language in Wycherley's Plays,* pp. 4, 114. For more on the play's language, see Barrie Hawkins, "*The Country Wife:* Metaphor Manifest," *Restoration & Eighteenth-Century Theatre Research,* second series, 11, no. 1 (1996): 40–63.

89. We expect Pinchwife to use "changeling" in the sense of one who is capricious or simple-minded, but its more formal meaning of one who is secretly exchanged for another also fits: the "country" Margery has been replaced—through the secret machinations of Alithea, Horner, and Margery herself—by the more frightening "city" Margery—she who threatens Pinchwife's masculinity. See his earlier allusion to her as a "changeling" (IV.ii.44).

90. Before Pinchwife arrives with "Alithea," Horner asserts to the Quack that "keeping a Cuckold company after you have had his Wife, is as tiresome as the company of a Country Squire to a witty fellow of the Town, when he has got all his Money" (V.ii.10–12), which suggests Horner's frequent, at least according to him, sexual adventures lately—and earlier, he wants the Quack to assume. And yet this picture does not square with the facts of the play. Horner does not keep Sir Jaspar or Pinchwife company (although the men come upon him without invitation). And we know of no males he must endure who are connected to Mrs. Squeamish or Mrs. Dainty Fidget. We may conclude, then, that Horner's depiction is a fictive construct—a vision intended for the Quack's benefit—at least to be distrusted if not disbelieved entirely.

91. That the ladies call themselves the "virtuous gang" is more than a sanctimonious reference to their publick "virtue" or "honour." We have seen Lady Fidget's ability to use *honour* as a code word for sex, and *virtue* is probably another esoteric reference to sexual proclivity at the expense of the dull-witted Jaspar.

92. This "mother-in-law" is most assuredly one female who is not part of the sisterhood. But there really is no such character in Wycherley. Mrs. Caution comes closest to filling the role, but as discussed, her character and motivations are complex enough to discourage our labeling her too simplistically.

93. Sir Wilfull says to Lady Wishfort, "I have no mind to marry. My cousin's a fine lady, and the gentleman loves her and she loves him, and they deserve one another"; and Lord Foppington observes to Lady Betty Modish, "Madam, to convince you that I am in an universal peace with mankind, since you own I have so far contributed to your happiness, give me leave to have the honor of

completing it by joining your hand [to Morelove] where you have already offered up your inclination." Congreve, *The Way of the World* (V.i.635–38); Cibber, *The Careless Husband* (V.vii.250–55).

94. Harold Weber writes that "this dinner party, in presenting an image of genuine community which the play's larger society moves to frustrate, displays the conception of human nature which the play assumes and the values it celebrates.... Within the context of the play, the honesty of the banquet's participants is a virtue, not a vice, and their frank acknowledgement of the sexual aspects of human nature marks a valuable departure from the negations of those characters who would deny the importance of their own desires and needs." Much of what Weber says here seems to me on the mark; I have trouble only with his assertion that "The dinner party, then, functions as a scene of revelation, creating an atmosphere in which the women no longer feel the necessity to lie to each other" (114). I believe they understand each other very well from the beginning, each comprehending the need for indirection and metaphoric speech. Derek Cohen finds that the scene provides significant commentary on the "threat of social collapse" and the "fragility of male-induced structures." Weber, "Horner and His 'Women of Honour': The Dinner Party in *The Country Wife*" (repeated in *The Restoration Rake Hero,* pp. 56–66), pp. 108, 110; Cohen, "*The Country Wife* and Social Danger," p. 2.

95. The sexual possessiveness again makes a small crack in the fortress of female sisterhood ("common women"), but there is no one woman they have in mind, no one who is attacked directly.

96. A similar reference is suggested in one of Rochester's "Songs" from the mid 1670s, where the man complains to his lady,

> While I, my passion to pursue,
> Am whole nights taking in
> The lusty juice of grapes, take you
> The lusty juice of men.

Vieth, *Poems,* p. 84. Regarding Wycherley's scene, Rose Zimbardo finds a Juvenalian parallel (in his Sixth Satire) in the Maenads "conducting their orgiastic rite" in the rite of *Bona Dea* (*Wycherley's Drama,* pp. 152, 160).

97. I cannot agree then with Michael Neill's assertion that "for a moment all four characters stand exposed and vulnerable to scorn: the ladies as victims of one another's duplicity and Horner's guile." Nor would I second Peggy Thompson's position that the women here "continue to exhibit the grossest sort of self-delusion." Neill, "Horned Beasts and China Oranges," p. 13; Thompson, "The Limits of Parody in *The Country Wife,*" p. 102. As Derek Cohen comments, "Nowhere in the play does [Horner] seem more like the object he ultimately becomes, the very plaything of a gang of female gallants.... The scene throws into doubt the entire question of the extent to which Horner manipulates the world about him." "The Revengers' Comedy: A Reading of *The Country Wife,*" pp. 31, 32. I think, however, that Horner's omnipotence was thrown in doubt much earlier in the play—indeed, in its very first scene.

98. Judith Milhous and Robert Hume comment that critics have "devoted singularly little thought to how the women in the audience are supposed to respond" to the play and that a Horner "contemptuous of his conquests would hardly appeal to the female part of the audience; if he seems genuinely to please and satisfy his women, then perhaps the identification would be with their in-

terests." I think it more to the pleasure of Restoration women to see Lady Fidget and her friends much as I see them here. Milhous and Hume, *Producible Interpretations,* p. 81, n. 15.

99. An insistence on seeing Alithea as "ideal" wrongly encourages anger over Horner's "betrayal" of her. Second, Margery has barely earned the designation "Mistress" (at least as modern readers construe the term) based on the "Orange and dried fruit" encounter and her being stuffed in Horner's "closet." And then, does Horner in any serious way *love* Margery Pinchwife? Earlier, he observed to the Quack that Margery was nothing but "a silly innocent"—not the supreme challenge he seemed to prefer (V.ii.22–24).

100. Some contend, to use Charles Hallet's words, that Alithea's "reputation is ruined" when Horner admits that she was brought to him and that "all the characters believe that Alithea has become Horner's mistress"—an assumption further held by Pat Gill: "While Harcourt's good name and offer of marriage deliver Alithea from shame, they do not acquit her from any charges." But the misunderstanding lasts only some forty lines before Margery arrives in Alithea's clothes to correct the false impression—hardly enough time to ruin a reputation—especially one as imposing as Alithea's. Hallet, "The Hobbesian Substructure of *The Country Wife,*" pp. 393–94; Gill, *Interpreting Ladies: Women, Wit, and Morality in the Restoration Comedy of Manners* (Athens: University of Georgia Press, 1994), p. 69.

101. Harcourt says to Horner that he must be concerned for Alithea's "Honour"—to which Horner answers, "And I must be concern'd for a Ladies Honour too":

Har. This Lady has her Honour, and I will protect it.
Hor. My Lady has not her Honour, but has given it me to keep, and I will preserve it.
Har. I understand you not.
Hor. I wou'd not have you.

(254–61)

Other than the further fragmentation of the brotherhood, this exchange suggests Horner's continuing Lady Fidget's use of "Honour" in the sexual sense and Harcourt's obtuseness, now that he has been "purified" by Alithea's accepting him, in not, openly at any rate, acknowledging its meaning.

102. Here we discover another intriguing connection between the adversaries. In the play's first scene, Horner ridiculed Jaspar's tag word *Sir* with "I will kiss no Man's Wife, Sir, for him, Sir; I have taken my eternal leave, Sir, of the Sex already, Sir" (I.i.70–71)—echoed now by Pinchwife's (again to Sir Jaspar) "Why my Wife has communicated Sir, as your Wife may have done too Sir, if she knows him Sir" (V.iv.294–95).

103. In this wild moment, an agitated Old Lady Squeamish comes up to her granddaughter: "An Hypocrite, a dissembler, speak young Harlotry, speak how?" And yet her next "assault" on Mrs. Squeamish allows for her dropping of the conventional senex pose and revealing an awareness of her granddaughter's natural promptings. The key to this interpretation is to read the first part of the line in a senex pose—then pause briefly—to deliver the second part in an exuberant interrogative, reflective of a young girl's questioning her older sister upon her return from a romantic assignation: "O thou Harloting Harlotry, [pause] hast thou done't then?" Such a reading reinforces in another way the play's delightful sorority.

104. Derek Cohen has likewise identified Lucy's power at this moment but supposes "for argument's sake, that Lucy is old and ugly"—which would make Horner's "enslavement" complete, a character "far more fettered than freed by sexual liberty." But there is no need to suppose Lucy as "old and ugly." Being younger and sexually attractive would suggest even more emphatically the power of her sex to rule Horner. "The Revengers' Comedy: A Reading of *The Country Wife*," p. 35. And more recently Cohen has argued that she "identifies with the illicit and subversive interests of the women of the drama in sabotaging the oppressive system of male control." "*The Country Wife* and Social Danger," p. 13. J. Douglas Canfield believes that she "remains a parasite on the political economy of the hegemonic system but exercises independent agency, serving not only her mistress but the Town Wits who reward her services." *Tricksters & Estates*, p. 191.

105. Yet Pinchwife has no relief from the realization of his humiliation—as Sparkish reminds him: "I was only deceiv'd by you, brother that shou'd have been, now man of conduct, who is a frank person now, to bring your Wife to her Lover—ha—" (324–26).

106. Aspasia Velissariou rightly asserts that the sexuality of Margery and the other women is "a factor potentially subversive of patriarchal arrangements" and that the play "insists on the self-determination of female desires outside such arrangements." She moreover notes that the play demonstrates the impossibility of a "'liberated' sexuality." "Patriarchal Tactics of Control and Female Desire in Wycherley's *The Gentleman Dancing-Master* and *The Country Wife*," *Texas Studies in Language and Literature* 37 (1995): 116, 125.

107. Horner's reaction makes it difficult to see the validity of J. Peter Verdurmen's claim that Horner "remains in the broad sense true to Margery, the mistress for whom he cares most." "Grasping for Permanence: Ideal Couples in *The Country Wife* and *Aureng-Zebe*," p. 345.

108. And as H. W. Matalene reminds us, from this point on the other characters have nothing to say to Horner. Matalene, "What Happens in *The Country Wife*," p. 409.

109. Helen M. Burke writes that "the resolution of normalcy—the comic resolution—then, demands the expulsion of this barbaric element [the women's overt sexual desire], the permanent exorcism of the consciousness that disturbs and disrupts. In the designation of Horner at the end of the play as the sole evil in the system, we see the process by which such a restoration can be carried out. Horner functions as the *pharmakos,* or ritual scapegoat, the man who is cast out of the city to save it. Like the *pharmakos,* Horner is expelled from the social system, his alienation being his public designation as eunuch. . . . But as Derrida has argued . . . the expulsion of the scapegoat also endlessly makes apparent the very difference it seeks to hide." Burke, "Wycherley's 'Tendentious Joke': The Discourse of Alterity in *The Country Wife*," *The Eighteenth Century: Theory and Interpretation* 29 (1988), 238.

110. W. R. Chadwick finds as a minor flaw the unlikelihood that Pinchwife "would not have heard of Horner's impotence before Act V." But owing to his perception and fears he may well have simply rejected the validity of the rumor. Chadwick, *The Four Plays of William Wycherley*, p. 104, n. 16.

111. These words are bitterly ironic in that he mouths the trite couplet as a way to concede his defeat without dwelling on the significance to his masculinity. I do not agree with A. N. Kaul that "From now on Pinchwife will be as well-adjusted and routinely jealous a husband as Sir Jasper Fidget"—for to take a

pair of horns back to the country would be unthinkable in part because the country had long viewed the male's reputation as a cuckold as "a slur both on his virility and his capacity to rule his own household." He would be defamed and denied public office—often, with his wife, suffering the indignation of a "skimmington" (public shame and punishment). Kaul, *The Action of English Comedy,* p. 127; Stone, *The Family, Sex and Marriage in England,* pp. 503–4.

112. Her remark "Come Brother your wife is yet innocent you see" (381) prompts one of her few detractors, Gerald Weales, to claim that "she is either as corrupt as Dorilant and the Quack, in covering for Horner, or as stupid as she has often seemed to be." *The Complete Works of William Wycherley,* p. xix. Her words, though, reflect neither corruption nor stupidity but rather that "sisterly" overture for Margery's sake. Nor would I agree with J. Peter Verdurmen's argument that here Alithea's "abrupt reversal" of character "can be understood only as an emotional reaction to the heavy pressure she has undergone." Verdurmen, "Grasping for Permanence: Ideal Couples in *The Country Wife* and *Aureng-Zebe,*" p. 342.

113. A dance consisting of Sir Jaspar, Pinchwife, and Sparkish? Horner's remark to the Quack—"Where are your Maskers" (401) conjures a separate troupe advancing on stage. To John Bowman the dance "seems to be a survival of the jigs and undoubtedly was an obscene and mocking short-hand for the play's action." John Harwood views it as an "icon of disorder, of loyalties forsaken and vows neglected." I would agree about the disorder, but where have we seen loyalties forsaken and vows broken to the extent that we are to feel regret (Alithea and Sparkish)? Bowman, "Dance, Chant and Mask in the Plays of Wycherley," p. 183; Harwood, *Critics, Values, and Restoration Comedy,* p. 111.

114. As "phallic symbol incarnate," writes Virginia Birdsall, Horner "represents, in all his impudence, the life force triumphant." On the other hand, John Harwood believes that Horner finds a hell in a "confinement to his own solitary being and the petty illusions by which he defines himself and of which he is master." Finally, I agree with the heart of Peggy Thompson's argument that the "dance and epilogue also resonate with the threatening power of female sexuality that Horner as hostile and inadequate lover cannot control." Birdsall, *Wild Civility,* p. 156; Harwood, *Critics, Values, and Restoration Comedy,* p. 111; Thompson, "The Limits of Parody in *The Country Wife,*" p. 113.

115. David Vieth does not go this far but does believe that Horner's "strikingly successful ruse limits the nature of his masculine activities so drastically that in a sense he becomes the eunuch he pretends to be" Vieth, "Wycherley's *The Country Wife:* An Anatomy of Masculinity," p. 346. We may find interesting if not significant the fact that Charles Hart (Horner) spoke the Prologue and Elizabth Knepp (Lady Fidget) the Epilogue—emphasizing a shift in power and ascendency at play's end. (The Epilogue chides the males for their inability to satisfy their women.)

116. I disagree, then, with Julie Stone Peters' assertion that here we see "the brilliant flash of Horner's final victory." Peters, "'Things Govern'd by Words': Late Seventeenth-Century Comedy and the Reformers," *English Studies* 68 (1987): 148.

117. The dance "Cuckolds all in a row"—explained in John Playford's *The English Dancing Master* (1650)—may be said to describe the play's movements, frenzied yet going nowhere, especially in the attempts of the male to put aside the woman, and the woman's redoubtable efforts to gain ground: "Men put the [contrary women] back by both hands, fall even on the [contrary's] side men cast

off to the right hand, your [women] following, come to the same place again . . put them back again, fall on your owne side, men cast off to the left hand, and come to your places, the [women] following" (p. 67).

118. Powell, *Restoration Theatre Production,* p 144.

CHAPTER 4: "SURROUNDED WITH SO MANY FEARS AND GRIEFS"

The quotation in the chapter title is from *Love in a Wood,* V.i.354.

1. The consensus view rejects the authority of the playwright's comment to Pope that he wrote this play as early as 1666. (See Joseph Spence, *Observations, Anecdotes, and Characters of Books and Men.* 2 vols., ed. James M. Osborn [Oxford: Clarendon Press, 1966], 1:34.) Robert Hume believes that a version of the comedy might have been composed earlier (around 1673), but that Wycherley revised it after the success of *The Country Wife.* See Friedman, *Plays,* pp. xiii–xvi; Hume, "William Wycherley: Text, Life, Interpretation," p. 401. Because the plays were performed within a relatively short time of one another—only five or six years (1671–1676) from the performance of *Love in a Wood* to that of *The Plain-Dealer*—Wycherley would have been, it seems, even more cognizant of their interrelationship, a connection he makes obvious in this play with the allusions to his own *Country Wife.* An excellent "handbook" to the comedy is found in Peter Holland's *The Ornament of Action: Text and Performance in Restoration Comedy,* pp. 170–203.

2. Katharine Rogers argues that whereas at first Wycherley portrays Manly as "a satiric butt," he later gives him a "moral stature." We are only confused because Wycherley vacillates between "detachment and indentification" in depicting him. Rose Zimbardo calls Manly a "satiric spokesman," not a hero. He is part of a "dark satiric design" of the English tradition. W. R. Chadwick points to Wycherley's having taken the name "Manly" later in his life as evidence that he intended him "to be, on balance, a sympathetic character." (But if others wished to make something out of Manly the play did not "intend," we cannot expect Wycherley to have held up his hands and begged, "No, no, don't give me that name. I meant it ironically in *The Plain-Dealer.*") Conversely, Norman Holland finds that Manly is a "blundering, blustering, and self-deceived" character—"a dupe, not a hero." Rogers, *William Wycherley,* pp. 77, 81, 88; Zimbardo, *Wycherley's Drama,* pp. 16, 79; Chadwick, *The Four Plays of William Wycherley,* p. 175; Holland, *The First Modern Comedies,* p. 98.

3. The comments of Peter Holland are worth repeating: "The audience in the theatre and the reader of the published text have no doubt that plain-dealing means not feigning. But even before the play itself starts, Wycherley confuses the audience, disorientates them, by joining the two incompatible ideas, plain-dealing and pretence, around the dual concept inherent in the word 'acting,' doing something and performing, pretending to do something in a play." *The Ornament of Action,* p. 171. Robert Markley adds that "Many of the interpretive problems that the play creates are foreshadowed (for readers, if not for the audience) in Wycherley's savagely ironic dedication to Mother Bennet." *Two-Edg'd Weapons,* p. 179.

4. And that this play, more than Wycherley's others, comes off better as dramatic literature than as staged drama may be inferred in some of the confused reaction when it was originally performed—though few have been so willing to

sweep it aside as Richard Bevis has recently done: "its plots are poorly integrated, and it is weakened by Wycherley's lack of distance from Manly. The female characters are generally unsatisfactory, and the brilliant stagecraft of *The Country Wife* is almost entirely lacking." Some critics have shared—and I believe rightly so—Ian Donaldson's point that the play is difficult "because of its strong feeling of contradictoriness. This contradictoriness seems to me to be deliberate and controlled, the source of the play's energy and brilliance." As for the name Manly, Donaldson adds that "Beneath the general, admiring connotations of the name gather more subversive suggestions." Derek Hughes too offers a valuable summation: "Of all the perplexing plays that the Restoration has left us, none can be more perplexing than Wycherley's *The Plain-Dealer* (1676), for where there is universal disagreement on every fundamental question, perplexity can go no further." Bevis, "Canon, Pedagogy, Prospectus: Redesigning 'Restoration and Eighteenth-Century Drama,'" *Comparative Drama* 31 (1997): 181; Donaldson, "'Tables Turned': *The Plain-Dealer*," *Essays in Criticism* 17 (1967): 308, 313; Hughes, "*The Plain-Dealer:* A Reappraisal," p. 315.

5. She is certainly correct, however, to argue that we must understand and not simply condemn the behavior of this "tormented" man. *Wild Civility,* pp. 165, 167. W. Gerald Marshall finds throughout the comedy "the elements of theatricality and madness": Manly's form of madness is his "obsession" with hypocrisy, which "leads him into an illusory perception not only of the world around him, but of himself; and it leads him into his own drama of madness." Marshall, "Wycherley's Drama of Madness: *The Plain-Dealer*," p. 32; reprinted in *Great Stage of Fools,* pp. 93–95. In another psychological reading, Anthony Kaufman argues that in Manly the playwright presents "a complex and dramatically powerful study of an exceptional man disbarred by his own anger and contempt for the world from experiencing friendship and love." Kaufman, "Idealization, Disillusion, and Narcissistic Rage in Wycherley's 'The Plain Dealer,'" p. 119.

6. John Harold Wilson sees a parallel between Manly and Almanzor (in Dryden's *Conquest of Granada* earlier in the decade), with Cynthia Matlack adding that Wycherley is offering a parody of the heroic play in his *Plain-Dealer.* But I would disagree with the view that the play is in the main, or even in part, a *conscious* parody of a genre—a state of mind, yes. Still, Robert Hume does well to remind us that "Modern critics have generally conceived Restoration comedy and heroic drama as contradictory extremes, but to study their connections as well as their differences can be instructive." Wilson, *A Preface to Restoration Drama,* p. 161; Matlack, "Parody and Burlesque of Heroic Ideals in Wycherley's Comedies," pp. 281–86; Hume, "Theory of Comedy in the Restoration," *Modern Philology* 70 (1973): 309.

7. In *Love in a Wood,* we might remember, Vincent offers the assessment, "for coyness in a woman is as little sign of true modesty, as huffing in a man, is of true courage" (II.i.185–87). Other than the traditional definitions of the adjective *manly,* one seventeenth-century usage was "human," another "grown up" or "mature." And there was the older medieval context of "Humane; charitable; generous"—all suggesting the potential for an ironic application of the name to Wycherley's character (see *OED*). Katharine Rogers finds Manly "a curiously inept choice" of names if the character were "intended to be primarily a butt" and that the "possibility of irony can be ruled out, since without exception Wycherley's other character names are to be taken literally." But Wycherley has shown that taking a name at its most literal level (a Lady Flippant, Mrs. Caution, Pinchwife, Alithea, or Horner) is to miss a number of ironic possibilities (or

probabilities). Rogers, "Fatal Inconsistency: Wycherley and *The Plain-Dealer,*" *ELH* 28 (1961): 152.

8. *Leviathan,* p. 24.

9. Anthony Kaufman sees in Manly's "illusion" the "psychological phenomenon" of "idealization" and offers Charles Ryscroft's view that the function of idealization is "to enable the ego to deny feelings of hopelessness and emptiness." (Ryscroft writes also of the "fear of the external object resulting from projection on to it of endogenous destructive impulses.") Kaufman, "Idealization, Disillusion, and Narcissistic Rage in Wycherley's 'The Plain Dealer,'" pp. 122–23. Ryscroft, "On Idealization, Illusion, and Catestrophic Disillusion," in *Imagination and Reality: Psycho-Analytic Essays, 1951–1961* (London: Hogarth Press, 1968), p. 35.

10. Rose Zimbardo concludes that the *Plain-Dealer* is a "darker, more deeply disturbing work, which verges on that end of the satiric spectrum that skirts nihilistic irony." Chadwick contends that Wycherley approved of Manly's fulminations against such an "unhealthy" society but also that the playwright's "satiric impulse" had "become so strong that it overbalanced that rational, ordering faculty that is so important to the creative process"—leading Wycherley to many dramaturgic flaws in the play. And Derek Cohen also sees the playwright championing his lead character: "In a world where social intercourse demands certain kinds of dishonesty, his capacity to speak his mind immediately and straightforwardly without regard for the consequence is like fresh air in an infected place"; "When Manly is onstage he dominates the action; he diminishes everyone around him by a large looming presence." Zimbardo, "William Wycherley," p. 277. Chadwick, *The Four Plays of William Wycherley,* pp. 176–77, 179–90; Cohen, "The Alternating Styles of *The Plain-Dealer,*" *Restoration and Eighteenth-Century Theatre Research,* second series, 2, no. 1 (1987): 19, 24. Other critics assume more of a middle ground: the play is a satire "in its tone and character," a comedy "in its movement toward a social resolution of the conflicts of characters." William McCarthy, *William Wycherley: A Biography* (Athens: Ohio University Press, 1979), p. 73. Laura Brown notes that the satire of the play "seems always to be retreating from a standard of behavior to one merely of honest admission of one's behavior." Wycherley is "thus able to criticize the satus quo, but unable or unwilling to stand by that criticism." Brown, *English Dramatic Form, 1660–1760: An Essay in Generic History* (New Haven: Yale University Press, 1981), pp. 56, 58. Finally, Kevin Cope believes that Manly is "too deep in the battle of the ideal with the vicious to assert a satirist's control over events." "The Conquest of Truth: Wycherley, Rochester, Butler, and Dryden and the Restoration Critique of Satire," *Restoration* 10 (1986): 26.

11. "For the first of many times in the play, an event is discussed and shown to be open to a variety of interpretations. It is clear that Manly's ship has sunk, but the motives and results, the meanings of the relationship of that act to the individuals involved in it, are not reconcilable. . . . Manly himself is beginning to be shown as an accumulation of irreconcilable contradictions." Peter Holland, *The Ornamant of Action,* pp. 187, 188.

12. On several occasions, these sailors refer to each other by name, Jack and Tom, as if to reject Manly's view that they are mere "Rascals" and "Dogs"—thereby countering his "heroic" misanthropy by their more "manly" sociability.

13. Zimbardo, *Wycherley's Drama,* pp. 127–28. In Virginia Birdsall's terms, if Manly is the satiric spokesman, Freeman is the "comic spokesman": "Thus the play is actually *about* both comedy and satire, as well as about realism and ide-

alism." *Wild Civility,* p. 158. James Thompson contends that Manly "stands out like a tourist in a foreign country, but Freeman blends in like a native, in England speaking as the English do"—later adding that Freeman's "expedience is shown to be corrupt, but Manly's idealism is impossible" and that in Freeman Wycherley "presents an even nastier picture: in his preditory acquisitiveness, we are forced to see the values celebrated by this age"—two points with which I cannot agree. Thompson, *Language in Wycherley's Plays,* p. 102; "Ideology and Dramatic Form," p. 170. I am more inclined to second Derek Cohen's view that "Freeman's ironic gaze refracts the society with a remarkably lucid result." His "self-knowledge" allows him "to understand the behaviour and the lapses of others." "The Alternating Styles of *The Plain-Dealer,*" p. 24.

14. I strongly disagree, then, with Laura Morrow's assertion that Freeman is held up for criticism for his "ready resignation to pragmatism": "Like his misanthropic friend, Freeman withdraws from society," which therefore justifies Manly's "desire for solitude"; and with Anthony Kaufman's view that "beneath the ceremonious flattery of compliments and hugs, lies malice" and that Freeman's "laughing detachment does not signal acceptance and toleration"—but "malice and hostility"—especially "towards women." Morrow, "Phenomenological Psychology and Comic Form in *The Plain-Dealer,*" *Restoration and Eighteenth-Century Theatre Research,* second series, 3, no. 2 (1988): 3–4; and Kaufman, "Idealization, Disillusion, and Narcissistic Rage in Wycherley's 'The Plain Dealer,'" pp. 130–31.

15. According to Derek Cohen, Manly "shows his obsessive concerns" largely by the "repeated use of the word *I.*" Cohen, "Alternating Styles in the *Plain-dealer,*" p. 26.

16. Helen Burke argues that Manly "at the beginning of the play, is thus recreating what Lacan would term the 'mirror stage' of subjectivity, the dyadic economy of the Imaginary, in which the one is preoccupied with the other as a guarantor of the unity of the self." Burke, "'Law-Suits,' 'Love-Suits,' and the Family Property in Wycherley's *The Plain-Dealer*" in J. Douglas Canfield and Deborah C. Payne, eds., *Cultural Readings of Restoration & Eighteenth-Century English Theatre* (Athens: University of Georgia Press, 1995), p. 103.

17. Katharine Rogers notes that Fidelia reflects an "exaggerated self-abnegation"; and Rose Zimbardo sees in her the "virtue of a past age to which the satirist always looks with longing." A. N. Kaul calls her "a Viola sentimentalized out of all credibility. A paragon of virtue and dullness, she surpasses even Alithea and Lydia in sheer lack of vitality." Rogers, *William Wycherley,* p. 87; Zimbardo, *Wycherley's Drama,* pp. 16, 144; Kaul, *The Action of English Comedy,* p. 110.

18. In Shakespeare we may find others besides Viola who dress as males to bring about comic resolution, most notably Rosalind in *As You Like It* and Portia in *The Merchant of Venice.* But we ought not forget Imogen in *Cymbeline,* not only because this "Fidele" is associated with a sordid "bed trick" but also because sexual revenge is motivation for much of the action. And Pisano's advice to Imogen on becoming a man not only sounds like advice Manly would give but also describes Manly fairly accurately:

> You must forget to be a woman; change
> Command into obedience; fear and niceness
> (The handmaidens of all women, or more truly
> Woman it pretty self) into a waggish courage,

> Ready in gibes, quick-answer'd, saucy, and
> As quarrellous as the weasel.
> (III.iv.154–59)

19. New spelling editions of Wycherley's play effectively strip the work of possible allegorical connotations by removing the capital letters, and this is one of several reasons why old spelling texts are to be preferred. I believe that Fidelia's words *Truth, Honour, Fame, Love, Faith,* and *Duty* are able to carry the weight of abstraction and allegory quite comfortably.

20. James Thompson likewise sees Fidelia's allegorical significance: it is, he writes, "a type of morality play." My point is that realism does accommodate the allegory (as Manly must learn to do). Thompson, *Language in Wycherley's Plays,* pp. 105–6. As for the difficulty of accepting an allegorical reading in "realistic" drama, Meredith Anne Skura offers the following caveat: "allegorical representation is not unnatural or artificial, though critics have always taken it to be so. It simply draws on the resources of a kind of thinking that differs from the one in which we construct a naturalistic, mimetic picture of reality." Skura, *The Literary Uses of the Psychoanalytic Process,* pp. 153–54.

21. At this point—and in the space of only fourteen lines—Wycherley uses "afraid" *eight* times. (338–52).

22. Jon Lance Bacon is correct to note that most "have judged the Widow Blackacre harshly." To Derek Hughes she is "the least attractive of the many women on the Restoration stage who struggle against institutionalized systems of justice, and who try to control the writing of their own fate. . . . [It is] doubtful whether she herself excites much sympathy." Katharine Rogers terms the law in the play "institutionalized falsity"; James Thompson sees as a theme the "corruption of law"—a central question being "will the play affirm or overcome the law?" Hughes also considers the "craving for legal form" in the play: "The rituals of law are ideally rituals of proof, and their debasement into bewildering chaos typifies a world in which empty words and meaningless forms veil the intrinsics of human existence." Bacon, "Wives, Widows, and Writing in Restoration Comedy," p. 435; Hughes, *English Drama,* pp. 190–91; Rogers, *William Wycherley,* p. 90; Thompson, *Language in Wycherley's Plays,* p. 94; Hughes, "The Plain-Dealer: A Reappraisal," p. 328. For further discussion on this matter consult Robert F. Bode, "'Try Me, At Least': The Dispensing of Justice in *The Plain-Dealer,*" *Restoration and Eighteenth-Century Theatre Research,* second series, 4, no. 1 (1989): 1–24. Bode argues that Wycherley has "created in the Widow a character who brings into the play an accurate and realistic representation of the contemporary operations of private law and equity in the courts, the corrupt state of which is virtually a byword in Restoration comedy" (p. 2).

23. The irony here is typically Wycherlean: he *should* have the same basic distrust of his "Love" as he does of her relation, the Widow Blackacre.

24. Although his topic is Dryden's heroic drama, Derek Hughes makes a point relevant to Wycherley's play: the heroic plays in short reveal "the disparity between Herculean aspiration and human reality." Hughes, *Dryden's Heroic Plays* (Lincoln: University of Nebraska Press, 1981), p. 2. We may note as well Manly's earlier reference to the fools who "seem to rehearse Bays's grand Dance" (I.i.288), which also stresses his heroic individuality (an emulation of an Alamanzor). Indeed, we would expect someone with such heroic sentiments to find little pleasure in Buckingham's *The Rehearsal.*

25. Such as Elizabeth, the wife of Henry VII and the last link to the once pow-

erful House of York, who with her husband lies in the beautiful Lady Chapel. And Westminster Abbey had far more lewd associations, as suggested in the anonymous poem, "The Westminster Whore" (c. 1610). See Burford, *Bawdy Verse,* pp. 63–64.

26. Lawrence Stone recounts that the women were not satisfied with the patronizing remarks coming from the Parliament: they "were making statements which revealed the development of a wholly new level of feminine consciousness." *The Family, Sex and Marriage in England,* pp. 338–40.

27. I disagree, then, with Derek Hughes's contention that the Widow is "a forbidding battle-ax," who "allows her verbose litigiousness to efface *all* traces of sexual . . . instinct" (my emphasis). "*The Plain-Dealer:* A Reappraisal," pp. 320, 323.

28. See Friedman, *Plays,* p. 423, n. 3. To help suggest Freeman's hostility toward women, Anthony Kaufman notes that the Widow is likely "old and ugly," but there is no good evidence that she is one or both—even though one gets the cheap laugh if she is either or both. J. Douglas Canfield adds that the part of the Widow was played by Katherine Cory, who "a few years earlier had created Duffett's fetid, grotesque amourous old woman [Strega] in the play of that name"—a fact that *cannot,* of course, prove that the Widow Blackacre is without any identifiable pulchritude. Corey had also played Octavia in *All for Love,* Doll Common in *The Alchemist,* and Lucy in *The Country Wife.* She was apparently larger than most of her fellow actresses, but no one suggested that she was hideous. Manner and make-up could indeed transform the pleasant face into the grotesque, but Wycherley's actors were able to depict characters of considerably different types—e.g., Michael Mohun (Dapperwit and Pinchwife), Charles Hart (Horner and Manly), Edward Kynaston (Valentine and Freeman), Betty Boutell (Christina and Margery Pinchwife), Elizabeth Knepp (Lady Fidget and Eliza), and Elizabeth James (Isabel and Alithea). The implication to me is more that the Widow Blackacre has at least some vestige of sexual attractiveness remaining to her. Kaufman, "Idealization, Disillusion, and Narcissistic Rage in Wycherley's 'The Plain Dealer,'" p. 131; Canfield, *Tricksters & Estates,* p. 138.

29. Derek Hughes writes of this speech: "This is an unexpected inversion of the theriophilic commonplace that beasts, 'who on others prey, their Kind will spare,' and that only man destroys his own species." He continues, "As his name suggests, Manly remains human, but he at times approaches each of Aristotle's extremes, alternating between heroic magnanimity and anarchic brutality." "*The Plain Dealer:* A Reappraisal," p. 317.

30. For more on the difficulty of applying a literal definition of the term, see Peter Holland's *The Ornament of Action,* pp. 171–80. William McCarthy argues that "plain-dealing" did not mean "speaking truth in all cases," but rather "speaking the truth in the most suitable manner or altering if circumstances necessitate such deception." McCarthy, *William Wycherley: A Biography,* p. 78. Of course, Manly's perception of the term seems more absolutist than McCarthy's qualified definition indicates. To Ben Ross Schneider, it "would be a pity if by the help of literary scholarship, Plain-dealing, the quality for which both Wycherley and his hero were admired in their own time, should be interpreted as a flaw in that hero's character and ignored as a salient feature of the whole class of plays which Wycherley's *The Plain-Dealer* in this respect epitomized." My answer would have to be, then—the more's the pity. Schneider, *The Ethos of Restoration Comedy,* p. 103.

31. A memorable parallel would be Harriet's completing for Dorimant a couplet from Waller, which becomes an emblem of both their fitness for each other and of her ascendancy. *Man of Mode,* V.ii.106–7.

32. Although our emphases are somewhat different, Derek Hughes also finds the motif of interruption highly significant: "In each case, fear of interruption—of society—coincides with some antisocial purpose.... The interruptions account for much of the apparent disjointedness of the play." *"The Plain-Dealer:* A Reappraisal," pp. 326–27. And of course coitus interruptus was known "particularly to the seventeenth century" as the common method of controlling births: "Within marriage, abstinence and *coitus interruptus* helped to trim family size to economic openings." Roy Porter, "Mixed Feelings," in Boucé, p. 3.

33. W. Gerald Marshall writes that Plausible "assumes a dramatic role—that of the supreme flatterer," although it is "generated by an obsessive idea which shapes his perception of the outer world and makes his performance more complex than Manly suggests." Marshall, "Wycherley's Drama of Madness: *The Plain-Dealer,*" pp. 29–30 and *Great Stage of Fools,* pp. 88–89.

34. Anthony Kaufman argues that the men's "desire to see in Olivia their own image perfectly reveals the mythic roots of psychological narcissism." Kaufman, "Idealization, Disillusion, and Narcissistic Rage in Wycherley's 'The Plain Dealer,'" p. 123.

35. We might recall Eliza's spirited entendre earlier in the scene: "Nay if you are for more *solid* pleasure, what think you of a rich, young Husband!" (emphasis added; 51–52). Peter Hynes argues that in the Eliza-Olivia scene, Wycherley "wants finally to endorse a self-conscious version of artifice which more or less successfully hides its traces and converts itself back into nature." Hynes, "Against Theory?: Knowledge and Action in Wycherley's Plays," p. 186.

36. Given that Elizabeth Barry was a little too young at the time, Wycherley could have no better actress assaying the role of Olivia than Rebecca Marshall. This "very handsome" performer (one of several that Pepys was much taken with) was often cast in "Queenly" and other dark, imposing, and passionate roles—such as Dryden's Lyndaraxa, Joyner's Fulvia, Crowne's Berenice, and Lee's Roxana. But she also played, between 1667–77, a number of "younger" roles: Dryden's Berenice, Lee's Gloriana, and Durfey's Maria. See Elizabeth Howe, *The First English Actresses* (Cambridge: University Press, 1992), pp. 152–53, 163–64, 187. The earlier study of the subject was John Harold Wilson's *All the King's Ladies* (Chicago: University of Chicago Press, 1958).

37. Just how old is Olivia? Manly's "tho' you were young" suggests that she might only have been in her later teens or at the most early twenties when he left. To Manly, her youth denoted innocence, that quality more conducive to being reshaped into a heroic paragon. The idea of a mature London woman is antithetical to Manly's creation—as it was to Pinchwife's.

38. Because Olivia has seen *The Country Wife,* this reference to "honour" most likely includes the sexual connotation Lady Fidget gave the term.

39. Manly might have benefitted from the advice Shakespeare's Olivia gives Malvolio (a literary cousin of Manly's we might argue): "O, you are sick of self-love, Malvolio, and taste with a distemper'd appetite. To be generous, guiltless, and of that free disposition, is to take those things for birdbolts that you deem cannon bullets. There is no slander in an allow'd fool, though he do nothing but rail; nor no railery in a known discreet man, though he do nothing but reprove" (*Twelfth Night,* I.v.82–88).

40. For Wycherley's audience, the latest pairing of Beck Marshall and Betty

Boutell would have been a special treat, given the memorable couplings in earlier plays: *The Roman Empress, The Conquest of Granada, The Tragedy of Nero, The Destruction of Jerusalem,* and particualry as Roxana and Statira in Lee's *Alexander the Great*—parts later played by Barry and Bracegirdle. Elizabeth Howe, *The First English Actresses,* pp. 152–54, 162–63.

41. A fanciful portrait of Manly may be likened to that done of Cromwell by Robert Walker (ca. 1649). The general looks impatient, annoyed, fatigued, and desirous of turning away from the artist. The aid tying his sash could well represent the benign presence of Fidelia—the prop against which the spiritually isolated figure of Cromwell [Manly] rests. See David Smurthwaite, *Battlefields of Britain* (Exeter: Webb & Bower, 1984), p. 134.

42. More than simple punning, Widow Blackacre's repetition of *court* (thrice in two lines) suggests her insistence and agitation—the initial consonant sound serving to punctuate her observations—pushing matters along with the harsh aspiration of the hard "c." In the section devoted to the Widow and the lawyers (III.i.135–265), one finds a healthy number of hard *c* words emitting from her mouth: *court* or *courts* (6 occurrences), *cause* or *causes* (10), *come* (5), *common* (3), *counsel* (3), *client* (3), and one each for *comparison, copiously, cavil, coughing, conversant, carrier, clerks, cuff, consider,* and *case.*

43. He might better have called her a "Fury," another who was much concerned with the "law," for we see here that she wishes to avenge the "murder" (the loss of her papers being a legal death) of a mother by the child. We can be sure she would pursue Jerry and Freeman with no less purpose than the Furies follwd Orestes or Alcmaeon. The Furies, we might also recall, were dressed in black robes when, in pursuit of Orestes, they appeared at one of the shrines of the Eringes in Arcadia. Aspasia Velissariou is one who agrees that the Widow Blackacre "arises as the possessor of phallic power." "Gender and the Circulation of Money and Desire in Wycherley's *The Plain-Dealer,*" *Restoration* 18 (1994): 29–30.

44. To Helen Burke, the "revelation that the mother can deceive also threatens to undermine the broader psychosexual fiction of paternal privilege." "'Law-Suits,' 'Love-Suits,' and the Family Property," p. 101.

45. Machiavelli's commentary on Fortune well describes Freeman's approach to his "fortune," the Widow Blackacre: "[F]ortune is a woman, and it is necessary, if you wish to master her, to conquer her by force; and it can be seen that she lets herself be overcome by the bold rather than by those who proceed coldly. And therefore, like a woman, she is always a friend to the young, because they are less cautious, fiercer, and master her with greater audacity." (*The Prince,* chap. 25)—although "mastering" the Widow is really not his goal; nor is it a possibility.

46. He certainly fares better in the agreement than did the hapless Monsieur de Paris in the face of the dominant Flirt (*The Gentleman Dancing-Master,* V.i.565ff).

47. And in the agreement for Jerry we also find merged the sexual and the legal: he must "have free ingress, egress, and regress to and from your Maids Garret" (474–75)—although considering the Jerry we have come to know, it is doubtful the maids have much to fear.

48. I cannot accept, then, Peter Holland's conclusion that "Freeman's success is out of all proportion to his place in the play. So strong has been the audience's feeling of contempt for the widow-hunting, for this capitualtion to the lowest of society's games, that Freeman's triumph has no relation to the moral attitude towards his activity." I cannot imagine more than a handful of any audience

from that time on who would have felt contempt for Freeman's "hunting"—especially given his quarry. *The Ornament of Action,* pp. 199–200.

49. As Pascal wrote in *The Pensées* (appearing in 1670), "We sail on a vast expanse, always drifting in uncertainty, and carried hither and thither. If there is any point to which we think we can attach ourselves to steady our position, it shifts and leaves us; if we pursue it, it escapes our grasp, slides past us, and vanishes on its eternal course. Nothing stays for us. This is our natural condition, and yet most contrary to our wishes."

50. Helen Burke believes that such neglect is "consistent with the critical perspectives of those critics who insist that Restoration comedies are not culturally or intellectually significant." She adds that the "unsettling effect of this strange play . . . can thus be attributed to a radical destabilization in the economic and sociosexual realm." We find a "Lacanian image of the male subject who is driven by the fear of expropriation." Through the Widow Blackacre, who represents the "economic threat posed by married women at this time because of changing property doctrine," Wycherley is "giving expression to the negative perception of such women in his society." "'Law-Suits,' 'Love-Suits,' and the Family Property in Wycherley's *The Plain-Dealer,*" pp. 90, 93–96.

51. Fidelia's hyperbole does Margery Pinchwife's one better: the Country Wife told her husband that Horner kissed her a "hundred" times. But in both cases the exaggeration is intended to intensify, or has the effect of intensifying, the male's distress. And Fidelia, at least, reveals that her hyperbole was intentional: "So! it works I find as I expected" (107).

52. B. Eugene McCarthy contends that Manly must come to accept the decorum of language as well as action and accept the direct speech of Fidelia. Ronald Berman sees the language of the play being employed to attack—as did Rochester—the period's "new values": "taste, grace, ease and the libertine capacity to distance emotional experience." Manly "speaks the language of feeling," and his rage, again like Rochester's, "is not only against the enemies of good sense. It is against the idea that certain conditions can be borne. It is against the limits of language." McCarthy, "Wycherley's *The Plain-Dealer* and the Limits of Wit," *English Miscellany* 22 (1971): 47–92. Berman, "Wycherley's Unheroic Society," *ELH* 51 (1984): 466–68.

53. James Thompson also notes the large number of interruptions in the play: "At times, it seems as if this play is composed entirely of interruption." But his emphasis is on verbal and providential interruption as opposed to mine—the frustration and tension in the parody of *sexual* interruption. *Language in Wycherley's Plays,* p. 107.

54. Perceptive like Pinchwife, Olivia offers a most telling assessment of Manly that embodies what may be seen as quintessential Wycherlean philosophy: "he that distrusts most the World, trusts most to himself, and is but the more easily deceiv'd, because he thinks he can't be deceiv'd: his cunning is like the Coward's Sword, by which he is oftner worsted, than defended" (IV.ii.201–4). W. Gerald Marshall writes that because she moves "*toward* the kind of madness reflected by other characters" and "consciously benefits from their obsessions," she "becomes one of the most interesting characters of the Restoration stage." Olivia's "ingenious use of theatricality enables her to become a *mirror of madness,* to actually act out the insane fictions and obsessions of the deranged characters." Marshall, "Wycherley's Drama of Madness: *The Plain Dealer,*" p. 33; *Great Stage of Fools,* pp. 87, 96–98.

55. The thinking "better on't" has led to a debate over whether Manly means thinking better of having sex or thinking better of a public revelation of the sex he has just had with Olivia. Derek Hughes believes that sexual relations have occurred, pointing to Manly's line "for if I barely shou'd publish it, she wou'd deny it with as much impudence, as she wou'd act it again with this young Fellow [Fidelia] here" (IV.ii.291–93). (Hughes, "*The Plain-Dealer:* A Reappraisal," p. 323, n. 17.) The *it* still remains ambiguous, though—actual sex, her infamy, thought of sex, planned sex act, false sex act—and the acting "it again" with Fideila may just as well refer to the lovemaking, stroking already having taken place in truth and in Manly's troubled mind. Hughes goes on to write that "we have no good reason to doubt Manly when he tells Vernish—whom he still trusts as a friend—that he has slept with Olivia" (V.ii.122–32). But I think we do have good reason. In Manly's state—with his masculinity so assailed and his sense of embarrassment over admitting that Olivia disdains him—he would most naturally embellish and twist the truth, if not lie outright, particularly about a matter that reflects on his manhood. Moreover, the plans for the second night would seem far less effective or at least superfluous had Manly already "raped" Olivia. Also, Olivia's breathless anticipation over sexual union with Fidelia well into the play's final act suggests that she has not lately (Act IV) shared her bed with any one. But the clinching evidence that he has not yet performed his sordid act may well be the fact that throughout the play we have been witness to frequent and varied occasions of coitus interruptus. Here, I would argue, is but one more instance. Robert Bode concludes that whatever happened in the bedroom, it was "not a 'rape' within the usually accepted defintion of the word," but that there *was* sexual intercourse: "for Manly's frame of mind makes it unlikely that he would have postponed having intercourse with Olivia even if he did postpone revealing it to people other than Fidelia immediately afterwards." Although I do not share this view, Bode's piece is one of the best arguments in favor of Manly's having had sex with Olivia. Bode, "A Rape and No Rape: Olivia's Bedroom Revisited," *Restoration* 12 (1988): 81–82. Still, the belief in the rape's having occurred has a number of vigorous supporters. Pat Gill offers the following to anyone who would argue differently: "To defend Manly's action from the charge of rape, one must ignore the subterfuge Manly uses to gain entrance into Olivia's arms and must argue against historical evidence that forcible assault is the only sexual violation deserving of the appellation of rape." *Interpreting Ladies,* p. 82. But one need not ignore the subterfuge nor the historical evidence of rape (whatever form) when one argues that there was *no* sexual intercourse between Manly and Olivia. For other views on the matter see Peter Holland, *The Ornament of Action,* pp. 197–99, and Percy Adams's most helpful essay "What Happened in Olivia's Bedroom? or Ambiguity in *The Plain-Dealer,*" in Thomas Austin Kirby and William John Oliver, eds., *Essays in Honor of Esmond Linworth Marilla* (Baton Rouge: Louisiana State University Press, 1970), pp. 174–87. Adams concludes that either choice may be defended—and that the ambiguity was likely deliberate. Finally, to Helen Burke, the play "affords no closure on the question of the sexual relation," although Manly's "proposed rape of Olivia (by pretending to be Fidelia) would effect the reimposition of [the] dialectic [the Hegelian model of the master-slave dialectic] and thus the return of the woman to her role as complement to the male." "'Law-Suits,' 'Love-Suits,' and Family Property," pp. 106–7.

56. Fidelia does speak with conviction—"Oh! oh! rather than you shall drag

me to a death so horrid, and so shameful, I'll die here a thousand deaths" (391–92)—but her words suggest one whose choices are severely limited to self-destruction or destruction by another. She is not like Shakespeare's Viola, who (though nervously) does draw her sword to protect herself from the likes of Aguecheek. It is not until the end of the play that Fidelia displays her physical mettle—but even there it is mitigated by her running at Vernish "behind" while he is struggling with Manly.

57. Eliza's calling theirs a "Plain-dealing" age continues to raise an interesting question. If we are to see plain-dealing as an admirable trait—one Manly has put considerable stock in—what do we make of Eliza's comment? If all or most are plain-dealers (meaning that the concept is the darling of the world but not in actuality practised), does this mean that the audience and reader is to put little stock in it? Is Manly trying to be the *only* one who truly speaks plain—again emphasizing his "heroic" aspirations? Or are Eliza and Freeman the only true plain dealers? If so, they think little of the term. It seems evident that Wycherley makes the concept an impossible one and those who are the healthiest in the play admit to that fact. James Thompson reminds us of Lord Halifax's comment that "A man that should call everything by its right Name, would hardly pass the streets without being knocked down as a common enemy." Finally, Sandra Sherman argues that in the play "plain dealing" is "reconfigured, not dispatched." Thompson. *Language in Wycherley's Plays,* p. 100. See also *The Works of Halifax,* ed. Walter Raleigh (Oxford: Oxford University Press, 1912), p. 246. Sherman, "Manly, Manliness, and Friendship in *The Plain-Dealer," Restoration* 20 (1996): 27.

58. Therefore, Manly shares Harcourt's and Dorliant's facility with the evocative and insulting simile. Derek Hughes has moreover determined that Manly is "less distinct from his antagonists than he imagines, and he becomes increasingly dependent upon the very linguistic process that he rejects." *English Drama,* p. 192.

59. The references to ships also call to mind their relationship to madness as well as to courage and adventure. As Foucault writes, "One thing at least is certain: water and madness have long been linked in the dreams of European man." And there is the "ship of fools" metaphor: "It is for the other world that the madman sets sail in his fool's boat; it is from the other world that he comes when he disembarks." In a most interesting passage, teasingly relevant to Wycherley's play, Foucault considers late medievel associations: "Soul as a skiff, abandoned on the infinite sea of desires. . . . a craft at the mercy of the sea's great madness, unless it throws out a solid anchor, faith, or raises its spiritual sails." Foucault moreover reminds us that the melancholy of the English "was easily explained by the influence of maritime climate, cold, humidity, the instability of the weather; all those fine droplets of water that penetrated the channels and fibers of the human body and made it lose its firmness, redisposed it to madness." Foucault, *Madness and Civilization: A History of Insanity in the Age of Reason,* trans. Richard Howard (New York: Random House, 1973), pp. 11–13. (This translation is of the edition [of *Histoire de la Folie,* 1961] abridged by Foucault.) Another perspective—one Wycherley would also have found congenial—is found in the bawdy lines from Oldham's "Sardanapulus":

> C——t was the Star that rul'd thy Fate,
> C——t the sole business and Affair of State,
> . . . .

> And C——t the sure unerring Card
> Which plac'd at Helm, the mighty Vessel and its motion steer'd.

Quoted in Thompson, *Unfit for Modest Ears,* p. 120.

60. Rose Zimbardo states that courage and cruelty go hand in hand in the Renaissance conception of the satirist. There is a "tinge of misanthropy" in "all heroes of Restoration comedy," adds Ben Ross Schneider. But the emphasis on satirical intent leads one to question in another way the matter of Manly's revenge on Olivia: according to T. W. Craik, "Confidence in Wycherley as a moral satirist is severely undermined if he so casually sacrifices his hero's character to exciting intrigue; and it is no less weakened if he does not recognize anything amiss with Manly's action except that it pains the disguised Fidelia." Anthony Kaufman argues, though, that because Manly is filled with "a sense of radical isolation and loneliness," the "psychoanalytic conceptions of narcissistic rage explain most fully and clearly the source of Manly's limitless rage at Olivia." Zimbardo. *Wycherley's Drama,* p. 85; Schneider, *The Ethos of Restoration Comedy,* p. 101; Craik, "Some Aspects of Satire in Wycherley's Plays," p. 176; Kaufman, "Idealization, Disillusion, and Narcissistic Rage in Wycherley's 'The Plain Dealer,'" pp. 124, 125.

61. Rose Zimbardo believes his vituperations often serve as a "release, a substitution for action," *society* having rendered him impotent. *Wycherley's Drama,* p. 83. For more on railery in the period's comedies see C. D. Cecil, "Raillery in Restoration Comedy," *Huntington Library Quarterly* 29 (1966): 147–59; and John Hayman, "Raillery in Restoration Satire," *Huntington Library Quarterly* 31 (1968): 107–22.

62. Olivia has presumably rejected the possibility that her husband was right about Fidelia's true sex. One could charge Wycherley with some excessive straining of credibility here or argue that her discomfort in the presence of Vernish was a ruse. But is seems more likely that her sexual longings—as is true with any predominant emotion or thought in these plays—obscures her better sense. In addition, Derek Hughes writes that "everyone in the play violates gender stereotype": "the stereotype of male and female are imprecise and over-schematic classifications of the manifold and unpredictable patterns of human life." *English Drama,* pp. 191, 195.

63. According to Rose Zimbardo, the "deterioration" of Manly's character—as evident in his exercising the vices he had decried—suggests his moving from Restoration hero to Renaissance satyr-satirist, a shift from fearless courage and honesty in the first two acts to "brutish sadism" in the last two. From another perspective, William McCarthy sees Manly moving from "malcontent to a true, plain-dealing gentleman," a view shared by both Katharine Rogers, who contends that by the last act, "although his personality has not changed, Manly is almost wholly to be admired"—and by Sandra Sherman: "[Manly] does progress, acknowledging a type of friendship consistent with a contingency of knowledge and power." Derek Cohen has written that "At the end of the play Manly is a far improved person in the conventional sense: he is nicer, more sociable, more capable of the softer emotions." As a result, he is "a tamer and infinitely more ordinary and unexceptional man too"—one who "shrivels into sudden mediocrity." My argument is instead that his character has been consistent for the most part—the potential for brute sadism and violence (stemming from his fear) always present—but with a slight movement forward toward acceptance. Zimbardo, *Wycherley's Drama,* pp. 86–87, 133–34; McCarthy, *William Wycherley: A*

Biography, p. 82; Rogers, "Fatal Inconsistency: Wycherley and *The Plain-Dealer,*" p. 154; Sherman, "Manly, Manliness, and Friendship," p. 18; Cohen, "Alternating Styles in *The Plain-Dealer,* pp. 28, 36.

64. James Thompson notes that at play's end we see Manly's using conditional, and not imperative, modes as he responds to Fidelia's revelations. He even begins to use the "language of civility." *Language in Wycherley's Plays,* pp. 105, 106.

65. Derek Cohen would add Shylock—like him the Widow Blackacre is "a throbbing presence in spite of her departure from sight." "Alternating Styles in *The Plain-Dealer,*" p. 36.

66. Olivia's philosophy might best be stated by Congreve's Millament: "One's cruelty is one's power, and when one parts with one's cruelty, one parts with one's power." *Way of the World,* II.i.434–36.

67. W. R. Chadwick finds the ending, as do most, problematic, especially in the rewards given to the "cynical" Freeman and the misanthropic Manly. Robert Markley asserts that the play "eliminates the middle ground of 'objective' detachment, forcing the audience into an ironic no-man's land among different forms of radical instability. . . . The ending of the play is an escapist fantasy that is played as part wish-fulfillment, part joke." And then there is Norman Holland's sentiment: Manly's reward is "the most outrageous kind of improbability." A far more pessimistic conclusion is that offered by Pat Gill: "The misogynistic principles that inform the action of *The Plain-Dealer* and are necessary in order to interpret it in a favorable light afford a glimpse into some of the more unsavory aspects of seventeenth-century theatrical culture and make this play difficult for some modern readers and viewers to enjoy." J. Douglas Canfield adds that the "lingering question of the play is how long can the Court party and its hired guns, among them the playwrights, hold the Restoration compromise together." Chadwick, *The Four Plays of William Wycherley,* pp. 173–74; Markley, *Two-Edg'd Weapons,* pp. 191, 193; Holland, *The First Modern Comedies,* p. 107; Gill, *Interpreting Ladies,* pp. 95–96; Canfield, *Tricksters & Estates,* p. 139.

68. Derek Hughes writes that Manly's acceptance of Fidelia "signifies the manly protagonist's acceptance of the principle of femininity: hence the decisive role of Fidelia's womanly hair in his conversion." "*The Plain-Dealer:* A Reappraisal," p. 333.

69. This fact is especially telling in light of James Thompson's tally of some one hundred uses of *friend* in the play. *Language in Wycherley's Plays,* p. 102. Sandra Sherman writes that the play "depicts the effect of moral prescriptions that infect male homosociality, depicting how conduct books for 'gentlemen' can derange conduct if followed to their logical conclusion." Nevertheless, *The Plain-Dealer* is "more optimistic about male homosociality than *The Country Wife*"—a point with which I strongly agree. "Manly, Manliness, and Friendship," pp. 20, 28.

70. Helen Burke concludes, "To disengage the complexity of *The Plain-Dealer,* an 'Other' kind of criticism is required, a criticism that is not 'proper.'" "'Law-Suits,' 'Love-Suits,' and Family Property," p. 109.

Chapter 5: Conclusions

The quotation in the conclusion title comes from *The Plain-Dealer,* IV.ii.347.

1. Rochester, *Ramble in St. James's Park* (ll.97–98) in Vieth, *Poems,* p. 43.

2. Foucault, *The History of Sexuality,* p. 53.

3. "All of us suffer always from 'a degree of sanity,'" Spacks continues, "a partial dominance of what can't be controlled over what is supposed to control it. Sexual activity may be one specific manifestation of this dominance." Spacks, "'Ev'ry Woman Is at Heart a Rake,'" pp. 36–38.

4. *The Brink of All We Hate,* p. 7.

5. As Aspasia Velissariou succinctly puts it, women's sexuality was "important for Wycherley." Two other recent critics still maintain, however, that Wycherley was capable of less-than-enlightened attitudes. J. Douglas Canfield points to *The Plain-Dealer's* "misogyny" and recommends the work of Pat Gill, who claims, as noted, not only this play's misogynistic leanings but those of *The Country Wife,* which "furnishes the stage with some of Restoration Comedy's most brutal depictions of female desire unrelieved by any clear alternatives." Arguing again for a satiric requirement, she adds that through "these unremitting depictions of wanton women, *The Country Wife* sustains an illusion of moral purpose and demonstrates the need for (patriarchal) order.... The play portrays despicable female behavior as both depraved and natural." Natural it most certainly is. As for the rest of her argument, I must take the fullest measure of exception. Velissariou, "Patriarchal Tactics of Control and Female Desire," p. 116; Canfield, *Tricksters & Estates,* p. 138; Gill, *Interpreting Ladies,* pp. 55, 56, 64, 74.

6. *Leviathan,* p. 105.

7. Zimbardo, "Wycherley: The Restoration's Juvenal," p. 26. See also "William Wycherley," p. 271.

8. Zimbardo, *Wycherley's Drama,* pp. 146–47.

9. As T. W. Craik sees it, "although Wycherley is, in a sense, a satirist, his satire is not intended to be more than a source of amusement for his fashionable audience, and does not spring from a consistently moral view of society." Virginia Birdsall believes that *The Plain-Dealer* "*is* a commentary on the futility of satire." Accordingly, I do not fit Zimbardo's portrayal on this point: "Those who have argued that Wycherley's plays cannot be satires have done so because they think that satirists should be more serious than Wycherley in 'lashing vice' and 'ridiculing folly' and in showing us how to behave ourselves." Craik, "Some Aspects of Satire in Wycherley's Plays," p. 179; Birdsall, *Wild Civility,* p. 175; Zimbardo, "William Wycherley," p. 271.

10. Frye, *Anatomy of Criticism,* p. 223. Kevin Cope has moreover argued that the period's satire in general "aggressively criticizes any simplistic attempt to fix a definition or complete an analysis of the genre." And in *The Plain-Dealer,* Wycherley criticized the "entire, reciprocal process of idealizing and disparaging, a process which is too often assumed to be the very essence of satire but which is the most frequent target of satire in Wycherley's plays." Cope, "The Conquest of Truth," pp. 19, 21. Obviously, a satiric vision and intention can be approached and defended from a host of angles. See, for example, chapter three of Zimbardo, *Wycherley's Drama;* Robert Elliott, *The Power of Satire* (Princeton: Princeton University Press, 1966); J. R. Sutherland, *English Satire* (Cambridge: Cambridge University Press, 1958); Peter Elkin, *The Augustan Defense of Satire* (New York: Oxford University Press, 1973); Ian Jack, *Augustan Satire* (Oxford: Oxford University Press, 1967); Alvin Kernan, *The Cankered Muse* (New Haven: Yale University Press, 1950); Lillian and Edward Bloom, *Satire's Persuasive Voice* (Ithaca: Cornell University Press, 1979); Michael Seidel, *Satiric Inheritance: Rabelais to Sterne* (Princeton: Princeton University Press, 1980); Leon

Guilhamet, *Satire and the Transformation of Genre* (Philadelphia: University of Pennsylvania Press, 1987); and Dustin Griffin, *Satire: A Critical Introduction* (Lexington: University Press of Kentucky, 1994). Griffin sees satire as less restricted in its assumptions and far more open ended in its aims. From these studies, one concludes that satire's best scholars are at odds as to what satire does and how it does it.

11. Bogel, "'Did you once see Johnson plain?: Reflections on Boswell's *Life* and the State of Eighteenth-Century Studies," in John A Vance, ed., *Boswell's 'Life of Johnson': New Questions, New Answers* (Athens: University of Georgia Press, 1985), p. 84.

12. Warton, "Ranelagh House" (1747), printed in John Wooll, *Biographical Memoirs of the Late Revd. Joseph Warton, D. D.* (London: T. Cadell and W. Davies, 1806), p. 190.

13. Chadwick, *The Four Plays of William Wycherley*, pp. 7, 51.

14. McCarthy, *William Wycherley: A Reference Guide*, pp. 46, 59, 63, 77, 83, 89, 138.

15. Hume, "Content and Meaning in the Drama" in *The Rakish Stage*, p. 10.

16. Wilson, *A Preface to Restoration Drama*, p. 131.

17. Scouten, "Plays and Playwrights" in *The Revels History of Drama in English,* eds. John Loftis, Richard Southern, Marion Jones, and A. H. Scouten (London: Methuen, 1976), 5:193–200; Vieth, *Poems,* p. xxxiv; Rogers, "Fatal Inconsistency: Wycherley and *The Plain-Dealer,*" p. 162.

18. Powell, *Restoration Theatre Production,* pp. 101, 129. And I might note here that my own portrayal of Pinchwife was influenced not only by my own critical perspective but also by my physical and vocal characteristics and those of the actress playing Margery, and the "styles" of the others with whom I interacted on stage.

19. Hawkins, *Likeness of Truth in Elizabethan and Restoration Drama* (Oxford: Clarendon Press, 1972), p. 22.

20. Holland, *The Ornament of Action,* pp. 170, 191.

21. Preface to the *Spanish Fryar* (1681).

22. Milhous and Hume, *Producible Interpretations,* pp. 73–87, 100–104. Hume adds elsewhere that "whatever the possibilities for the reader ensconced in his study, any interpreter owes us a clear sense of whether his reading is stageable or not." Hume, "Content and Meaning in the Drama" in *The Rakish Stage,* p. 41. I would not agree that the critic has this *obligation*—again given the fact that printed drama enters the realm of literature, shedding a number of the restraints imposed on stage drama. It is simply metamorphosed into another creature. (And the same would be true of, say, fiction which is made into a motion picture.) And yet I believe that my interpretation of Wycherley—and many of the others I have read—could be stageable (certainly filmable), although this does not satisfy what would be Hume's first qualification: stageable *in the 1670s.*

23. See Peter Holland, *The Ornamant of Action,* p. 170.

24. Harwood, *Critics, Values, and Restoration Comedy,* p. 139.

25. Muir, *The Comedy of Manners,* p. 78.

26. See Hume, "William Wycherley: Text, Life, Interpretation," pp. 410, 413, 415.

27. *Producible Interpretations,* p. 104. Two other remarks in this engaging chapter might be noted. The first concerns one of Anne Righter's conclusions about *The Country Wife:* "How she deduces Wycherley's intentions with such assurance she does not explain" (p. 92). Did Righter actually imply that she knew

for certain what the playwright was thinking? Is it not a given that one is allowed to write, "Wycherley believed that . . . " without assuming a certitude about intentions? And then there is the authors' summation that "the many critics who have quarrelled so long and inconclusively over *The Country-Wife* are for the most part neither stupid nor totally wrong-headed about the play" (p. 104). This is certainly good to know.

28. Johnson, *Idler* 85, in *The Idler and The Adventurer*, eds. W. J. Bate, J. M. Bullitt, and L. F. Powell (New Haven: Yale University Press, 1963), p. 265.

29. Zimbardo, "William Wycherley," p. 283.

30. Kermode, *Forms of Attention* (Chicago: University of Chicago Press, 1985), p. 62.

31. Harwood, *Critics, Values, and Restoration Comedy,* p. 18.

32. Hume, *The Development of English Drama in the Late Seventeenth Century,* p. 104.

33. Hawkins, *Likeness and Truth in Elizabethan and Restoration Drama,* pp. 17–18.

34. Vieth, *Poems,* p. xxxiv. See also Vieth, "Divided Consciousness: The Trauma and Triumph of Restoration Culture," *Tennessee Studies in Literature* 22 (1974): 46–62. Hagstrum, *Sex and Sensibility: Ideal and Erotic Love from Milton to Mozart,* p. 72; Stone, *The Family, Sex and Marriage in England,* p. 177.

35. Powell, *Restoration Theatre Production,* p. 25.

Bibliography

Adams, Percy. "What Happened in Olivia's Bedroom? or Ambiguity in *The Plain-Dealer*." In *Essays in Honor of Esmond Linworth Marilla,* edited by Thomas Austin Kirby and William John Oliver, 174–87. Baton Rouge: Louisiana State University Press, 1970.

Arcangeli, Alessandro. "Dance and Punishment." *Dance Research* 10 (Autumn 1992): 30–42.

Atkins, G. Douglas. *Reading Deconstruction, Deconstructive Reading.* Lexington: University Press of Kentucky, 1983.

Bacon, Jon Lance. "Wives, Widows, and Writings in Restoration Comedy." *Studies in English Literature* 31 (1991): 427–43.

Bate, W. J., J. M. Bullitt, and L. F. Powell, eds. *The Idler and The Adventurer.* New Haven: Yale University Press, 1963.

Beauchamp, Gorman. "The Amorous Machiavellism of *The Country Wife*." *Comparative Drama* 11 (1978–79): 316–30.

Berman, Ronald. "The Ethic of *The Country Wife*." *Texas Studies in Language and Literature* 9 (1967): 47–55.

———. "Wycherley's Unheroic Society." *ELH* 51 (1984): 465–78.

Bevis, Richard. "Canon, Pedagogy, Prospectus: Redesigning 'Restoration and Eighteenth-Century Drama.'" *Comparative Drama* 31 (1997): 178–91.

Birdsall, Virginia Ogden. *Wild Civility: The English Comic Spirit on the Restoration Stage.* Bloomington: Indiana University Press, 1970.

Bloom, Lillian, and Edward Bloom. *Satire's Persuasive Voice.* Ithaca: Cornell University Press, 1979.

Bode, Robert F. "A Rape and No Rape: Olivia's Bedroom Revisited." *Restoration* 12 (1988): 80–86.

———. "'Try Me, At Least': The Dispensing of Justice in *The Plain-Dealer*." *Restoration and Eighteenth-Century Theatre Research,* second series, 4, no. 1 (1989): 1–24.

Bogel, Fredric V. "'Did you once see Johnson plain?': Reflections on Boswell's *Life* and the State of Eighteenth-Century Studies." In *Boswell's 'Life of Johnson': New Questions, New Answers,* edited by John A. Vance, 73–93. Athens: University of Georgia Press, 1985.

Bowman, John. "Dance, Chant and Mask in the Plays of Wycherley." *Drama Survey* 3 (1963): 181–205.

Brown, Laura. *English Dramatic Form, 1660–1760: An Essay in Generic History.* New Haven: Yale University Press, 1981.

Bruce, Donald. *Topics of Restoration Comedy.* London: Victor Gollancz LTD, 1974.

Burford, E. L., ed. *Bawdy Verse: A Pleasant Collection.* Harmondsworth: Penguin Books, 1982.

Burke, Helen M. "'Law-Suits,' 'Love-Suits,' and the Family Property in Wycherley's *The Plain-Dealer.*" In *Cultural Readings of Restoration & Eighteenth-Century English Theatre,* edited by J. Douglas Canfield and Deborah C. Payne, 89–113. Athens: University of Georgia Press, 1995.

———. "Wycherley's 'Tendentious Joke': The Discourse of Alterity in *The Country Wife.*" *The Eighteenth Century: Theory and Interpretation* 29 (1988): 227–41.

Candido, Joseph. "Theatricality and Satire in *The Country Wife.*" *Essays in Literature* 4 (1977): 27–36.

Canfield, J. Douglas. *Tricksters & Estates: On the Ideology of Restoration Comedy.* Lexington: University Press of Kentucky, 1997.

Castiglione, Baldesar. *The Book of the Courtier.* Trans. by George Bull. Harmondsworth: Penguin Books, 1976.

Cecil, C. D. "Delicate and Indelicate Puns in Restoration Comedy." *Modern Language Review* 61 (1966): 572–78.

———. "Raillery in Restoration Comedy." *Huntington Library Quarterly* 29 (1966): 147–59.

Chadwick, W. R. *The Four Plays of William Wycherley.* The Hague: Mouton, 1975.

Cohen, Derek. "The Alternating Styles of *The Plain-Dealer.*" *Restoration and Eighteenth-Century Theatre Research,* second series, 2, no. 1 (1987): 19–37.

———. "*The Country Wife* and Social Danger." *Restoration and Eighteenth-Century Theatre Research,* second series, 10, no. 1 (1995): 1–14.

———. "The Farce Pattern of Wycherley's *Love in a Wood.*" *English Studies in Canada* 3 (1977): 267–77.

———. "The Revengers' Comedy: A Reading of *The Country Wife.*" *Durham University Journal* 76 (1983): 31–36.

Collier, Jeremy. *A Short View of the Immorality, and Profaneness of the English Stage.* London: S. Keble, 1698.

Cope, Kevin. "The Conquest of Truth: Wycherley, Rochester, Butler, and Dryden and the Restoration Critique of Satire." *Restoration* 10 (1986): 19–40.

Corman, Brian. *Genre and Generic Change in English Comedy.* Toronto: University of Toronto Press, 1993.

Craik, T. W. "Some Aspects of Satire in Wycherley's Plays." *English Studies* 41 (1960): 168–79.

Cunningham, John E. *Restoration Drama.* London: Evans Brothers, 1966.

Dixon, Peter, ed. *The Country Wife and Other Plays.* Oxford: Oxford University Press, 1996.

Dobrée, Bonamy. *Restoration Comedy.* Oxford: Clarendon Press, 1924.

Donaldson, Ian. "'Tables Turned': *The Plain-Dealer.*" *Essays in Criticism* 17 (1967): 304–21.

Duncan, Douglas. "Mythic Parody in *The Country Wife.*" *Essays in Criticism* 31 (1981): 299–312.

Elkin, Peter. *The Augustan Defense of Satire.* New York: Oxford University Press, 1973.

Elliott, Robert. *The Power of Satire*. Princeton: Princeton University Press, 1966.

Farrell, William J. "The Role of Mandeville's Bee Analogy in 'The Grumbling Hive.'" *Studies in English Literature* 25 (1985): 511–27.

Ford, Douglas. "*The Country Wife:* Rake Hero as Artist." *Restoration* 17 (1993): 77–84.

Foucault, Michel. *The History of Sexuality.* Volume 1: *An Introduction.* Trans. by Robert Hurley. New York: Random House, 1978.

———. *Madness and Civilization: A History of Insanity in the Age of Reason.* Trans. by Richard Howard. New York: Random House, 1973.

Foxon, David. *Libertine Literature in England, 1660–1745.* New York: University Books, 1965.

Fraser, Antonia. *The Weaker Vessel.* New York: Alfred A. Knopf, 1984.

Freedman, William. "Impotence and Self-Destruction in *The Country Wife.*" *English Studies* 53 (1972): 421–31.

Freud, Sigmund. *Jokes and Their Relation to the Unconscious* (1905). Vol. 8, *The Standard Edition of the Complete Psychological Works of Sigmund Freud.* London: Hogarth Press, 1953.

Friedman, Arthur, ed. *The Plays of William Wycherley.* Oxford: Clarendon Press, 1979.

Friedson, A. M. "Wycherley and Molière: Satirical Point of View in *The Plain Dealer.*" *Modern Philology* 64 (1967): 189–97.

Frye, Northrop. *Anatomy of Criticism: Four Essays.* Princeton: Princeton University Press, 1957.

Fujimura, Thomas. *The Restoration Comedy of Wit.* Princeton: Princeton University Press, 1952.

Gagen, Jean. *The New Woman: Her Emergence in English Drama.* New York: Twayne, 1954.

Gill, Pat. *Interpreting Ladies: Women, Wit, and Morality in the Restoration Comedy of Manners.* Athens: University of Georgia Press, 1994.

Green, Peter, trans. *Juvenal: The Sixteen Satires.* Harmondsworth: Penguin Books, 1974.

Griffin, Dustin. *Satire: A Critical Introduction.* Lexington: University Press of Kentucky, 1994.

Guilhamet, Leon. *Satire and the Transformation of Genre.* Philadelphia: University of Pennsylvania Press, 1987.

Hagstrum, Jean. "Pictures to the Heart: The Psychological Picturesque in Ann Radcliffe's *The Mystery of Udolpho.*" In *Greene Centennial Studies,* edited by Paul J. Korshin and Robert R. Allen, 434–41. Charlottesville: University Press of Virginia, 1984.

———. *Sex and Sensibility: Ideal and Erotic Love from Milton to Mozart.* Chicago: University of Chicago Press, 1980.

Hallet, Charles. "The Hobbesian Substructure of *The Country Wife.*" *Papers on Language and Literature* 9 (1973): 380–95.

Hammond, N. G. L., and H. H. Sculland, eds. *The Oxford Classical Dictionary.* 2nd. ed. Oxford: Clarendon Press, 1970.

Harwood, John T. *Critics, Values, and Restoration Comedy.* Carbondale and Edwardsville: Southern Illinois University Press, 1983.

Hawkins, Barrie. "*The Country Wife:* Metaphor Manifest." *Restoration and Eighteenth-Century Theatre Research,* second series, 11, no. 1 (1996): 40–63.

Hawkins, Harriet. *Likeness of Truth in Elizabethan and Restoration Drama.* Oxford: Clarendon Press, 1972.

Hayman, John. "Raillery in Restoration Satire." *Huntington Library Quarterly* 31 (1968): 107–22.

Hee, Carol L. "'The Sign of a Jest': Freudian Jokes in Wycherley's *The Country Wife.*" *Literature and Psychology* 30 (1980): 8–17.

Highfill, Philip H., Jr., Kalman A. Burnim, and Edward A. Langhans. *A Biographical Dictionary of Actors, Actresses, Musicians, Dancers, Managers, and Other Stage Personnel in London, 1660–1800.* Vol. 9. Carbondale: Southern Illinois University Press, 1973–.

Hill, George Birkbeck, ed. *[Boswell's] Life of Samuel Johnson, LL.D.* Rev. by L. F. Powell. 6 vols. Oxford: Clarendon Press, 1934–64.

Hobbes, Thomas. *Leviathan.* Everyman Edition. London: J. M. Dent & Sons, 1973.

Holland, Norman. *The First Modern Comedies: The Significance of Etherege, Wycherley, and Congreve.* Cambridge: Harvard University Press, 1959.

Holland, Peter. *The Ornament of Action: Text and Performance in Restoration Comedy.* Cambridge: Cambridge University Press, 1979.

Holland, Peter, ed. *The Plays of William Wycherley.* Cambridge: Cambridge University Press, 1981.

Howe, Elizabeth. *The First English Actresses.* Cambridge: University Press, 1992.

Howe, P. P., ed. *The Complete Works of William Hazlitt.* 21 vols. London: Dent, 1930–34.

Hughes, Derek. *Dryden's Heroic Plays.* Lincoln: University of Nebraska Press, 1981.

———. *English Drama, 1660–1700.* Oxford: Clarendon Press, 1996.

———. "Naming and Entitlement in Wycherley, Etherege, and Dryden." *Comparative Literature* 21 (1987): 259–89.

———. "*The Plain-Dealer:* A Reappraisal." *Modern Language Quarterly* 43 (1982): 315–36.

Hume, Robert D. "Content and Meaning in the Drama." In *The Rakish Stage: Studies in English Drama, 1660–1800,* edited by Robert D. Hume, 1–45. Carbondale and Edwardsville: Southern Illinois University Press, 1983.

———.*The Development of English Comedy in the Late Seventeenth Century.* Oxford: Clarendon Press, 1976.

———. "Diversity and Development in Restoration Comedy, 1660–1679." *Eighteenth-Century Studies* 5 (1972): 365–97.

———. "Marital Discord in English Comedy from Dryden to Fielding." In *The Rakish Stage: Studies in English Drama, 1660–1800,* edited by Robert D. Hume, 176–213. Carbondale and Edwardsville: Southern Illinois University Press, 1983.

———. "The Myth of the Rake in 'Restoration Comedy.'" In *The Rakish Stage: Studies in English Drama, 1660–1800,* edited by Robert D. Hume, 138–75. Carbondale and Edwardsville: Southern Illinois University Press, 1983.

———. "Theory of Comedy in the Restoration." *Modern Philology* 70 (1973): 302–18.

———. "William Wycherley: Text, Life, Interpretation." *Modern Philology* 78 (1981): 399–415.

Hynes, Peter. "Against Theory?: Knowledge and Action in Wycherley's Plays." *Modern Philology* 94 (1996): 163–89.

Jack, Ian. *Augustan Satire*. Oxford: Oxford University Press, 1967.

Jackson, Wallace. "*The Country Wife:* The Premises of Love and Lust." *South Atlantic Quarterly* 72 (1973): 540–46.

Jenyns, Soame. *The Art of Dancing*. Edited by Anne Cottis. London: Dance Books, 1978.

Kaufman, Anthony. "Idealization, Disillusion, and Narcissistic Rage in Wycherley's 'The Plain Dealer.'" *Criticism* 21 (1979): 119–33.

———. "The Shadow of the Burlador: Don Juan on the Continent and in England." In *Comedy from Shakespeare to Sheridan,* edited by A. R. Braunmuller and J. C. Bulman, 229–54. Newark: University of Delaware Press, 1986.

———. "Wycherley's *The Country Wife* and the Don Juan Character." *Eighteenth-Century Studies* 9 (1975): 216–31.

Kaul, A. N., *The Action of English Comedy*. New Haven: Yale University Press, 1970.

Keller, Katherine Zapantis. "Re-reading and Re-playing: An Approach to Restoration Comedy." *Restoration* 6 (1982): 64–71.

Kermode, Frank. *Forms of Attention*. Chicago: University of Chicago Press, 1985.

Kernan, Alvin. *The Cankered Muse*. New Haven: Yale University Press, 1950.

Latham, Robert, and William Matthews, eds. *The Diary of Samuel Pepys*. 11 vols. Berkeley: University of California Press, 1970–83.

Loftis, John. *The Spanish Plays of Neoclassical England*. New Haven: Yale University Press, 1973.

McCarthy, B. Eugene. *William Wycherley: A Reference Guide*. Boston: G. K. Hall, 1985.

———. "Wycherley's *The Plain-Dealer* and the Limits of Wit." *English Miscellany* 22 (1971): 47–92.

McCarthy, William. *William Wycherley: A Biography*. Athens: Ohio University Press, 1979.

McDonald, Charles. "Restoration Comedy as Drama of Satire: An Investigation into Seventeenth Century Aesthetics." *Studies in Philology* 61 (1964): 522–44.

McMillin, Scott, ed. *Restoration and Eighteenth-Century Comedy*. New York: W. W. Norton, 1973.

McNamara, Peter. "The Witty Company: Wycherley's *The Country Wife.*" *A Review of International English Literature* 7 (1976): 59–72.

Macaulay, Thomas. "Comic Dramatists of the Restoration." *Edinburgh Review* 72 (1841): 490–528.

Mann, David D. "The Function of the Quack in *The Country Wife.*" *Restoration* 7 (1983): 19–22.

Marius, Richard. *Thomas More*. New York: Alfred A. Knopf, 1984.

Markley, Robert. *Two-Edg'd Weapons: Style and Ideology in the Comedies of Etherege, Wycherley, and Congreve*. Oxford: Clarendon Press, 1988.

Marshall, W. Gerald. *A Great Stage of Fools: Theatricality and Madness in the Plays of William Wycherley.* New York: AMS Press, 1993.

———. "The Idea of Theatre in Wycherley's *The Gentleman Dancing Master.*" *Restoration* 6 (1982): 1–10.

———. "Wycherley's Drama of Madness: *The Plain-Dealer.*" *Philological Quarterly* 59 (1980): 26–37.

———. "Wycherley's 'Great Stage of Fools': Madness and Theatricality in *The Country Wife.*" *Studies in English Literature* 29 (1989): 409–29.

———. "Wycherley's *Love in a Wood* and the Designs of Providence." *Restoration* 3 (1979): 8–16.

Matalene, "What Happens in *The Country Wife.*" *Studies in English Literature* 22 (1982): 395–411.

Matlack, Cynthia. "Parody and Burlesque of Heroic Ideals in Wycherley's Comedies: A Critical Reinterpretation of Contemporary Evidence." *Papers on Language and Literature* 8 (1972): 273–86.

Milhous, Judith, and Robert D. Hume. *Producible Interpretations: Eight English Plays, 1675–1707.* Carbondale and Edwardsville: Southern Illinois University Press, 1985.

Morford, Mark, and Robert Lenardon. *Classical Mythology.* New York: David McKay, 1971.

Morris, David B. "Language and Honor in 'The Country Wife.'" *South Atlantic Bulletin* 37, no. 4 (1972): 3–10.

Morrow, Laura. "Phenomenological Psychology and Comic Form in *The Plain-Dealer.*" *Restoration and Eighteenth-Century Theatre Research,* second series, 3, no. 2 (1988): 1–10.

Muir, Kenneth. *The Comedy of Manners.* London: Hutchinson, 1970.

Neill, Michael. "Horned Beats and China Oranges: Reading the Signs in *The Country Wife.*" *Eighteenth-Century Life,* n.s. 12 (1988): 3–17.

Novak, "Margery Pinchwife's 'London Disease': Restoration Comedy and the Libertine Offensive of the 1670s." *Studies in the Literary Imagination* 10 (1977): 1–23.

Nussbaum, Felicity. *The Brink of All We Hate: English Satires on Women.* Lexington: University Press of Kentucky, 1984.

Onions, C. T., ed. *The Oxford Dictionary of English Etymologies.* New York: Oxford University Press, 1966.

Palmer, John. *The Comedy of Manners.* London: G. Bell and Sons, 1913.

Payne, Deborah C. "Reading the Signs in *The Country Wife.*" *Studies in English Literature* 26 (1986): 403–19.

Peters, Julie Stone. "'Things Govern'd by Words': Late Seventeenth-Century Comedy and the Reformers." *English Studies* 68 (1987): 142–53.

Playford, John. *The English Dancing Master.* London: Thomas Harper, 1650.

Porter, Roy. "Mixed Feelings: the Enlightenment and Sexuality in Eighteenth-Century Britain." In *Sexuality in Eighteenth-Century Britain,* edited by Paul-Gabriel Boucé, 1–27. Manchester: Manchester University Press, 1982.

Pottle, Frederick A., ed. *Boswell's London Journal.* New York: McGraw-Hill, 1950.

Powell, Jocelyn. *Restoration Theatre Production.* London: Routledge & Kegan Paul, 1984.

Raleigh, Walter, ed. *The Works of Halifax.* Oxford: Oxford University Press, 1912.

Rawson, Claude. *Henry Fielding and the Augustan Ideal under Stress.* London: Routledge and Kegan Paul, 1972.

Righter, Anne. "William Wycherley." In *Restoration Dramatists,* edited by Earl Miner, 105–22. Englewood Cliffs: Prentice-Hall, Inc., 1966.

Roberts, Nickie. *Whores in History: Prostitution in Western Society.* London: Harper Collins, 1992.

Rogers, Katherine M. "Fatal Inconsistency: Wycherley and *The Plain-Dealer.*" *ELH* 28 (1961): 148–62.

———.*William Wycherley.* New York: Twayne, 1972.

Rogers, Pat. "The Breeches Part." In *Sexuality in Eighteenth-Century Britain,* edited by Paul-Gabriel Boucé, 244–58. Manchester: Manchester University Press, 1982.

Roper, Alan. "Sir Harbottle Grimstone and *The Country Wife.*" *Studies in the Literary Imagination* 10 (1977): 109–23.

Rump, Eric S. "Theme and Structure in Wycherley's *Love in a Wood*" *English Studies* 54 (1973): 326–33.

Rundle, J. U. "Wycherley and Calderón: A Source for *Love in a Wood.*" *PMLA* 64 (1949): 701–7.

Ryscroft, Charles. *Imagination and Reality: Psycho-Analytic Essays, 1951–1961.* London: Hogarth Press, 1968.

Sachs, Curt. *World History of the Dance.* Trans. by Bessie Schonberg. New York: W. W. Norton, 1937.

Schafer, Yvonne. "Restoration Heroines: Reflections of Social Change." *Restoration and Eighteenth-Century Theatre Research,* second series, 12, no. 1 (1987): 38–53.

Schneider, Ben Ross, Jr. *The Ethos of Restoration Comedy.* Urbana: University of Illinois Press, 1971.

Scouten, Arthur. "Plays and Playwrights." In *The Revels History of Drama in English.* Vol. 5. Edited by John Loftis, Richard Southern, Marion Jones, and A. H. Scouten, 159–229. London: Methuen, 1976.

Sedgwick, Eve Kosofsky. "Sexualism and the Citizen of the World: Wycherley, Sterne, and Male Homosocial Desire." *Critical Inquiry* 11 (1984): 226–45.

Seidel, Michael. *Satiric Inheritance: Rabelais to Sterne.* Princeton: Princeton University Press, 1980.

Sherman, Sandra. "Manly, Manliness, and Friendship in *The Plain-Dealer.*" *Restoration* 20 (1996): 18–30.

Skura, Meredith Anne. *The Literary Use of the Psychoanalytic Process.* New Haven: Yale University Press, 1981.

Slade, Giles. "The Two Backed Beast: Eunuchus and Priapus in *The Country Wife.*" *Restoration and Eighteenth-Century Theatre Research* second series, 7, no. 1 (1992): 23–34.

Spacks, Patricia Meyer. "'Ev'ry Woman Is at Heart a Rake.'" *Eighteenth-Century Studies* 8 (1974–75): 27–46.

Spence, Joseph. *Observations, Anecdotes, and Characters of Books and Men.* Edited by James M. Osborn. 2 vols. Oxford: Clarendon Press, 1966.

Stanley, Eric. "Dance, Dancers, and Dancing in Anglo-Saxon England." *Dance Research* 9 (Autumn 1991): 18–31.

Staves, Susan. "A Few Kind Words for the Fop." *Studies in English Literature* 22 (1982): 395–428.

———. *Players' Scepters: Fictions of Authority in the Restoration.* Lincoln: University of Nebraska Press, 1979.

Steiger, Richard. "'Wit in a Corner': Hypocrisy in *The Country Wife.*" *Tennessee Studies in Literature* 24 (1979): 56–70.

Stone, Lawrence. *The Family, Sex, and Marriage in England, 1500–1800.* New York: Harper and Row, 1977.

Stonehill, Charles, ed. *The Complete Works of George Farquhar.* Vol. 2. London: Nunsuch Press, 1930.

Sutherland, James. *English Literature of the Late Seventeenth Century.* Oxford: Clarendon Press, 1969.

———. *English Satire.* Cambridge: Cambridge University Press, 1958.

Terry, Sam. "The Comic Standard in Wycherley's *The Gentleman Dancing-Master.*" *Enlightenment Essays* 6 (Spring 1975): 3–11.

Thompson, James. "Ideology and Dramatic Form: The Case of Wycherley." *Studies in the Literary Imagination* 17 (1984): 49–62. Rpt. in *Reader Entrapment in Eighteenth-Century Literature,* edited by Carl R. Kropf, 159–75. New York: AMS Press, 1992.

———. *Language in Wycherley's Plays.* University: University of Alabama Press, 1984.

Thompson, Peggy. "The Limits of Parody in *The Country Wife.*" *Studies in Philology* 89 (1992): 100–114.

Thompson, Roger. *Unfit for Modest Ears.* Totowa: Rowman and Littlefield, 1979.

Underwood, Dale. *Etherege and the Seventeenth-Century Comedy of Manners.* New Haven: Yale University Press, 1957.

Velissariou, Aspasia. "Gender and the Circulation of Money and Desire in Wycherley's *The Plain-Dealer.*" *Restoration* 18 (1994): 27–36.

———. "Patriarchal Tactics of Control and Female Desire in Wycherley's *The Gentleman Dancing-Master* and *The Country Wife.*" *Texas Studies in Language and Literature* 37 (1995): 115–26.

Verdurmen, J. Peter. "Grasping for Permanence: Ideal Couples in *The Country Wife* and *Aureng-Zebe.*" *Huntington Library Quarterly* 42 (1979): 329–47.

Vernon, P. F. *William Wycherley.* London: Longmans, Green, 1965.

———. "Wycherley's First Comedy and Its Spanish Source." *Comparative Literature* 18 (1966): 132–44.

Vieth, David. "Divided Consciousness: The Trauma and Triumph of Restoration Culture." *Tennessee Studies in Literature* 22 (1974): 46–62.

———. "Introduction." *Papers on Language and Literature* 18 (1982): 227–33.

———. "Wycherley's *The Country Wife:* An Anatomy of Masculinity." *Papers on Language and Literature* 2 (1966): 335–50.

Vieth, David, ed. *The Complete Poems of John Wilmot, Earl of Rochester.* New Haven and London: Yale University Press, 1968.

Warton, Joseph. *Adventurer 105* (6 November 1753).

Weales, Gerald, ed. *The Complete Plays of William Wycherley.* New York: New York University Press, 1967.

Weber, Harold. "Horner and His 'Women of Honour': The Dinner Party in *The Country Wife.*" *Modern Language Quarterly* 43 (1982): 107–20.

———. "The Rake Hero in Wycherley and Congreve." *Philological Quarterly* 61 (1982): 143–60.

———. *The Restoration Rake Hero.* Madison: University of Wisconsin Press, 1986.

White, T. H. *The Bestiary: A Book of Beasts, Being a Translation from a Latin Bestiary of the Twelfth Century.* New York: G. P. Putnam's Sons, 1960.

Wilkinson, D. R. M. *The Comedy of Habit: An Essay on the Use of Courtesy Literature in a Study of Restoration Comic Drama.* Leiden: University Press, 1964.

Williams, Aubrey. "The 'Fall' of China and *The Rape of the Lock.*" *Philological Quarterly* 41 (1962): 412–25.

Wilson, John Harold. *All the King's Ladies.* Chicago: University of Chicago Press, 1958.

———. *A Preface to Restoration Drama.* Cambridge: Harvard University Press, 1968.

Woods, Karen. "Dance in England through a Study of Selected Eighteenth-Century Texts." Ph.D. diss., University of Georgia, 1995.

Wooll, John. *Biographical Memoirs of the Late Revd. Joseph Warton, D. D.* London: T. Cadell and W. Davies, 1806.

Zimbardo, Rose. "William Wycherley." In *Restoration and Eighteenth-Century Dramatists, First Series,* edited by Paula R. Backscheider, 263–300. Detroit: Bruccoli Clark Layman, 1989.

———. "Wycherley: The Restoration's Juvenal." *Forum* 17, no. 1 (1979): 17–26.

———. *Wycherley's Drama: A Link in the Development of English Satire.* New Haven: Yale University Press, 1965.

Index

Adams, Percy, 239 n.55
Armin, Robert, 178
Atkins, G. Douglas, 222 n.68

Bacon, Francis, 212 n.13
Bacon, Jon Lance, 222 n.69, 234 n.22
Barker, Jane, 206 n.37
Barry, Elizabeth, 178, 236 n.36, 237 n.40
Beauchamp, Gorman, 223 n.75
Berman, Ronald, 212 n.13, 238 n.52
Bevis, Richard, 231 n.4
Birdsall, Virginia, 131, 185 n.2, 189 n.11, 200 nn. 5 and 7, 201 n.8, 206 n.39, 207 n.47, 208 n.51, 209 n.57, 210 n.2, 214 n.21, 222 n.71, 223 n.72, 229 n.114, 231 n.5, 232 n.13, 243 n.9
Birkenhead, Sir John, 204 n.27
Bode, Robert F., 232 n.22, 239 n.55
Bogel, Fredric, 177
Boswell, James, 190 nn.18 and 20, 193 n.33
Boutell, Elizabeth, 137, 178, 195 n.38, 235 n.28, 236 n.40
Bowman, John, 188 n.2, 192 n.24, 198 n.62, 199 n.3, 229 n.113
Bracegirdle, Anne, 178, 237 n.40
Branagh, Kenneth, 178
Brown, Ivor, 179
Brown, Laura, 232 n.10
Buckingham, duke of, 234 n.24
Burbage, Richard, 178
Burke, Helen M., 228 n.109, 233 n.16, 237 n.44, 238 n.50, 239 n.55, 242 n.70
Butler, Samuel, 202 n.15, 222 n.71

Calderón de la Barca, Pedro, 201 n.10
Candido, Joseph, 216 n.33

Canfield, J. Douglas, 188 n.4, 228 n.104, 235 n.28, 242 n.67, 243 n.5
Cartwright, William, 200 n.5
Cary, Philadelphia, 225 n.86
Castiglione, Baldesar, 205 n.35
Castlemaine, Lady, 210 n.3
Cecil, C. D., 224 n.81
Chadwick, W. R., 178, 191 n.23, 197 n.55, 198 n.62, 200 n.5, 205 n.31, 208 nn.52 and 54, 210 n.2, 212 n.13, 214 n.21, 216 n.32, 218 n.42, 228 n.110, 230 n.2, 232 n.10, 242 n.67
Charles II, king of England, 208 n.49, 210 n.3
Chesterfield, earl of, 198 n.1
Chorier, Nicholas, 196 n.44
Cibber, Colley, 32, 67, 121, 178, 225 n.93
Cohen, Derek, 211 n.7, 220 n.57, 226 nn.94 and 97, 228 n.104, 232 n.10, 233 nn.13 and 15, 241 n.63, 242 n.65
Collier, Jeremy, 9
Congreve, William, 26, 27, 32, 56, 103, 121, 172, 178, 184, 185 n.1, 216 n.29, 225 n.93, 242 n.66
Cope, Kevin, 232 n.10, 243 n.10
Corman, Brian, 188 n.3, 193 n.28, 195 n.38, 210 n.2, 217 nn.36 and 38
Corneille, Pierre, 101
Cory, Katherine, 235 n.28
Cowley, Abraham, 189 n.8
Craik, T. W., 188 n.4, 201 n.7, 202 n.18, 241 n.60, 243 n.9
Cromwell, Oliver, 237 n.41
Crowne, John, 214 n.22, 236 n.36
Cunningham, John, 214 n.21

Dennis, John, 181
Derrida, Jacques, 228 n.109

256 INDEX

Dobrée, Bonamy, 200 n.7, 209 n.57, 210 n.2
Domitian, emperor of Rome, 48
Donaldson, Ian, 231 n.4
Dryden, John, 9, 176, 180, 184, 220 n.59, 231 n.6, 234 n.24, 235 n.28, 236 n.36
Duffett, Thomas, 235 n.28
Durfey, Thomas 236 n.36

Edward III, King of England, 199 n.2
Elizabeth I, Queen of England, 141, 153
Elizabeth of York, 234 n.25
Erasmus, 215 n.26
Etherege, George, 9, 26, 27, 32, 56, 67, 78, 98, 103, 172, 184, 216 n.33, 236 n.31

Farquhar, George, 214 n.19
Farrell, William J., 214 n.19
Fletcher, John, 137, 188 n.3, 194 n.34, 200 n.5
Ford, Douglas, 210 n.2, 216 n.28
Foreman, Simon, 201 n.11
Foucault, Michel, 175, 192 n.27, 193 n.30, 196 n.48, 201 n.8, 205 n.37, 211 n.4, 222 n.72, 224 n.81, 240 n.59
Fraser, Antonia, 203 n.21, 224 n.86
Freedman, William, 211 n.5, 214 n.20, 222 n.68
Freud, Sigmund, 10, 175, 187 n.15, 215 n.23, 216 n.30, 222 n.68
Friedman, Arthur, 49, 195 n.43, 201 n.10, 208 n.55, 215 n.28, 221 n.65, 223 n.77
Friedson, A. M., 10
Frye, Northrop, 176, 192 n.24
Fujimura, Thomas, 185 n.2, 193 nn.28 and 29, 195 n.39, 202 n.12, 203 n.18, 208 n.52, 212 n.13, 216 n.32, 218 n.49, 224 n.83

Garrick, David, 178
Gielgud, John, 178
Gill, Pat, 227 n.100, 239 n.55, 242 n.67, 243 n.5
Goldsmith, Oliver, 13, 187 n.11
Gould, Robert, 57

Griffin, Dustin, 244 n.10
Gwyn, Nell, 198 n.60

Hagstrum, Jean, 183, 211 n.9, 221 n.64
Halifax, Lord, 218 n.42, 240 n.57
Hallet, Charles, 215 n.23, 218 n.45, 227 n.100
Hart, Charles, 178, 181, 229 n.115, 235 n.28
Harwood, John, 181, 182, 229 nn.113 and 114
Hawkins, Harriet, 180, 183
Hazlitt, William, 191 n.21
Hegel, Georg Wilhelm Friedrich, 239 n.55
Henry VII, king of England, 234 n.25
Herod, 199 n.2
Herodia, 199 n.2
Hobbes, Thomas, 12, 20, 47, 89, 98, 111, 131, 176, 187 n.13, 187 n.15, 189 n.11, 190 n.14, 201 n.11, 202 n.12, 214 n.20, 215 n.23, 216 n.31
Holland, Norman, 191 n.22, 193 n.34, 195 n.39, 199 n.3, 202 n.18, 204 n.26, 209 n.57, 230 n.2, 242 n.67
Holland, Peter, 180, 195 n.43, 210 n.2, 230 n.3, 232 n.11, 237 n.48
Holyday, Barton, 199 n.3
Horace, 209 n.57, 217 n.38
Howard, Edward, 200 n.5
Howard, James, 26
Howard, Robert, 19
Hughes, Derek, 187 n.1, 189 n.6, 217 n.39, 218 n.43, 220 n.61, 231 n.4, 234 nn.22 and 24, 235 nn.27 and 29, 236 n.32, 239 n.55, 240 n.58, 241 n.62, 242 n.68
Hume, Robert, 10, 179, 180, 181, 183, 187 n.2, 195 n.39, 208 n.53, 210 n.1, 226 n.98, 230 n.1, 231 n.6, 244 nn.22 and 27
Hynes, Peter, 186 n.3, 236 n.35

Jackson, Wallace, 216 n.31
James, Elizabeth, 235 n.28
Jennings, Frances, 221 n.63
Jenyns, Soame, 199 n.2

Johnson, Samuel, 48, 182, 198 n.1
Jonson, Ben, 188 n.3, 201 n.10, 235 n.28
Joyner, William, 236 n.36
Juvenal, 23, 48, 175, 199 n.3

Kaufman, Anthony, 10, 182, 210 n.2, 211 nn.5 and 7, 212 n.10, 231 n.5, 232 n.9, 233 n.14, 235 n.28, 236 n.34, 241 n.60
Kaul, A. N., 189 n.8, 195 n.38, 197 n.55, 228 n.111, 233 n.17
Kean, Edmund, 178
Keller, Katherine Zapantis, 223 n.72
Kermode, Frank, 182
Killigrew, Henry, 221 n.63
Knepp, Elizabeth, 105, 178, 193 n.28, 229 n.115, 235 n.28
Kynaston, Edward, 195 n.38, 235 n.28

Lacan, Jacques, 233 n.16, 238 n.50
Le Sage, Alain René, 178
Lee, Nathaniel, 236 n.36, 237 n.40
Leigh, Ashton, 179
Lenardon, Robert, 191 n.23
Lillo, George, 70, 203 n.20
Loftis, John, 189 n.8, 201 n.10
Lydal, Edward, 181
Lyly, Peter, 113, 146, 221 n.64

Macaulay, Thomas, 9
Machiavelli, Niccolò, 223 n.75, 237 n.45
Mann, David D., 211 n.4
Markley, Robert, 188 n.6, 190 nn.14 and 15, 194 n.34, 195 n.38, 200 n.7, 204 n.30, 205 n.32, 206 n.38, 213 n.18, 218 n.47, 222 n.70, 223 n.73, 230 n.3, 242 n.67
Marshall, Rebecca, 198 n.60, 236 nn.36 and 40
Marshall, Stephen, 198 n.60
Marshall, W. Gerald, 188 nn.2 and 3, 193 n.34, 195 n.38, 197 n.56, 198 n.60, 200 nn.3 and 7, 205 nn.32 and 36, 207 n.44, 209 n.57, 210 n.2, 231 n.5, 236 n.33, 238 n.54
Marston, John, 201 n.10
Mary Tudor, queen of England, 141
Mary, queen of Scots, 141
Massinger, Philip, 200 n.5

Matalene, W. H., 212 n.13, 228 n.108
Matlack, Cynthia, 194 n.38, 217 n.39, 231 n.6
McCarthy, B. Eugene, 178, 232 n.10, 235 n.30, 238 n.52, 241 n.63
McDonald, Charles O., 221 n.62
McMillin, Scott, 11
McNamara, Peter, 221 n.64, 223 n.76
Milhous, Judith, 180, 181, 226 n.98, 244 n.27
Milton, John, 51
Mohun, Michael, 22, 178, 180, 181, 235 n.28
Molière, 135, 147, 215 n.28
Monmouth, James, duke of, 224 n.86
Morford, Mark, 191 n.23
Morris, David, 217 n.38
Morrow, Laura, 233 n.14
Muir, Kenneth, 181, 186 n.10, 188 n.4, 198 n.58, 202 n.18, 208 n.51, 219 n.53, 222 n.71

Nashe, Thomas, 202 n.15, 222 n.71
Naylor, James, 203 n.21
Needham, Lady Jane, 221 n.64
Neill, Michael, 221 n.64, 226 n.97
Nokes, James, 178, 208 n.54
Novak, Maximillian, 214 n.22, 225 n.87
Nussbaum, Felicity, 175

Oldfield, Nan, 178
Oldham, John, 240 n.59
Olivier, Laurence, 178
Otway, Thomas, 178, 184

Palmer, John, 209 n.1
Pascal, Blaise, 238 n.49
Payne, Deborah C., 220 n.61
Payne, Henry Neville, 219 n.50
Pepys, Samuel, 48, 193 n.28, 198 n.60, 211 n.9, 236 n.36
Peters, Julie Stone, 229 n.116
Petrarch, 30
Playford, John, 209 n.58, 229 n.117
Pope, Alexander, 230 n.1
Porter, Roy, 191 n.20, 196 n.44, 202 n.15, 224 n.80, 236 n.32
Powell, Jocelyn, 10, 126, 180, 183, 190 n.16

Price, Goditha, 221 n.63
Prynne, William, 49

Ravenscroft, Edward, 220 n.59
Rawson, Claude, 198 n.1
Righter, Anne, 202 n.18, 244 n.27
Rochester, earl of, 12, 24, 175,
    191 n.21, 202 n.15, 222 n.71,
    224 n.82, 226 n.96, 238 n.52
Rogers, Katharine, 10, 179,
    194 n.34, 198 n.60, 207 n.48,
    209 n.57, 224 n.80, 230 n.2,
    231 n.7, 233 n.17, 234 n.22,
    241 n.63
Romano, Giulio, 211 n.9
Roper, Alan, 213 n.18
Rowe, Nicholas, 209 n.56
Rubens, Peter Paul, 183
Rump, Eric, 198 n.58
Rundle, J. U., 187 n.1
Ryscroft, Charles, 232 n.9

Schneider, Ben Ross, 189 n.11,
    235 n.30, 241 n.60
Sedgwick, Eve Kosofsky, 212 n.13
Segneri, Paolo, 201 n.11
Shadwell, Thomas, 18
Shafer, Yvonne, 200 n.7, 203 n.26
Shakespeare, William, 17, 30, 40,
    49, 66, 118, 137, 151, 152, 170,
    172, 178, 182, 187 n.2, 189 n.8,
    190 n.18, 194 n.35, 198 n.61,
    214 n.21, 221 n.64, 233 nn.17 and
    18, 236 n.39, 240 n.56, 242 n.65
Shanks, Edward, 179
Sharp, Jane, 224 n.86
Sheridan, Richard Brinsley, 13,
    187 n.11
Sherman, Sandra, 240 n.57, 241 n.63,
    242 n.69
Skura, Meredith Anne, 10, 186 n.7,
    234 n.20
Spacks, Patricia Meyer, 175, 201 n.12,
    204 n.28, 206 nn.37, 42, 216 n.33,
    222 n.72, 243 n.3
Stapylton, Robert, 199 n.3
Staves, Susan, 195 n.40, 219 n.53
Steiger, Richard, 186 n.3, 218 n.42,
    219 n.53, 221 n.63, 224 n.78
Stone, Lawrence, 183, 192 n.25,
    201 n.8, 206 n.37, 213 n.17,
    215 n.24, 218 n.48, 219 n.50,
    235 n.26
Sutherland, James, 10, 191 n.23
Swift, Jonathan, 134

Tatham, John, 189 n.8
Terry, Sam, 204 n.28
Thompson, James, 10, 188 n.3,
    190 n.14, 193 n.34, 194 n.38,
    198 n.62, 200 n.5, 204 n.26,
    209 n.57, 212 n.11, 215 n.25,
    217 n.38, 225 n.88, 233 n.13,
    234 nn.20 and 22, 238 n.53,
    240 n.57, 242 nn.64 and 69
Thompson, Peggy, 212 n.12,
    217 n.38, 222 n.67, 226 n.97,
    229 n.114
Thompson, Roger, 189 n.7, 196 n.44,
    201 n.11, 211 n.7
Tour, Georges de la, 184
Tuke, Samuel, 205 n.32

Underwood, Dale, 211 n.8

Vanbrugh, John, 9, 48, 184, 185 n.1
Vance, John A., 187 n.11, 244 n.18
Vaughn, Lord John, 217 n.37
Velissariou, Aspasia, 228 n.106,
    237 n.43, 243 n.5
Verdurmen, J. Peter, 213 n.15,
    215 n.25, 228 n.107, 229 n.112
Vermeer, Jan, 183
Vernon, P. F., 187 n.1, 194 n.34,
    197 n.55, 198 n.62, 219 n.53
Vieth, David, 179, 183, 186 n.6,
    197 n.54, 213 n.18, 215 n.27,
    217 n.38, 224 n.82, 229 n.115

Walker, Robert, 237 n.41
Ward, A. C., 179
Warton, Joseph, 178, 185 n.1
Weales, Gerald, 179, 209 n.57,
    229 n.112
Weber, Harold, 212 n.10, 222 n.71,
    223 n.72, 224 n.80, 226 n.94
Weston, James, 200 n.5
Wilkinson, D. R. M., 218 n.42
Williams, Aubrey, 223 n.77
Wilson, John, 189 n.8, 196 n.47
Wilson, John Harold, 179, 231 n.6
Woods, Karen, 200 n.4

Wycherley, William. Plays: *The Country Wife,* 20, 23, 24, 30, 31, 57, 59, 75, 78, 81-129, 130, 136, 137, 142, 147-49, 150, 162, 167, 173, 175, 176, 177, 178, 179, 180, 181, 182, 183, 186 n.6, 187 n.14, 193 nn.28, 30, 203 n.22, 230 n.1, 231 nn.4 and 7, 233 n.17, 235 n.28, 236 nn.37 and 38, 238 nn.51 and 54, 240 n.58, 242 n.69, 243 n.5, 245 n.27; *The Gentleman Dancing-Master,* 23, 24, 31, 48-80, 81, 82, 89, 91, 93, 105, 115, 122, 142, 148, 175, 177, 179, 187 n.14, 209 n.1, 216 n.35, 222 n.69, 224 n.79, 225 n.92, 231 n.7, 237 n.46; *Love in a Wood,* 17-47, 48, 49, 51, 53, 57, 66, 69, 80, 89, 96, 136, 175, 179, 187 n.14, 205 n.33, 209 n.57, 209 n.1, 230 n.1, 231 n.7, 233 n.17, 235 n.28; *The Plain-Dealer,* 10, 20, 21, 22, 31, 36, 37, 59, 108, 130-74, 175, 176, 177, 178, 180, 181, 182, 184, 186 n.10, 187 n.14, 193 nn.28, 31, 243 nn.5, 9 and 10; Poetry, 187 n.16

Zimbardo, Rose, 10, 176, 182, 185 n.2, 186 n.9, 187 n.2, 188 nn.3 and 4, 193 n.34, 200 n.7, 203 n.19, 204 n.26, 207 n.48, 209 n.57, 210 n.2, 212 n.11, 217 n.38, 226 n.96, 230 nn.2 and 10, 233 n.17, 241 nn.60, 61 and 63, 243 n.9